SIGNLL Conference on Computational Natural Language Learning 2019

Proceedings of the Shared Task on Cross-Framework Meaning Representation Parsing at the 2019 Conference on Natural Language Learning

Hong Kong, China
3 November 2019

ISBN: 978-1-7138-0090-3

Preface

We are excited (and a little relieved) to present the proceedings from the 2019 Shared Task on *Cross-Framework Meaning Representation Parsing* (MRP) at the Conference for Computational Language Learning (CoNLL). This volume provides linguistic, methodological, and technical background to the target representations, mode of operation, and participating systems in a 'system bake-off' for *data-driven parsing* into *graph-structured* representations of *sentence meaning*.

The task received submissions from eighteen teams, of which two involved task co-organizers and do not participate in the official ranking of submissions. Three teams declined the invitation to submit a system description for publication in the proceedings, such that the volume in total comprises an in-depth task overview, two 'system descriptions' by task co-organizers, and thirteen system descriptions by task participants. All system descriptions were reviewed by at least three experts, drawing from among the task participants and an external pool of colleagues working in meaning representation parsing.

We much look forward to the presentation of results and meeting with task participants in person at CoNLL in early November 2019. The conference has allocated a 90-minute slot for oral presentations from the shared task, where all teams will have the opportunity to present a 'blitz' overview of their work. Following this plenary session, there will be poster presentations by all teams, allowing for more detailed technical discussions.

The shared task has been an intensive experience for organizers and participants alike, with data preparation, definition of evaluation metrics, system development, submission of parser outputs, scoring and compilation of the task proceedings—running near-continuously between March and October 2019. We are deeply grateful to all participants (including several who in the end did not make a submission) for the time and effort they have invested in system development and documentation. With no less than five distinct linguistic frameworks for graph-based meaning representation combined for the first time in a uniform training and evaluation setting, this was not an easy competition to enter. As co-organizers of the MRP 2019 competition, we will continue to work on facilitating cross-framework meaning representation parsing and enabling participants to further build on their work. We are delighted (and a litte scared) to confirm that there will be a follow-up shared task MRP 2020 at the next CoNLL meeting a year from now.

Many colleagues have made essential contributions to the task organization along the way. We gratefully acknowledge assistance by Emily M. Bender, Jayeol Chun, Dan Flickinger, Andrey Kutuzov, Sebastian Schuster, Milan Straka, and Zdeňka Urešová.

Oslo, Jerusalem, Prague, Copenhagen,
Linköping, Boulder, and Brandeis;
October 2019

Stephan Oepen, Omri Abend, Jan Hajič, Daniel Hershcovich,
Marco Kuhlmann, Tim O'Gorman, and Nianwen Xue

Organizers:

Stephan Oepen, University of Oslo
Omri Abend, The Hebrew University of Jerusalem
Jan Hajic, Charles University, Prague
Daniel Hershcovich, University of Copenhagen
Marco Kuhlmann, Linköping University
Tim O'Gorman, University of Colorado in Boulder
Nianwen Xue, Brandeis University

Program Committee:

Omri Abend
Hongxiao Bai
Miguel Ballesteros
Bernd Bohnet
Jan Buys
Jie Cao
Yufei Chen
Shay B. Cohen
Timothy Dozat
Daniel Hershcovich
Zixia Jia
Wei Jiang
Alexander Koller
Yuta Koreeda
Marco Kuhlmann
Sunny Lai
Zuchao Li
Matthias Lindemann
Gaku Morio
Seung-Hoon Na
Tim O'Gorman
Stephan Oepen
Hiroaki Ozaki
Hao Peng
Nathan Schneider
Djamé Seddah
Gabriel Stanovsky
Jana Straková
Weiwei Sun
Rik van Noord
Xinyu Wang
Nianwen Xue
Daniel Zeman
Sheng Zhang
Yi Zhang

Table of Contents

Conference Program

Sunday, November 3, 2019

Meaning Representation Parsing (MRP) Shared Task at CoNLL 2019

14:00–14:30   *MRP 2019: Cross-Framework Meaning Representation Parsing*
Stephan Oepen, Omri Abend, Jan Hajic, Daniel Hershcovich, Marco Kuhlmann, Tim O'Gorman, Nianwen Xue, Jayeol Chun, Milan Straka and Zdenka Uresova

14:30–14:33   *TUPA at MRP 2019: A Multi-Task Baseline System*
Daniel Hershcovich and Ofir Arviv

14:33–14:36   *The ERG at MRP 2019: Radically Compositional Semantic Dependencies*
Stephan Oepen and Dan Flickinger

14:36–14:39   *SJTU-NICT at MRP 2019: Multi-Task Learning for End-to-End Uniform Semantic Graph Parsing*
Zuchao Li, Hai Zhao, Zhuosheng Zhang, Rui Wang, Masao Utiyama and Eiichiro Sumita

14:39–14:42   *ShanghaiTech at MRP 2019: Sequence-to-Graph Transduction with Second-Order Edge Inference for Cross-Framework Meaning Representation Parsing*
Xinyu Wang, Yixian Liu, Zixia Jia, Chengyue Jiang and Kewei Tu

14:42–14:45   *Saarland at MRP 2019: Compositional parsing across all graphbanks*
Lucia Donatelli, Meaghan Fowlie, Jonas Groschwitz, Alexander Koller, Matthias Lindemann, Mario Mina and Pia Weißenhorn

14:45–14:48   *HIT-SCIR at MRP 2019: A Unified Pipeline for Meaning Representation Parsing via Efficient Training and Effective Encoding*
Wanxiang Che, Longxu Dou, Yang Xu, Yuxuan Wang, Yijia Liu and Ting Liu

14:48–14:51   *SJTU at MRP 2019: A Transition-Based Multi-Task Parser for Cross-Framework Meaning Representation Parsing*
Hongxiao Bai and Hai Zhao

14:51–14:54   *JBNU at MRP 2019: Multi-level Biaffine Attention for Semantic Dependency Parsing*
Seung-Hoon Na, Jinwoon Min, Kwanghyeon Park, Jong-Hun Shin and Young-Kil Kim

14:54–14:57   *CUHK at MRP 2019: Transition-Based Parser with Cross-Framework Variable-Arity Resolve Action*
Sunny Lai, Chun Hei Lo, Kwong Sak Leung and Yee Leung

14:57–15:00   *Hitachi at MRP 2019: Unified Encoder-to-Biaffine Network for Cross-Framework Meaning Representation Parsing*
Yuta Koreeda, Gaku Morio, Terufumi Morishita, Hiroaki Ozaki and Kohsuke Yanai

15:00–15:03   *ÚFAL MRPipe at MRP 2019: UDPipe Goes Semantic in the Meaning Representation Parsing Shared Task*
Milan Straka and Jana Straková

15:03–15:06   *Amazon at MRP 2019: Parsing Meaning Representations with Lexical and Phrasal Anchoring*
Jie Cao, Yi Zhang, Adel Youssef and Vivek Srikumar

15:06–15:09   *SUDA-Alibaba at MRP 2019: Graph-Based Models with BERT*
Yue Zhang, Wei Jiang, Qingrong Xia, Junjie Cao, Rui Wang, Zhenghua Li and Min Zhang

15:09–15:12   *ÚFAL-Oslo at MRP 2019: Garage Sale Semantic Parsing*
Kira Droganova, Andrey Kutuzov, Nikita Mediankin and Daniel Zeman

15:12–15:15   *Peking at MRP 2019: Factorization- and Composition-Based Parsing for Elementary Dependency Structures*
Yufei Chen, Yajie Ye and Weiwei Sun

Final Discussion (15:15-15:30)

Poster Session

Please note that due to the travel restrictions caused by the Hongkong situation the program might change at a short notice.

MRP 2019: Cross-Framework Meaning Representation Parsing

Stephan Oepen♣, Omri Abend♠, Jan Hajič♡, Daniel Hershcovich◇, Marco Kuhlmann°,
Tim O'Gorman⋆, Nianwen Xue•, Jayeol Chun•, Milan Straka♡, and Zdeňka Urešová♡

♣ University of Oslo, Department of Informatics
♠ The Hebrew University of Jerusalem, School of Computer Science and Engineering
♡ Charles University in Prague, Faculty of Mathematics and Physics, Institute of Formal and Applied Linguistics
◇ University of Copenhagen, Department of Computer Science
° Linköping University, Department of Computer and Information Science
⋆ University of Colorado at Boulder, Department of Linguistics
• Brandeis University, Department of Computer Science

`mrp-organizers@nlpl.eu,`
`jchun@brandeis.edu, {straka|uresova}@ufal.mff.cuni.cz`

Abstract

The 2019 Shared Task at the Conference for
Computational Language Learning (CoNLL)
was devoted to Meaning Representation Parsing (MRP) across frameworks. Five distinct
approaches to the representation of sentence
meaning in the form of directed graphs were
represented in the training and evaluation data
for the task, packaged in a uniform graph abstraction and serialization. The task received
submissions from eighteen teams, of which
five do not participate in the official ranking
because they arrived after the closing deadline,
made use of extra training data, or involved
one of the task co-organizers. All technical information regarding the task, including system
submissions, official results, and links to supporting resources and software are available
from the task web site at:

`http://mrp.nlpl.eu`

1 Background and Motivation

All things semantic are receiving heightened attention in recent years, and despite remarkable advances in vector-based (continuous and distributed)
encodings of meaning, 'classic' (discrete and hier-
archically structured) semantic representations will
continue to play an important role in 'making sense'
of natural language. While parsing has long been
dominated by tree-structured target representations,
there is now growing interest in general graphs as
more expressive and arguably more adequate target
structures for sentence-level analysis beyond surface syntax, and in particular for the representation
of semantic structure.

The 2019 Conference on Computational Language Learning (CoNLL) hosts a shared task (or
'system bake-off') on Cross-Framework Meaning
Representation Parsing (MRP 2019). The goal
of the task is to advance data-driven parsing into
graph-structured representations of *sentence meaning*. For the first time, this task combines *formally*
and *linguistically* different approaches to meaning
representation in graph form in a uniform training and evaluation setup. Participants were invited
to develop parsing systems that support five distinct semantic graph frameworks (see §3 below)—
which all encode core predicate–argument structure, among other things—in the same implementation. Ideally, these parsers predict sentence-level
meaning representations in all frameworks in parallel. Architectures utilizing complementary knowledge sources (e.g. via parameter sharing) were encouraged, though not required. Learning from multiple flavors of meaning representation in tandem
has hardly been explored (with notable exceptions,
e.g. the parsers of Peng et al., 2017; Hershcovich
et al., 2018; or Stanovsky and Dagan, 2018).

Training and evaluation data were provided for
all five frameworks. The task design aims to reduce
framework-specific 'balkanization' in the field of
meaning representation parsing. Its contributions
include (a) a unifying formal model over different semantic graph banks (§2), (b) uniform representations and scoring (§4 and §6), (c) contrastive evaluation across frameworks (§5), and
(d) increased cross-fertilization via transfer and
multi-task learning (§7). Thus, the task engages
the combined community of parser developers for
graph-structured output representations, including
from prior framework-specific tasks at the Semantic Evaluation (SemEval) exercises between 2014
and 2019 (Oepen et al., 2014, 2015; May, 2016;
May and Priyadarshi, 2017; Hershcovich et al.,
2019). Owing to the scarcity of semantic anno-

Proceedings of the Shared Task on Cross-Framework Meaning Representation Parsing at the 2019 CoNLL, pages 1–27
Hong Kong, November 3, 2019. ©2019 Association for Computational Linguistics
https://doi.org/10.18653/v1/K19-2001

tations across frameworks, the MRP 2019 shared task is regrettably limited to parsing English for the time being.

2 Definitions: Graphs and Flavors

Reflecting different traditions and communities, there is wide variation in how individual meaning representation frameworks think (and talk) about semantic graphs, down to the level of visual conventions used in rendering graph structures. The following paragraphs provide semi-formal definitions of core graph-theoretic concepts that can be meaningfully applied across the range of frameworks represented in the shared task.

Basic Terminology Semantic graphs (across different frameworks) can be viewed as directed graphs or *digraphs*. A semantic digraph is a triple (T, N, E) where N is a set of *nodes* and $E \subseteq N \times N$ is a set of *edges*. The *in-* and *out-degree* of a node count the number of edges arriving at or leaving from the node, respectively. In contrast to the unique *root* node in trees, graphs can have multiple (structural) roots, which we define as nodes with in-degree zero. The majority of semantic graphs are structurally multi-rooted. Thus, we distinguish one or several nodes in each graph as *top* nodes, $T \subset N$; the top(s) correspond(s) to the most central semantic entities in the graph, usually the main predication(s).

In a tree, every node except the root has in-degree one. In semantic graphs, nodes can have in-degree two or higher (indicating shared arguments), which constitutes a *reentrancy* in the graph. In contrast to trees, general digraphs may contain *cycles*, i.e. a directed path leading from a node to itself. Another central property of trees is that they are *connected*, meaning that there exists an undirected path between any pair of nodes. In contrast, semantic graphs need not generally be connected.

Finally, in some semantic graph frameworks there is a (total) linear order on the nodes, typically induced by the surface order of corresponding tokens. Such graphs are conventionally called *bi-lexical dependencies* and formally constitute ordered graphs. A natural way to visualize a bi-lexical dependency graph is to draw its edges as semicircles in the halfplane above the sentence. An ordered graph is called *noncrossing* if in such a drawing, the semicircles intersect only at their endpoints (this property is a natural generalization of projectivity as it is known from dependency trees).

A natural generalization of the noncrossing property, where one is allowed to also use the halfplane below the sentence for drawing edges is a property called *pagenumber two*. Kuhlmann and Oepen (2016) provide additional definitions and a quantitative summary of various formal graph properties across frameworks.

Hierarchy of Formal Flavors In the context of the shared task, we distinguish different *flavors* of semantic graphs based on the nature of the relationship they assume between the linguistic surface signal (typically a written sentence, i.e. a string) and the nodes of the graph. We refer to this relation as *anchoring* (of nodes onto sub-strings); other commonly used terms include alignment, correspondence, or lexicalization.

Flavor (0) is the strongest form of anchoring, obtained in bi-lexical dependency graphs, where graph nodes injectively correspond to surface lexical units (i.e. tokens or 'words'). In such graphs, each node is directly linked to one specific token (conversely, there may be semantically empty tokens), and the nodes inherit the linear order of their corresponding tokens.

Flavor (1) includes a more general form of anchored semantic graphs, characterized by relaxing the correspondence between nodes and tokens, allowing arbitrary parts of the sentence (e.g. sub-token or multi-token sequences) as node anchors, as well as multiple nodes anchored to overlapping sub-strings. These graphs afford greater flexibility in the representation of meaning contributed by, for example, (derivational) affixes or phrasal constructions and facilitate lexical decomposition (e.g. of causatives or comparatives).

Finally, Flavor (2) semantic graphs do not consider the correspondence between nodes and the surface string as part of the representation of meaning (thus backgrounding notions of derivation and compositionality). Such semantic graphs are simply unanchored.

While different flavors refer to formally defined sub-classes of semantic graphs, we reserve the term *framework* for specific linguistic approaches to graph-based meaning representation (typically encoded in a particular graph flavor, of course).

3 Meaning Representation Frameworks

The shared task combines five frameworks for graph-based meaning representation, each with its specific formal and linguistic assumptions. This

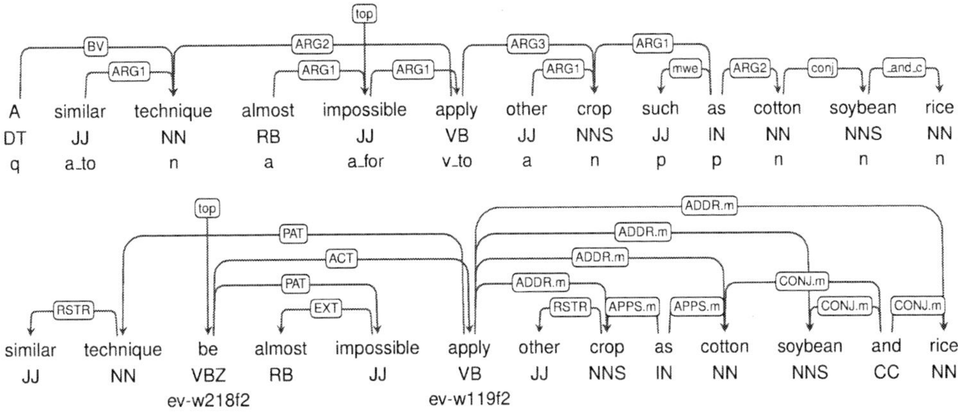

Figure 1: Bi-lexical semantic dependencies for the running example *A similar technique is almost impossible to apply to other crops, such as cotton, soybeans and rice*: DELPH-IN MRS Bi-Lexical Dependencies (DM; top) and Prague Semantic Dependencies (PSD; bottom).

section reviews the frameworks and presents example graphs for sentence #20209013 from the venerable Wall Street Journal (WSJ) Corpus from the Penn Treebank (PTB; Marcus et al., 1993):

> (1) *A similar technique is almost impossible to apply to other crops, such as cotton, soybeans and rice.*

The example exhibits some interesting linguistic complexity, including what is called a tough adjective (*impossible*), a scopal adverb (*almost*), a tripartite coordinate structure, and apposition. The example graphs in Figures 1 through 3 are presented in order of (arguably) increasing 'abstraction' from the surface string, i.e. ranging from ordered Flavor (0) to unanchored Flavor (2).

Two of the frameworks in the shared task present simplifications into bi-lexical semantic dependencies (i.e. lossy reductions) of independently developed syntactico-semantic annotations. These representations were first prepared for the Semantic Dependency Parsing (SDP) tasks at the 2014 and 2015 SemEval campaigns (Oepen et al., 2014, 2015). The SDP graph banks were originally released through the Linguistic Data Consortium (as catalogue entry LDC 2016T10); they comprise four distinct bi-lexical semantic dependency frameworks, from which the MRP 2019 shared task selects two (a) DELPH-IN MRS Bi-Lexical Dependencies (DM) and (b) Prague Semantic Dependencies (PSD).[1]

DELPH-IN MRS Bi-Lexical Dependencies
The DM bi-lexical dependencies (Ivanova et al., 2012) originally derive from the underspecified logical forms computed by the English Resource Grammar (Flickinger et al., 2017; Copestake et al., 2005). These logical forms are not in and of themselves semantic graphs (in the sense of § 2 above) and are often refered to as English Resource Semantics (ERS; Bender et al., 2015). The underlying grammar is rooted in the general linguistic theory of Head-Driven Phrase Structure Grammar (HPSG; Pollard and Sag, 1994).

Ivanova et al. (2012) propose a two-stage conversion from ERS into bi-lexical semantic dependency graphs, where ERS logical forms are first recast as Elementary Dependency Structures (EDS; Oepen and Lønning, 2006; see below) and then further simplified into pure bi-lexical semantic dependencies, dubbed DELPH-IN MRS Bi-Lexical Dependencies (or DM). As a Flavor (0) framework, graph nodes in DM are restricted to surface tokens. But DM graphs are neither lexically fully covering nor rooted trees, i.e. some tokens do not contribute to the graph, and for some nodes there are multiple incoming edges. In the example DM graph in Figure 1, *technique* semantically depends on the determiner (the quantificational locus), the modifier *similar*, and the predicate *apply*. Conversely, the predicative copula, infinitival *to*, and the vacu-

---

[1]Note, however, that the parsing problem for these frameworks is harder in the current shared task than in the ealier SDP 2014 and 2015 tasks, because gold-standard tokenization, lemmas, and parts of speech are not available as part of the parser input data. Also, some minor lemmatization errors have been corrected for both the DM and PSD graphs, in comparison to the original SDP releases.

ous preposition marking the deep object of *apply* (in the top of Figure 1) are analyzed as not having a semantic contribution of their own. The top node in the DM graph is the degree adverb *almost*, reflecting the underlying logical form, where *almost* has operator-like status scoping over the full proposition.

In DM, edge labels predominantly indicate semantic argument positions (ARG1, ARG2, . . .) into the relation corresponding to their source node, but there are some more specialized edge labels too, like BV (bound variable) as a reflection of quantification in the underlying logic, conj and others for coordinate structures, and mwe to structurally tie together multi-token predicates. Node labels are tripartite, combining the lemmatized surface form with a part of speech (pos) and a framework-specific frame identifier. Together, these encode grammaticalized word sense distinctions, such as those between the nominal vs. verbal usages of *crop* or the distinct valency frames for three-place *apply . . . to* (e.g. paint, to the wall) vs. binary *apply for* (e.g. promotion).

Prague Semantic Dependencies Another instance of simplification from richer syntactico-semantic representations into Flavor (0) bi-lexical semantic dependencies is the reduction of *tectogrammatical trees* (or t-trees) from the linguistic school of Functional Generative Description (FGD; Sgall et al., 1986; Hajič et al., 2012) into what are called Prague Semantic Dependencies (or PSD). Miyao et al. (2014) sketch the nature of this conversion, which essentially collapses empty (or *generated*, in FGD terminology) t-tree nodes with corresponding surface nodes and forward-projects incoming dependencies onto all members of paratactic constructions, e.g. the appositive and coordinate structures in the bottom of Figure 1.

The PSD graph for our running example has many of the same dependency edges as the DM one (albeit using a different labeling scheme and inverse directionality in a few cases), but it analyzes the predicative copula as semantically contentful and does not treat *almost* as 'scoping' over the entire graph. The ADDR.m(ember) argument relation to the *apply* predicate has been recursively propagated to both elements of the apposition and to all members of the coordinate structure. Accordingly, edge labels in PSD are not in general functional, in the sense of allowing multiple outgoing edges from one node with the same label.

In FGD, role labels (called *functors*) ACT(or), PAT(ient), ADDR(essee), ORIG(in), and EFF(ect) indicate 'participant' positions in an underlying valency frame and, thus, correspond more closely to the numbered argument positions in other frameworks than their names might suggest.[2] The PSD annotations are grounded in a machine-readable valency lexicon (Urešová et al., 2016), and the frame values on verbal nodes in Figure 1 indicate specific verbal senses in the lexicon.

Elementary Dependency Structures Elementary Dependency Structures (EDS; Oepen and Lønning, 2006) encode English Resource Semantics in a variable-free semantic dependency graph—not limited to bi-lexical dependencies—where graph nodes correspond to logical predications and edges to labeled argument positions. The EDS conversion from underspecified logical forms to directed graphs discards partial information on semantic scope from the full ERS, which makes these graphs abstractly—if not linguistically—similar to Abstract Meaning Representation (see below).

Nodes in EDS are in principle independent of surface lexical units, but for each node there is an explicit, many-to-many anchoring onto sub-strings of the underlying sentence. Thus, EDS instantiates Flavor (1) in our hierarchy of different formal types of semantic graphs. Breaking free of the Flavor (0) one-to-one correspondence between graph nodes and surface lexical units enables EDS to more adequately represent, among other things, lexical decomposition (e.g. of comparatives), sub-lexical or construction semantics, and covert (e.g. elided) meaning contributions. All nodes in the example EDS in the top of Figure 2 make explicit their anchoring onto sub-strings of the underlying input, for example span $\langle 2 : 9 \rangle$ for *similar*.

In the EDS analysis for the running example, nodes representing covert quantifiers (e.g. on bare nominals, labeled udef_q[3]), the two-place such+as_p relation, as well as the implicit_conj(unction) relation (which reflects recursive decomposition of the coordinate structure

---

[2]Accordingly, multiple instances of the same core participant role—as ADDR.m in Figure 1—will only occur with propagation of dependencies into paratactic constructions.

[3]In the EDS example in the top of Figure 2, all nodes corresponding to instances of bare 'nominal' meanings are bound by a covert quantificational predicate, including the group-forming implicit_conj and _and_c nodes that represent the nested, binary-branching coordinate structure. This practice of uniform quantifier introduction in ERS is acknowledged as "particularly exuberant" by Steedman (2011, p. 21).

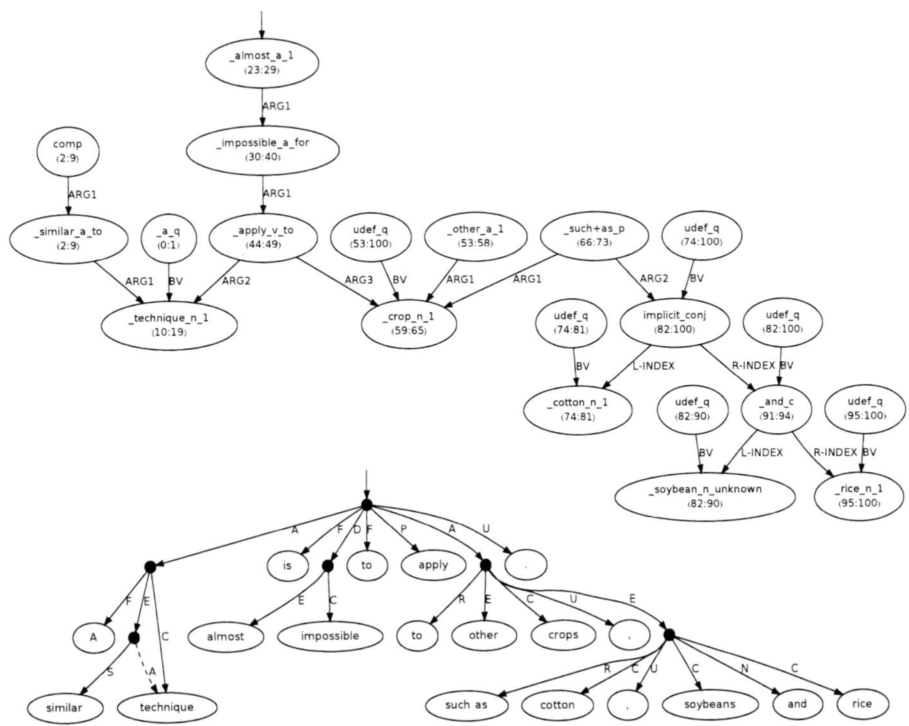

Figure 2: Semantic dependency graphs for the running example *A similar technique is almost impossible to apply to other crops, such as cotton, soybeans and rice*: Elementary Dependency Structures (EDS; top) and Universal Conceptual Cognitive Annotation (UCCA; bottom).

into binary predications) do not correspond to individual surface tokens (but are anchored on larger spans, overlapping with anchors from other nodes). Conversely, the two nodes associated with *similar* indicate lexical decomposition as a comparative predicate, where the second argument of the comp relation (the 'point of reference') remains unexpressed in Example (1).

Universal Conceptual Cognitive Annotation
Universal Cognitive Conceptual Annotation (UCCA; Abend and Rappoport, 2013) is based on cognitive linguistic and typological theories, primarily Basic Linguistic Theory (Dixon, 2010/2012). The shared task targets the UCCA foundational layer, which focuses on argument structure phenomena (where predicates may be verbal, nominal, adjectival, or otherwise). This coarse grained level of semantics has been shown to be preserved well across translations (Sulem et al., 2015). It has also been successfully used

for improving text simplification (Sulem et al., 2018b), as well as to the evaluation of a number of text-to-text generation tasks (Birch et al., 2016; Sulem et al., 2018a; Choshen and Abend, 2018).

The basic unit of annotation is the *scene*, denoting a situation mentioned in the sentence, typically involving a predicate, participants, and potentially modifiers. Linguistically, UCCA adopts a notion of semantic constituency that transcends pure dependency graphs, in the sense of introducing separate, unlabeled nodes, called *units*. One or more labels are assigned to each edge. Formally, UCCA has a Type (1) flavor, where leaf (or terminal) nodes of the graph are anchored to possibly discontinuous sequences of surface sub-strings, while interior (or 'phrasal') graph nodes are formally unanchored.

The UCCA graph for the running example (see the bottom of Figure 2) includes a single scene, whose main relation is the Process (P) evoked by *apply*. It also contains a secondary relation labeled Adverbial (D), *almost impossible*, which is broken

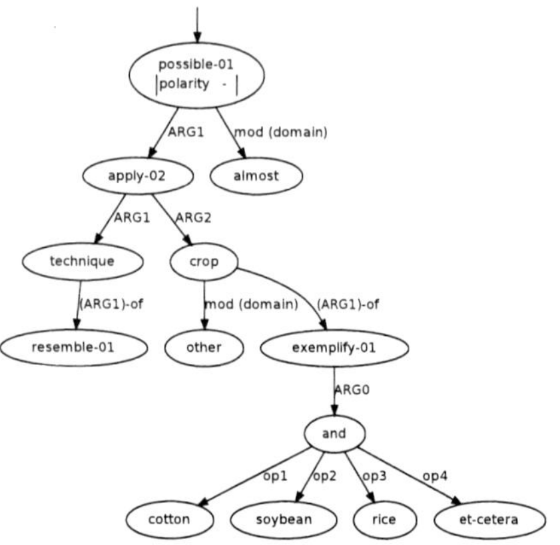

Figure 3: Abstract Meaning Representation (AMR) for the running example *A similar technique is almost impossible to apply to other crops, such as cotton, soybeans and rice.*

down into its Center (C) and Elaborator (E); as well as two complex arguments, labeled as Participants (A). Unlike the other frameworks in the task, the UCCA foundational layer integrates all surface tokens into the graph, possibly as the targets of semantically bleached Function (F) and Punctuation (U) edges. UCCA graphs need not be rooted trees: Argument sharing across units will give rise to reentrant nodes much like in the other frameworks. For example, *technique* in Figure 2 is both a Participant in the scene evoked by *similar* and a Center in the parent unit. UCCA in principle also supports implicit (unexpressed) units which do not correspond to any tokens, but these are currently excluded from parsing evaluation and, thus, suppressed in the UCCA graphs distributed in the context of the shared task.

Abstract Meaning Representation   Finally, the shared task includes Abstract Meaning Representation (AMR; Banarescu et al., 2013), which in the MRP hierarchy of different formal types of semantic graphs (see § 2 above) is simply unanchored, i.e. represents Flavor (2). The AMR framework is independent of particular approaches to derivation and compositionality and, accordingly, does not make explicit how elements of the graph correspond to the surface utterance. Although most AMR parsing research presupposes a pre-processing step that 'aligns' graph nodes with (possibly discontinuous) sets of tokens in the underlying input, this anchor-

ing is not part of the meaning representation proper.

At the same time, AMR frequently invokes lexical decomposition and normalization towards verbal senses, such that AMR graphs often appear to 'abstract' furthest from the surface signal. Since the first general release of an AMR graph bank in 2014, the framework has provided a popular target for data-driven meaning representation parsing and has been the subject of two consecutive tasks at SemEval 2016 and 2017 (May, 2016; May and Priyadarshi, 2017).

The AMR example graph in Figure 3 has a topology broadly comparable to EDS, with some notable differences. Similar to the UCCA example graph (and unlike EDS), the AMR representation of the coordinate structure is flat. Although most lemmas are linked to derivationally related forms in the sense lexicon, this is not universal, as seen by the nodes corresponding to *similar* and *such as*, which are labeled as resemble-01 and exemplify-01, respectively. These sense distinctions (primarily for verbal predicates) are grounded in the inventory of predicates from the PropBank lexicon (Kingsbury and Palmer, 2002; Hovy et al., 2006).

Role labels in AMR encode semantic argument positions, with the particular roles defined according to each PropBank sense, though the counting in AMR is zero-based such that the ARG1 and ARG2 roles in Figure 3 often correspond to ARG2 and ARG3, respectively, in the EDS of Figure 2. PropBank distinguishes such numbered arguments from non-core roles labeled from a general semantic inventory, such as frequency, duration, or domain.

Figure 3 also shows the use of inverted edges in AMR, for example ARG1-of and mod. These serve to allow annotators (and in principle also parsing systems) to view the graph as a tree-like structure (with occasional reentrancies) but are formally merely considered notational variants. Therefore, the MRP rendering of the AMR example graph also provides an unambiguous indication of the underlying, normalized graph: Edges with a label component shown in parentheses are to be reversed in normalization, e.g. representing an actual ARG0 edge from resemble-01 to technique or a domain edge from other to crop.

Given the non-compositionality of AMR annotation, AMR allows the introduction of semantic concepts which have no explicit lexicalization in the text, for example the et-cetera element in the coordinate structure in Figure 3. Conversely, like

		DM	PSD	EDS	UCCA	AMR
	Flavor	0	0	1	1	2
TRAIN	Text Type	newspaper	newspaper	newspaper	mixed	mixed
	Sentences	35,656	35,656	35,656	6,572	56,240
	Tokens	802,717	802,717	802,717	138,268	1,000,217
TEST	Text Type	mixed	mixed	mixed	mixed	mixed
	Sentences	3,359	3,359	3,359	1,131	1,998
	Tokens	64,853	64,853	64,853	21,647	39,520

Table 1: Quantitative summary of gold-standard training and evaluation data for the five frameworks.

in the other frameworks (except UCCA), some surface tokens are analyzed as semantically vacuous. For example, parallel to the PSD graph in Figure 1, there is no meaning contribution annotated for the determiner *a* (let alone for covert determiners in bare nominals, as are made explicit as quantificational nodes in EDS).

4 Task Setup

The following paragraphs summarize the 'logistics' of the MRP 2019 shared task, including data and software provided to participants, the schedule, and rules of participation.

Training and Evaluation Data Table 1 summarizes the primary training and evaluation data provided to task participants. The DM and PSD data sets are annotations over the exact same selection of texts, which for the earler SemEval tasks have been aligned at the sentence and token levels. As DM was originally derived from EDS, the EDS graphs also cover the same texts. The training data for these frameworks draws from a homogeneous source, WSJ Sections 00–20 from the PTB. As a common point of reference, a sample of 100 WSJ sentences annotated in all five frameworks is available for public download from the task web site (see §9 below).

UCCA training annotations are over web reviews from the English Web Treebank (LDC 2012T13), and from English Wikipedia articles on celebrities. While in principle UCCA structures are not confined to a single sentence (about 0.18 percent of edges cross sentence boundaries), in the MRP context passages are split to individual sentences, discarding inter-relations between them, to create a standard setting across the frameworks.

AMR annotations are drawn from a wide variety of texts, with the majority of sentences coming from on-line discussion forums. The training corpus also contains newswire, folktales, fiction, and Wikipedia articles.

Table 2 provides a quantitative side-by-side comparison of the training data, using some of the graph-theoretic properties discussed by Kuhlmann and Oepen (2016); see §2 for semi-formal definitions (the row indices in Table 2 correspond to the numbering used by Kuhlmann and Oepen, 2016). The table indicates clear differences among the frameworks. The underlying input strings for AMR (where text selection is more varied), for example, are shorter; and EDS and UCCA have many more nodes per token, on average, than the other frameworks—reflecting lexical decomposition and 'phrasal' grouping, respectively, as evident in Figure 2. In some respects, the PSD and UCCA graphs are more tree-like than graphs in the other frameworks, for example in their proportions of actual rooted trees, the frequencies of reentrant nodes, and the lower percentages of multi-rooted structures. At the same time, PSD exhibits comparatively high average and maximal treewidth. Finally, the properties applicable to the ordered bi-lexical frameworks only are largely comparable, though PSD edges on average span over larger distances; propagation of dependencies into paratactic structures observed in Figure 1 may well contribute substantially to this quantitative difference.

Evaluation data for the five frameworks (also summarized in Table 1) draws on many of the same domains and genres, with two major additions: For DM, PSD, and EDS (where the training data is homogeneously comprised of newspaper texts), a little more than half of the evaluation data are taken from 'out-of-domain' texts, viz. a balanced sample of documents from the Brown Corpus (Francis and Kučera, 1982). Additionally, a fresh random selection of 100 sentences from the novel *The Little Prince* (by Antoine de Saint-Exupéry) was manually annotated with gold-standard semantic graphs

			DM	PSD	EDS	UCCA	AMR^{-1}
COUNTS	(02)	Average Tokens per Graph	22.51	22.51	22.51	21.03	17.78
	(03)	Average Nodes per Token	0.77	0.64	1.29	1.37	0.65
	(04)	Number of Edge Labels	59	90	10	15	101
TREENESS	(05)	$\%_g$ Rooted Trees	2.31	42.26	0.09	34.83	22.24
	(06)	$\%_g$ Treewidth One	69.82	43.08	68.99	41.57	50.00
	(07)	Average Treewidth	1.30	1.61	1.31	1.61	1.56
	(08)	Maximal Treewidth	3	7	3	4	5
	(09)	Average Edge Density	1.019	1.073	1.015	1.053	1.092
	(10)	$\%_n$ Reentrant	27.43	11.41	32.78	4.98	19.89
	(11)	$\%_g$ Cyclic	0.00	0.00	0.12	0.00	0.38
	(12)	$\%_g$ Not Connected	6.57	0.70	1.74	0.00	0.00
	(13)	$\%_g$ Multi-Rooted	97.47	40.60	99.93	0.00	71.37
ORDER	(15)	Average Edge Length	2.684	3.320	–	–	–
	(16)	$\%_g$ Noncrossing	69.21	64.61	–	–	–
	(17)	$\%_g$ Pagenumber Two	99.59	98.08	–	–	–

Table 2: Contrastive graph statistics for the MRP 2019 training data using a subset of the properties defined by Kuhlmann and Oepen (2016). Here, $\%_g$ and $\%_n$ indicate percentages of all graphs and nodes, respectively, in each framework; AMR^{-1} refers to the *normalized* form of the graphs, with inverted edges reversed, as discussed in § 3.

in all five frameworks.[4] This subset of the evaluation data is available for download from the task site.

Because some of the semantic graph banks involved in the shared task had originally been released by the Linguistic Data Consortium (LDC), the training data was made available to task participants by the LDC under no-cost evaluation licenses. Upon completion of the competition, all task data (including system submissions and evaluation results) are being prepared for general release through the LDC, while those subsets that are copyright-free will also become available for direct, open-source download.

Additional Resources For reasons of comparability and fairness, the shared task constrained which additional data or pre-trained models (e.g. corpora, word embeddings, lexica, or other annotations) can be legitimately used besides the resources distributed by the task organizers. The overall goal was that all participants should in principle be able to use the same range of data. However, to keep such constraints to the minimum required, a 'white-list' of legitimate resources was compiled from nominations by participants (with a cut-off date six weeks before the end of the evalua-

tion period).[5] Thus, the task design reflects what is at times called a *closed track*, where participants are constrained in which additional data and pre-trained models can be used in system development.

At a technical level, training (and evaluation) data were distributed in two formats, (a) as sequences of 'raw' sentence strings and (b) in pre-tokenized, part-of-speech–tagged, lemmatized, and syntactically parsed form. For the latter, premium-quality English morpho-syntactic analyses were provided to participants, described in more detail below. These parser outputs are referred to as the MRP 2019 morpho-syntactic companion trees. Additional companion data available to participants includes automatically generated reference anchorings (commonly called 'alignments' in AMR parsing) for the AMR graphs in the training data, obtained from the JAMR and ISI tools of Flanigan et al. (2016) and Pourdamghani et al. (2014), respectively.

Companion Dependency Trees The optional morpho-syntactic trees were generated from the combination of a rule-based PTB-style tokenizer and a high-accuracy dependency parser trained on the union of (the majority of) available English syntactic treebanks. Notably, we applied an updated version of the converter by Schuster and Manning (2016) to the PTB annotations of the Brown Corpus (Francis and Kučera, 1982) and of the WSJ

---

[4] Annotations of the full novel have long served as a common reference point for AMR, and gold-standard DM and EDS graphs could be converted from the ERS inter-annotator agreement study by Bender et al. (2015). For PSD and UCCA, the 100-sentence subset used for MRP evaluation has been annotated specifically for the shared task.

[5] See http://svn.nlpl.eu/mrp/2019/public/resources.txt for the full list of seventeen generally available third-party resources, including a broad range of large English corpora and distributed word representations.

Corpus, as well as to the PTB-style annotations of the GENIA Corpus (Tateisi et al., 2005). This conversion targets Universal Dependencies (UD; McDonald et al., 2013; Nivre, 2015) version 2.x, so that the resulting gold-standard annotations could be concatenated with the UD English Web Treebank (Silveira et al., 2014), for a total of 2.2 million tokens annotated with lemmas, Universal and PTB-style parts of speech, and UD labeled dependency trees.

We then trained the currently best-performing UDPipe architecture (Straka, 2018; Straka et al., 2019), which implements a joint part-of-speech tagger, lemmatizer, and dependency parser employing contextualized BERT embeddings. To avoid overlap of morpho-syntactic training data with the texts underlying the semantic graphs of the shared task, we performed five-fold jack-knifing on the WSJ and EWT corpora. For compatibility with the majority of the training data, the 'raw' input strings for the MRP semantic graphs were tokenized using the PTB-style REPP rules of Dridan and Oepen (2012) and input to UDPipe in pre-tokenized form. Whether as merely a source of state-of-the-art PTB-style tokenization, or as a vantage point for approaches to meaning representation parsing that start from explicit syntactic structure, the optional morpho-syntactic companion data offers community value in its own right.

Graph Interchange Format Besides differences in anchoring, the frameworks also vary in how they label nodes and edges, and to what degree they allow multiple edges between two nodes, multiple outgoing edges of the same label, or multiple instances of the same property on a node. Node labels for Flavor (0) graphs typically are lemmas, optionally combined with a (morpho-syntactic) part of speech and a (syntactico-semantic) frame (or sense) identifier. Node labels for the other graph flavors tend to be more abstract, i.e. are interpreted as concept or relation identifiers (where for the vast majority, of course, there also is a systematic relationship to lemmas, lexical categories, and (sub-)senses). Graph nodes in UCCA are formally unlabeled, and anchoring is used to relate leaf nodes of these graphs to input sub-strings. Conversely, edge labels in all cases come from a fixed and relatively small inventory of (semantic) argument names, though there is stark variation in label granularity, ranging between about a dozen in UCCA and around 90 or 100 in PSD and AMR,

respectively; see Table 2. The shared task has, for the first time, repackaged the five graph banks into a uniform and normalized abstract representation with a common serialization format.

The common interchange format for semantic graphs implements the abstract model of Kuhlmann and Oepen (2016) as a JSON-based serialization for graphs across frameworks. This format describes general directed graphs, with structured node and edge labels, and optional anchoring and ordering of nodes. JSON is easily manipulated in all programming languages and offers parser developers the option of 'in situ' augmentation of the graph representations from the task with system-specific additional information, e.g. by adding private properties to the JSON objects. The MRP interchange format is based on the JSON Lines format, where a stream of objects is serialized with line breaks as the separator character.

Each MRP graph is represented as a JSON object with top-level properties `tops`, `nodes`, and `edges`, reflecting the definitions in §2 above. Additionally, an `input` property on all graphs presents the 'raw' surface string corresponding to this graph; thus, parser inputs for the task are effectively assumed to be sentence-segmented but not pre-tokenized. Additional information about each graph is provided as properties `id` (a string), `flavor` (an integer in the range 0–2), `framework` (a string), `version` (a decimal number), and `time` (a string, encoding when the graph was serialized).

The `nodes` and `edges` values on graphs each are list-valued, but the order among list elements is only meaningful for the nodes of Flavor (0) graphs. Node objects have an obligatory `id` property (an integer) and optional properties called `label`, `properties` and `values`, as well as `anchors`. The `label` (a string) has a distinguished status in evaluation; the `properties` and `values` are both list-valued, such that elements between the lists correspond by position. Together, the two lists present a framework-specific, non-recursive attribute–value matrix (where duplicate properties are in principle allowed). The `anchors` list, if present, contains pairs of `from`–`to` sub-string indices into the `input` string of the graph. Finally, the edge objects in the top-level `edges` list all have two integer-valued properties: `source` and `target`, which encode the start and end nodes, respectively, to which the edge is incident. All edges in the MRP collection further have a (string-valued) `label` property, although formally this is considered optional. Parallel to graph nodes, edges can carry framework-specific `attributes` and `values` lists; in MRP 2019, only the UCCA framework makes use of edge attributes, viz. a boolean `remote` flag (corresponding to dashed edges in the bottom of Figure 2).

Rules of Participation The shared task was first announced in early March 2019, the initial release of the unified training data became available in mid-April, and the evaluation period ran between July 8 and 25, 2019; during this period, teams obtained the unannotated input strings for the evaluation data and had available a little more than two weeks to prepare and submit parser outputs. Submission of semantic graphs for evaluation was through the on-line CodaLab infrastructure, which proved a sub-optimal choice—in part due to limited transparency and customization options of the service, in part because technical problems on the CodaLab site caused the entire infrastructure to be unavailable for five days during the MRP evaluation period.

Teams were allowed to make repeated submissions, but only the most recent successful upload to CodaLab within the evaluation period was considered for the official, primary ranking of submissions. Task participants were encouraged to process all inputs using the same general parsing system, but—owing to inevitable fuzziness about what constitutes 'one' parser—this constraint was not formally enforced. Unlike in recent years of other CoNLL shared tasks, processing of the evaluation data was not tied to a uniform virtualization platform (such as TIRA; Potthast et al., 2014), because GPU computing resources are a prerequisite to modern, neural parsing architectures but are not currently available on such platforms.

5 Evaluation

For each of the individual frameworks, there are established ways of evaluating the quality of parser outputs in terms of graph similarity to gold-standard target representations called EDM (Dridan and Oepen, 2011), SMATCH (Cai and Knight, 2013), SDP (Oepen et al., 2014), and UCCA (Hershcovich et al., 2019). There is broad similarity between the framework-specific evaluation metrics used to date, but also some subtle differences. Meaning representation parsing is commonly evaluated in terms of a graph similarity F_1 score at

	DM	PSD	EDS	UCCA	AMR
Top Nodes	✓	✓	✓	✓	✓
Node Labels	✓	✓	✓	✗	✓
Node Properties	✓	✓	✓	✗	✓
Node Anchoring	✓	✓	✓	✓	✗
Labeled Edges	✓	✓	✓	✓	✓
Edge Attributes	✗	✗	✗	✓	✗

Table 3: Different tuple types per framework.

the level of individual node–edge–node and node–property–value triples. Variations in extant metrics relate to among others, how node correspondences across two graphs are established, whether edge labels can optionally be ignored in triple comparison, and how top nodes (and other node properties, including anchoring) are evaluated.

Background In a nutshell, semantic graphs in all frameworks can be broken down into 'atomic' component pieces, i.e. tuples capturing (a) top nodes, (b) node labels, (c) node properties, (d) node anchoring, (e) labeled edges, and (f) edge attributes.[6] Not all tuple types apply to all frameworks, however, as is summarized in Table 3.

To evaluate any of these tuple types, a correspondence relation must be established between nodes (and edges) from the gold-standard vs. the system graphs. This relation presupposes a notion of node (and edge) identities, which is where the various flavors and frameworks differ. In bi-lexical (semantic) dependencies—e.g. DM and PSD, our Flavor (0)—the nodes are surface lexical units (tokens); their identities are uniquely determined as the character range of the corresponding sub-strings (rather than by token indices, which would not be robust to tokenization mis-matches). In the Flavor (1) graphs (EDS and UCCA), multiple distinct nodes can have overlapping or even identical anchors; in EDS, for example, the semantics of an adverb like *today* is decomposed into four nodes, all anchored to the same substring:

$$\text{implicit\_q } x : \text{time\_n}(x) \land$$
$$\text{\_today\_a\_1}(x) \land \text{temp\_loc}(e, x) .$$

The standard EDS and UCCA evaluation metrics determine node identities through anchors (and

---

[6]In principle, one could further view unlabeled edges and their labels as two distinct pieces of information, but the task design shies away from such formal purity for both linguistic and practical reasons. First, it does not appear desirable to try and give credit for edges with incompatible labels (e.g. an ARG1 with an ARG3); and, second, it would make the search for node-to-node correspondences somewhat less tractable.

transitively the union of child anchors, in the case of UCCA) and allow many-to-many correspondences across the gold-standard and system graphs (Oepen et al., 2014; Hershcovich et al., 2019). Finally, as a Flavor (2) framework, nodes in AMR graphs are unanchored. Thus, node-to-node correspondences need to be established (as one-to-one equivalence classes of node identifiers), to maximize the set of shared tuples between each pair of graphs. Abstractly, this is an instance of the NP-hard maximum common edge subgraph isomorphism problem (where node-local tuples can be modeled as 'pseudo-edges' with globally unique target nodes). The standard SMATCH scorer for AMR approximates a solution through a hill-climbing search for high-scoring correspondences, with a fixed number of random restarts (Cai and Knight, 2013).

Unified Evaluation For the shared task, we have implemented a generalization of existing, framework-specific metrics, along the lines above. Our goal is for the unified MRP metric to (a) be applicable across different flavors of semantic graphs, (b) enable labeled and unlabeled variants, as much as possible, (c) not require corresponding node anchoring, but (d) minimize the impact of non-deterministic approximations, and (e) take advantage of anchoring information when available. The official MRP metric for the task is the average F_1 score across frameworks over all tuple types.

The basic principle is that all information presented in the MRP graph representations is scored with equal weight, i.e. all applicable tuple types for each framework. There is no special status (or 'primacy') to anchoring in this scheme: Unlike the original SDP, EDM, and UCCA metrics, the MRP scorer searches for a correspondence relation between the gold-standard and system graphs that maximizes tuple overlap. Thus, the MRP approach is abstractly similar to SMATCH, but using a search algorithm that considers the full range of different tuple types and finds an exact solution in the majority of cases.[7]

Anchoring (for all frameworks but AMR) in this scheme is treated on a par with node labels and properties, labeled edges, and edge attributes. Likewise, the `pos` and `frame` (or sense) node properties in DM and PSD are scored with equal weight as

the node labels (which are lemmas for the bi-lexical semantic graphs), given that the three properties jointly determine the semantic predicate.

For AMR evaluation, there is an exception to the above principle that all information in MRP graphs be scored equally: The MRP encodings of AMR graphs preserve the tree-like topology used in AMR annotations, using 'inverted' edges with labels like ARG0-of (see § 3 above). To make explicit which AMR edges actually are inverted, the MRP encoding in JSON provides an additional `normal` property, which is present only an inverted edges and provides the effective 'base' label (e.g. ARG0). AMR graphs are standardly evaluated in normalized form, i.e. with inverted edges restored to their 'base' directionality and label.

Software Support MRP scoring is implemented in the open-source `mtool` software (the Swiss Army Knife of Meaning Representation), which is hosted in a public Microsoft GitHub repository to stimulate community engagement.[8] `mtool` implements a refinement of the maximum common edge subgraph (MCES) algorithm by McGregor (1982), initializing and scheduling candidate node-to-node correspondences based on pre-computed per-node rewards and upper bounds on adjacent edge correspondences.[9] In addition to the cross-framework MRP metric, the tool also provides reference implementations of the SDP, EDM, SMATCH, and UCCA metrics, in the case of SDP and UCCA generalized to support character-based anchoring (rather than using token indices).

Value comparison in MRP evaluation is robust to 'uninteresting' variation, i.e. different encodings of essentially the same information. Specifically, literal values will always be compared as case-insensitive strings, such that for example 42 (an integer) and "42" (a string) are considered equivalent, as are "Pierre" and "pierre"; this applies to node and edge labels, node properties, and edge attributes. Anchor values are normalized for comparison into sets of non-whitespace character positions. For example, assuming the underlying

---

[7] The MRP scorer further avoids a few known implementation issues in SMATCH related to over-counting, incomplete normalization, and top nodes.

[8] See `https://github.com/cfmrp/mtool` for access to the software and available documentation.

[9] For the *ordered* DM and PSD graphs, an optimal initialization regarding node-local information can be efficiently computed, using an adaptation of the dynamic programming algorithm for minimum-edit–distance problems For these graphs, scheduling of variant correspondences is further constrained to search for local variations first, i.e. alternate node–node pairings are considered in increasing node distance relative to the initial candidate correspondences.

Teams	DM	PSD	EDS	UCCA	AMR	MTL	Approach	Reference
ERG[‖§†]	✓	✗	✓	✗	✗	✗	Composition	Oepen and Flickinger (2019)
TUPA[§†]	✓	✓	✓	✓	✓	✗	Transition	Hershcovich and Arviv (2019)
TUPA[§†]	✓	✓	✓	✓	✓	✓	Transition	Hershcovich and Arviv (2019)
HIT-SCIR	✓	✓	✓	✓	✓	✗	Transition	Che et al. (2019)
SJTU–NICT	✓	✓	✓	✓	✓	✗	Factorization	Li et al. (2019)
SUDA–Alibaba	✓	✓	✓	✓	✓	(✓)	Factorization	Zhang et al. (2019c)
Saarland	✓	✓	✓	✓	✓	✗	Composition	Donatelli et al. (2019)
Hitachi	✓	✓	✓	✓	✓	(✓)	Factorization	Koreeda et al. (2019)
ÚFAL MRPipe	✓	✓	✓	✓	✓	✗	Transition	Straka and Straková (2019)
ShanghaiTech	✓	✓	✓	✗	✓	✗	Factorization	Wang et al. (2019)
Amazon	✓	✓	✗	✗	✓	✗	Factorization	Cao et al. (2019)
JBNU	✓	✓	✗	✓	✗	✗	Factorization	Na et al. (2019)
SJTU	✓	✓	✓	✓	✓	✓	Transition	Bai and Zhao (2019)
ÚFAL–Oslo	✓	✓	✓	✗	✗	✗	Transition	Droganova et al. (2019)
HKUST	✓	✓	✗	✓	✗	?		
Bocharov	✗	✗	✗	✗	✓	?		
ÚFAL MRPipe[§]	✓	✓	✓	✓	✓	✗	Transition	Straka and Straková (2019)
Peking[‖]	✓	✓	✓	✓	✗	✗	Factorization	Chen et al. (2019)
ÚFAL–Oslo[§]	✓	✓	✓	✓	✓	✗	Transition	Droganova et al. (2019)
CUHK[§]	✓	✓	✓	✓	✓	✓	Transition	Lai et al. (2019)
Anonymous[§]	✗	✓	✗	✗	✗	?		
Peking[‖§]	✓	✓	✓	✓	✗	✗	Composition	Chen et al. (2019)

Table 4: Overview of participating teams. The top and bottom blocks represent 'unofficial' submissions, which are not considered for the *primary* ranking because they used training data beyond the white-listed resources (indicated by the symbol "‖"), arrived after the closing deadline ("§"), or were prepared by the task co-organizers as points of reference ("†"). The *secondary* ranking (see §6) considers *all* submissions by genuine task participants (excluding co-organizers), i.e. both the middle and bottom blocks (but not the 'reference' systems from the top block).

input string contains whitespace at character position 6, the following are considered equivalent: $\{\langle 0 : 13 \rangle\}$ and $\{\langle 0 : 6 \rangle, \langle 7 : 13 \rangle\}$.

Furthermore, character positions corresponding to basic punctuation marks in the left or right periphery of a normalized anchor are discarded for comparison:

$$. \; ? \; ! \; : \; ; \; , \; \text{“ " ” ‘ ’} \; (\;) \; [\;] \; \{ \; \}$$

6 Submissions and Results

The task received submissions from sixteen teams, plus another two 'reference' submissions prepared by the task co-organizers (Hershcovich and Arviv, 2019; Oepen and Flickinger, 2019). These reference points are not considered in the overall ranking. Non-reference submissions are further subdivided into 'official' and 'unofficial' ones, where the latter are characterized by either arriving after the closing deadline of the evaluation period or using training data beyond the official resources provided (and white-listed) for the task; see §4 above.

Table 4 provides an inventory of participating teams, where the top block corresponds to reference submissions from the co-organizers, and the bottom block shows unofficial submissions by task participants. In two cases, participants discovered serialization or other technical issues in their submissions shortly after the closing date and provided corrected parser outputs (ÚFAL MRPipe and ÚFAL–Oslo). The two submissions from the Peking team are considered unofficial because they incorporate EDS-specific training data beyond the white-listed resources for the shared task (see §4 above).[10] And, finally, the Anonymous and CUHK submissions only became available a few days after the closing date of the evaluation period.

It is evident in Table 4 that some submissions are partial, in the sense of not providing parser outputs for all target frameworks. Albeit not the ultimate goal of the cross-framework shared task design, such partiality was explicitly allowed to lower the technical barrier to entry and make it possible to include framework-specific parsers in the comparison. Seven (of thirteen) of the official submissions, as well as the two TUPA baselines, provide semantic graphs for all five frameworks. Three highly par-

---

[10]In the case of the factorization-based Peking submission, the extra training data is limited to gold-standard tokenization from the original EDS annotations, which in hindsight could in principle have been white-listed.

tial submissions declined the invitation to submit a system description for publication in the shared task proceedings (and one team asked to remain anonymous), such that only limited information is available about these parsers, and they will not be considered in further detail in §7.

Finally, based on input by task participants, Table 4 also provides an indication of which submissions employed multi-task learning (MTL) and a high-level characterization of the overall parsing approach. The distinction between *transition-*, *factorization-*, and *composition*-based architectures follows Koller et al. (2019) and is discussed in more detail in §7 below. In some submissions there can of course be elements of more than one of these high-level architecture types. Also, not all of the teams who indicate the use of multi-task learning actually apply it across different semantic graph frameworks, but in some cases rather to multiple sub-tasks within the parsing architecture for a single framework.[11]

The main task results are summarized in Table 6, showing average MRP scores across frameworks, broken down by the different component pieces (see §5 above). These cross-framework averages can only be meaningfully compared for parsers that support all five frameworks, indicated with italics in the table. The top-three submissions achieve performance levels in the mid-80s F_1 range, followed by a competitive middle field of complete submissions that perform comparably to the TUPA baselines and well above. Despite fundamental architectural differences, there are emergent patterns in the average performance levels for different graph elements. Except for the binary top property, node-local information (fine-grained labels and properties) tend to be harder to predict than labeled edges. Edge attributes are only present in UCCA, encoding a binary distinction between primary and remote edges, which none of the parsers appear to predict successfully.

The correlation between the primary ranking of the official submissions (by overall average MRP F_1) and per-framework ranks is indicated in Table 5. The top-performing HIT-SCIR submission performs best on only one of the five frameworks (UCCA), but achieves uniformly strong results

---

[11]In the case of the SUDA–Alibaba submission, multi-task learning is only applied for the two bi-lexical frameworks; and for the Hitachi team it was only enabled in follow-up work after completion of the official evaluation period, as discussed in the system description by Koreeda et al. (2019).

System	DM	PSD	EDS	UCCA	AMR
HIT-SCIR	2 : 2	4 : 3	2 : 3	1 : 1	2 : 2
SJTU–NICT	1 : 3	3 : 1	3 : 2	3 : 3	3 : 4
SUDA–Alibaba	7 : 7	8 : 8	1 : 1	2 : 2	5 : 5
Saarland	4 : 6	1 : 6	4 : 5	6 : 6	6 : 6
Hitachi	8 : 4	2 : 4	6 : 6	5 : 5	8 : 8
ÚFAL MRPipe	9 : 10	9 : 10	7 : 7	4 : 4	4 : 3
ShanghaiTech	3 : 1	6 : 2	5 : 4	10 : 10	7 : 7
Amazon	6 : 9	5 : 9	10 : 10	10 : 10	1 : 1
JBNU	5 : 5	7 : 5	10 : 10	7 : 8	11 : 11
SJTU	11 : 11	11 : 12	8 : 8	9 : 9	9 : 9
ÚFAL–Oslo	10 : 8	10 : 7	9 : 9	10 : 10	11 : 11
HKUST	12 : 12	12 : 11	10 : 10	8 : 7	11 : 11
Bocharov	13 : 13	13 : 13	10 : 10	10 : 10	10 : 10

Table 5: Per-framework rankings of the official submissions, contrasting the cross-framework MRP metric (first in each cell) and framework-specific evaluation (second). The order of entries reflects the primary ranking by overall average MRP F_1. Team names in italics indicate submissions that support all five frameworks.

across the board; the picture is similar for the second-ranked SJTU–NICT submission (which has the best performance on DM). For the other top-performing submissions, there is more variation across frameworks: SUDA–Alibaba is strongest on the Flavor (1) EDS and UCCA graphs, and Saarland and Hitachi rank first and second, respectively, on the PSD graphs, but are not among the top-three ranks for the other frameworks.

As indicated, Table 5 shows the primary ranking, and unofficial submissions are not included. The complete summary of quantitative results from the task (see §9 below) also provides a secondary ranking, considering all submissions (but not reference points) and excluding those entries that are superseded by others from the same team, viz. the earlier submissions from ÚFAL MRPipe and ÚFAL–Oslo and the EDS-only composition-based entry from Peking. In terms of secondary ranks, the unofficial ÚFAL MRPipe entry (correcting a minor bug in the original submission) would come in third overall (outranking SUDA–Alibaba), and the factorization-based Peking submission would take an overall seventh rank (outranking ShanghaiTech, and notably showing overall best performance for the EDS framework). Remaining secondary ranks are eleventh, thirteenth, and sixth, for ÚFAL–Oslo, CUHK, and Anonymous, respectively.

Table 5 also contrasts the ranking obtained from the official, cross-framework MRP metric in comparison to the pre-existing framework-specific metrics. For EDS, UCCA, and AMR there are only few

	Tops			Labels			Properties			Anchors			Edges			Attributes			All		
	P	R	F	P	R	F	P	R	F	P	R	F	P	R	F	P	R	F	P	R	F
ERG	.36	.36	.364	.39	.39	.390	.38	.38	.383	.39	.39	.391	.37	.37	.368	–	–	–	.38	.38	.383
	.38	.38	.376	.39	.39	.390	.36	.37	.368	.39	.40	.396	.37	.37	.372	–	–	–	.39	.39	.386
TUPA single	.65	.56	.603	.59	.76	.664	.41	.58	.479	.87	.81	.837	.34	.54	.414	.12	.22	.152	.51	.67	.577
	.76	.68	.718	.61	.76	.677	.43	.61	.501	.90	.79	.842	.31	.56	.401	.24	.24	.240	.50	.67	.575
TUPA multi	.67	.57	.616	.40	.55	.457	.29	.42	.327	.68	.60	.626	.30	.45	.347	.02	.02	.018	.39	.57	.453
	.75	.68	.714	.43	.55	.470	.21	.36	.234	.69	.64	.658	.35	.48	.390	.06	.03	.037	.45	.61	.506
HIT-SCIR	.91	.90	.904	.72	.70	.709	.70	.69	.699	.78	.77	.776	.81	.78	.794	.13	.12	.124	.87	.85	.862
	.93	.93	.932	.69	.68	.685	.60	.66	.625	.78	.78	.779	.80	.78	.786	.11	.08	.097	.85	.85	.848
SJTU–NICT	.92	.91	.915	.73	.70	.712	.71	.67	.687	.78	.77	.776	.80	.75	.777	.13	.07	.094	.87	.83	.853
	.94	.92	.931	.71	.70	.702	.50	.52	.505	.78	.77	.778	.79	.76	.773	.10	.05	.069	.85	.84	.842
SUDA–Alibaba	.88	.84	.860	.69	.70	.695	.68	.68	.682	.77	.77	.771	.77	.76	.768	.11	.07	.082	.84	.84	.840
	.90	.87	.884	.65	.67	.662	.60	.67	.636	.77	.78	.775	.77	.77	.770	.13	.05	.076	.82	.84	.832
Saarland	.83	.92	.867	.72	.71	.713	.72	.56	.611	.76	.75	.751	.76	.74	.750	–	–	–	.83	.80	.819
	.88	.93	.905	.72	.72	.723	.61	.58	.586	.77	.77	.771	.79	.77	.778	–	–	–	.85	.85	.849
Hitachi	.89	.90	.893	.64	.64	.641	.56	.54	.519	.75	.75	.755	.70	.69	.696	.08	.03	.042	.77	.75	.760
	.91	.92	.917	.62	.63	.624	.48	.43	.374	.75	.77	.760	.71	.70	.703	.10	.02	.034	.75	.77	.762
ÚFAL MRPipe	.83	.71	.751	.71	.59	.640	.70	.50	.565	.76	.64	.695	.70	.56	.622	.10	.06	.079	.83	.69	.747
	.85	.72	.758	.67	.55	.604	.68	.47	.539	.76	.63	.686	.69	.55	.608	.12	.05	.068	.80	.67	.729
ShanghaiTech	.73	.73	.733	.66	.67	.668	.59	.69	.633	.58	.57	.577	.63	.63	.628	–	–	–	.66	.68	.670
	.75	.75	.748	.65	.65	.649	.48	.61	.507	.58	.58	.578	.64	.64	.640	–	–	–	.66	.68	.668
Amazon	.45	.42	.438	.55	.54	.547	.53	.52	.525	.39	.39	.394	.46	.44	.450	–	–	–	.52	.51	.513
	.49	.47	.484	.52	.53	.526	.45	.49	.471	.39	.39	.392	.45	.46	.454	–	–	–	.50	.51	.502
JBNU	.56	.56	.560	.35	.35	.353	.37	.36	.365	.55	.55	.551	.41	.39	.400	.04	.02	.028	.47	.46	.465
	.57	.57	.566	.33	.33	.331	.34	.37	.355	.57	.58	.575	.44	.43	.431	.03	.01	.018	.48	.48	.483
SJTU	.68	.44	.527	.45	.42	.428	.29	.38	.321	.69	.45	.547	.36	.27	.295	.00	.00	.002	.46	.43	.430
	.74	.52	.602	.45	.45	.443	.22	.31	.249	.70	.47	.560	.37	.29	.308	.00	.00	.001	.47	.46	.451
ÚFAL–Oslo	.51	.51	.514	.20	.29	.239	.21	.37	.261	.43	.53	.464	.48	.40	.432	–	–	–	.30	.42	.344
	.53	.54	.534	.18	.28	.222	.19	.38	.239	.40	.54	.455	.50	.43	.459	–	–	–	.28	.43	.334
HKUST	.48	.45	.463	.20	.29	.238	–	–	–	.36	.49	.417	.25	.22	.230	.09	.04	.057	.22	.28	.245
	.43	.41	.420	.18	.28	.222	–	–	–	.37	.51	.426	.27	.23	.248	.07	.03	.046	.24	.30	.258
Bocharov	.17	.17	.167	.09	.07	.079	.01	.01	.011	–	–	–	.06	.05	.057	–	–	–	.07	.06	.065
	.17	.17	.172	.07	.09	.076	.02	.06	.027	–	–	–	.04	.07	.055	–	–	–	.06	.09	.068
ÚFAL MRPipe	.89	.78	.815	.74	.72	.731	.71	.69	.700	.77	.77	.772	.75	.73	.739	.10	.06	.079	.85	.83	.840
	.91	.78	.822	.71	.71	.710	.62	.65	.634	.77	.78	.775	.75	.74	.744	.12	.05	.068	.84	.83	.833
Peking	.74	.71	.725	.55	.54	.544	.56	.56	.560	.78	.78	.779	.67	.66	.666	.05	.07	.062	.71	.71	.711
	.76	.73	.744	.51	.52	.515	.43	.55	.480	.78	.78	.781	.67	.66	.663	.06	.03	.041	.70	.70	.702
ÚFAL–Oslo	.86	.78	.812	.34	.36	.332	.35	.42	.326	.49	.56	.502	.57	.44	.484	–	–	–	.46	.49	.439
	.88	.87	.871	.32	.42	.357	.33	.45	.335	.46	.60	.513	.57	.49	.527	–	–	–	.43	.56	.473
CUHK	.51	.50	.502	.34	.40	.365	.29	.35	.317	.55	.59	.568	.10	.10	.095	–	–	–	.36	.41	.378
	.51	.51	.514	.30	.39	.340	.24	.35	.283	.52	.62	.565	.09	.09	.087	–	–	–	.33	.42	.365
Anonymous	.04	.03	.035	.08	.13	.101	–	–	–	–	–	–	–	–	–	–	–	–	.02	.03	.022
	.04	.04	.038	.07	.11	.084	–	–	–	–	–	–	–	–	–	–	–	–	.01	.03	.019
Peking	.16	.16	.163	.19	.18	.185	.19	.19	.188	.19	.19	.187	.18	.18	.179	–	–	–	.18	.18	.184
	.17	.17	.174	.18	.18	.181	.16	.18	.166	.19	.19	.190	.18	.18	.178	–	–	–	.18	.19	.183

Table 6: Official results using the cross-framework MRP metric, broken down by 'atomic' component pieces. For each component we report precision (P), recall (R), and F_1 score (F). Entries are split into the same three blocks as in Table 4: references (top), official submissions (middle), and unofficial submissions (bottom). For each system, the first row shows MRP scores on the full evaluation set, while the second shows results on the public 100-sentence subset sampled from *The Little Prince*. The official and unofficial submissions are sorted by overall average F_1. Team names in italics indicate submissions that support all five frameworks.

and 'local' divergences in the rankings obtained from the different scoring approaches: In total, there are four instances of pairs of teams swapping ranks when comparing MRP vs. framework-specific results (the absolute per-framework scores in Table 7 suggest that such 'fluctuation' primarily reflects minor differences in performance). For DM and PSD, on the other hand, Table 5 reveals greater differences between the two ranks indicated in each cell: ShanghaiTech, for example, ranks much higher in the framework-specific SDP metric than in the official MRP ranks. These divergences likely reflect the more limited scope of the SDP approach to scoring, which essentially only considers labeled edges (and top nodes, as a pseudo-edge) but ignores node labels, properties, and anchors (which all used to be provided as part of the parser inputs in the original SDP parsing tasks; see §3 above).

Finally, Tables 7 and 8 complement the breakdown of official results from the shared task with two per-framework views, using the official MRP metric and earlier framework-specific metrics, respectively. On both views, there are stark differences in overall parser accuracy across frameworks—ranging from the low-70s to mid-90s F_1 ranges—with mostly decreasing performance when moving from the bi-lexical Flavor (0) graphs to the unanchored Flavor (2) ones. Given the cross-framework MRP metric, these results become comparable for the first time (within the same parsing system at least, and assuming optimistically that it has been engineered and tuned at comparable effort levels for all frameworks). As such, it is tempting to interpret these differences as indicative of framework-specific parsing difficulty.

However, the volume, uniformity, and quality of available training data (and its similarity to evaluation data, in each framework) inevitably also must factor into such comparison; for example, gold-standard UCCA annotations count at less than one fifth the tokens of the other frameworks. Breaking down results further, viz. into component-wise per-framework scores (available through the task web site; see §9), suggests that scoring the more technical anchoring information at equal weight as the genuinely linguistic node and edge properties contributes to higher average MRP accuracies, in particular for the bi-lexical frameworks where anchors essentially encode tokenization. Ultimately, to put these differences into perspective more, con-trastive, phenomena-oriented studies would likely be called for, as for example the comparison of parsing accuracies for EDS vs. AMR by Lin and Xue (2019).

7 Overview of Approaches

The participating systems in the shared task have approached this multi-meaning representation task in a variety of ways, which we characterize into three broad families of approaches: transition-, factorization-, or composition-based architectures.

Transition-Based Architectures In these parsing system, the meaning representation graph is generated via a series of actions, in a process that is very similar to dependency tree parsing, with the difference being that the actions for graph parsing need to allow reentrancies, as well as (possibly) non-token nodes, labels, properties, and attributes. At any given point in the parsing process, a parser state, which typically consists of a stack that holds already processed elements in the input and a buffer for yet-to-be processed elements, needs to be maintained. Which action to take next is predicted by a classifier using a representation of the parser state as input. When this parsing procedure is complete, the sequence of parsing actions will be used to deterministically reconstitute the meaning representation graph.

This basic method allows variations in various aspects of the parsing process. First of all, the set of actions can vary from system to system. Apart from the standard actions used in syntactic dependency parsing such as SHIFT, LEFTARC, RIGHTARC, and REDUCE (Nivre, 2003; Yamada and Matsumoto, 2003), transition systems in meaning representation parsing also include actions to create reentrant edges, such as LEFTREMOTE and RIGHTREMOTE from the pre-task version of TUPA (Hershcovich et al., 2017). It may also include actions to create abstract concepts that do not correspond to a word token in the input sentence, such as the NODE action from TUPA, and actions that allow the transition to skip a word token in the input when it does not have semantic content, such as the PASS action from HIT-SCIR. The transition set may also include actions that label the nodes or edges, such as LABEL in the version of TUPA used in the shared task. CUHK developed a transition-based parser with a general transition system suited for all five frameworks, by including a variable-arity RESOLVE action.

	DM			PSD			EDS			UCCA			AMR		
	P	R	F	P	R	F	P	R	F	P	R	F	P	R	F
ERG	.96	.96	.961	–	–	–	.95	.95	.952	–	–	–	–	–	–
	.97	.97	.973	–	–	–	.96	.96	.959	–	–	–	–	–	–
TUPA single	.47	.67	.555	.44	.63	.518	.83	.79	.810	.20	.45	.276	.42	.48	.447
	.50	.70	.586	.52	.68	.589	.83	.79	.814	.31	.57	.401	.43	.51	.470
TUPA multi	.31	.69	.427	.45	.63	.526	.74	.74	.740	.17	.38	.236	.29	.41	.338
	.28	.68	.395	.47	.65	.545	.74	.76	.748	.34	.52	.410	.45	.42	.434
HIT-SCIR	.95	.95	.951	.90	.91	.905	.91	.90	.907	.83	.81	.817	.77	.69	.729
	.95	.95	.950	.85	.90	.874	.89	.90	.898	.84	.82	.826	.72	.66	.690
SJTU–NICT	.96	.95	.955	.91	.91	.912	.95	.86	.899	.80	.76	.778	.75	.69	.720
	.95	.95	.949	.86	.91	.885	.94	.88	.912	.77	.74	.755	.72	.70	.706
SUDA–Alibaba	.91	.93	.923	.85	.86	.856	.92	.92	.918	.81	.76	.784	.73	.70	.717
	.89	.92	.907	.79	.87	.828	.92	.93	.925	.85	.80	.821	.67	.69	.679
Saarland	.95	.95	.947	.91	.91	.913	.90	.88	.891	.71	.65	.675	.70	.63	.667
	.94	.95	.948	.86	.91	.883	.93	.91	.920	.78	.74	.762	.74	.72	.731
Hitachi	.91	.91	.910	.91	.92	.912	.84	.84	.837	.72	.68	.704	.47	.41	.439
	.89	.90	.894	.86	.91	.884	.78	.84	.811	.78	.73	.750	.47	.47	.470
ÚFAL MRPipe	.91	.79	.850	.87	.68	.763	.82	.57	.674	.76	.71	.732	.77	.67	.718
	.91	.80	.854	.82	.60	.691	.77	.57	.651	.78	.71	.741	.74	.67	.707
ShanghaiTech	.95	.95	.949	.90	.89	.895	.86	.88	.869	–	–	–	.61	.66	.636
	.94	.94	.943	.83	.88	.852	.86	.89	.875	–	–	–	.66	.67	.668
Amazon	.94	.93	.933	.90	.90	.900	–	–	–	–	–	–	.75	.71	.734
	.92	.92	.921	.85	.91	.879	–	–	–	–	–	–	.71	.72	.711
JBNU	.94	.94	.940	.88	.88	.879	–	–	–	.53	.49	.507	–	–	–
	.92	.92	.924	.84	.88	.857	–	–	–	.66	.62	.636	–	–	–
SJTU	.36	.53	.431	.48	.48	.476	.75	.41	.532	.31	.35	.327	.40	.37	.385
	.35	.53	.419	.47	.51	.488	.74	.44	.553	.31	.40	.353	.46	.42	.441
ÚFAL–Oslo	.72	.91	.805	.48	.83	.609	.27	.35	.306	–	–	–	–	–	–
	.68	.91	.778	.43	.83	.566	.26	.43	.326	–	–	–	–	–	–
HKUST	.34	.41	.370	.28	.48	.353	–	–	–	.51	.50	.502	–	–	–
	.32	.42	.364	.26	.48	.334	–	–	–	.61	.58	.592	–	–	–
Bocharov	–	–	–	–	–	–	–	–	–	–	–	–	.37	.29	.327
	–	–	–	–	–	–	–	–	–	–	–	–	.28	.44	.342
ÚFAL MRPipe	.94	.95	.947	.90	.92	.910	.90	.89	.891	.76	.71	.732	.77	.67	.718
	.93	.95	.943	.85	.91	.878	.89	.90	.896	.78	.71	.740	.74	.67	.707
Peking	.94	.94	.944	.90	.89	.893	.95	.94	.945	.78	.77	.772	–	–	–
	.92	.93	.925	.83	.88	.853	.92	.93	.928	.82	.78	.803	–	–	–
ÚFAL–Oslo	.72	.91	.805	.48	.83	.609	.27	.35	.306	.23	.07	.112	.58	.27	.364
	.68	.91	.778	.43	.83	.566	.26	.43	.326	.23	.14	.175	.54	.50	.519
CUHK	.63	.75	.687	.60	.71	.648	.31	.25	.276	.18	.22	.196	.06	.12	.081
	.57	.73	.644	.51	.70	.590	.31	.32	.313	.22	.26	.235	.03	.08	.042
Anonymous	–	–	–	.08	.16	.109	–	–	–	–	–	–	–	–	–
	–	–	–	.07	.15	.095	–	–	–	–	–	–	–	–	–
Peking	–	–	–	–	–	–	.92	.92	.918	–	–	–	–	–	–
	–	–	–	–	–	–	.90	.93	.914	–	–	–	–	–	–

Table 7: Per-framework results using the official MRP metric. For each framework we report precision (P), recall (R), and F_1 score (F). Entries are split and sorted into the same three blocks as in Tables 4 and 6, and again the two rows per submission correspond to the full evaluation data and the *Little Prince* subset.

	DM			PSD			EDS			UCCA			AMR		
	P	R	F	P	R	F	P	R	F	P	R	F	P	R	F
ERG	.91	.91	.912	–	–	–	.93	.92	.926	–	–	–	–	–	–
	.93	.93	.929	–	–	–	.94	.95	.944	–	–	–	–	–	–
TUPA single	.65	.69	.670	.51	.60	.552	.77	.71	.741	.28	.19	.224	.41	.47	.438
	.66	.71	.690	.55	.63	.585	.77	.72	.744	.32	.25	.284	.42	.49	.451
TUPA multi	.51	.62	.562	.47	.53	.501	.68	.64	.656	.28	.19	.224	.28	.39	.328
	.50	.63	.557	.52	.59	.553	.67	.65	.660	.32	.25	.284	.42	.40	.411
HIT-SCIR	.93	.92	.925	.81	.81	.810	.87	.86	.866	.68	.66	.667	.77	.69	.725
	.94	.94	.937	.79	.80	.794	.85	.86	.857	.66	.63	.644	.71	.65	.680
SJTU–NICT	.93	.92	.924	.82	.81	.817	.93	.83	.877	.63	.59	.609	.75	.68	.714
	.94	.93	.936	.81	.81	.810	.93	.87	.897	.63	.57	.597	.71	.69	.696
SUDA–Alibaba	.89	.91	.898	.76	.76	.760	.90	.89	.893	.66	.62	.639	.73	.70	.713
	.88	.91	.895	.75	.77	.759	.90	.91	.903	.69	.63	.662	.66	.69	.674
Saarland	.90	.91	.906	.80	.80	.796	.80	.78	.794	.34	.31	.324	.70	.63	.661
	.91	.93	.919	.79	.80	.798	.87	.85	.860	.52	.49	.505	.73	.71	.722
Hitachi	.91	.93	.919	.80	.82	.808	.78	.78	.783	.39	.37	.381	.46	.40	.425
	.92	.94	.927	.80	.82	.807	.73	.79	.757	.47	.44	.454	.45	.45	.453
ÚFAL MRPipe	.80	.70	.745	.69	.52	.594	.73	.49	.587	.42	.38	.396	.77	.67	.716
	.81	.72	.759	.68	.45	.539	.67	.48	.560	.48	.42	.445	.74	.67	.700
ShanghaiTech	.94	.92	.930	.83	.81	.816	.81	.82	.814	–	–	–	.61	.66	.631
	.95	.94	.945	.82	.82	.819	.81	.84	.825	–	–	–	.65	.66	.659
Amazon	.87	.86	.866	.76	.72	.742	–	–	–	–	–	–	.75	.71	.730
	.87	.87	.869	.77	.78	.771	–	–	–	–	–	–	.70	.71	.704
JBNU	.92	.90	.912	.80	.80	.800	–	–	–	.19	.17	.177	–	–	–
	.93	.92	.926	.82	.81	.815	–	–	–	.34	.31	.325	–	–	–
SJTU	.51	.30	.379	.49	.26	.340	.66	.33	.435	.05	.04	.045	.39	.36	.373
	.45	.27	.335	.52	.28	.359	.64	.34	.449	.06	.05	.055	.43	.39	.411
ÚFAL–Oslo	.90	.86	.880	.81	.73	.769	.14	.21	.168	–	–	–	–	–	–
	.90	.88	.888	.82	.77	.795	.15	.27	.192	–	–	–	–	–	–
HKUST	.33	.27	.297	.45	.36	.398	–	–	–	.21	.20	.203	–	–	–
	.33	.27	.299	.47	.36	.412	–	–	–	.25	.24	.244	–	–	–
Bocharov	–	–	–	–	–	–	–	–	–	–	–	–	.35	.28	.314
	–	–	–	–	–	–	–	–	–	–	–	–	.26	.41	.321
ÚFAL MRPipe	.87	.90	.881	.76	.79	.775	.87	.85	.859	.42	.38	.396	.77	.67	.716
	.87	.91	893	.77	.80	.782	.87	.87	.869	.48	.41	.442	.73	.67	.699
Peking	.92	.92	.924	.81	.80	.808	.93	.91	.919	.63	.61	.620	–	–	–
	.93	.93	.925	.80	.80	.797	.90	.91	.906	.67	.62	.640	–	–	–
ÚFAL–Oslo	.90	.86	.880	.81	.73	.769	.14	.21	.168	–	–	.002	.56	.26	.351
	.90	.88	.888	.82	.77	.795	.15	.27	.192	–	–	.001	.53	.49	.508
CUHK	.10	.12	.108	.06	.06	.057	.05	.04	.047	.01	.01	.007	.05	.09	.060
	.10	.12	.109	.04	.05	.042	.08	.08	.083	.02	.01	.018	–	.01	.005
Anonymous	–	–	–	–	–	–	–	–	–	–	–	–	–	–	–
	–	–	–	–	–	–	–	–	–	–	–	–	–	–	–
Peking	–	–	–	–	–	–	.88	.88	.879	–	–	–	–	–	–
	–	–	–	–	–	–	.88	.90	.890	–	–	–	–	–	–

Table 8: Results using the framework-specific (labeled) metrics: SDP (for DM and PSD), EDM (for EDS), UCCA, and SMTACH (for AMR); see § 5 above. For each framework (and its metric) we report precision (P), recall (R), and F_1 score (F). Entries are split and sorted into the same three blocks as in Tables 4 and 6, and again the two rows per submission correspond to the full evaluation data and the *Little Prince* subset.

Second, the classifier used to predict the action for any given state can also vary a great deal. For example, the HIT-SCIR system aggregates information from the action history, the stack, the list, and the buffer with a stack LSTM and then predicts the action by taking a softmax over the output of the LSTM. The CUHK system uses a regular LSTM to aggregate information from the stack, the sequence of words before the current word token, and the sequence of words after the current token, and then predict the action with a softmax. The TUPA system uses a BiLSTM with an MLP and softmax layer, with the BiLSTM running over the sequence of input tokens.

Factorization-Based Architectures These parsing models for meaning representation also have their roots in syntactic dependency parsing (where they are often called *graph-based*; McDonald and Pereira, 2006). Given a set of nodes, the basic idea of the factorization-based approach is to find the graph that has the highest score among all possible graphs. In the case of dependency parsing, the goal is to find the Maximum Spanning Tree, and this has been extended to meaning representation parsing, where the goal is to find the Maximum Spanning Connected Subgraphs (Flanigan et al., 2014). To make the computation of the score of a graph practical, the typical strategy is to factorize the score of a graph into the sum of the scores of its subgraphs, and in the case of first-order factorization, into the sum of the scores of its nodes and edges. A popular choice for predicting the edge is to feed the output of an LSTM encoder to a biaffine classifier to predict if an edge exists between a pair of nodes as well as the label of the edge (SJTU–NICT, SUDA–Alibaba, Hitachi, and JBNU), with slight variations as to the input to the LSTM encoder. Due to the difference in anchoring between the nodes in the graph and the word tokens in the sentence, the way to identify nodes also differs from framework to framework. ÚFAL–Oslo used the factorization-based NeurboParser (Peng et al., 2017) for DM and PSD, and for EDS they simply submitted graphs identical to the DM ones. They also used the factorization-based JAMR (Flanigan et al., 2014, 2016) for AMR, and further adjusted JAMR to support UCCA graphs, by converting UCCA to the standard AMR serialization.

Composition-Based Architectures Finally, this approach to meaning representation parsing emphasizes the principle of compositionality in meaning construction and assumes an explict inventory of operations that combine pieces of meaning into larger fragments. Typically grounded in some kind of formal derivation process, composition-based architectures associate meaning fragments with lexical items (leaf nodes in the derivation) and apply a designated composition operation for each step in the derivation. What differentiates composition-based approaches from transition-based or factorization-based ones is that the derivations are licensed by some form of 'grammar' (explicit or implicit), where illegitimate derivations can be ruled out by the structural constraints over the lexical items and the rules of derivation. The MRP shared task attracted two (and a half) composition-based systems, the Apply-Modify (AM) algebra based system from Saarland and the Peking parser based on Synchronous Hyperedge Replacement Grammar (SHRG) for EDS.[12] For composition-based approaches, the extraction of lexical items from a sentence is a crucial component of the system. In the case of the Saarland parser, the lexical items are produced by a BiLSTM-based supertagger, and the best derivation is selected in a tree dependency parsing process where the edge between a head and its argument or modifier is labeled with the derivation operation. In the case of the Peking system, the SHRG rules are extracted with a context-free parser, and the derivation is scored by a sum of the scores of its subgraphs.

Other Approaches The transition-, factorization-, and composition-based systems represent the main approaches in the shared task, but there are a few systems that stretch the dividing lines of this this categorization. When parsing the UCCA framework, a number of systems—e.g. SJTU–NICT, SUDA–Alibaba, and Amazon—adopt an approach where 'remote' (reentrancy) edges are first removed to create constituent tree structures to train standard constituent tree parsers using neural network–based models, and then in a postprocessing stage, the remote edges are added back with a separate classifier, following Jiang et al. (2019).

The MRPipe system could be said to define its own category. It differs from transition-based systems in that it does not use the typical actions

---

[12]The unofficial submission of DM and EDS reference graphs obtained from parsing with the ERG also represents a composition-based approach.

used in transition-based systems and it also does not maintain a typical parser state. It also differs from factorization-based systems in that it builds the meaning representation iteratively, while in a factorization-based systems all possible graphs are (conceptually) enumerated at once and the focus is on finding the graph with the highest score.

Anchoring One difference among the five meaning representation frameworks covered in the shared task is the correspondence relation between the concepts (graph nodes) and word tokens in the sentence (see §2). In Flavors (0) and (1) (DM, PSD, EDS, and UCCA), this alignment is explicit, while in Flavor (2) AMRs there is no explicit anchoring. How to tackle anchoring in the parsing system has a significant impact on parser performance. Some of the participating systems follow early approaches in AMR parsing and use a separate 'alignment' model to provide hard anchorings and then proceed with the rest of the parsing process (e.g. the HIT-SCIR system) assuming the alignments are already in place. Other submissions use a soft alignment component that is trained jointly with other components of their systems. For example, the Amazon and the SUDA–Alibaba parsers jointly model anchoring, node detection, and edge detection, adopting the approach of Lyu and Titov (2018), while the SJTU–NICT system uses a sequence-to-sequence model with a pointer-generator network to predict the concepts in AMR, following Zhang et al. (2019a). That sequence-to-sequence model is trained jointly with other components of their system.

Cross-Framework Architecture Design One question that the co-organizers would like to help answer through the shared task is to what degree the same general architecture can be used to effectively parse all five meaning representation frameworks. The answer to this question is tentatively in the affirmative. The HIT-SCIR and TUPA systems use a transition-based system to parse all five meaning representations, with the caveat that the transitions for the five meaning representations vary in the actions that are used. The CUHK parser, on the other hand, uses a uniform transition set for all frameworks. The Saarland system uses the same AM algebra composition system to parse all five meaning representations, but has to do a considerable amount of pre-processing to convert the meaning representations into well-formed terms of the AM algrebra (accordingly, some of the pre-processing effects need to be undone in post-processing). The MRPipe system adopts an approach in which the meaning representation graph is built up iteratively with two operations, ADDNODES and ADDEDGES, and applies this model successfully to all five meaning representations. Other participating systems adopt the strategy of using the model that they consider to be the most appropriate for a particular flavor of meaning representation. For example, the SJTU–NICT submission uses a factorization-based model for DM, PSD, and EDS parsing, but uses a constituent tree parsing approach for UCCA, as it is not obvious how a factorization-based model would be extended to also handle UCCA parsing. The Amazon system uses a factorization-based model for DM, PSD, and AMR while adopting a constituent tree parsing approach for UCCA and EDS. The SUDA–Alibaba system also adopts a constituent tree parsing approach to UCCA, similar to Jiang et al. (2019).

Benefits of Multi-Task Learning Another research question the shared task seeks to advance is whether and how multi-task learning (MTL) helps with multi-framework meaning representation parsing. The term, in fact, seems to be applied somewhat variably in the system descriptions. In one sense, it is equated with traditional joint learning, where different components of the SUDA–Alibaba system are trained jointly by combining their objectives. The sense of the term that was intended by the organizers is whether pooling the training data for all five frameworks in a multi-task learning framework can improve the parser performance of one particular framework. A number of participating systems attempted MTL in the latter sense, and the results are mixed and not definitive. The MTL version of the TUPA system performs much worse than its single-task version, but this might be attributed to inadequate training strategies and incomplete tuning. The Hitachi systems (in a post-competition experiment) show MTL results that are slightly better than single framework results, but the difference is probably not statistically significant.

8 On the State of the Art

Prior to the shared task, various methods have been proposed for semantic graph parsing, including transition-, factorization-, and composition-based, as well as sequence-to-sequence systems. Existing parsers also diverge in terms of their assumptions regarding the syntax–semantics interface, some parsing raw text directly to meaning representation graphs, and some producing the graphs from or in parallel with syntactic derivations.

While some meaning representations have parsers for languages other than English (Oepen et al., 2015; Wang et al., 2018; Damonte and Cohen, 2018; Hershcovich et al., 2019), we limit the discussion here to the state of the art in English meaning representation parsing, as has been the focus of the current shared task.

DM and PSD were both among the representations targeted in two SemEval shared tasks on Semantic Dependency Parsing (Oepen et al., 2014, 2015), where the winning system (Kanerva et al., 2015) utilized SVM-based sequence labeling. The runner-up (Du et al., 2014, 2015) used an ensemble based on factorization-based weighted tree approximation. More recently, Peng et al. (2017, 2018a,b) improved upon previous approaches by using a neural factorization-based multi-task system, sharing parameters between representations and applying joint inference. Stanovsky and Dagan (2018) linearized the bi-lexical graphs and modeled the parsing task as a sequence-to-sequence problem. They also used multi-task learning, adapting multilingual machine translation algorithms to 'translate' between text and meaning representations, outperforming the previous best results on PSD. Lindemann et al. (2019) trained a composition-based parser on DM, PAS, PSD, AMR and EDS, using the Apply–Modify algebra, on which the Saarland submission to the shared task is based. They employed multi-task training with all tackled semantic frameworks and UD, establishing the state of the art on all graph banks but AMR 2017.

AMR has been a challenging target representation for parsing, due to the fact that AMRs are Flavor (2), unanchored graphs. AMR parsing was pioneered by Flanigan et al. (2014), who performed alignment as a preprocessing step during training. They developed their own rule-based alignment method, complemented by Pourdamghani et al. (2014), who adapted methods from machine translation. Some transition-based AMR parsers also perform rule-based alignment (Damonte et al., 2017; Damonte and Cohen, 2018; Ballesteros and Al-Onaizan, 2017; Naseem et al., 2019), while others derive AMRs from syntactic dependencies by applying transitions (Wang et al., 2015; Wang

and Xue, 2017). The latter approach reached the best performance (Wang et al., 2016; Nguyen and Nguyen, 2017) in two SemEval shared tasks on AMR parsing (May, 2016; May and Priyadarshi, 2017), where in the former it performed as well as a novel character-level neural translation based AMR parser (Barzdins and Gosko, 2016). Composition-based AMR parsers include Artzi et al. (2015), who combined CCG grammar induction with AMR parsing. Sequence-to-sequence attention-based approaches (Konstas et al., 2017; van Noord and Bos, 2017) use techniques from machine translation to directly generate (linearized) graphs from text. Lyu and Titov (2018) parsed AMR using a joint probabilistic model with latent alignments, avoiding cascading errors due to alignment inaccuracies and outperforming previous approaches. The factorization-based parser by Zhang et al. (2019a,b) uses an attention-based architecture, but derives target graphs directly instead of a linearization, also treating alignment as a latent variable with a copy mechanism. Their parser additionally supports UCCA and SDP, and establishes the state-of-the-art in AMR parsing, though without using multi-task training across frameworks.

UCCA parsing was first tackled by Hershcovich et al. (2017), who used a neural transition-based parser. Hershcovich et al. (2018) further showed that multi-task learning with AMR, DM, and UD as auxiliary tasks improves UCCA parsing performance. UCCA also recently featured in a SemEval shared task (Hershcovich et al., 2019), where the composition-based best system (Jiang et al., 2019) outperformed the transition-based baseline by treating the task as constituency tree parsing with the recovery of remote edges as a postprocessing task.

EDS, being a result of automatic conversion from English Resource Semantics (Bender et al., 2015), can be derived by any ERG parser (e.g. Callmeier, 2002; Packard, 2012). Buys and Blunsom (2017) were the first to build a purely data-driven EDS parser, combining graph linearization with a custom transition system. Chen et al. (2018) established the state of the art on data-driven EDS parsing, using a neural SHRG-based, ERG-guided parser. Their comparison on in-domain WSJ evaluation data showed parsing accuracies on par or in excess of the full, grammar-based ACE parser of Packard (2012).

While some shared task submissions are based on existing systems that have been specifically improved, direct comparison to previously published results is impossible: Our definition of the SDP task, for example, is different from Oepen et al. (2014, 2015); prior EDS work has mostly tested on WSJ only; the UCCA annotations have been revised and extended; we are using a new, forthcoming version of AMRbank; and gold-standard tokenization is not provided for any of the frameworks. Also, even some of our framework-specific metrics are not exactly what was used previously: We have made SDP and UCCA character-based (for increased robustness to tokenization mismatches), and we un-invert edges more thoroughly in AMR graphs before calling SMATCH for scoring. However, overall performance levels and general trends observed in § 6 appear consistent with recent developments in the field: By and large, the transition-, factorization-, and composition-based approaches all can yield competitive parsers, where cross-framework multi-task learning sometimes helps but only slightly so. While general methods for meaning representation graph parsing are clearly beneficial, there is yet progress to be made (so far) in sharing information between parsers for different frameworks and making better use of their overlap.

9   Reflections and Outlook

The MRP 2019 shared task was a first step in a new direction, aiming to more closely (inter)relate the representations and parsing approaches across a diverse range of semantic graph frameworks. Despite new uniformity in packaging and evaluation, cumulative overall complexity and inherent technical and linguistic diversity of the frameworks deemed participation in the competition a demanding challenge. The problem attracted broad interest: Some 140 individuals have subscribed to the shared task mailing list, and 38 teams obtained the training data package from the LDC (of these, sixteen submitted parser outputs for evaluation). In a post-evaluation questionnaire and through informal communication, several prospective participants have indicated that they had started to work towards a system submission but in the end simply ran out of time for the official evaluation period.

Possibly related to the high technological barrier to participation is the comparatively low proportion of submissions that successfully utilize multi-task learning (across frameworks). Even though some of the participating teams have previously applied multi-task learning for semantic graph parsing, it appears some may have shied away from increased training times and tuning effort and instead had to focus their work on developing strong end-to-end parsers for individual frameworks. As task co-organizers, we remain committed to enabling continued research along these lines, and we will ultimately make all training and evaluation data generally available. In the interim, however, we are delighted (and a little frightened) to confirm that CoNLL has invited us to orchestrate a follow-up shared task on Cross-Framework Meaning Representation Parsing in 2020.

Deciding on the task parameters for MRP 2020 will be a balancing act between keeping overall complexity manageable, in particular for 'newcomer' participants, and pushing further in the direction of learning from complementary knowledge sources. Above all, the mid- to long-term goals of the cross-framework meaning representation initiative are to advance our understanding of degrees of complementarity among the various frameworks. Current plans foresee inclusion of one additional framework, viz. a graph-based encoding of the Discourse Representation Structures of Basile et al. (2012). Further, we plan on refining and extending the available training data (in particular for UCCA) and will put greater focus on the systematic exploration of variant evaluation perspectives, for example scoring at the level of larger sub-graphs in the spirit of the 'complete predications' metric of Oepen et al. (2015), or 'semantic n-grams' along the lines of the SemBleu proposal by Song and Gildea (2019). Aiming for increased linguistic diversity, it will of course also be tempting to seek to include meaning representations for additional languages. For each of the frameworks involved (six in total for MRP 2020), gold-standard annotations are in principle available for at least one language besides English, but in most cases these would be different languages for each framework. Thus, it remains yet to be decided how best to balance cross-linguistic and multi-task perspectives on the MRP problem.

All technical information regarding the MRP 2019 shared task, including system submissions, detailed official results, and links to supporting resources and software are available from the task web site at:

```
http://mrp.nlpl.eu
```

Acknowledgments

Many colleagues have assisted in designing the task and preparing its data and software resources. Emily M. Bender and Dan Flickinger provided a critical review of (a sample of) the DM and EDS graphs. Sebastian Schuster made available a pre-release of the converter from PTB-style constituent trees to (basic) UD 2.x dependency graphs. Dotan Dvir has coordinated the team of UCCA annotators, always ensuring that the corpora were ready in time. Andrey Kutuzov helped with the preparation of morpho-syntactic companion trees for the evaluation data.

The task design and implementation has benefited from input by the Steering Committee of the ACL Special Interest Group on Natural Language Learning, notably Xavier Carreras and Julia Hockenmaier, as well as by the CoNLL 2019 Programme Chairs, Mohit Bansal and Aline Villavicencio.

We are grateful to the Nordic e-Infrastructure Collaboration for their support to the Nordic Language Processing Laboratory (NLPL), which has provided technical infrastructure for the MRP 2019 task. Also, we thankfully acknowledge the assistance of the Linguistic Data Consortium in distributing the training data for the task to participants at no cost to anyone.

We acknowledge the support of the Czech Ministry of Education, Youth, and Sports, through project CZ.02.1.01/0.0/0.0/16_013/0001781 (EF16_013/0001781); Czech Ministry of Culture, project DG16P02R019, the support for the data and services used by the Research Infrastructure projects LM2015071 and LM2018101, also of the Czech Ministry of Education, Youth, and Sports, and the support of the Grant Agency of the Czech Republic, project No. GA17-07313S. The work on UCCA and TUPA was partially supported by the Israel Science Foundation (grant no. 929/17). We also acknowledge the support of the US National Science Foundation on the Uniform Meaning Representation project via Award No. 1763926. All views expressed in this paper are those of the authors and do not necessarily represent the view of the National Science Foundation.

References

Omri Abend and Ari Rappoport. 2013. UCCA. A semantics-based grammatical annotation scheme. In *Proceedings of the 10th International Conference on Computational Semantics*, pages 1–12, Potsdam, Germany.

Yoav Artzi, Kenton Lee, and Luke Zettlemoyer. 2015. Broad-coverage CCG semantic parsing with AMR. In *Proceedings of the 2015 Conference on Empirical Methods in Natural Language Processing*, pages 1699–1710, Lisbon, Portugal.

Hongxiao Bai and Hai Zhao. 2019. SJTU at MRP 2019: A transition-based multi-task parser for cross-framework meaning representation parsing. In *Proceedings of the Shared Task on Cross-Framework Meaning Representation Parsing at the 2019 Conference on Natural Language Learning*, pages 86–94, Hong Kong, China.

Miguel Ballesteros and Yaser Al-Onaizan. 2017. AMR parsing using stack-LSTMs. In *Proceedings of the 2017 Conference on Empirical Methods in Natural Language Processing*, pages 1269–1275, Copenhagen, Denmark.

Laura Banarescu, Claire Bonial, Shu Cai, Madalina Georgescu, Kira Griffitt, Ulf Hermjakob, Kevin Knight, Philipp Koehn, Martha Palmer, and Nathan Schneider. 2013. Abstract Meaning Representation for sembanking. In *Proceedings of the 7th Linguistic Annotation Workshop and Interoperability with Discourse*, pages 178–186, Sofia, Bulgaria.

Guntis Barzdins and Didzis Gosko. 2016. RIGA at SemEval-2016 task 8: Impact of Smatch extensions and character-level neural translation on AMR parsing accuracy. In *Proceedings of the 10th International Workshop on Semantic Evaluation*, pages 1143–1147, San Diego, CA, USA.

Valerio Basile, Johan Bos, Kilian Evang, and Noortje Venhuizen. 2012. Developing a large semantically annotated corpus. In *Proceedings of the 8th International Conference on Language Resources and Evaluation*, pages 3196–3200, Istanbul, Turkey.

Emily M. Bender, Dan Flickinger, Stephan Oepen, Woodley Packard, and Ann Copestake. 2015. Layers of interpretation. On grammar and compositionality. In *Proceedings of the 11th International Conference on Computational Semantics*, pages 239–249, London, UK.

Alexandra Birch, Omri Abend, Ondřej Bojar, and Barry Haddow. 2016. HUME. Human UCCA-based evaluation of machine translation. In *Proceedings of the 2016 Conference on Empirical Methods in Natural Language Processing*, pages 1264–1274, Austin, TX, USA.

Jan Buys and Phil Blunsom. 2017. Robust incremental neural semantic graph parsing. In *Proceedings* of the 55th Meeting of the Association for Computational Linguistics*, pages 158–167, Vancouver, Canada.

Shu Cai and Kevin Knight. 2013. Smatch. An evaluation metric for semantic feature structures. In *Proceedings of the 51th Meeting of the Association for Computational Linguistics*, pages 748–752, Sofia, Bulgaria.

Ulrich Callmeier. 2002. Preprocessing and encoding techniques in PET. In Stephan Oepen, Daniel Flickinger, J. Tsujii, and Hans Uszkoreit, editors, *Collaborative Language Engineering. A Case Study in Efficient Grammar-based Processing*, pages 127–140. CSLI Publications, Stanford, CA.

Jie Cao, Yi Zhang, Adel Youssef, and Vivek Srikumar. 2019. Amazon at MRP 2019: Parsing meaning representations with lexical and phrasal anchoring. In *Proceedings of the Shared Task on Cross-Framework Meaning Representation Parsing at the 2019 Conference on Natural Language Learning*, pages 138–148, Hong Kong, China.

Wanxiang Che, Longxu Dou, Yang Xu, Yuxuan Wang, Yijia Liu, and Ting Liu. 2019. HIT-SCIR at MRP 2019: A unified pipeline for meaning representation parsing via efficient training and effective encoding. In *Proceedings of the Shared Task on Cross-Framework Meaning Representation Parsing at the 2019 Conference on Natural Language Learning*, pages 76–85, Hong Kong, China.

Yufei Chen, Weiwei Sun, and Xiaojun Wan. 2018. Accurate SHRG-based semantic parsing. In *Proceedings of the 56th Meeting of the Association for Computational Linguistics*, pages 408–418, Melbourne, Australia.

Yufei Chen, Yajie Ye, and Weiwei Sun. 2019. Peking at MRP 2019: Factorization- and composition-based parsing for Elementary Dependency Structures. In *Proceedings of the Shared Task on Cross-Framework Meaning Representation Parsing at the 2019 Conference on Natural Language Learning*, pages 166–176, Hong Kong, China.

Leshem Choshen and Omri Abend. 2018. Reference-less measure of faithfulness for grammatical error correction. In *Proceedings of the 2015 Conference of the North American Chapter of the Association for Computational Linguistics*, New Orleans, LA, USA.

Ann Copestake, Dan Flickinger, Carl Pollard, and Ivan A. Sag. 2005. Minimal Recursion Semantics. An introduction. *Research on Language and Computation*, 3(4):281–332.

Marco Damonte and Shay B. Cohen. 2018. Cross-lingual abstract meaning representation parsing. In *Proceedings of the 2015 Conference of the North American Chapter of the Association for Computational Linguistics*, pages 1146–1155, New Orleans, LA, USA.

Marco Damonte, Shay B. Cohen, and Giorgio Satta. 2017. An incremental parser for abstract meaning representation. In *Proceedings of the 15th Meeting of the European Chapter of the Association for Computational Linguistics*, pages 536–546, Valencia, Spain.

Robert M. W. Dixon. 2010/2012. *Basic Linguistic Theory*. Oxford University Press.

Lucia Donatelli, Meaghan Fowlie, Jonas Groschwitz, Alexander Koller, Matthias Lindemann, Mario Mina, and Pia Weißenhorn. 2019. Saarland at MRP 2019: Compositional parsing across all graphbanks. In *Proceedings of the Shared Task on Cross-Framework Meaning Representation Parsing at the 2019 Conference on Natural Language Learning*, pages 66–75, Hong Kong, China.

Rebecca Dridan and Stephan Oepen. 2011. Parser evaluation using elementary dependency matching. In *Proceedings of the 12th International Conference on Parsing Technologies*, pages 225–230, Dublin, Ireland.

Rebecca Dridan and Stephan Oepen. 2012. Tokenization. Returning to a long solved problem. A survey, contrastive experiment, recommendations, and toolkit. In *Proceedings of the 50th Meeting of the Association for Computational Linguistics*, pages 378–382, Jeju, Republic of Korea.

Kira Droganova, Andrey Kutuzov, Nikita Mediankin, and Daniel Zeman. 2019. ÚFAL–oslo at MRP 2019: Garage sale semantic parsing. In *Proceedings of the Shared Task on Cross-Framework Meaning Representation Parsing at the 2019 Conference on Natural Language Learning*, pages 158–165, Hong Kong, China.

Yantao Du, Fan Zhang, Weiwei Sun, and Xiaojun Wan. 2014. Peking: Profiling syntactic tree parsing techniques for semantic graph parsing. In *Proceedings of the 8th International Workshop on Semantic Evaluation*, pages 459–464, Dublin, Ireland. Association for Computational Linguistics.

Yantao Du, Fan Zhang, Xun Zhang, Weiwei Sun, and Xiaojun Wan. 2015. Peking: Building semantic dependency graphs with a hybrid parser. In *Proceedings of the 9th International Workshop on Semantic Evaluation*, pages 927–931, Denver, CO, USA.

Jeffrey Flanigan, Chris Dyer, Noah A. Smith, and Jaime Carbonell. 2016. CMU at SemEval-2016 task 8. Graph-based AMR parsing with infinite ramp loss. In *Proceedings of the 10th International Workshop on Semantic Evaluation*, pages 1202–1206, San Diego, CA, USA.

Jeffrey Flanigan, Sam Thomson, Jaime Carbonell, Chris Dyer, and Noah A. Smith. 2014. A discriminative graph based parser for the Abstract Meaning Representation. In *Proceedings of the 52nd Meeting of the Association for Computational Linguistics*, pages 1426–1436, Baltimore, MD, USA.

Dan Flickinger, Stephan Oepen, and Emily M. Bender. 2017. Sustainable development and refinement of complex linguistic annotations at scale. In Nancy Ide and James Pustejovsky, editors, *Handbook of Linguistic Annotation*, pages 353–377. Springer, Dordrecht, The Netherlands.

W. Nelson Francis and Henry Kučera. 1982. *Frequency Analysis of English Usage. Lexicon and Grammar.* Houghton Mifflin, New York, USA.

Jan Hajič, Eva Hajičová, Jarmila Panevová, Petr Sgall, Ondřej Bojar, Silvie Cinková, Eva Fučíková, Marie Mikulová, Petr Pajas, Jan Popelka, Jiří Semecký, Jana Šindlerová, Jan Štěpánek, Josef Toman, Zdeňka Urešová, and Zdeněk Žabokrtský. 2012. Announcing Prague Czech-English Dependency Treebank 2.0. In *Proceedings of the 8th International Conference on Language Resources and Evaluation*, pages 3153–3160, Istanbul, Turkey.

Daniel Hershcovich, Omri Abend, and Ari Rappoport. 2017. A transition-based directed acyclic graph parser for UCCA. In *Proceedings of the 55th Meeting of the Association for Computational Linguistics*, pages 1127–1138, Vancouver, Canada.

Daniel Hershcovich, Omri Abend, and Ari Rappoport. 2018. Multitask parsing across semantic representations. In *Proceedings of the 56th Meeting of the Association for Computational Linguistics*, pages 373–385, Melbourne, Australia.

Daniel Hershcovich, Zohar Aizenbud, Leshem Choshen, Elior Sulem, Ari Rappoport, and Omri Abend. 2019. SemEval-2019 task 1. Cross-lingual semantic parsing with UCCA. In *Proceedings of the 13th International Workshop on Semantic Evaluation*, pages 1–10, Minneapolis, MN, USA.

Daniel Hershcovich and Ofir Arviv. 2019. TUPA at MRP 2019: A multi-task baseline system. In *Proceedings of the Shared Task on Cross-Framework Meaning Representation Parsing at the 2019 Conference on Natural Language Learning*, pages 28–39, Hong Kong, China.

Eduard Hovy, Mitchell Marcus, Martha Palmer, Lance Ramshaw, and Ralph Weischedel. 2006. OntoNotes. The 90% solution. In *Proceedings of Human Language Technologies: The 2006 Annual Conference of the North American Chapter of the Association for Computational Linguistics, Companion Volume: Short Papers*, pages 57–60, New York City, USA.

Angelina Ivanova, Stephan Oepen, Lilja Øvrelid, and Dan Flickinger. 2012. Who did what to whom? A contrastive study of syntacto-semantic dependencies. In *Proceedings of the 6th Linguistic Annotation Workshop*, pages 2–11, Jeju, Republic of Korea.

Wei Jiang, Zhenghua Li, Yu Zhang, and Min Zhang. 2019. HLT@SUDA at SemEval-2019 task 1: UCCA graph parsing as constituent tree parsing. In *Proceedings of the 13th International Workshop on Semantic Evaluation*, pages 11–15, Minneapolis, MI, USA.

Jenna Kanerva, Juhani Luotolahti, and Filip Ginter. 2015. Turku: Semantic dependency parsing as a sequence classification. In *Proceedings of the 9th International Workshop on Semantic Evaluation*, pages 965–969, Denver, CO, USA.

Paul Kingsbury and Martha Palmer. 2002. From Tree-Bank to PropBank. In *Proceedings of the 3rd International Conference on Language Resources and Evaluation*, pages 1989–1993, Las Palmas, Spain.

Alexander Koller, Stephan Oepen, and Weiwei Sun. 2019. Graph-based meaning representations. Design and processing. In *Proceedings of the 57th Meeting of the Association for Computational Linguistics: Tutorial Abstracts*, pages 6–11, Florence, Italy.

Ioannis Konstas, Srinivasan Iyer, Mark Yatskar, Yejin Choi, and Luke Zettlemoyer. 2017. Neural AMR: Sequence-to-sequence models for parsing and generation. In *Proceedings of the 55th Meeting of the Association for Computational Linguistics*, pages 146–157, Vancouver, Canada.

Yuta Koreeda, Gaku Morio, Terufumi Morishita, Hiroaki Ozaki, and Kohsuke Yanai. 2019. Hitachi at MRP 2019: Unified encoder-to-biaffine network for cross-framework meaning representation parsing. In *Proceedings of the Shared Task on Cross-Framework Meaning Representation Parsing at the 2019 Conference on Natural Language Learning*, pages 114–126, Hong Kong, China.

Marco Kuhlmann and Stephan Oepen. 2016. Towards a catalogue of linguistic graph banks. *Computational Linguistics*, 42(4):819–827.

Sunny Lai, Chun Hei Lo, Kwong Sak Leung, and Yee Leung. 2019. CUHK at MRP 2019: Transition-based parser with cross-framework variable-arity resolve action. In *Proceedings of the Shared Task on Cross-Framework Meaning Representation Parsing at the 2019 Conference on Natural Language Learning*, pages 104–113, Hong Kong, China.

Zuchao Li, Hai Zhao, Zhuosheng Zhang, Rui Wang, Masao Utiyama, and Eiichiro Sumita. 2019. SJTU–NICT at MRP 2019: Multi-task learning for end-to-end uniform semantic graph parsing. In *Proceedings of the Shared Task on Cross-Framework Meaning Representation Parsing at the 2019 Conference on Natural Language Learning*, pages 45–54, Hong Kong, China.

Zi Lin and Nianwen Xue. 2019. Parsing meaning representations. Is easier always better? In *Proceedings of the First International Workshop on Designing Meaning Representations*, pages 34–43, Florence, Italy.

Matthias Lindemann, Jonas Groschwitz, and Alexander Koller. 2019. Compositional semantic parsing across graphbanks. In *Proceedings of the 57th Annual Meeting of the Association for Computational Linguistics*, pages 4576–4585, Florence, Italy. Association for Computational Linguistics.

Chunchuan Lyu and Ivan Titov. 2018. AMR parsing as graph prediction with latent alignment. In *Proceedings of the 56th Meeting of the Association for Computational Linguistics*, pages 397–407, Melbourne, Australia.

Mitchell Marcus, Beatrice Santorini, and Mary Ann Marcinkiewicz. 1993. Building a large annotated corpus of English. The Penn Treebank. *Computational Linguistics*, 19:313–330.

Jonathan May. 2016. SemEval-2016 Task 8. Meaning representation parsing. In *Proceedings of the 10th International Workshop on Semantic Evaluation*, pages 1063–1073, San Diego, CA, USA.

Jonathan May and Jay Priyadarshi. 2017. SemEval-2017 Task 9. Abstract Meaning Representation parsing and generation. In *Proceedings of the 11th International Workshop on Semantic Evaluation*, pages 536–545.

Ryan McDonald, Joakim Nivre, Yvonne Quirmbach-Brundage, Yoav Goldberg, Dipanjan Das, Kuzman Ganchev, Keith Hall, Slav Petrov, Hao Zhang, and Oscar Täckström. 2013. Universal dependency annotation for multilingual parsing. In *Proceedings of the 51th Meeting of the Association for Computational Linguistics*, pages 92–97, Sofia, Bulgaria.

Ryan McDonald and Fernando Pereira. 2006. Online learning of approximate dependency parsing algorithms. In *Proceedings of the 11th Meeting of the European Chapter of the Association for Computational Linguistics*, pages 81–88, Trento, Italy.

James J. McGregor. 1982. Backtrack search algorithms and the maximal common subgraph problem. *Journal of Software: Practice and Experience*, 12:23–34.

Yusuke Miyao, Stephan Oepen, and Daniel Zeman. 2014. In-House. An ensemble of pre-existing off-the-shelf parsers. In *Proceedings of the 8th International Workshop on Semantic Evaluation*, pages 63–72, Dublin, Ireland.

Seung-Hoon Na, Jinwoo Min, Kwanghyeon Park, Jong-Hun Shin, and Young-Kil Kim. 2019. Jbnu at MRP 2019: Multi-level biaffine attention for semantic dependency parsing. In *Proceedings of the Shared Task on Cross-Framework Meaning Representation Parsing at the 2019 Conference on Natural Language Learning*, pages 95–103, Hong Kong, China.

Tahira Naseem, Abhishek Shah, Hui Wan, Radu Florian, Salim Roukos, and Miguel Ballesteros. 2019. Rewarding Smatch: Transition-based AMR parsing

with reinforcement learning. In *Proceedings of the 57th Meeting of the Association for Computational Linguistics*, pages 4586–4592, Florence, Italy.

Khoa Nguyen and Dang Nguyen. 2017. UIT-DANGNT-CLNLP at SemEval-2017 task 9: Building scientific concept fixing patterns for improving CAMR. In *Proceedings of the 11th International Workshop on Semantic Evaluation*, pages 909–913, Vancouver, Canada.

Joakim Nivre. 2003. An efficient algorithm for projective dependency parsing. In *Proceedings of the 8th International Conference on Parsing Technologies*, pages 149–160, Nancy, France.

Joakim Nivre. 2015. Towards a universal grammar of natural language processing. In *Proceedings of the 16th International Conference on Intelligent Text Processing and Computational Linguistics*, Cairo, Egypt.

Rik van Noord and Johan Bos. 2017. Dealing with co-reference in neural semantic parsing. In *Proceedings of the 2nd Workshop on Semantic Deep Learning (SemDeep-2)*, pages 41–49, Montpellier, France.

Stephan Oepen and Dan Flickinger. 2019. The ERG at MRP 2019: Radically compositional semantic dependencies. In *Proceedings of the Shared Task on Cross-Framework Meaning Representation Parsing at the 2019 Conference on Natural Language Learning*, pages 40–44, Hong Kong, China.

Stephan Oepen, Marco Kuhlmann, Yusuke Miyao, Daniel Zeman, Silvie Cinková, Dan Flickinger, Jan Hajič, and Zdeňka Urešová. 2015. SemEval 2015 Task 18. Broad-coverage semantic dependency parsing. In *Proceedings of the 9th International Workshop on Semantic Evaluation*, pages 915–926, Denver, CO, USA.

Stephan Oepen, Marco Kuhlmann, Yusuke Miyao, Daniel Zeman, Dan Flickinger, Jan Hajič, Angelina Ivanova, and Yi Zhang. 2014. SemEval 2014 Task 8. Broad-coverage semantic dependency parsing. In *Proceedings of the 8th International Workshop on Semantic Evaluation*, pages 63–72, Dublin, Ireland.

Stephan Oepen and Jan Tore Lønning. 2006. Discriminant-based MRS banking. In *Proceedings of the 5th International Conference on Language Resources and Evaluation*, pages 1250–1255, Genoa, Italy.

Woodley Packard. 2012. Choosing an evaluation metric for parser design. In *Proceedings of Human Language Technologies: The 2012 Annual Conference of the North American Chapter of the Association for Computational Linguistics*, pages 29–34, Montréal, Canada.

Hao Peng, Sam Thomson, and Noah A. Smith. 2017. Deep multitask learning for semantic dependency parsing. In *Proceedings of the 55th Meeting of the

Association for Computational Linguistics, pages 2037–2048, Vancouver, Canada.

Hao Peng, Sam Thomson, and Noah A. Smith. 2018a. Backpropagating through structured argmax using a SPIGOT. In *Proceedings of the 56th Meeting of the Association for Computational Linguistics*, pages 1863–1873, Melbourne, Australia.

Hao Peng, Sam Thomson, Swabha Swayamdipta, and Noah A. Smith. 2018b. Learning joint semantic parsers from disjoint data. In *Proceedings of the 2015 Conference of the North American Chapter of the Association for Computational Linguistics*, pages 1492–1502, New Orleans, LA, USA.

Carl Pollard and Ivan A. Sag. 1994. *Head-Driven Phrase Structure Grammar*. Studies in Contemporary Linguistics. The University of Chicago Press, Chicago, USA.

Martin Potthast, Tim Gollub, Francisco Rangel, Paolo Rosso, Efstathios Stamatatos, and Benno Stein. 2014. Improving the reproducibility of PAN's shared tasks. Plagiarism detection, author identification, and author profiling. In *Information Access Evaluation meets Multilinguality, Multimodality, and Visualization. 5th International Conference of the CLEF Initiative*, pages 268–299, Berlin, Germany. Springer.

Nima Pourdamghani, Yang Gao, Ulf Hermjakob, and Kevin Knight. 2014. Aligning English strings with Abstract Meaning Representation graphs. In *Proceedings of the 2014 Conference on Empirical Methods in Natural Language Processing*, pages 425–429, Doha, Qatar.

Sebastian Schuster and Christopher D. Manning. 2016. Enhanced English Universal Dependencies. An improved representation for natural language understanding tasks. In *Proceedings of the 10th International Conference on Language Resources and Evaluation*, Portorož, Slovenia.

Petr Sgall, Eva Hajičová, and Jarmila Panevová. 1986. *The Meaning of the Sentence and Its Semantic and Pragmatic Aspects*. D. Reidel Publishing Company, Dordrecht, The Netherlands.

Natalia Silveira, Timothy Dozat, Marie-Catherine de Marneffe, Samuel Bowman, Miriam Connor, John Bauer, and Christopher D. Manning. 2014. A gold standard dependency corpus for English. In *Proceedings of the 9th International Conference on Language Resources and Evaluation*, Reykjavik, Iceland.

Linfeng Song and Dan Gildea. 2019. SemBleu: A robust metric for AMR parsing evaluation. In *Proceedings of the 57th Meeting of the Association for Computational Linguistics*, pages 4547–4552, Florence, Italy.

Gabriel Stanovsky and Ido Dagan. 2018. Semantics as a foreign language. In *Proceedings of the 2018 Conference on Empirical Methods in Natural Language Processing*, pages 2412–2421, Brussels, Belgium.

Mark Steedman. 2011. *Taking Scope*. MIT Press, Cambridge, MA, USA.

Milan Straka. 2018. UDPipe 2.0 prototype at CoNLL 2018 UD shared task. In *Proceedings of the CoNLL 2018 Shared Task: Multilingual Parsing from Raw Text to Universal Dependencies*, pages 197–207.

Milan Straka and Jana Straková. 2019. ÚFAL MRPipe at MRP 2019: UDPipe goes semantic in the Meaning Representation Parsing shared task. In *Proceedings of the Shared Task on Cross-Framework Meaning Representation Parsing at the 2019 Conference on Natural Language Learning*, pages 127–137, Hong Kong, China.

Milan Straka, Jana Straková, and Jan Hajič. 2019. Evaluating Contextualized Embeddings on 54 Languages in POS Tagging, Lemmatization and Dependency Parsing. *arXiv preprint arXiv:1908.07448*.

Elior Sulem, Omri Abend, and Ari Rappoport. 2015. Conceptual annotations preserve structure across translations. A French–English case study. In *Proceedings of the 1st Workshop on Semantics-Driven Statistical Machine Translation*, pages 11–22.

Elior Sulem, Omri Abend, and Ari Rappoport. 2018a. Semantic structural annotation for text simplification. In *Proceedings of the 2015 Conference of the North American Chapter of the Association for Computational Linguistics*, New Orleans, LA, USA.

Elior Sulem, Omri Abend, and Ari Rappoport. 2018b. Simple and effective text simplification using semantic and neural methods. In *Proceedings of the 56th Meeting of the Association for Computational Linguistics*, Melbourne, Australia.

Yuka Tateisi, Akane Yakushiji, Tomoko Ohta, and J. Tsujii. 2005. Syntax annotation for the GENIA corpus. In *Proceedings of the 2nd International Joint Conference on Natural Language Processing*, pages 220–225, Jeju, Korea.

Zdeňka Urešová, Eva Fučíková, and Jana Šindlerová. 2016. CzEngVallex. A bilingual Czech–English valency lexicon. *The Prague Bulletin of Mathematical Linguistics*, 105:17–50.

Chuan Wang, Bin Li, and Nianwen Xue. 2018. Transition-based Chinese AMR parsing. In *Proceedings of the 2015 Conference of the North American Chapter of the Association for Computational Linguistics*, pages 247–252, New Orleans, LA, USA.

Chuan Wang, Sameer Pradhan, Xiaoman Pan, Heng Ji, and Nianwen Xue. 2016. CAMR at SemEval-2016 task 8: An extended transition-based AMR parser. In *Proceedings of the 10th International Workshop on Semantic Evaluation*, pages 1173–1178, San Diego, CA, USA.

Chuan Wang and Nianwen Xue. 2017. Getting the most out of AMR parsing. In *Proceedings of the 2017 Conference on Empirical Methods in Natural Language Processing*, pages 1257–1268, Copenhagen, Denmark.

Chuan Wang, Nianwen Xue, and Sameer Pradhan. 2015. A transition-based algorithm for AMR parsing. In *Proceedings of the 2015 Conference of the North American Chapter of the Association for Computational Linguistics*, pages 366–375, Denver, CO, USA.

Xinyu Wang, Yixian Liu, Zixia Jia, Chengyue Jiang, and Kewei Tu. 2019. ShanghaiTech at MRP 2019: Sequence-to-graph transduction with second-order edge inference for cross-framework meaning representation parsing. In *Proceedings of the Shared Task on Cross-Framework Meaning Representation Parsing at the 2019 Conference on Natural Language Learning*, pages 55–65, Hong Kong, China.

Hiroyasu Yamada and Yuji Matsumoto. 2003. Statistical dependency analysis with support vector machines. In *Proceedings of the 8th International Conference on Parsing Technologies*, pages 195–206, Nancy, France.

Sheng Zhang, Xutai Ma, Kevin Duh, and Benjamin Van Durme. 2019a. AMR parsing as sequence-to-graph transduction. In *Proceedings of the 57th Meeting of the Association for Computational Linguistics*, pages 80–94, Florence, Italy.

Sheng Zhang, Xutai Ma, Kevin Duh, and Benjamin Van Durme. 2019b. Broad-coverage semantic parsing as transduction. In *Proceedings of the 2019 Conference on Empirical Methods in Natural Language Processing*, Hong Kong, China.

Yue Zhang, Wei Jiang, Qingrong Xia, Junjie Cao, Rui Wang, Zhenghua Li, and Min Zhang. 2019c. Suda–alibaba at MRP 2019: Graph-based models with BERT. In *Proceedings of the Shared Task on Cross-Framework Meaning Representation Parsing at the 2019 Conference on Natural Language Learning*, pages 149–157, Hong Kong, China.

TUPA at MRP 2019: A Multi-Task Baseline System

Daniel Hershcovich[*] and **Ofir Arviv**[**]

[*]University of Copenhagen, Department of Computer Science
[**]Hebrew University of Jerusalem, School of Computer Science and Engineering
`hershcovich@di.ku.dk`, `ofir.arviv@mail.huji.ac.il`

Abstract

This paper describes the TUPA system submission to the shared task on Cross-Framework Meaning Representation Parsing (MRP) at the 2019 Conference for Computational Language Learning (CoNLL). TUPA provides a baseline point of comparison and is not considered in the official ranking of participating systems. While originally developed for UCCA only, TUPA has been generalized to support all MRP frameworks included in the task, and trained using multi-task learning to parse them all with a shared model. It is a transition-based parser with a BiLSTM encoder, augmented with BERT contextualized embeddings.

1 Introduction

TUPA (Transition-based UCCA/Universal Parser; Hershcovich et al., 2017) is a general transition-based parser for directed acyclic graphs (DAGs), originally designed for parsing text to graphs in the UCCA framework (Universal Conceptual Cognitive Annotation; Abend and Rappoport, 2013). It was used as the baseline system in SemEval 2019 Task 1: Cross-lingual Semantic Parsing with UCCA (Hershcovich et al., 2019b), where it was outranked by participating team submissions in all tracks (open and closed in English, German and French), but was also among the top 5 best-scoring systems in all tracks, and reached second place in the English closed tracks.

Being a general DAG parser, TUPA has been shown (Hershcovich et al., 2018a,b) to support other graph-based meaning representations and similar frameworks, including UD (Universal Dependencies; Nivre et al., 2019), which was the focus of CoNLL 2017 and 2018 Shared Tasks (Zeman et al., 2017, 2018); AMR (Abstract Meaning Representation; Banarescu et al., 2013), targeted in SemEval 2016 and 2017 Shared Tasks

(May, 2016; May and Priyadarshi, 2017); and DM (DELPH-IN MRS Bi-Lexical Dependencies; Ivanova et al., 2012), one of the target representations, among PAS and PSD (Prague Semantic Dependencies; Hajic et al., 2012; Miyao et al., 2014), in the SemEval 2014 and 2015 Shared Tasks on SDP (Semantic Dependency Parsing; Oepen et al., 2014, 2015, 2016). DM is converted from DeepBank (Flickinger et al., 2012), a corpus of hand-corrected parses from LinGO ERG (Copestake and Flickinger, 2000), an HPSG (Pollard and Sag, 1994) using Minimal Recursion Semantics (Copestake et al., 2005). EDS (Elementary Dependency Structures; Oepen and Lønning, 2006) is another framework derived from ERG, encoding English Resource Semantics in a variable-free semantic dependency graph.

The CoNLL 2019 Shared Task (Oepen et al., 2019) combines five frameworks for graph-based meaning representation: DM, PSD, EDS, UCCA and AMR. For the task, TUPA was extended to support the MRP format and frameworks, and is used as a baseline system, both as a single-task system trained separately on each framework, and as a multi-task system trained on all of them. The code is publicly available.[1]

2 Intermediate Graph Representation

Meaning representation graphs in the shared tasks are distributed in, and expected to be parsed to, a uniform graph interchange format, serialized as JSON Lines.[2]

The formalism encapsulates annotation for graphs containing nodes (corresponding either to text tokens, concepts, or logical predications), with the following components: top nodes, node

---

[1] `https://github.com/danielhers/tupa/tree/mrp`
[2] `http://mrp.nlpl.eu/index.php?page=4`

Proceedings of the Shared Task on Cross-Framework Meaning Representation Parsing at the 2019 CoNLL, pages 28–39
Hong Kong, November 3, 2019. ©2019 Association for Computational Linguistics
https://doi.org/10.18653/v1/K19-2002

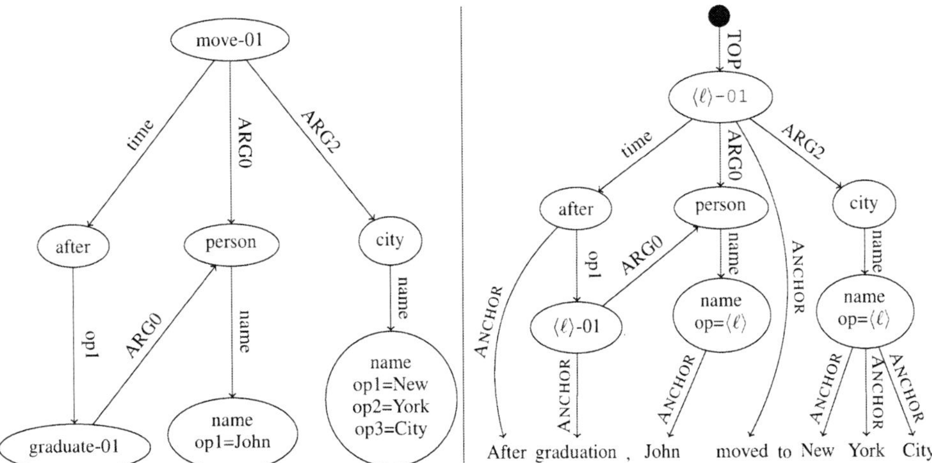

Figure 1: Left: AMR graph, in the MRP formalism, for the sentence "After graduation, John moved to New York City." Edge labels are shown on the edges. Node labels are shown inside the nodes, along with any node properties (in the form `property=value`). The text tokens are not part of the graph, and are matched to nodes by automatic alignment (anchoring). Right: converted AMR graph in the intermediate graph representation. Same as in the intermediate graph representation for all frameworks, it contains a virtual root node attached to the graph's top node with a TOP edge, and virtual terminal nodes corresponding to text tokens, attached according to the anchoring (or, for AMR, the provided automatic alignments) with ANCHOR edges. Same as for all frameworks with node labels and properties (i.e., all but UCCA), labels and properties are replaced with placeholders corresponding to anchored tokens, where possible. The placeholder $\langle\ell\rangle$ corresponds to the concatenated lemmas of anchored tokens. Specifically for AMR, name operator properties (e.g., op* for New York City) are collapsed to single properties.

labels, node properties, node anchoring, directed edges, edge labels, and edge attributes.

While all frameworks represent top nodes, and include directed, labeled edges, UCCA does not contain node labels and properties, AMR lacks node anchoring, and only UCCA has edge attributes (distinguishing primary/remote edges).

2.1 Roots and Anchors

TUPA supports parsing to rooted graphs with labeled edges, and with the text tokens as terminals (leaves), which is the standard format for UCCA graphs. However, MRP graphs are not given in this format, since there may be multiple roots and the text tokens are only matched to the nodes by anchoring (and not by explicit edges).

For the CoNLL 2019 Shared Task, TUPA was extended to support node labels, node properties, and edge attributes (see §3.1). Top nodes and anchoring are combined into the graph by adding a virtual root node and virtual terminal nodes, respectively, during preprocessing.

A virtual terminal node is created per token according to the tokenization predicted by UDPipe (Straka and Straková, 2017) and provided as com-

panion data by the task organizers. All top nodes are attached as children of the virtual root with a TOP-labeled edge.

Nodes with anchoring are attached to the virtual terminals associated with the tokens whose character spans intersect with their anchoring, with ANCHOR-labeled edges. Note that anchoring is automatically determined for training in the case of AMR, using the alignments from the companion data, computed by the ISI aligner (Pourdamghani et al., 2014). There is no special treatment of non-trivial anchoring for EDS: in case a node is anchored to multiple tokens (as is the case for multi-word expressions), they are all attached with ANCHOR-labeled edges, resulting in possibly multiple parents for some virtual terminal nodes.

During inference, after TUPA returns an output graph, the virtual root and terminals are removed as postprocessing to return the final graph. Top nodes and anchoring are then inserted accordingly.

2.2 Placeholder Insertion

The number of distinct node labels and properties is very large for most frameworks, resulting in severe sparsity, as they are taken from an open vo-

Before Transition				Transition	After Transition				
Stack	Buffer	N.	Edges		Stack	Buffer	Nodes	Edges	Extra Effect
S	$x \mid B$	V	E	SHIFT	$S \mid x$	B	V	E	
$S \mid x$	B	V	E	REDUCE	S	B	V	E	
$S \mid x$	B	V	E	NODE$_X$	$S \mid x$	$y \mid B$	$V \cup \{y\}$	$E \mid (y, x)$	$\ell_E(y, x) \leftarrow X$
$S \mid x$	B	V	E	CHILD$_X$	$S \mid x$	$y \mid B$	$V \cup \{y\}$	$E \mid (x, y)$	$\ell_E(x, y) \leftarrow X$
$S \mid x$	B	V	E	LABEL$_X$	$S \mid x$	B	V	E	$\ell_V(x) \leftarrow X$
$S \mid x$	B	V	E	PROPERTY$_X$	$S \mid x$	B	V	E	$p(x) \leftarrow X$
$S \mid y, x$	B	V	E	LEFT-EDGE$_X$	$S \mid y, x$	B	V	$E \mid (x, y)$	$\ell_E(x, y) \leftarrow X$
$S \mid x, y$	B	V	E	RIGHT-EDGE$_X$	$S \mid x, y$	B	V	$E \mid (x, y)$	$\ell_E(x, y) \leftarrow X$
S	B	V	$E \mid (x, y)$	ATTRIBUTE$_X$	S	B	V	$E \mid (x, y)$	$a(x) \leftarrow X$
$S \mid x, y$	B	V	E	SWAP	$S \mid y$	$x \mid B$	V	E	
[root]	$\emptyset$	V	E	FINISH	$\emptyset$	$\emptyset$	V	E	terminal state

Figure 2: The TUPA-MRP transition set. We write the stack with its top to the right and the buffer with its head to the left; the set of edges is also ordered with the latest edge on the right. NODE, LABEL, PROPERTY and ATTRIBUTE require that $x \neq$ root; CHILD, LABEL, PROPERTY, LEFT-EDGE and RIGHT-EDGE require that $x \notin w_{1:n}$; ATTRIBUTE requires that $y \notin w_{1:n}$; LEFT-EDGE and RIGHT-EDGE require that $y \neq$ root and that there is no directed path from y to x; and SWAP requires that $i(x) < i(y)$, where $i(x)$ is the swap index (see §3.5).

cabulary of e.g. word senses and named entities. However, many are simply copies of text tokens and their lemmas.

To reduce the number of unique node labels and properties, we use the (possibly automatic) anchoring and UDPipe preprocessing to introduce placeholders in the values. For example, a node labeled `move-01` anchored to the token `moved` will be instead labeled $\langle \ell \rangle$`-01`, where $\langle \ell \rangle$ is a placeholder for the token's lemma. In this way we reduce the number of node labels in the AMR training set, for example, from tens of thousands to 7,300, of which 2,000 occur only once and are treated as unknown. We use similar placeholders for the token's surface form. Placeholders are resolved back to the full value after an output graph is produced by the parser, according to the anchoring in the graph. While nodes labels and properties sometimes have a non-trivial relationship to the text tokens, in most cases they contain the lemma or surface form, making this a simple and effective solution.

While more sophisticated alignment rules have been developed (Flanigan et al., 2014; Pourdamghani et al., 2014), such as using entity linking (Daiber et al., 2013), as employed by Bjerva et al. (2016); van Noord and Bos (2017), in this baseline system we are employing a simple strategy without relying on external, potentially non-whitelisted resources.

Named entities in AMR are expressed by `name`-labeled nodes, with a property for each token in the name, with keys `op1`, `op2`, etc. We in-

stead collapse these properties to a single `op` property whose label is the concatenation of the name tokens, with special separator symbols. This value is in turn replaced by a placeholder, if the node is anchored and the anchored tokens match the property. Figure 1 demonstrates an AMR graph before and after the conversion to the intermediate graph representation.

3 Transition-based Meaning Representation Parser

TUPA is a transition-based parser (Nivre, 2003), constructing graphs incrementally from input tokens by applying *transitions* (*actions*) to the *parser state* (*configuration*). The parser state is composed of a buffer B of tokens and nodes to be processed, a stack S of nodes currently being processed, and an incrementally constructed graph G. Some states are marked as *terminal*, meaning that G is the final output. The input to the parser is a sequence of tokens: $w_1, \ldots, w_n$. Parsing starts with a (virtual) root node on the stack, and the input tokens in the buffer, as (virtual) terminal nodes.

Given a gold-standard graph and a parser state, an *oracle* returns the set of gold transitions to apply at the next step, i.e., all transitions that preserve the reachability of the gold target graph.[3] A classifier is trained using the oracle to select

---

[3] This type of oracle is similar to a *dynamic oracle* (Goldberg and Nivre, 2012; Goldberg, 2013), but in TUPA it only supports the case where the current parser state is valid, i.e., only gold transitions have been applied since the initial state. Training with exploration is thus not supported (yet).

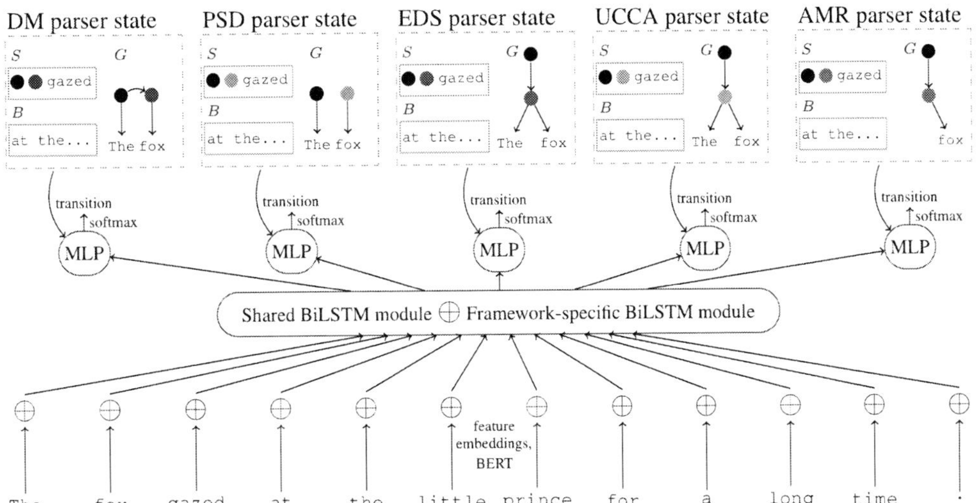

Figure 3: Illustration of the TUPA model, adapted from Hershcovich et al. (2018a), at an intermediate point in the process of parsing the sentence "The fox gazed at the little prince for a long time." Top: parser state (stack, buffer and intermediate graph) for each framework. Bottom: encoder architecture. Input feature embeddings are concatenate with BERT embeddings for each token. Vector representations for the input tokens are then computed by two layers of shared and framework-specific bidirectional LSTMs. At each point in the parsing process, the encoded vectors for specific tokens (from specific location in the stack/buffer) are concatenated with embedding and numeric features from the parser state (for existing edge labels, number of children, etc.), and fed into the MLP for selecting the next transition. Note that parsing the different frameworks is not performed jointly; the illustration only expresses the parameter sharing scheme.

the next transition based on features encoding the parser's current state, where the training objective is to maximize the sum of log-likelihoods of all gold transitions at each step. If there are multiple gold transitions, the highest-scoring one is taken in training. Inference is performed greedily: the highest-scoring transition is always taken.

Formally, the incrementally constructed graph G consists of $(V, E, \ell_V, \ell_E, p, a)$, where V is the set of *nodes*, E is the sequence of directed *edges*, $\ell_V : V \to L_V$ is the *node label* function, L_V being the set of possible node labels, $\ell_E : E \to L_E$ is the *edge label* function, L_E being the set of possible edge labels, $p : V \to \mathcal{P}(P)$ is the *node property* function, P being the set of possible node property-value pairs, and $a : E \to \mathcal{P}(A)$ is the *edge attribute* function, A being the set of possible edge attribute-value pairs (a node may have any number of properties; an edge may have any number of attributes).

3.1 Transition Set

The set of possible transitions in TUPA is based on a combination of transition sets from other parsers, designed to support reentrancies (Sagae and Tsujii, 2008; Tokgöz and Eryiğit, 2015), discontinuities (Nivre, 2009; Maier, 2015; Maier and Lichte, 2016) and non-terminal nodes (Zhu et al., 2013). Beyond the original TUPA transitions (Hershcovich et al., 2017, 2018a), for the CoNLL 2019 Shared Task, transitions are added to support node labels, node properties, and edge attributes. Additionally, top nodes and node anchoring are encoded by special edges from a virtual root node and to virtual terminal nodes (corresponding to text tokens), respectively (see §2).

The TUPA-MRP transition set is shown in Figure 2. It includes the following original TUPA transitions: the standard SHIFT and REDUCE operations (to move a node from the buffer to the stack and to discard a stack node, respectively), NODE$_X$ for creating a new non-terminal node and an X-labeled edge (so that the new node is a parent of the stack top), LEFT-EDGE$_X$ and RIGHT-EDGE$_X$ to create a new X-labeled edge, SWAP to handle discontinuous nodes (moving the second topmost stack node back to the buffer), and FIN-ISH to mark the state as terminal.

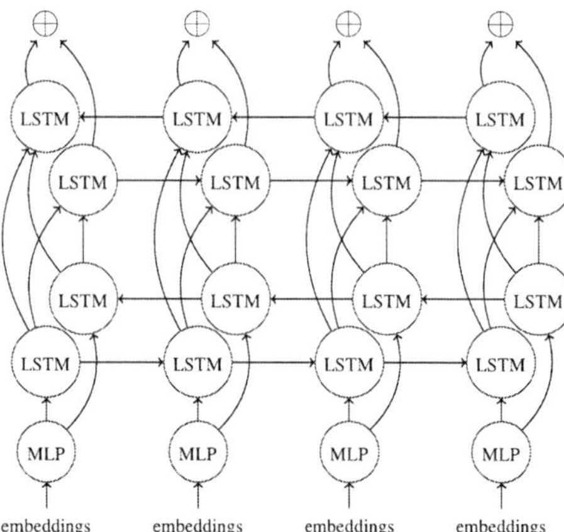

Figure 4: BiLSTM module, illustrated for an input sequence of four tokens.

Besides the original TUPA transitions, TUPA-MRP contains a CHILD transition to create unanchored children for existing nodes (like NODE, but the new node is a *child* of the stack top),[4] a LABEL transition to select a label for an existing node (either the stack top of the second topmost stack node), a PROPERTY transition to select a property-value pair for an existing node, and an ATTRIBUTE transition to select an attribute-value pair for an existing edge (the last created edge).

The original TUPA transitions LEFT-REMOTE$_X$ and RIGHT-REMOTE$_X$, creating new *remote* edges (a UCCA-specific distinction), are omitted. Remote edges are encoded instead as edges with the `remote` attribute, and are supported by the combination of EDGE and ATTRIBUTE transitions. In contrast to the original TUPA transitions, EDGE transitions are allowed to attach multiple parents to a node.

3.2 Transition Classifier

To predict the next transition at each step, TUPA uses a BiLSTM module followed by an MLP and a softmax layer for classification (Kiperwasser and Goldberg, 2016). The model is illustrated in Figure 3.

The BiLSTM module (illustrated in more detail in Figure 4) is applied before the transition se-

---

[4]While UCCA contains unanchored (*implicit*) nodes corresponding to non-instantiated arguments or predicates, the original TUPA disregards them as they are not included in standard UCCA evaluation. The CoNLL 2019 Shared Task omits implicit UCCA nodes too, in fact, but the CHILD transition is included to support unanchored nodes in AMR, and is not used otherwise.

quence starts, running over the input tokenized sequence. It consists of a pre-BiLSTM MLP with feature embeddings (§3.3) and pre-trained contextualized embeddings (§3.4) concatenated as inputs, followed by (multiple layers of) a bidirectional recurrent neural network (Schuster and Paliwal, 1997; Graves, 2008) with a long short-term memory cell (Hochreiter and Schmidhuber, 1997).

While edge labels are combined into the identity of the transition (so that for example, LEFT-EDGE$_P$ and LEFT-EDGE$_S$ are separate transitions in the output), there is just one transition for each of LABEL, PROPERTY and ATTRIBUTE. After each time one of these transition is selected, an additional classifier is evoked with the set of possible values for the currently parsed framework. This hard separation is made due to the large number of node labels and properties in the MRP frameworks. Since there is only one possible edge attribute value (`remote` for UCCA), performing this transition always results in this value being selected.

3.3 Features

In both training and testing, we use vector embeddings representing the lemmas, coarse POS tags (UPOS) and fine-grained POS tags (XPOS). These feature values are provided by UDPipe as companion data by the task organizers. In addition, we use punctuation and gap type features (Maier and Lichte, 2016), and previously predicted node and edge labels, node properties, edge attributes and parser actions. These embeddings are initialized randomly (Glorot and Bengio, 2010).

To the feature embeddings, we concatenate numeric features representing the node height, number of parents and children, and the ratio between the number of terminals to total number of nodes in the graph G. Numeric features are taken as they are, whereas categorical features are mapped to real-valued embedding vectors. For each non-terminal node, we select a *head terminal* for feature extraction, by traversing down the graph, selecting the first outgoing edge each time according to alphabetical order of labels.

3.4 Pre-trained Contextualized Embeddings

Contextualized representation models such as BERT (Devlin et al., 2019) have recently achieved state-of-the-art results on a diverse array of downstream NLP tasks, gaining improved results compared to non-contextual representations. We use the weighted sum of last four hidden layers of a BERT pre-trained model as extra input features.[5]

BERT uses a wordpiece tokenizer (Wu et al., 2016), which segments all text into sub-word units, while TUPA uses the UDPipe tokenization. To maintain alignment between wordpieces and tokens, we use a summation of the outputs of BERT vectors corresponding to the wordpieces of each token as its representation.

3.5 Constraints

As each annotation scheme has different constraints on the allowed graph structures, we apply these constraints separately for each task. During training and parsing, the relevant constraint set rules out some of the transitions according to the parser state.

Some constraints are task-specific, others are generic. For example, in AMR, a node with an incoming NAME edge must have the NAME label. In UCCA, a node may have at most one outgoing edge with label $\in \{$PROCESS, STATE$\}$.

An example of a generic constraint is that stack nodes that have been swapped should not be swapped again, to avoid infinite loops in inference. To implement this constraint, we define a *swap index* for each node, assigned when the node is created. At initialization, only the root node and terminals exist. We assign the root a swap index of 0, and for each terminal, its position in the text (starting at 1). Whenever a node is created as a result of a NODE or CHILD transition, its swap index is the arithmetic mean of the swap indices of the stack top and buffer head. While this constraint may theoretically limit the ability to parse arbitrary graphs, in practice we find that all graphs in the shared task training set can still be reached without violating it.

4 Multi-Task Learning

Whereas in the single-task setting TUPA is trained separately on each framework as described above, in the multi-task setting, all frameworks share a BiLSTM for encoding the input. In addition, each framework has a framework-specific BiLSTM, private to it. Each framework has its own MLP on top of the concatenation of the shared and framework-specific BiLSTM (see Figure 3).

---

[5]We used the `bert-large-cased` model from `https://github.com/huggingface/pytorch-transformers`.

Hyperparameter	Value	
Lemma dim.	200	
UPOS dim.	20	
XPOS dim.	20	
Dep. rel. dim.	10	
Punct. dim.	1	
Action dim.	3	
Node label dim.	20	
Node prop. dim.	20	
Edge label dim.	20	
Edge attrib. dim.	1	
MLP layers	2	
MLP dim.	50	
Shared BiLSTM layers	2	
Shared BiLSTM dim.	500	
Shared pre-BiLSTM MLP layers	1	
Shared pre-BiLSTM MLP dim.	300	
Private BiLSTM layers	2	
Private BiLSTM dim.	500	
Private pre-BiLSTM MLP layers	1	
Private pre-BiLSTM MLP dim.	300	

Table 1: Hyperparameter settings.

For node labels and properties and for edge attributes (when applicable), an additional "axis" (private BiLSTM and MLP) is added per framework (e.g., AMR node labels are predicted separately and with an identical architecture to AMR transitions, except the output dimension is different). This is true for the single-task setting too, so in fact the single-task setting is multi-task over {transitions, node labels, node properties, edge attributes}.

5 Training details

The model is implemented using DyNet v2.1 (Neubig et al., 2017).[6] Unless otherwise noted, we use the default values provided by the package. We use the same hyperparameters as used in previous experiments on UCCA parsing (Hershcovich et al., 2018a), without any hyperparameter tuning on the CoNLL 2019 data.

5.1 Hyperparameters

We use dropout (Srivastava et al., 2014) between MLP layers, and recurrent dropout (Gal and Ghahramani, 2016) between BiLSTM layers, both with $p = 0.4$. We also use word, lemma, coarse- and fine-grained POS tag dropout with $\alpha = 0.2$

---

[6]`http://dynet.io`

Offi-cial	TUPA (single-task)		TUPA (multi-task)		Best System	
	ALL	LPPS	ALL	LPPS	ALL	LPPS
DM	55.54	58.60	42.69	39.45	95.50 (Bai and Zhao, 2019)	94.96 (Che et al., 2019)
PSD	51.76	58.87	52.65	54.53	91.28 (Donatelli et al., 2019)	88.46 (Li et al., 2019)
EDS	81.00	81.36	73.95	74.81	91.85 (Zhang et al., 2019)	92.55 (Zhang et al., 2019)
UCCA	27.56	40.06	23.65	41.03	81.67 (Che et al., 2019)	82.61 (Che et al., 2019)
AMR	44.73	47.04	33.75	43.37	73.38 (Cao et al., 2019)	73.11 (Donatelli et al., 2019)
Overall	57.70	57.55	45.34	50.64	86.20 (Che et al., 2019)	84.88 (Donatelli et al., 2019)

Table 2: Official test MRP F-scores (in %) for TUPA (single-task and multi-task). For comparison, the highest score achieved for each framework and evaluation set is shown.

(Kiperwasser and Goldberg, 2016): in training, the embedding for a feature value w is replaced with a zero vector with a probability of $\frac{\alpha}{\#(w)+\alpha}$, where $\#(w)$ is the number of occurrences of w observed. In addition, we use *node dropout* (Hershcovich et al., 2018a): with a probability of 0.1 at each step, all features associated with a single node in the parser state are replaced with zero vectors. For optimization we use a minibatch size of 100, decaying all weights by 10^{-5} at each update, and train with stochastic gradient descent for 50 epochs with a learning rate of 0.1, followed by AMSGrad (Sashank J. Reddi, 2018) for 250 epochs with $\alpha = 0.001, \beta_1 = 0.9$ and $\beta_2 = 0.999$. Table 1 lists other hyperparameter settings.

5.2 Official Evaluation

For the official evaluation, we did not use a development set, and trained on the full training set for as many epochs as the evaluation period allowed for. The multi-task model completed just 3 epoch of training. The single task models completed 12 epochs for DM, 22 epochs for PSD, 14 epochs for EDS, 100 epochs for UCCA (the maximum number we allowed) and 13 epochs for AMR.

Due to an oversight resulting from code re-use, in the official evaluation we used non-whitelisted resources. Specifically, for AMR, we used a constraint forcing any node whose label corresponds to a PropBank (Palmer et al., 2005) frame to only have the core arguments defined for the frame. We obtained the possible arguments per frame from the PropBank frame files.[7] Additionally, for the intermediate graph representation, we used placeholders for tokens' negation, verb, noun and adjective form, as well as organizational and relational roles, from a pre-defined lexicon included in the

AMR official resources.[8] This is similar to the delexicalization employed by Buys and Blunsom (2017a) for AMR parsing.

5.3 Post-evaluation Training

After the evaluation period, we continued training for a longer period of time, using a slightly modified system: we used only resources whitelisted by the task organizers in the post-evaluation training, removing the constraints and placeholders based on PropBank and AMR lexicons.

In this setting, training is done over a shuffled mix of the training set for all frameworks (no special sampling is done to balance the number of instances per framework), and a development set of 500 instances per framework (see §5.1). We select the epoch with the best average MRP F-score score on a development set, selected by sampling 500 random training instances from each framework (the development instances are excluded from the training set). The large multi-task model only completed 4 training epochs in the available time, the single-task models completed 24 epochs for DM, 31 epochs for PSD, 25 epochs for EDS, 69 epochs for UCCA and 23 epochs for AMR.

6 Results

Table 2 presents the averaged scores on the test sets in the official evaluation (§5.2), for TUPA and for the best-performing system in each framework and evaluation set. Since non-whitelisted resources were used, the TUPA scores cannot be taken as a baseline. Furthermore, due to insufficient training time, all models but the UCCA one are underfitting, while the UCCA model is overfitting due to excessive training without early stopping (no development set was used in this setting).

Post-Evalua-tion	MRP Test Scores				Native Evaluation Test Scores				Trans./ Token Ratio
	TUPA (single-task)		TUPA (multi-task)		TUPA (single-task)		TUPA (multi-task)		
	ALL	LPPS	ALL	LPPS	ALL	LPPS	ALL	LPPS	
DM	75.57	80.46	62.16	66.07	77.16	79.27	72.65	71.80	8.4
PSD	70.86	70.62	65.95	68.05	69.53	72.03	61.27	65.81	6.7
EDS	84.85	85.36	79.39	80.25	72.38	72.68	79.84	80.29	12.8
UCCA	77.69	82.15	64.05	73.11	57.42	65.90	35.60	50.29	8.4
AMR	53.85	53.47	39.00	42.62	53.05	52.52	38.11	40.47	6.6
Overall	75.73	77.63	66.01	68.58					8.4

Table 3: Post-evaluation test scores (in %) for TUPA (single-task and multi-task), using the MRP F-score (left), and using Native Evaluation (middle): labeled SDP F-score for DM and PSD, EDM F-score for EDS, primary labeled F-score for UCCA, and Smatch for AMR. The rightmost column (Trans./Token Ratio) shows the mean ratio between length of oracle transition sequence and sentence length, over the training set.

6.1 Post-evaluation Results

Table 3 presents the averaged scores on the test sets for the post-evaluation trained models (§5.3). Strikingly, the multi-task TUPA consistently falls behind the single-task one, for each framework separately and in the overall score. This stems from several factors, namely that the sharing strategy could be improved, but mainly since the multi-task model is probably underfitting due to insufficient training. We conclude that better efficiency and faster training is crucial for practical applicability of this approach. Perhaps a smaller multi-task model would have performed better by training on more data in the available time frame.

6.2 Diagnostic Evaluation

The rightmost column of Table 3 displays the mean ratio between length of oracle transitions sequence and sentence length by framework, over the shared task training set. Scores are clearly better as the framework has longer oracle transition sequences, perhaps because many of the transitions are "easy" as they correspond to structural elements of the graphs or properties copied from the input tokens.

6.3 Comparability with Previous Results

Previous published results of applying TUPA to UCCA parsing (Hershcovich et al., 2017, 2018a, 2019b,a) used a different version of the parser, without contextualized word representations from BERT.

For comparability with previous results, we train and test an identical model to the one presented in this paper, on the SemEval 2019 Task 1 data (Hershcovich et al., 2019b), which is UCCA-only, but contains tracks in English, German and French. For this experiment, we use `bert-multilingual` instead of `bert-large-cased`, and train a shared model over all three languages. A 50-dimensional learned language embedding vector is concatenated to the input. Word, lemma and XPOS features are not used. No multi-task learning with other frameworks is employed. The results are shown in Table 4. While improvement is achieved uniformly over the previous TUPA scores, even with BERT, TUPA is outperformed by the shared task winners (Jiang et al., 2019). Note that Jiang et al. (2019) also used `bert-multilingual` in the open tracks.

We also train and test TUPA with BERT embeddings on v1.0 of the UCCA English Web Tree bank (EWT) reviews dataset (Hershcovich et al., 2019a). While the EWT reviews are included in the MRP shared task UCCA data, the different format and preprocessing makes for slightly different scores, so we report the scores for comparability with previous work in Table 5. We again see pronounced improvements from incorporating pretrained contextualized embeddings into the model.

7 Related Work

Transition-based meaning representation parsing dates back already to semantic dependency parsing work by Sagae and Tsujii (2008); Tokgöz and Eryiğit (2015), who support a DAG structure by allowing multiple parents to be created by EDGE transitions, and by Titov et al. (2009), who applied a SWAP transition (Nivre, 2008) for online reordering of nodes to support non-projectivity.

Transition-based parsing was applied to AMR

SemEval 2019	All	Prim.	Rem.
English-Wiki (open)			
TUPA (w/o BERT)	73.5	73.9	53.5
TUPA (w/ BERT)	77.8	78.3	57.4
Jiang et al. (2019)	**80.5**	**81.0**	**58.8**
English-20K (open)			
TUPA (w/o BERT)	68.4	69.4	25.9
TUPA (w/ BERT)	74.9	75.7	**44.0**
Jiang et al. (2019)	**76.7**	**77.7**	39.2
German-20K (open)			
TUPA (w/o BERT)	79.1	79.6	59.9
TUPA (w/ BERT)	81.3	81.6	**69.2**
Jiang et al. (2019)	**84.9**	**85.4**	64.1
French-20K (open)			
TUPA (w/o BERT)	48.7	49.6	2.4
TUPA (w/ BERT)	72.0	72.8	**45.8**
Jiang et al. (2019)	**75.2**	**76.0**	43.3

Table 4: Test UCCA F-score scores (in %) on all edges, primary edges and remote edges, on the SemEval 2019 Task 1 data. The previous published TUPA scores are shown (TUPA w/o BERT), as well as scores for TUPA with BERT contextualized embeddings, TUPA (w/ BERT), averaged over three separately trained models in each setting, differing only by random seed (standard deviation < 0.03); and the scores for the best-scoring system from that shared task.

by Wang et al. (2015b,a, 2016); Wang and Xue (2017); Guo and Lu (2018), who transformed syntactic dependencies into AMRs by a sequence of transitions. Subsequent work used transition-based parsing to create AMRs from text directly (Damonte et al., 2017; Ballesteros and Al-Onaizan, 2017; Naseem et al., 2019). Buys and Blunsom (2017b) developed a transition-based parser supporting both AMR and EDS.

8 Conclusion

We have presented TUPA, a baseline system in the CoNLL 2019 shared task on Cross-Framework Meaning Representation. TUPA is a general transition-based DAG parser, which is trained with multi-task learning on multiple frameworks. Its input representation is augmented with BERT contextualized embeddings.

Acknowledgments

We are grateful for the valuable feedback from the anonymous reviewers. We would like to thank the other task organizers, Stephan Oepen, Omri Abend, Jan Hajič, Tim O'Gorman and Nianwen

EWT	All	Prim.	Rem.
TUPA (w/o BERT)	71.0	72.1	47.0
TUPA (w/ BERT)	**75.2**	**76.1**	**54.8**

Table 5: Test UCCA F-score scores (in %) on all edges, primary edges and remote edges, on the UCCA EWT reviews data. TUPA (w/o BERT) is from (Hershcovich et al., 2019a). TUPA (w/ BERT) is averaged over three separately trained models in each setting, differing only by random seed (standard deviation < 0.03).

Xue, for valuable discussions and tips on developing the baseline systems, as well as for providing the data, evaluation metrics and information on the various frameworks.

References

Omri Abend and Ari Rappoport. 2013. Universal Conceptual Cognitive Annotation (UCCA). In *Proc. of ACL*, pages 228–238.

Joakim Nivre et al. 2019. Universal dependencies 2.4. LINDAT/CLARIN digital library at the Institute of Formal and Applied Linguistics (ÚFAL), Faculty of Mathematics and Physics, Charles University.

Hongxiao Bai and Hai Zhao. 2019. SJTU at MRP 2019: A transition-based multi-task parser for cross-framework meaning representation parsing. In *Proceedings of the Shared Task on Cross-Framework Meaning Representation Parsing at the 2019 Conference on Natural Language Learning*, pages 86 – 94, Hong Kong, China.

Miguel Ballesteros and Yaser Al-Onaizan. 2017. AMR parsing using stack-LSTMs. In *Proceedings of the 2017 Conference on Empirical Methods in Natural Language Processing*, pages 1269–1275, Copenhagen, Denmark. Association for Computational Linguistics.

Laura Banarescu, Claire Bonial, Shu Cai, Madalina Georgescu, Kira Griffitt, Ulf Hermjakob, Kevin Knight, Martha Palmer, and Nathan Schneider. 2013. Abstract Meaning Representation for sembanking. In *Proc. of the Linguistic Annotation Workshop*.

Johannes Bjerva, Johan Bos, and Hessel Haagsma. 2016. The meaning factory at SemEval-2016 task 8: Producing AMRs with boxer. In *Proceedings of the 10th International Workshop on Semantic Evaluation (SemEval-2016)*, pages 1179–1184, San Diego, California. Association for Computational Linguistics.

Jan Buys and Phil Blunsom. 2017a. Oxford at SemEval-2017 task 9: Neural AMR parsing with pointer-augmented attention. In *Proc. of SemEval*, pages 914–919.

Jan Buys and Phil Blunsom. 2017b. Robust incremental neural semantic graph parsing. In *Proc. of ACL*, pages 1215–1226.

Jie Cao, Yi Zhang, Adel Youssef, and Vivek Srikumar. 2019. Amazon at MRP 2019: Parsing meaning representations with lexical and phrasal anchoring. In *Proceedings of the Shared Task on Cross-Framework Meaning Representation Parsing at the 2019 Conference on Natural Language Learning*, pages 138 – 148, Hong Kong, China.

Wanxiang Che, Longxu Dou, Yang Xu, Yuxuan Wang, Yijia Liu, and Ting Liu. 2019. HIT-SCIR at MRP 2019: A unified pipeline for meaning representation parsing via efficient training and effective encoding. In *Proceedings of the Shared Task on Cross-Framework Meaning Representation Parsing at the 2019 Conference on Natural Language Learning*, pages 76 – 85, Hong Kong, China.

Ann Copestake and Dan Flickinger. 2000. An open source grammar development environment and broad-coverage English grammar using HPSG. In *Proc. of LREC*, pages 591–600.

Ann Copestake, Dan Flickinger, Carl Pollard, and Ivan A. Sag. 2005. Minimal recursion semantics: An introduction. *Research on Language and Computation*, 3(2):281–332.

Joachim Daiber, Max Jakob, Chris Hokamp, and Pablo N. Mendes. 2013. Improving efficiency and accuracy in multilingual entity extraction. In *Proc. of I-Semantics*.

Marco Damonte, Shay B. Cohen, and Giorgio Satta. 2017. An incremental parser for Abstract Meaning Representation. In *Proc. of EACL*.

Jacob Devlin, Ming-Wei Chang, Kenton Lee, and Kristina Toutanova. 2019. BERT: Pre training of deep bidirectional transformers for language understanding. In *Proceedings of the 2019 Conference of the North American Chapter of the Association for Computational Linguistics: Human Language Technologies, Volume 1 (Long and Short Papers)*, pages 4171–4186, Minneapolis, Minnesota. Association for Computational Linguistics.

Lucia Donatelli, Meaghan Fowlie, Jonas Groschwitz, Alexander Koller, Matthias Lindemann, Mario Mina, and Pia WeiSSenhorn. 2019. Saarland at MRP 2019: Compositional parsing across all graphbanks. In *Proceedings of the Shared Task on Cross-Framework Meaning Representation Parsing at the 2019 Conference on Natural Language Learning*, pages 66 – 75, Hong Kong, China.

Jeffrey Flanigan, Sam Thomson, Jaime Carbonell, Chris Dyer, and Noah A. Smith. 2014. A discriminative graph-based parser for the Abstract Meaning Representation. In *Proc. of ACL*, pages 1426–1436.

Daniel Flickinger, Yi Zhang, and Valia Kordoni. 2012. DeepBank: A dynamically annotated treebank of the Wall Street Journal. In *Proc. of Workshop on Treebanks and Linguistic Theories*, pages 85–96.

Yarin Gal and Zoubin Ghahramani. 2016. A Theoretically Grounded Application of Dropout in Recurrent Neural Networks. In D D Lee, M Sugiyama, U V Luxburg, I Guyon, and R Garnett, editors, *Advances in Neural Information Processing Systems 29*, pages 1019–1027. Curran Associates, Inc.

Xavier Glorot and Yoshua Bengio. 2010. Understanding the difficulty of training deep feedforward neural networks. In *Proceedings of the thirteenth international conference on artificial intelligence and statistics*, pages 249–256.

Yoav Goldberg. 2013. Dynamic-oracle transition-based parsing with calibrated probabilistic output. In *Proc. of IWPT*.

Yoav Goldberg and Joakim Nivre. 2012. A dynamic oracle for arc-eager dependency parsing. In *Proc. of COLING*, pages 959–976.

Alex Graves. 2008. Supervised sequence labelling with recurrent neural networks. *Ph. D. thesis*.

Zhijiang Guo and Wei Lu. 2018. Better transition-based AMR parsing with a refined search space. In *Proceedings of the 2018 Conference on Empirical Methods in Natural Language Processing*, pages 1712–1722, Brussels, Belgium. Association for Computational Linguistics.

Jan Hajic, Eva Hajicová, Jarmila Panevová, Petr Sgall, Ondrej Bojar, Silvie Cinková, Eva Fucíková, Marie Mikulová, Petr Pajas, Jan Popelka, et al. 2012. Announcing prague czech-english dependency treebank 2.0. In *LREC*, pages 3153–3160.

Daniel Hershcovich, Omri Abend, and Ari Rappoport. 2017. A transition-based directed acyclic graph parser for UCCA. In *Proc. of ACL*, pages 1127–1138.

Daniel Hershcovich, Omri Abend, and Ari Rappoport. 2018a. Multitask parsing across semantic representations. In *Proc. of ACL*, pages 373–385.

Daniel Hershcovich, Omri Abend, and Ari Rappoport. 2018b. Universal dependency parsing with a general transition-based DAG parser. In *Proc. of CoNLL UD Shared Task*, pages 103–112.

Daniel Hershcovich, Omri Abend, and Ari Rappoport. 2019a. Content differences in syntactic and semantic representation. In *Proc. of NAACL-HLT*, pages 478–488, Minneapolis, Minnesota. Association for Computational Linguistics.

Daniel Hershcovich, Zohar Aizenbud, Leshem Choshen, Elior Sulem, Ari Rappoport, and Omri Abend. 2019b. SemEval-2019 task 1: Cross-lingual semantic parsing with UCCA. In *Proc. of SemEval*, pages 1–10.

Sepp Hochreiter and Jürgen Schmidhuber. 1997. Long short-term memory. *Neural computation*, 9(8):1735–1780.

Angelina Ivanova, Stephan Oepen, Lilja Øvrelid, and Dan Flickinger. 2012. Who did what to whom? A contrastive study of syntacto-semantic dependencies. In *Proc. of LAW*, pages 2–11.

Wei Jiang, Zhenghua Li, Yu Zhang, and Min Zhang. 2019. HLT@SUDA at SemEval-2019 task 1: UCCA graph parsing as constituent tree parsing. In *Proceedings of the 13th International Workshop on Semantic Evaluation*, pages 11–15, Minneapolis, Minnesota, USA. Association for Computational Linguistics.

Eliyahu Kiperwasser and Yoav Goldberg. 2016. Simple and accurate dependency parsing using bidirectional LSTM feature representations. *TACL*, 4:313–327.

Zuchao Li, Hai Zhao, Zhuosheng Zhang, Rui Wang, Masao Utiyama, and Eiichiro Sumita. 2019. SJTU–NICT at MRP 2019: Multi-task learning for end-to-end uniform semantic graph parsing. In *Proceedings of the Shared Task on Cross-Framework Meaning Representation Parsing at the 2019 Conference on Natural Language Learning*, pages 45–54, Hong Kong, China.

Wolfgang Maier. 2015. Discontinuous incremental shift-reduce parsing. In *Proc. of ACL*, pages 1202–1212.

Wolfgang Maier and Timm Lichte. 2016. Discontinuous parsing with continuous trees. In *Proc. of Workshop on Discontinuous Structures in NLP*, pages 47–57.

Jonathan May. 2016. SemEval-2016 task 8: Meaning representation parsing. In *Proc. of SemEval*, pages 1063–1073.

Jonathan May and Jay Priyadarshi. 2017. SemEval-2017 task 9: Abstract Meaning Representation parsing and generation. In *Proc. of SemEval*, pages 536–545.

Yusuke Miyao, Stephan Oepen, and Daniel Zeman. 2014. In-house: An ensemble of pre-existing off-the-shelf parsers. In *Proceedings of the 8th International Workshop on Semantic Evaluation (SemEval 2014)*, pages 335–340.

Tahira Naseem, Abhishek Shah, Hui Wan, Radu Florian, Salim Roukos, and Miguel Ballesteros. 2019. Rewarding Smatch: Transition-based AMR parsing with reinforcement learning. In *Proceedings of the 57th Annual Meeting of the Association for Computational Linguistics*, pages 4586–4592, Florence, Italy. Association for Computational Linguistics.

Graham Neubig, Chris Dyer, Yoav Goldberg, Austin Matthews, Waleed Ammar, Antonios Anastasopoulos, Miguel Ballesteros, David Chiang, Daniel Clothiaux, Trevor Cohn, Kevin Duh, Manaal Faruqui, Cynthia Gan, Dan Garrette, Yangfeng Ji, Lingpeng Kong, Adhiguna Kuncoro, Gaurav Kumar, Chaitanya Malaviya, Paul Michel, Yusuke Oda, Matthew Richardson, Naomi Saphra, Swabha Swayamdipta, and Pengcheng Yin. 2017. DyNet: The dynamic neural network toolkit. *CoRR*, abs/1701.03980.

Joakim Nivre. 2003. An efficient algorithm for projective dependency parsing. In *Proc. of IWPT*, pages 149–160.

Joakim Nivre. 2008. Algorithms for deterministic incremental dependency parsing. *Computational Linguistics*, 34(4):513–553.

Joakim Nivre. 2009. Non-projective dependency parsing in expected linear time. In *Proc. of ACL*, pages 351–359.

Rik van Noord and Johan Bos. 2017. Dealing with co-reference in neural semantic parsing. In *Proc. of SemDeep*, pages 41–49.

Stephan Oepen, Omri Abend, Jan Hajič, Daniel Hershcovich, Marco Kuhlmann, Tim O'Gorman, Nianwen Xue, Jayeol Chun, Milan Straka, and Zdeňka Urešová. 2019. MRP 2019: Cross-framework Meaning Representation Parsing. In *Proceedings of the Shared Task on Cross-Framework Meaning Representation Parsing at the 2019 Conference on Natural Language Learning*, pages 1–27, Hong Kong, China.

Stephan Oepen, Marco Kuhlmann, Yusuke Miyao, Daniel Zeman, Silvie Cinkova, Dan Flickinger, Jan Hajic, Angelina Ivanova, and Zdenka Uresova. 2016. Towards comparability of linguistic graph banks for semantic parsing. In *Proc. of LREC*.

Stephan Oepen, Marco Kuhlmann, Yusuke Miyao, Daniel Zeman, Silvie Cinková, Dan Flickinger, Jan Hajič, and Zdeňka Urešová. 2015. SemEval 2015 task 18: Broad-coverage semantic dependency parsing. In *Proc. of SemEval*, pages 915–926.

Stephan Oepen, Marco Kuhlmann, Yusuke Miyao, Daniel Zeman, Dan Flickinger, Jan Hajič, Angelina Ivanova, and Yi Zhang. 2014. SemEval 2014 task 8: Broad-coverage semantic dependency parsing. In *Proc. of SemEval*, pages 63–72.

Stephan Oepen and Jan Tore Lønning. 2006. Discriminant-based mrs banking. In *LREC*, pages 1250–1255.

Martha Palmer, Daniel Gildea, and Paul Kingsbury. 2005. The proposition bank: An annotated corpus of semantic roles. *Computational Linguistics*, 31(1).

Carl Pollard and Ivan A Sag. 1994. *Head-driven phrase structure grammar*. University of Chicago Press.

Nima Pourdamghani, Yang Gao, Ulf Hermjakob, and Kevin Knight. 2014. Aligning English strings with Abstract Meaning Representation graphs. In *Proc. of EMNLP*, pages 425–429.

Kenji Sagae and Jun'ichi Tsujii. 2008. Shift-reduce dependency DAG parsing. In *Proc. of COLING*, pages 753–760.

Sanjiv Kumar Sashank J. Reddi, Satyen Kale. 2018. On the convergence of Adam and beyond. *ICLR*.

Mike Schuster and Kuldip K Paliwal. 1997. Bidirectional recurrent neural networks. *IEEE Transactions on Signal Processing*, 45(11):2673–2681.

Nitish Srivastava, Geoffrey Hinton, Alex Krizhevsky, Ilya Sutskever, and Ruslan Salakhutdinov. 2014. Dropout: A simple way to prevent neural networks from overfitting. *Journal of Machine Learning Research*, 15:1929–1958.

Milan Straka and Jana Straková. 2017. Tokenizing, POS tagging, lemmatizing and parsing UD 2.0 with UDPipe. In *Proc. of CoNLL UD Shared Task*, pages 88–99, Vancouver, Canada.

Ivan Titov, James Henderson, Paola Merlo, and Gabriele Musillo. 2009. Online graph planarisation for synchronous parsing of semantic and syntactic dependencies. In *Twenty-First International Joint Conference on Artificial Intelligence*.

Alper Tokgöz and Gülsen Eryiğit. 2015. Transition-based dependency DAG parsing using dynamic oracles. In *Proc. of ACL Student Research Workshop*, pages 22–27.

Chuan Wang, Sameer Pradhan, Xiaoman Pan, Heng Ji, and Nianwen Xue. 2016. CAMR at SemEval-2016 task 8: An extended transition based AMR parser. In *Proc. of SemEval*, pages 1173–1178.

Chuan Wang and Nianwen Xue. 2017. Getting the most out of AMR parsing. In *Proc. of EMNLP*, pages 1257–1268.

Chuan Wang, Nianwen Xue, and Sameer Pradhan. 2015a. Boosting transition-based AMR parsing with refined actions and auxiliary analyzers. In *Proc. of ACL*, pages 857–862.

Chuan Wang, Nianwen Xue, and Sameer Pradhan. 2015b. A transition-based algorithm for AMR parsing. In *Proc. of NAACL*, pages 366–375.

Yonghui Wu, Mike Schuster, Zhifeng Chen, Quoc V. Le, Mohammad Norouzi, Wolfgang Macherey, Maxim Krikun, Yuan Cao, Qin Gao, Klaus Macherey, Jeff Klingner, Apurva Shah, Melvin Johnson, Xiaobing Liu, Lukasz Kaiser, Stephan Gouws, Yoshikiyo Kato, Taku Kudo, Hideto Kazawa, Keith Stevens, George Kurian, Nishant Patil, Wei Wang, Cliff Young, Jason Smith, Jason Riesa, Alex Rudnick, Oriol Vinyals, Greg Corrado, Macduff Hughes, and Jeffrey Dean. 2016. Google's neural machine translation system: Bridging the gap between human and machine translation. *CoRR*, abs/1609.08144.

Daniel Zeman, Jan Hajič, Martin Popel, Martin Potthast, Milan Straka, Filip Ginter, Joakim Nivre, and Slav Petrov. 2018. CoNLL 2018 shared task: Multilingual parsing from raw text to universal dependencies. In *Proc. of CoNLL UD Shared Task*, pages 1–21.

Daniel Zeman, Martin Popel, Milan Straka, Jan Hajič, Joakim Nivre, Filip Ginter, Juhani Luotolahti, Sampo Pyysalo, Slav Petrov, Martin Potthast, Francis Tyers, Elena Badmaeva, Memduh Gökırmak, Anna Nedoluzhko, Silvie Cinková, Jan Hajič jr., Jaroslava Hlaváčová, Václava Kettnerová, Zdeňka Urešová, Jenna Kanerva, Stina Ojala, Anna Missilä, Christopher Manning, Sebastian Schuster, Siva Reddy, Dima Taji, Nizar Habash, Herman Leung, Marie-Catherine de Marneffe, Manuela Sanguinetti, Maria Simi, Hiroshi Kanayama, Valeria de Paiva, Kira Droganova, Héctor Martínez Alonso, Çağrı Çöltekin, Umut Sulubacak, Hans Uszkoreit, Vivien Macketanz, Aljoscha Burchardt, Kim Harris, Katrin Marheinecke, Georg Rehm, Tolga Kayadelen, Mohammed Attia, Ali Elkahky, Zhuoran Yu, Emily Pitler, Saran Lertpradit, Michael Mandl, Jesse Kirchner, Hector Fernandez Alcalde, Jana Strnadova, Esha Banerjee, Ruli Manurung, Antonio Stella, Atsuko Shimada, Sookyoung Kwak, Gustavo Mendonça, Tatiana Lando, Rattima Nitisaroj, and Josie Li. 2017. CoNLL 2017 Shared Task: Multilingual Parsing from Raw Text to Universal Dependencies. In *Proceedings of the CoNLL 2017 Shared Task: Multilingual Parsing from Raw Text to Universal Dependencies*, pages 1–19, Vancouver, Canada. Association for Computational Linguistics.

Yue Zhang, Wei Jiang, Qingrong Xia, Junjie Cao, Rui Wang, Zhenghua Li, and Min Zhang. 2019. Suda-alibaba at MRP 2019: Graph-based models with BERT. In *Proceedings of the Shared Task on Cross-Framework Meaning Representation Parsing at the 2019 Conference on Natural Language Learning*, pages 149–157, Hong Kong, China.

Muhua Zhu, Yue Zhang, Wenliang Chen, Min Zhang, and Jingbo Zhu. 2013. Fast and accurate shift-reduce constituent parsing. In *Proc. of ACL*, pages 434–443.

The ERG at MRP 2019:
Radically Compositional Semantic Dependencies

Stephan Oepen♣ and **Dan Flickinger**♠

♣ University of Oslo, Department of Informatics
♠ Stanford University, Center for the Study of Language and Information
`oe@ifi.uio.no, danf@stanford.edu`

Abstract

The English Resource Grammar (ERG) is a broad-coverage computational grammar of English that derives underspecified logical-form representations of meaning. Elementary Dependency Structures (EDS) and DELPH-IN MRS Bi-Lexical Dependencies (DM) are graph-based simplifications of ERG meaning representations. As a point of reference outside the official competition of the 2019 Shared Task on Cross-Framework Meaning Representation Parsing, we evaluate ERG-derived EDS and DM graphs. These graphs yield higher accuracy scores than the purely data-driven parsers in the shared task, suggesting that the general-purpose grammatical knowledge encoded in the ERG aids parsing into these meaning representations.

1 Introduction

Two of the target representations in the 2019 Shared Task on Cross-Framework Meaning Representation Parsing (MRP 2019; Oepen et al., 2019) derive from the framework dubbed English Resource Semantics (ERS; Flickinger et al., 2014; Bender et al., 2015). ERS instantiates the designer logic for scopally underspecified meaning representation called Minimal Recursion Semantics (MRS; Copestake et al., 2005); in and of themselves, ERS terms are logic- rather than graph-based, i.e. require conversion into graph-structured representations of meaning in the context of the MRP shared task. Elementary Dependency Structures (EDS; Oepen and Lønning, 2006) and DELPH-IN MRS Bi-Lexical Dependencies (DM; Ivanova et al., 2012) achieve simplification of ERS into labeled directed graphs by elimination of most of the information regarding scope underspecification and, in the case of DM, further reduction into pure bi-lexical graphs. Oepen et al. (2019) provide additional background on these representations. This paper gives some linguistic and technical background on ERS parsing (§2), summarizes the processes used in deriving EDS and DM graphs for the MRP evaluation data

(§3), and puts quantitative ERS parsing results into the perspective of the shared task at large (§4).

2 The LinGO English Resource Grammar and Redwoods Treebank

At the core of this work are two linguistic resources that have been under continuous development for multiple decades now, as part of the world-wide Deep Linguistic Processing with HPSG Initiative (DELPH-IN; `http://delph-in.net`). First, the LinGO English Resource Grammar (ERG; Flickinger, 2000) is an implementation of the grammatical theory of Head-Driven Phrase Structure Grammar (HPSG; Pollard and Sag, 1994) for English, i.e. a computational grammar that can be used for parsing and generation. Development of the ERG started in 1993, building conceptually on earlier work on unification-based grammar engineering for English at Hewlett Packard Laboratories (Gawron et al., 1982). The ERG has continuously evolved through a series of R&D projects (and a small handful of commercial applications) and today allows the grammatical analysis of running text across domains and genres. The hand-built ERG lexicon of some 38,000 lemmata (for 27,000 distinct citation forms) aims for complete coverage of function words and open-class words with 'non-standard' syntactic properties (e.g. argument structure). Built-in support for light-weight named entity recognition and an unknown word mechanism combining statistical PoS tagging and on-the-fly lexical instantiation for 'standard' open-class words (e.g. names or non-relational common nouns and adjectives) typically enable the grammar to derive complete syntactico-semantic analyses for $85-95$ percent of all utterances in standard corpora, including newspaper text, the English Wikipedia, or bio-medical research literature (Flickinger et al., 2017). Parsing times for these data sets measure in seconds per sentence, time comparable to human production or comprehension.

Second, since around 2001 the ERG has been accompanied by a selection of development cor-

Proceedings of the Shared Task on Cross-Framework Meaning Representation Parsing at the 2019 CoNLL, pages 40–44
Hong Kong, November 3, 2019. ©2019 Association for Computational Linguistics
https://doi.org/10.18653/v1/K19-2003

pora, where for each sentence an annotator has selected the intended analysis among the alternatives provided by the grammar (or has recorded that no appropriate analysis is available, in a given version of the grammar). This companion resource is called the LinGO Redwoods Treebank (Oepen et al., 2004). For each release of the ERG, a corresponding version of the treebank has been produced, manually validating and updating existing analyses to reflect changes in the underlying grammar, as well as 'picking up' analyses for previously out-of-scope inputs and new development corpora. Since mid-2016, the current version of Redwoods (dubbed Ninth Growth, corresponding to ERG release 1214) encompasses gold-standard analyses for some 85,400 utterances (or close to 1.3 million tokens) of running text from half a dozen different genres and domains, including the first 22 sections of the venerable Wall Street Journal (WSJ) text in the Penn Treebank (PTB; Marcus et al., 1993).

The original motivation for treebanking ERG analyses was to enable training discriminative parse ranking models, i.e. a conditional probability distribution over ERG derivations (Johnson et al., 1999). For this purpose, the treebank must disambiguate at the same level of granularity as is maintained in the grammar, i.e. encode its exact linguistic distinctions. Furthermore, to train discriminative (i.e. conditional) stochastic models, both the intended as well as the dispreferred analyses are needed.

The Redwoods treebank is built exclusively from ERG analyses, i.e. full HPSG syntactico-semantic signs. Annotation in Redwoods amounts to disambiguation among the candidate analyses derived by the grammar (identifying the intended parse) and, of course, analytical validation of the final result. To make this task practical, a specialized tree selection tool extracts a set of what are called *discriminants* from the complete set of analyses. Discriminants encode contrasts among alternate analyses—for example whether to treat a word like *crop* as nominal or verbal, or where to attach a prepositional phrase modifier. While picking one full analysis (among a set of hundreds or thousands of trees) would be daunting (to say the least), the isolated contrasts presented as discriminants are comparatively easy to judge for a human annotator.

Discriminant-based tree selection was first proposed by Carter (1997) and has since been successfully applied to a range of grammatical frameworks. To the best of our knowledge, Redwoods is the most comprehensive such effort, complementing the original proposal by Carter (1997) with the notion of *dynamic* treebanking, in two senses of this term. First, different views can be projected from the multi-stratal HPSG analyses at the core of the treebank, highlighting subsets of the syntactic or semantic properties of each analysis, e.g. HPSG derivations, more conventional phrase structure trees, full logical-form meaning representations, and various variable-free forms of semantic dependency graphs—including EDS and DM.

Second, the dynamic treebank is extended and refined *over time*. As the grammar (the core repository of knowledge about derivation and composition) evolves, dynamic refinement refers to the ability to mostly automatically update the Redwoods treebank, to for example add detail to the linguistic analyses or apply targeted error correction while minimizing any loss of manual input from previous annotation cycles. Although we can by no means quantify precisely the effort devoted to ERG and Redwoods development to date, we estimate that in excess of thirty person years have been accumulated between 1993 and 2019.

3 Parsing with the ERG

There are several highly engineered implementations of the DELPH-IN feature structure reference formalism; for our experiments we used the PET parser of Callmeier (2002), as bundled in the open-source distribution of DELPH-IN resources called LOGON (Lønning and Oepen, 2006).[1] At its core, PET is a classic, agenda-driven chart parser (Kay, 1986), synthesizing a large body of algorithm design for efficient feature structure manipulation and unification-based parsing by among others Tomabechi (1995), Malouf et al. (2000), Erbach (1991), Kiefer et al. (1999), and Oepen and Callmeier (2000). The parser achieves exact inference by constructing the complete *parse forest*, factoring local ambiguity under feature structure subsumption (a technique termed *retroactive packing* by Oepen and Carroll, 2000) and subsequently enumerating n-best full derivations from the forest according to a discriminative parse ranking model in the tradition of Johnson et al. (1999) and Toutanova et al. (2005).

Despite the non-local nature of features (of ERG derivations) used in parse ranking, the *selective unpacking* procedure of Carroll and Oepen (2005)

---

[1] See http://moin.delph-in.net/LogonTop.

		Tops			Labels			Properties			Anchors			Edges			Attributes			All		
		P	R	F_1	P	R	F_1	P	R	F_1	P	R	F_1	P	R	F_1	P	R	F_1	P	R	F
DM	ERG	.92	.92	.918	.99	.99	**.987**	.96	.96	**.956**	.99	.99	**.994**	.91	.91	.912	–	–	–	.96	.96	**.961**
		.95	.95	.950	.99	.99	**.987**	.98	.98	**.978**	.99	.00	**.995**	.93	.93	.927	–	–	–	.97	.97	**.973**
	SJTU–NICT	.93	.93	**.933**	.95	.95	.949	.96	.95	.955	.99	.99	.993	.93	.92	.924	–	–	–	.96	.95	.955
		.97	.96	**.965**	.93	.93	.933	.94	.94	.944	.99	.99	.990	.93	.93	.933	–	–	–	.95	.95	.949
	HIT-SCIR	.93	.93	.926	.93	.93	.930	.95	.95	.953	.99	.99	.993	.93	.92	**.925**	–	–	–	.95	.95	.951
		.95	.95	.950	.93	.93	.928	.95	.95	.947	.99	.99	.990	.94	.94	**.935**	–	–	–	.95	.95	.950
	SUDA–Alibaba	.91	.91	.911	.90	.91	.903	.91	.92	.915	.97	.99	.982	.89	.91	.898	–	–	–	.91	.93	.923
		.91	.88	.893	.86	.89	.872	.88	.91	.895	.96	.99	.979	.88	.92	.896	–	–	–	.89	.92	.907
	Peking	.93	.93	.927	.92	.91	.915	.95	.94	.945	.99	.99	.991	.92	.92	.924	–	–	–	.94	.94	.944
		.96	.96	.960	.88	.88	.882	.91	.92	.914	.99	.99	.989	.92	.92	.921	–	–	–	.92	.93	.925
EDS	ERG	.90	.90	**.902**	.97	.96	**.965**	.96	.96	**.960**	.96	.96	**.963**	.93	.93	.929	–	–	–	.95	.95	**.952**
		.93	.93	.930	.96	.97	**.964**	.85	.88	**.863**	.98	.99	**.983**	.93	.94	**.932**	–	–	–	.96	.96	**.959**
	SUDA–Alibaba	.90	.90	.899	.91	.91	.912	.89	.91	.897	.95	.95	.949	.90	.90	.897	–	–	–	.92	.92	.918
		.94	.94	**.940**	.91	.92	.913	.72	.84	.778	.95	.96	.953	.91	.91	.911	–	–	–	.92	.93	.925
	HIT-SCIR	.88	.82	.852	.90	.89	.894	.89	.91	.895	.95	.94	.943	.89	.88	.888	–	–	–	.91	.90	.907
		.92	.91	.915	.85	.86	.854	.76	.88	.815	.95	.96	.950	.89	.89	.890	–	–	–	.89	.90	.898
	SJTU–NICT	.91	.85	.877	.93	.86	.894	.79	.76	.775	.97	.90	.934	.95	.82	.878	–	–	–	.95	.86	.899
		.97	.89	.927	.93	.88	.904	.27	.24	.255	.97	.93	.949	.94	.86	.894	–	–	–	.94	.88	.912
	Peking	.83	.83	.829	.95	.94	.946	.91	.96	.936	.96	.96	.961	.94	.93	**.933**	–	–	–	.95	.94	.945
		.89	.89	.890	.91	.92	.918	.49	.88	.629	.95	.96	.959	.92	.92	.918	–	–	–	.92	.93	.928

Table 1: MRP results for DM (top) and EDS (bottom), with precision (P), recall (R), and F_1 for different types of graph components: top nodes, node labels, other node properties, anchoring into the surface string, labeled edges, and all of these combined (neither DM nor EDS use edge attributes). Best F_1 scores in each category are in bold. The pair of rows per submission indicate the full MRP evaluation data vs. the 100-sentence *Little Prince* subset.

guarantees n-best enumeration from the parse forest in globally correct rank order. At its core, this is a specialized search procedure on a weighted and–or graph (the forest), where for packed (i.e. disjunctive) nodes local contexts of optimization are established on demand. Although worst-case complexity for both forest construction and unpacking is in principle exponential, parsing times (for small values of n) with the ERG in practice mostly grow polynomially in input length. For example, parser throughput for the sentences from the *Little Prince* subset of the MRP evaluation data (see Oepen et al., 2019) averages at two sentences per second, whereas average parse times for the much longer 100-sentence MRP sample of WSJ text lie around four seconds per sentence.

For parsing the MRP evaluation data, we applied ERG release 1214 with its bundled WSJ parse ranking model, which uses the feature configuration of Zhang et al. (2007) and was trained on Sections 00–20 of the Redwoods Ninth Growth using the Maximum Entropy estimation toolkit of Malouf (2002). We use the LOGON distribution as of August 2019

to parse in one-best mode the 'raw' strings for the MRP evaluation data whose target representations were indicated as DM or EDS. The resulting HPSG derivations each uniquely determine an ERS meaning representation in underspecified logic, which we subsequently convert to EDS and DM.[2]

Given the formal nature of this process, the resulting graphs are guaranteed to reflect the composition algebra of the ERG, recursively building larger fragments of meaning from smaller parts.

4 Experimental Results

Parsing accuracies for PET and the ERG are summarized in Table 1, for both the DM (top) and EDS (bottom) evaluation graphs. The table compares ERG parsing results to a selection of 'real' submissions to the shared task, viz. the top performers within each framework and for the task

---

[2]The ERS-to-EDS converter of Oepen and Lønning (2006) is part of the LOGON distribution, as is the converter of Ivanova et al. (2012) for further simplification to bi-lexical DM. Exact command-line incantations for all tools and their parameterization are specified as part of the submission archive in the MRP 2019 data release.

overall: HIT-SCIR (Che et al., 2019), Peking (Chen et al., 2019)[3], SJTU–NICT (Bai and Zhao, 2019), and SUDA–Alibaba (Zhang et al., 2019). In contrast to the ERG parser, all of these systems are purely *data-driven*, in the sense that they do not incorporate manually curated linguistic knowledge (beyond finite-state tokenization rules, maybe) but rather learn all their parameters exclusively from the shared task training data.

By and large, the data-driven parsers are competitive to the ERG, in particular the SJTU–NICT and HIT-SCIR systems for DM, and the Peking parser for EDS. For some structural types of graph components (tops and edges), the ERG is in fact outperformed by some submissions, whereas it holds at times commanding leads on node-local types of information, e.g. labels, properties, and achors. It could be argued that comparison for some of these graph components favors the ERG, seeing as it embodies the exact principles of deriving these values that were used in creating the Redwoods annotations. However, for DM at least, node labels are essentially lemmas, and it is prima facie surprising that none of the data-driven parsers succeeds very well in replicating ERG-style lemmatization.

Likewise, anchoring for EDS is a many-to-many relation between graph nodes and (arbitrary) input sub-strings, where one can speculate that at least some of the conventions used in the ERG may be linguistically idiosyncratic. Inasmuch as that may (or may not) be the case, the Peking parser shows anchoring accuracies comparable to the ERG.

The *Little Prince* subset of the evaluation data is comprised of much shorter sentences, and observed accuracies for some types of graph components may appear to correlate with input complexity, notably top node and (to a lesser) degree edge prediction. At the same time, the novelistic style of this subset most likely makes it least similar to the WSJ-derived training data for the data-driven parsers, hence some submissions can seem to suffer from detrimental cross-domain effects.

5 Reflections

As long-term co-developers of the ERG and its PET parser, we are impressed by the overall performance levels of the data-driven submissions to the MRP 2019 shared task. We hope to conduct more contrastive error-analysis, possibly in collaboration with other parser developers, to further isolate effects of domain variation, for example, and generally gauge the contributions (if any) of the explicit body of linguistic knowledge in the ERG.

References

Hongxiao Bai and Hai Zhao. 2019. SJTU at MRP 2019: A transition-based multi-task parser for cross-framework meaning representation parsing. In *Proceedings of the Shared Task on Cross-Framework Meaning Representation Parsing at the 2019 Conference on Natural Language Learning*, pages 86–94, Hong Kong, China.

Emily M. Bender, Dan Flickinger, Stephan Oepen, Woodley Packard, and Ann Copestake. 2015. Layers of interpretation. On grammar and compositionality. In *Proceedings of the 11th International Conference on Computational Semantics*, pages 239–249, London, UK.

Ulrich Callmeier. 2002. Preprocessing and encoding techniques in PET. In *Collaborative Language Engineering. A Case Study in Efficient Grammar-based Processing*, pages 127–140, Stanford, CA. CSLI Publications.

John Carroll and Stephan Oepen. 2005. High-efficiency realization for a wide-coverage unification grammar. In *Proceedings of the 2nd International Joint Conference on Natural Language Processing*, pages 165–176, Jeju, Korea.

David Carter. 1997. The TreeBanker. A tool for supervised training of parsed corpora. In *Proceedings of the Workshop on Computational Environments for Grammar Development and Linguistic Engineering*, pages 9–15, Madrid, Spain.

Wanxiang Che, Longxu Dou, Yang Xu, Yuxuan Wang, Yijia Liu, and Ting Liu. 2019. HIT-SCIR at MRP 2019: A unified pipeline for meaning representation parsing via efficient training and effective encoding. In *Proceedings of the Shared Task on Cross-Framework Meaning Representation Parsing at the 2019 Conference on Natural Language Learning*, pages 76–85, Hong Kong, China.

Yufei Chen, Yajie Ye, and Weiwei Sun. 2019. Peking at MRP 2019: Factorization- and composition-based parsing for Elementary Dependency Structures. In *Proceedings of the Shared Task on Cross-Framework Meaning Representation Parsing at the 2019 Conference on Natural Language Learning*, pages 166–176, Hong Kong, China.

Ann Copestake, Dan Flickinger, Carl Pollard, and Ivan A. Sag. 2005. Minimal Recursion Semantics. An introduction. *Research on Language and Computation*, 3(4):281–332.

Gregor Erbach. 1991. A flexible parser for a linguistic development environment. In Otthein Herzog and

---

[3]The Peking submission is not considered in the *primary* ranking of the official shared task results, because the team inadvertently used tokenization training data beyond the 'whitelisted' resources for task participants

Claus-Rainer Rollinger, editors, *Text Understanding in LILOG*, pages 74–87. Springer, Berlin, Germany.

Dan Flickinger. 2000. On building a more efficient grammar by exploiting types. *Natural Language Engineering*, 6 (1):15–28.

Dan Flickinger, Emily M. Bender, and Stephan Oepen. 2014. Towards an encyclopedia of compositional semantics. Documenting the interface of the English Resource Grammar. In *Proceedings of the 9th International Conference on Language Resources and Evaluation*, pages 875–881, Reykjavik, Iceland.

Dan Flickinger, Stephan Oepen, and Emily M. Bender. 2017. Sustainable development and refinement of complex linguistic annotations at scale. In *Handbook of Linguistic Annotation*, pages 353–377, Dordrecht, The Netherlands. Springer.

Jean Mark Gawron, Jonathan King, John Lamping, Egon Loebner, E. Anne Paulson, Geoffrey K. Pullum, Ivan A. Sag, and Thomas Wasow. 1982. Processing English with a Generalized Phrase Structure Grammar. In *Proceedings of the 20th Meeting of the Association for Computational Linguistics*, pages 74–81, Toronto, Canada.

Angelina Ivanova, Stephan Oepen, Lilja Øvrelid, and Dan Flickinger. 2012. Who did what to whom? A contrastive study of syntacto-semantic dependencies. In *Proceedings of the 6th Linguistic Annotation Workshop*, pages 2–11, Jeju, Republic of Korea.

Mark Johnson, Stuart Geman, Stephen Canon, Zhiyi Chi, and Stefan Riezler. 1999. Estimators for stochastic 'unification-based' grammars. In *Proceedings of the 37th Meeting of the Association for Computational Linguistics*, pages 535–541, College Park, MD, USA.

Martin Kay. 1986. Algorithm schemata and data structures in syntactic processing. In In Barbara J. Grosz, Karen Spärck Jones, and Bonnie Lynn Weber, editors, *Readings in Natural Language Processing*, pages 35–70. Morgan Kaufmann, San Francisco, CA, USA.

Bernd Kiefer, Hans-Ulrich Krieger, John Carroll, and Robert Malouf. 1999. A bag of useful techniques for efficient and robust parsing. In *Proceedings of the 37th Meeting of the Association for Computational Linguistics*, pages 473–480, College Park, MD, USA.

Jan Tore Lønning and Stephan Oepen. 2006. Re-usable tools for precision machine translation. In *Proceedings of the COLING|ACL 2006 Interactive Presentation Sessions*, pages 53–56, Sydney, Australia.

Robert Malouf. 2002. A comparison of algorithms for maximum entropy parameter estimation. In *Proceedings of the 6th Conference on Natural Language Learning*, pages 49–55, Taipei, Taiwan.

Robert Malouf, John Carroll, and Ann Copestake. 2000. Efficient feature structure operations without compilation. *Natural Language Engineering*, 6(1):29–46.

Mitchell Marcus, Beatrice Santorini, and Mary Ann Marcinkiewicz. 1993. Building a large annotated corpus of English. The Penn Treebank. *Computational Linguistics*, 19:313–330.

Stephan Oepen, Omri Abend, Jan Hajič, Daniel Hershcovich, Marco Kuhlmann, Tim O'Gorman, Nianwen Xue, Jayeol Chun, Milan Straka, and Zdeňka Urešová. 2019. MRP 2019: Cross-framework Meaning Representation Parsing. In *Proceedings of the Shared Task on Cross-Framework Meaning Representation Parsing at the 2019 Conference on Natural Language Learning*, pages 1–27, Hong Kong, China.

Stephan Oepen and Ulrich Callmeier. 2000. Measure for measure: Parser cross-fertilization. Towards increased component comparability and exchange. In *Proceedings of the 6th International Conference on Parsing Technologies*, pages 183–194, Trento, Italy.

Stephan Oepen and John Carroll. 2000. Ambiguity packing in constraint-based parsing. Practical results. In *Proceedings of the 1st Meeting of the North American Chapter of the Association for Computational Linguistics*, pages 162–169, Seattle, WA, USA.

Stephan Oepen, Daniel Flickinger, Kristina Toutanova, and Christopher D. Manning. 2004. LinGO Redwoods. A rich and dynamic treebank for HPSG. *Research on Language and Computation*, 2(4):575–596.

Stephan Oepen and Jan Tore Lønning. 2006. Discriminant-based MRS banking. In *Proceedings of the 5th International Conference on Language Resources and Evaluation*, pages 1250–1255, Genoa, Italy.

Carl Pollard and Ivan A. Sag. 1994. *Head-Driven Phrase Structure Grammar*. Studies in Contemporary Linguistics. The University of Chicago Press, Chicago, USA.

Hideto Tomabechi. 1995. Design of efficient unification for natural language. *Journal of Natural Language Processing*, 2(2):23–58.

Kristina Toutanova, Christopher D. Manning, Dan Flickinger, and Stephan Oepen. 2005. Stochastic HPSG Parse Disambiguation using the Redwoods Corpus. *Research on Language and Computation*, 3:83–105.

Yi Zhang, Stephan Oepen, and John Carroll. 2007. Efficiency in unification-based n-best parsing. In *Proceedings of the 10th International Conference on Parsing Technologies*, pages 48–59, Prague, Czech Republic.

Yue Zhang, Wei Jiang, Qingrong Xia, Junjie Cao, Rui Wang, Zhenghua Li, and Min Zhang. 2019. Sudaalibaba at MRP 2019: Graph-based models with BERT. In *Proceedings of the Shared Task on Cross-Framework Meaning Representation Parsing at the 2019 Conference on Natural Language Learning*, pages 149–157, Hong Kong, China.

SJTU-NICT at MRP 2019: Multi-Task Learning for End-to-End Uniform Semantic Graph Parsing

Zuchao Li[1,2,3], **Hai Zhao**[1,2,3,*], **Zhuosheng Zhang**[1,2,3],
Rui Wang[4,*], **Masao Utiyama**[4], and **Eiichiro Sumita**[4]
[1]Department of Computer Science and Engineering, Shanghai Jiao Tong University (SJTU)
[2]Key Laboratory of Shanghai Education Commission for Intelligent Interaction
and Cognitive Engineering, Shanghai Jiao Tong University, Shanghai, China
[3]MoE Key Lab of Artificial Intelligence, AI Institude, Shanghai Jiao Tong University, China
[4]National Institute of Information and Communications Technology (NICT), Kyoto, Japan

Abstract

This paper describes our SJTU-NICT's system for participating in the shared task on Cross-Framework Meaning Representation Parsing (MRP) at the 2019 Conference for Computational Language Learning (CoNLL). Our system uses a graph-based approach to model a variety of semantic graph parsing tasks. Our main contributions in the submitted system are summarized as follows: 1. Our model is fully end-to-end and is capable of being trained only on the given training set which does not rely on any other extra training source including the companion data provided by the organizer; 2. We extend our graph pruning algorithm to a variety of semantic graphs, solving the problem of excessive semantic graph search space; 3. We introduce multi-task learning for multiple objectives within the same framework. The evaluation results show that our system achieved second place in the overall F_1 score and achieved the best F_1 score on the DM framework.

1 Introduction

In recent years, the semantic graph parsing has received a lot of attention from researchers.

However, due to the variety of semantic graph flavors, the framework-specific "balkanization" of semantic parsing is worth noting. The 2019 Conference on Computational Language Learning (CoNLL) hosts a shared task on Cross-Framework Meaning Representation Parsing (MRP 2019) (Oepen et al., 2019). From the perspective of the formal representation of semantic graphs, MRP 2019 uses the directed graphs to unify the five different semantic representation frameworks: DELPH-IN MRS Bi-Lexical Dependencies (DM), Prague Semantic Dependencies (PSD), Elementary Dependency Structures (EDS), Universal Conceptual Cognitive Annotation (UCCA), and Abstract Meaning Representation (AMR). Wherein, the directed graph is represented by a $\langle \mathcal{T}, \mathcal{N}, \mathcal{E} \rangle$ triplet, $\mathcal{N}$ represents a set of nodes that constitutes the semantic graph, $\mathcal{E} \subseteq \mathcal{N} \times \mathcal{N}$ represents a set of edges that express a specific semantic relationship ($\mathcal{N}$, $\mathcal{E}$ contains a specific attribute corresponding to the semantic framework), and $\mathcal{T}$ represents nodes with a degree of zero in $\mathcal{N}$, usually corresponding to the most central semantic entity.

Though the semantic graph parsing task is uniformly modeled into a directed graph generation task, according to the relationship between nodes in the directed graph and the surface lexical units in the sentence, the five semantic graph frameworks can be divided into three different categories according to the alignment degree between graph nodes and lexical semantics: (1) graph nodes and surface lexical units anchor correspondence strictly (i.e., DM, PSD, EDS), (2) partial graph nodes and surface lexical units anchor correspondence strictly (i.e., UCCA), and (3) graph nodes and surface lexical units have no anchor correspondence (i.e., AMR). As there is a case of anchoring multiple nodes in the

* Corresponding authors. [†]This work was conductd when Zuchao Li and Zhuosheng Zhang visited NICT as internship students. Email: charlee@sjtu.edu.cn, zhaohai@cs.sjtu.edu.cn, zhangzs@sjtu.edu.cn, {wangrui, mutiyama, eiichiro.sumita}@nict.go.jp. This paper was partially supported by National Key Research and Development Program of China (No. 2017YFB0304100) and Key Projects of National Natural Science Foundation of China (U1836222 and 61733011). This work was partially conducted under the program "Research and Development of Enhanced Multilingual and Multipurpose Speech Translation Systems" of the Ministry of Internal Affairs and Communications (MIC), Japan. Masao Utiyama is partly supported by JSPS KAKENHI Grant Number 19H05660. Rui Wang was partially supported by JSPS grant-in-aid for early-career scientists (19K20354): "Unsupervised Neural Machine Translation in Universal Scenarios" and NICT tenure-track researcher startup fund "Toward Intelligent Machine Translation".

Proceedings of the Shared Task on Cross-Framework Meaning Representation Parsing at the 2019 CoNLL, pages 45–54
Hong Kong, November 3, 2019. ©2019 Association for Computational Linguistics
https://doi.org/10.18653/v1/K19-2004

corresponding graph of the directed graph of EDS, our system further treats EDS as one type, and DM and PSD as another type.

Based on the experiences of Jiang et al. (2019) and Zhang et al. (2019a) and our previous works on the *Dependency Parsing* (Li et al., 2018a,b,d; Zhou and Zhao, 2019; Zhou et al., 2019), *Semantic Role Labeling* (He et al., 2018b; Cai et al., 2018; Li et al., 2018c, 2019b; He et al., 2019), *Universal Conceptual Cognitive Annotation* (Jiang et al., 2019), *Abstract Mean Representation* (Zhang et al., 2019a), *Machine Translation* (Xiao et al., 2019; Sun et al., 2019; Chen et al., 2019), *Language Modeling* (Li et al., 2019a; Zhang et al., 2019c,b) tasks, we create three graph parsing models based on the semantic graph flavors: (1) Strictly anchored (DM, PSD, EDS): scores the surface lexical units as nodes of the graph, and performs edge training based on the expression of the candidate graph nodes, (2) Non-strictly anchored (UCCA): treats it as a special constituent tree parsing task and uses an additional component to recover the remote edges, and (3) Completely unanchored (i.e., AMR): uses the Seq2seq model to generate the nodes and then performs edge scoring on the generated graph nodes. In order to maintain the end-to-end style of our system, we use the multi-task learning method to jointly train and predict the attributes of nodes and edges together with themselves. We use the pre-trained language model BERT as the encoder. In the training phase, in order to prevent the nodes from falling into local optimum and the edges unable to get enough training, we use the random sampling method on the golden graph nodes to push as many correct nodes as possible to join the edge training. According to the official results of the evaluation, our system ranked second place in the overall F_1 metric among the 16 participating systems. On the DM framework, our system achieved the best results. Our system on other 4 frameworks (PSD, EDS, UCCA, and AMR) are all ranked the third place.

2 Tasks and Modeling

In this section, we will introduce this shared task and our modeling approach. Our key idea is to use a graph-based approach rather than a transition-based one; therefore, all the modeling and optimization methods we have on these frameworks are graph-based. The CoNLL shared task combines the following five frameworks for graph-based meaning representation: DM, PSD, EDS, UCCA, and AMR.

2.1 DM and PSD

The DM (Ivanova et al., 2012) and PSD (Hajic et al., 2012; Miyao et al., 2014) are two independently developed syntactic-semantic annotations which project semantic forms onto bi-lexical dependencies in a lossy manner.

In the representation of the DM and PSD frameworks, the graph nodes and surface lexical units are strictly anchored. There is an explicit, one-to-many anchoring onto sub-strings of the underlying sentence. These graphs are neither fully connected nor rooted. The graphs of DM and PSD have the following features:

- There is only a one-to-one correspondence[1] between the graph node and the span in the sentence.

- Graph nodes can have multiple in-edges or out-edges.

- Graph nodes can be completely isolated, with no in-edges or out-edges.

- There is at most one edge between any two graph nodes.

According to the above properties, the task is modeled as follows: Given a sentence $S = \{w_1, w_2, ..., w_n\}$, enumerate all the span in the sentence $span_{i,j} = \{w_i, w_{i+1}, ..., w_j\}, (i <= j)$, which is used as a candidate graph node and is fed into the node classifier $classifier_n$[2] to filter the truly graph nodes: $node_k = classifier_n(span_{i,j})$, and then uses the edge classifier $classifier_e$ to obtain the semantic relationship between the two graph nodes $edge_{k_1,k_2} = classifier_e(node_{k_1}, node_{k_2})$.

2.2 EDS

EDS is a variable-free semantic dependency graph representation proposed by Oepen and Lønning

---

[1] Due to one span in the sentence includes several surface lexical units; therefore the one-to-many anchoring becomes one-to-one correspondence.

[2] Here, we summarize the general terminology of using only the *classifier*. In practice, it is possible that the *classifier* contains several attribute classifiers, depending on how many attributes of the node or edge need to be predicted.

(2006) which encode the English Resource Semantics (ERS) (Flickinger et al., 2014). The EDS conversion from under-specified logical forms of the full ERS to variable-free graphs discards partial semantic information which makes the graph abstractly.

In the representation of the EDS framework, the graph nodes are independent of surface lexical units. For each graph node, there is an explicit, many-to-many anchoring onto sub-strings of the underlying sentence. The EDS graph has the following features:

- There is a many-to-one correspondence between the graph node and the span in the sentence.

- Graph nodes do not correspond to individual surface tokens in the sentence.

- Graph nodes can not be completely isolated and have at least one in- or out-edge.

According to the above features, since there is a many-to-one correspondence between the graph nodes and the spans in the sentences, it is impossible to use the modeling method of DM and PSD simply. Therefore, we adopt a `pseudo` node method to solve the problem. The transformation is carried out: the pseudo node has a one-to-one relationship with the span in the sentence. The edge between nodes in the graph is transformed into the edge of the pseudo node, and two attributes are added for the edge: the source node label and the target node label which are used to indicate the node label in the original EDS graph. In this way, the many-to-one relationship is converted into a one-to-one relationship. After conversion, we can model the problem using in the same way as DM and PSD as described in Subsection 2.1.

2.3 UCCA

UCCA is a multi-layer linguistic framework for semantic annotation proposed by Abend and Rappoport (2013). UCCA aims to recognize the level of semantic granularity which abstracts away from syntactic paraphrases in a typologically-motivated, cross-linguistic fashion and does not need to rely on language-specific resources.

In the representation of the UCCA framework, some nodes have a one-to-one correspondence with the span in the sentence, which is called terminal nodes[3]. Other nodes do not have any corresponding relationship with the span, which is introduced as a notion of a semantic constituency that transcends the pure dependency graphs to represent the semantic granularity. The UCCA graph has the following features:

- There is a one-to-one correspondence between the terminal nodes and the spans in the sentence.

- Graph nodes may have multiple parents, among which one is annotated as the primary parent and others as remote parents.

- The primary edges between nodes and their primary parents form a tree structure, whereas the remote edges between nodes and their remote parents enable the reentrancy, forming directed acyclic graphs (DAGs).

- The non-terminal nodes may exist discontinuous leaves; in which some terminal nodes are not its descendants.

Based on the above features and inspired by Nivre and Nilsson (2005), we transform the tree composed of primary edges (and nodes) into a constituent syntax tree structure, which is modeled using the constituent syntax tree parsing schema. Use an additional classifier for the remote edges prediction and recovery.

2.4 AMR

Abstract Meaning Representation (AMR) (Banarescu et al., 2013) parsing is the task of transducing natural language text into AMR, which is a graph-based formalism used for capturing sentence-level semantics. The AMR framework backgrounds notions of compositionality and derivation, therefore, without explicit correspondence between graph nodes and lexical units.

In the representation of AMR framework, the graph nodes are obtained by composition, derivation, lexical decomposition, normalization towards verb senses and so on. The features of the AMR graphs built on these graph nodes is similar

---

[3]MRP-transformed UCCA graph differs from on the terminal nodes from the original UCCA graph. In the original UCCA graph representation, terminal nodes refer to words, and in the MRP-transformed UCCA graph, terminal nodes refer to the lowest layer of non-terminal nodes in the original UCCA graph due to a node can contain multiple words in the MRP-transformed UCCA graph.

to the dependency syntax tree except for the reentrancy. Therefore, if the node is determined, modeling can be performed using the method of dependency syntax parsing. However, we can't get the nodes of the graph directly from the sentence due to the nature of the AMR framework. Therefore, inspired by Zhang et al. (2019a), we model the nodes determination as sequence generation tasks using the Seq2seq model and then parse the tree structure on the generated nodes.

3 Data and Preprocessing

3.1 Data

The CoNLL shared task provides a training dataset of 5 subtasks, of which DM, PSD, and EDS are from Wall Street Journal (WSJ) text of Penn Treebank (Marcus et al., 1993) and contain 35,656 sentences. The UCCA training data comes from the English Web Treebank's reviews text (Bies et al., 2012) and the English Wikipedia celebrity articles, with a total data volume of 5,672 sentences. AMR annotation data are drawn from a variety of texts, including online discussion forums, newswires, folktales, novels, and Wikipedia articles, which contain a total of 56,240 sentences.

3.2 Tokenization, Lemmatization, and Anchor conversion

Since the sentence in the training dataset is the original text and no tokenization is performed, and the subsequent processing requires the word root form, we use the Stanford NLP toolkit[4] (Manning et al., 2014) to tokenize and lemmatize the original text. As the graph node anchor in the original data is defined at the character level, we need to convert the anchor to the word level. In this process, due to the difference in tokenization criteria and the existence of tokenizing errors, some graph nodes will be converted into the same one in the process of conversion to word-level anchor. Therefore, we performed some post-processing modifications on the tokenization results of the Stanford NLP toolkit to ensure that the graph nodes after the conversion to the word level anchor correspond to the previous character level, without increasing or decreasing the nodes.

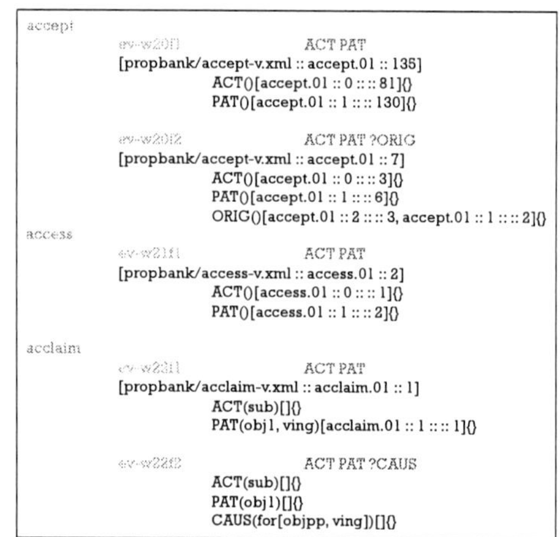

Figure 1: Examples of the most frequent frame-to-frameset mapping extracted from "rng_pb_links.txt".

3.3 Frame Label Projection in PSD Framework

The node label in the PSD framework is a special item id for Engvallex-to-PropBank mapping dictionary. The node label contains the item id of the item in the dictionary and the format id of the item. Such as: [access: ev-w22f1 ACT PAT] where 22 is the item id (word id) and 1 is the format id. Therefore, it is not convenient to use the classifier directly for prediction on the raw node label. Due to the word has a one-to-many relationship with the item id, we cannot obtain this item id by word directly. By observing "rng_pb_links.txt"[5] as shown in Figure 1, the item id has a one-to-one correspondence with its usage pattern string (like "ACT PAT") in the case of word determination, and the usage pattern has duplicates among different words, the number is much smaller than all item ids size; thus it is more suitable as a learning goal. In the subsequent recovery process, we can use lemma and the usage pattern to restore to the item id.

3.4 Graph to Constituent Tree Conversion in UCCA Framework

As described in subsection 2.3, the features, and modeling approach, we need to preprocess the UCCA graph in the training set, transforming the graph into a constituent tree by removing the remote edges and the edges that cause the

---

[4]https://stanfordnlp.github.io/
CoreNLP/index.html.

[5]https://ufal.mff.cuni.cz/pcedt2.0/
publications/eng_pb_links.txt

discontinuous leaves. We have adopted the same transformation method as Jiang et al. (2019). The simple steps are as follows:

1) Remote edges removal. In the UCCA MRP representation graph, we remove all edges with the $remote = True$ attribute. The label of the primary edge corresponding to the remote edge is added with a "remote" suffix to distinguish the node with the remote relationship from the ordinary node and subsequent recovery of the remote edge.

2) Constituency continuity formation. Since the current mainstream constituent parsing method requires continuity of constituency, we need to process the discontinuous nodes of the tree species obtained in the previous step. For detailed conversion steps, see Algorithm 1.

Algorithm 1 Constituency continuity formation

Input:
    A tree with discontinuous leaves, T_d;
Output:
    A constituent tree, T_c;
1: set $T(t) = T_d$
2: **repeat**
3:    set $n(t)$ is a non-descendant node with discontinuous leaves;
4:    find the discontinuous spans S_d in the range of $n(t)$;
5:    **for** each span $s \in S_d$ **do**
6:      **for** each word $w \in s$ **do**
7:        find a maximum range parent node n_p of word w whose range size is less than s;
8:        move node n_p to be the child of $n(t)$, and concatenate the original edge label with "ancestor-d" where d represents the original number of edges between the ancestor of n_p and $n(t)$;
9:        remove all the children words of n_p from s;
10:      **end for**
11:    **end for**
12: **until** $T(t)$ is a constituent tree
13: set $T_c = T(t)$

---

3) Edge labels move down. Constituent syntax parsing generally uses parenthetical notation to represent the constituent syntax tree structure, so in order to keep the model consistent, we also move the edge label down to the child node. Since the UCCA graphs need not be rooted trees, we add a "ROOT" dummy node to ensure that the transformed tree is a rooted tree.

3.5 Graph to Tree Conversion in AMR Framework

AMR graph is rooted, directed, and most acyclic. However, AMR is a graph instead of a tree due to it allows re-entrant semantic relations. In order to adopt the tree model for AMR parsing, we need to convert the AMR graph to a tree in the preprocessing step. Following the practice of Zhang et al. (2019a), we duplicate the nodes that have a re-entrant relation. In order to recover the original graph, we assign an index to each node, named `reentrancy index`. Duplicate nodes will be assigned the same index.

3.6 Anonymization in AMR Framework

Anonymization is an important AMR preprocessing method to reduce the data sparsity issue (Werling et al., 2015; Peng et al., 2017; Guo and Lu, 2018). Following the practice of Zhang et al. (2019a), we first remove senses, wiki links, and polarity attributes in the training dataset. Secondly, we anonymize sub-graphs of named entities which is labeled by one of AMR's fine-grained entity types that contain a `name` role, and other entities which end with `-entity`[6].

4 Models

To handle different flavors of representation, our system has three types of models: `Anchoring-based Pruning Parsing Model`, `Constituent Parsing Model`, `Seq2seq-based Parsing Model`.

4.1 Anchoring-based Pruning Parsing Model

The anchoring-based pruning parsing model is suitable for frameworks where the graph nodes are strictly one-to-one with the sentence span, such as DM, PSD, and the transformed EDS framework. The key idea of the anchoring-based pruning parsing model is to obtain the candidate graph nodes by enumerating the sentence span, and then use a scorer to pruning the candidate graph nodes and perform parsing on these graph nodes.

---

[6]For details of preprocessing, please refer to (Zhang et al., 2019a).

Formally, for major structural parsing goals, given a sentence $S = \{w_1, w_2, ..., w_n\}$, where n is the sequence length, we aim to predict a set of labeled graph node-pair (sentence span-pair) relations $Y \subseteq \mathcal{N} \times \mathcal{N} \times \mathcal{L}$, where $\mathcal{N} = \{(w_i, ..., w_j)|1 \leq i \leq j \leq n\}$ contains all the spans (graph nodes), and $\mathcal{L}$ is the space of the edge labels (semantic roles), including a null label ϵ indicating no edge between the node-pairs.

As our model deals with $\mathcal{O}(n^2)$ possible sentence spans (graph nodes), it needs to consider $\mathcal{O}(n^4|\mathcal{L}|)$ possible relations, which is computationally impractical. To overcome this issue, motivated by our previous work (Li et al., 2019b) and the work of (He et al., 2018a), we limit the maximum width of the candidate spans to fixed number W, which reduces the overall number of relational factors need to be considered by the model to $\mathcal{O}(n^2|\mathcal{L}|)$. In order to make the training goal denser, we also introduce a unary scorer $\phi_{node}(\cdot)$ and the candidate nodes are ranked and pruned by their unary score in descending order. The size of candidates reserved after the pruning operation is limited to λn. Candidates that are pruned do not participate in computing the edge relation prediction, which can also further reduce the computational complexity and memory requirements. These parameters W and λ are determined based on the statistics on the training dataset of each framework.

Neural Architecture Our model builds the candidate graph nodes representation based on the BERT (Devlin et al., 2019) encoder outputs, i.e., for each token w_i, the contextualized vector from BERT encoder is denoted as x_i. The candidate span (i, j) representation h consists of two endpoint contextualized vectors (x_i, x_j) where i and j are the start and end position of the span in the sentence:

$$h = [x_i; x_j]. \tag{1}$$

The node unary scorer $\phi_{node}(\cdot)$ is implemented with feed-forward networks based on the candidate graph nodes representation h:

$$\phi_{node}(\cdot) = sigmoid(\mathbf{MLP}_{node}(h)). \tag{2}$$

The edge relation classifier $\phi_{rel}(\cdot)$ is implemented with biaffine attention mechanism. Following Dozat and Manning (2017), we apply two seperate MLPs to the source and target nodes respectively, producing identity-specified representation:

$r_{src} = \mathbf{MLP}_{src}(h)$ and $r_{tgt} = \mathbf{MLP}_{tgt}(h)$. We perform a biaffine operation to compute the relation labeling score.

$$\phi_{rel}(\cdot) = r_{src}^T \mathbf{W}_{rel} r_{tgt} + \mathbf{U}_{rel}^T r_{src} + \mathbf{V}_{rel}^T r_{tgt} + \mathbf{b}_{rel}, \tag{3}$$

where $\mathbf{W}_{rel}$, $\mathbf{U}_{rel}$, $\mathbf{V}_{rel}$, and $\mathbf{b}_{rel}$ are the weight matrix of the bi-linear term, the two weight vectors of the linear terms, and the bias vector, respectively.

Training Loss For the node scoring goal, we use the binary cross-entropy loss between the target and the output. For the edge classification, we implement it with the standard cross-entropy loss.

Multi-Task Learning Each framework still has some other goals to learn. The DM framework in-cludes `top node`, `node pos tag`, and `node frame label`. The PSD includes `top node`, `node pos tag`, and `node frame label`. The EDS includes `edge source label` and `edge target label`. Overall, we use multi-tasking learning strategy, shared hidden representation, The `top node` uses the same mechanism as node scoring, using binary cross-entropy as loss implementation. The `node pos tag` and `node frame label` use independent feed-forward classifier, using cross-entropy as loss implementation. The `edge source label` and `edge target label` use a biaffine scorer consistent with the edge label, using cross-entropy loss as well. We accumulate the loss of all goals together.

4.2 Constituent Parsing Model

For the UCCA framework, we directly adopt the minimal span-based parser of Stern et al. (2017) on the converted constituent trees. A constituency tree can be regarded as a collection of labeled spans over a sentence. There are two components in the constituent parsing model: one is to assign the scores directly to span existence which determines the tree structure, and the other one assigns scores to span labels which provides the labeled outputs.

Neural Architecture In this model, we also build the candidate span representation h based on the BERT encoder outputs due to a span's correct label and its quality as a constituent depend heavily on the context in which it appears. Different from the previous span representation, in this model, the representation h of span (i, j) is the concatenation of the two endpoint contextualized vectors differences:

$$h = x_j - x_i. \tag{4}$$

The span splitting unary scorer $\phi_{split}(\cdot)$ and the span label scorer $\phi_{label}(\cdot)$ are both implemented as feed-forward networks which take as input the span representation and output either a single span score or a vector of labeling scores. For the tree inference, we adopt the greedy top-down searching strategy introduced in Stern et al. (2017).

In order to recover the full UCCA graph, the model needs to learn the remote edge target. The remote edge target is similar to the previous edge target, which is to predict the relationship between the node pairs, so we also use the relational classifier $\phi_{rel}(\cdot)$. As the same in the previous model, there is also a null label ϵ indicating no edge between the node-pairs.

4.3 Seq2seq-based Parsing Model

The AMR framework backgrounds notions of compositionality and derivation and, accordingly, declines to make explicit how elements of the graph correspond to the surface utterance. Although most AMR parsing research presupposes a preprocessing step that aligns graph nodes with (possibly discontinuous) sets of tokens in the underlying input, these correspondences need extra annotation and training. This does not match our requirements for the model to be end-to-end. Therefore, we consider the AMR tree with indexed nodes as the prediction target (proposed by Zhang et al. (2019a)). The approach of AMR parsing is formulized as a two-stage process: node prediction (concept identification) and edge prediction (relation identification).

Formally, given a sentence $S = \{w_1, w_2, ..., w_n\}$, the model sequentially decodes a list of nodes $N = \{u_1, u_2, ..., u_m\}$ and their reentrancy indices $D = \{d_1, d_2, .., d_m\}$. Then, the model is required to search for the highest scoring parsing tree similar to dependency parsing.

Neural Architecture For node prediction, we adopt the widely-used Seq2seq model $Seq2seq(\cdot)$ with pointer-generator network (Vinyals et al., 2015). The pointer-network has the advantage of copying words from the source text while still retaining the ability to produce novel words

DM & PSD & EDS	
node_space_dim	128
max_seq_len	100
DM & PSD	
max_span_width (W)	5
pruning_reserve_ratio[*] (λ)	1.0
EDS	
max_span_width (W)	8
pruning_reserve_ratio[*] (λ)	1.2
UCCA	
split_space_dim (W)	128
AMR	
decoder_type	RNN
decoder_hidden_dim	512
decoder_num_layers	3
Deep biaffine classfier	
edge_space_dim	512
edge_label_space_dim	128
Optimizer	
optimizer_type	Adam
learning_rate	$5e^{-5}$
max_grad_norm	1.0

Table 1: Hyper-parameter settings for our final submission. [*]*pruning_reserve_ratio* (λ) is for the sentence length n, not the number of candidate nodes.

through the generator. The node representation h is obtained as the decoder hidden state of the Seq2seq model:

$$h - Seq2seq(\cdot). \tag{5}$$

For the edge prediction, we also adopt the biaffine attention mechanism to score all possible head-dependent pairs like dependency parsing. The relation classifier $\phi_{rel}(\cdot)$ is the same as the previous:

$$\phi_{arc}(\cdot) = h_{head}^T \mathbf{W}_{arc} h_{dep} + \mathbf{U}_{arc}^T h_{head} \\ + \mathbf{V}_{arc}^T h_{dep} + \mathbf{b}_{arc}, \tag{6}$$

where $\mathbf{W}_{arc}$, $\mathbf{U}_{arc}$, $\mathbf{V}_{arc}$, and $\mathbf{b}_{arc}$ are the weight matrix of the bi-linear term, the two weight vectors of the linear terms, and the bias vector, respectively.

5 Experiments

5.1 Setup

We first describe the final setup used for our final submission. We use the

	P	R	F_1	RANK
tops	0.92	0.91	0.915	**1**
labels	0.73	0.70	0.712	2
properties	0.70	0.67	0.687	2
anchors	0.78	0.77	0.776	1
edges	0.80	0.75	0.777	2
attributes	0.13	0.07	0.094	2
all	0.87	0.83	0.853	**2**

Table 2: The official evaluation scores of different "atomic" component pieces on all the test dataset.

	P	R	F_1	RANK
DM	0.96	0.95	0.9550	**1**
PSD	0.91	0.91	0.9119	3
EDS	0.95	0.86	0.8990	3
UCCA	0.80	0.76	0.7780	3
AMR	0.75	0.69	0.7197	3
all	0.87	0.83	0.853	**2**

Table 3: The official evaluation scores of different frameworks on all the test dataset.

`pytorch-transformers`[7] as our codebase to develop the downstream parsing models. The weights of pre-trained language model BERT with whole word masking[8] are used to initialize the encoder of our models. Due to the absence of development dataset, we split the training dataset to 10 sections and 0-8 for training and 9 for development. Our model is trained using Adam (Kingma and Ba, 2014) up to 30 epochs for DM, PSD, and EDS, and 20 epochs for UCCA and 120 epochs for AMR, with early stopping strategy based on the MRP F_1 score[9] on the development dataset with `mtool`[10] toolkit. Table 1 lists the hyperparameters used in our full model. We apply the hidden dropout ($dropout\_rate = 0.1$) to the outputs of each module in our model.

5.2 Main Results

We list our official evaluation scores[11] on the all test dataset in Tables 2 and 3. Table 2 summarizes the MRP F_1 scores of the 6 graph components. The results listed in Table 2 shows that we obtained the state-of-the-art MRP F_1 score on the `top nodes` component. In Table 3, we assess the quality on each frameworks. Our model also achieved the best results on the DM framework. We observed a notable phenomenon that as the anchoring relationship between the graph node and the surface lexical units is getting farther, the difficulty of parsing is getting higher.

From the results of parsing on different frameworks, our results on the EDS framework have the biggest gap with other priority teams, probably because of the existence of multiple edges between the same pair of `pseudo` nodes in the EDS framework after our modeling transformation. Therefore, our subsequent experiments modeled the edges of EDS as multi-classification problems, and our results on the development dataset have been improved.

6 Conclusion and Future Work

In this paper, we present our end-to-end graph-based system participated in the CoNLL 2019 shared task on Cross-Framework Meaning Representation Parsing (MRP 2019). We extend existing models and make our model be end-to-end and does not depend on any other information (including the companion data provided by the organizer). We introduce our previous graph pruning algorithm to a variety of semantic graphs, solving the problem of excessive semantic graph search space and adopt multi-task learning for multiple objectives within the same framework. Specifically, we model the semantic graph task as a multi-objective learning task of nodes, edges, node attributes, and edge attributes. The nodes candidates are scored and then pruned within the model, thus controlling the overall graph search space, and finally forming an end-to-end style parsing system. We achieve state-of-the-art results on the `top nodes` component and DM framework.

For future work, we are going to integrate all the different frameworks into one single model, not just the same modeling approach. Based on the MRP representation method, a single model is used to generate various semantic graphs. Furthermore, we would like to extend our model to other more semantic parsing tasks.

---

[7] `https://github.com/huggingface/pytorch-transformers`.

[8] In our experiments, we use the BERT-Large, uncased (Whole Word Masking) with 24-layer, 1024-hidden, 16-heads, and 340M parameters released by Google, `https://github.com/google-research/bert`.

[9] `http://mrp.nlpl.eu/index.php`.

[10] `https://github.com/cfmrp/mtool`.

[11] The official evaluation results are at `http://bit.ly/cfmrp19`.

References

Omri Abend and Ari Rappoport. 2013. Universal conceptual cognitive annotation (ucca). In *Proceedings of the 51st Annual Meeting of the Association for Computational Linguistics (Volume 1: Long Papers)*, pages 228–238.

Laura Banarescu, Claire Bonial, Shu Cai, Madalina Georgescu, Kira Griffitt, Ulf Hermjakob, Kevin Knight, Philipp Koehn, Martha Palmer, and Nathan Schneider. 2013. Abstract meaning representation for sembanking. In *Proceedings of the 7th Linguistic Annotation Workshop and Interoperability with Discourse*, pages 178–186.

Ann Bies, Justin Mott, Colin Warner, and Seth Kulick. 2012. English web treebank. *Linguistic Data Consortium, Philadelphia, PA*.

Jiaxun Cai, Shexia He, Zuchao Li, and Hai Zhao. 2018. A full end-to-end semantic role labeler, syntactic-agnostic over syntactic-aware? In *Proceedings of the 27th International Conference on Computational Linguistics*, pages 2753–2765.

Kehai Chen, Rui Wang, Masao Utiyama, Eiichiro Sumita, and Tiejun Zhao. 2019. Neural machine translation with sentence-level topic context. *IEEE/ACM Transactions on Audio, Speech, and Language Processing*.

Jacob Devlin, Ming-Wei Chang, Kenton Lee, and Kristina Toutanova. 2019. BERT: Pre-training of deep bidirectional transformers for language understanding. In *Proceedings of the 2019 Conference of the North American Chapter of the Association for Computational Linguistics: Human Language Technologies, Volume 1 (Long and Short Papers)*, pages 4171–4186, Minneapolis, Minnesota. Association for Computational Linguistics.

Timothy Dozat and Christopher D. Manning. 2017. Deep biaffine attention for neural dependency parsing. In *Proceedings of the 5th International Conference on Learning Representations*, Toulon, France.

Dan Flickinger, Emily M Bender, and Stephan Oepen. 2014. Towards an encyclopedia of compositional semantics: Documenting the interface of the english resource grammar. In *LREC*, pages 875–881.

Zhijiang Guo and Wei Lu. 2018. Better transition-based amr parsing with a refined search space. In *Proceedings of the 2018 Conference on Empirical Methods in Natural Language Processing*, pages 1712–1722.

Jan Hajic, Eva Hajicová, Jarmila Panevová, Petr Sgall, Ondrej Bojar, Silvie Cinková, Eva Fucíková, Marie Mikulová, Petr Pajas, Jan Popelka, et al. 2012. Announcing prague czech-english dependency treebank 2.0. In *LREC*, pages 3153–3160.

Luheng He, Kenton Lee, Omer Levy, and Luke Zettlemoyer. 2018a. Jointly predicting predicates and arguments in neural semantic role labeling. In *Proceedings of the 56th Annual Meeting of the Association for Computational Linguistics (Volume 2: Short Papers)*, pages 364–369, Melbourne, Australia. Association for Computational Linguistics.

Shexia He, Zuchao Li, and Hai Zhao. 2019. Syntax-aware multilingual semantic role labeling. *arXiv preprint arXiv:1909.00310*.

Shexia He, Zuchao Li, Hai Zhao, and Hongxiao Bai. 2018b. Syntax for semantic role labeling, to be, or not to be. In *Proceedings of the 56th Annual Meeting of the Association for Computational Linguistics (Volume 1: Long Papers)*, pages 2061–2071.

Angelina Ivanova, Stephan Oepen, Lilja Øvrelid, and Dan Flickinger. 2012. Who did what to whom?: A contrastive study of syntacto-semantic dependencies. In *Proceedings of the sixth linguistic annotation workshop*, pages 2–11. Association for Computational Linguistics.

Wei Jiang, Zhenghua Li, Yu Zhang, and Min Zhang. 2019. Hlt@ suda at semeval-2019 task 1: Ucca graph parsing as constituent tree parsing. In *Proceedings of the 13th International Workshop on Semantic Evaluation*, pages 11–15.

Diederik P Kingma and Jimmy Ba. 2014. Adam: A method for stochastic optimization. *arXiv preprint arXiv:1412.6980*.

Jiangtong Li, Hai Zhao, Zuchao Li, Wei Bi, and Xiaojiang Liu. 2019a. Subword elmo. *ArXiv*, abs/1909.08357.

Zuchao Li, Jiaxun Cai, Shexia He, and Hai Zhao. 2018a. Seq2seq dependency parsing. In *Proceedings of the 27th International Conference on Computational Linguistics*, pages 3203–3214.

Zuchao Li, Jiaxun Cai, and Hai Zhao. 2018b. Effective representation for easy-first dependency parsing. *arXiv preprint arXiv:1811.03511*.

Zuchao Li, Shexia He, Jiaxun Cai, Zhuosheng Zhang, Hai Zhao, Gongshen Liu, Linlin Li, and Luo Si. 2018c. A unified syntax-aware framework for semantic role labeling. In *Proceedings of the 2018 Conference on Empirical Methods in Natural Language Processing*, pages 2401–2411.

Zuchao Li, Shexia He, Zhuosheng Zhang, and Hai Zhao. 2018d. Joint learning of pos and dependencies for multilingual universal dependency parsing. In *Proceedings of the CoNLL 2018 Shared Task: Multilingual Parsing from Raw Text to Universal Dependencies*, pages 65–73.

Zuchao Li, Shexia He, Hai Zhao, Yiqing Zhang, Zhuosheng Zhang, Xi Zhou, and Xiang Zhou. 2019b. Dependency or span, end-to-end uniform semantic role labeling. *arXiv preprint arXiv:1901.05280*.

Christopher Manning, Mihai Surdeanu, John Bauer, Jenny Finkel, Steven Bethard, and David McClosky. 2014. The stanford corenlp natural language processing toolkit. In *Proceedings of 52nd annual meeting of the association for computational linguistics: system demonstrations*, pages 55–60.

Mitchell Marcus, Beatrice Santorini, and Mary Ann Marcinkiewicz. 1993. Building a large annotated corpus of english: The penn treebank.

Yusuke Miyao, Stephan Oepen, and Daniel Zeman. 2014. In-house: An ensemble of pre-existing off-the-shelf parsers. In *Proceedings of the 8th International Workshop on Semantic Evaluation (SemEval 2014)*, pages 335–340.

Joakim Nivre and Jens Nilsson. 2005. Pseudo-projective dependency parsing. In *Proceedings of the 43rd Annual Meeting on Association for Computational Linguistics*, pages 99–106. Association for Computational Linguistics.

Stephan Oepen, Omri Abend, Jan Hajič, Daniel Hershcovich, Marco Kuhlmann, Tim O'Gorman, Nianwen Xue, and Milan Straka. 2019. MRP 2019: Cross-framework Meaning Representation Parsing. In *Proceedings of the Shared Task on Cross-Framework Meaning Representation Parsing at the 2019 Conference on Natural Language Learning*, pages 1 – 26, Hong Kong, China.

Stephan Oepen and Jan Tore Lønning. 2006. Discriminant-based mrs banking. In *LREC*, pages 1250–1255.

Xiaochang Peng, Chuan Wang, Daniel Gildea, and Nianwen Xue. 2017. Addressing the data sparsity issue in neural amr parsing. In *Proceedings of the 15th Conference of the European Chapter of the Association for Computational Linguistics: Volume 1, Long Papers*, pages 366–375.

Mitchell Stern, Jacob Andreas, and Dan Klein. 2017. A minimal span-based neural constituency parser. In *Proceedings of the 55th Annual Meeting of the Association for Computational Linguistics (Volume 1: Long Papers)*, pages 818–827, Vancouver, Canada. Association for Computational Linguistics.

Haipeng Sun, Rui Wang, Kehai Chen, Masao Utiyama, Eiichiro Sumita, and Tiejun Zhao. 2019. Unsupervised bilingual word embedding agreement for unsupervised neural machine translation. In *Proceedings of the 57th Annual Meeting of the Association for Computational Linguistics*, pages 1235–1245.

Oriol Vinyals, Meire Fortunato, and Navdeep Jaitly. 2015. Pointer networks. In *Advances in Neural Information Processing Systems*, pages 2692–2700.

Keenon Werling, Gabor Angeli, and Christopher D Manning. 2015. Robust subgraph generation improves abstract meaning representation parsing. In *Proceedings of the 53rd Annual Meeting of*

the Association for Computational Linguistics and the 7th International Joint Conference on Natural Language Processing (Volume 1: Long Papers), pages 982–991.

Fengshun Xiao, Jiangtong Li, Hai Zhao, Rui Wang, and Kehai Chen. 2019. Lattice-based transformer encoder for neural machine translation. *arXiv preprint arXiv:1906.01282*.

Sheng Zhang, Xutai Ma, Kevin Duh, and Benjamin Van Durme. 2019a. AMR parsing as sequence-to-graph transduction. In *Proceedings of the 57th Annual Meeting of the Association for Computational Linguistics*, pages 80–94, Florence, Italy. Association for Computational Linguistics.

Zhuosheng Zhang, Yuwei Wu, Hai Zhao, Zuchao Li, Shuailiang Zhang, Xi Zhou, and Xiang Zhou. 2019b. Semantics-aware bert for language understanding. *arXiv preprint arXiv:1909.02209*.

Zhuosheng Zhang, Hai Zhao, Kangwei Ling, Jiangtong Li, Zuchao Li, Shexia He, and Guohong Fu. 2019c. Effective subword segmentation for text comprehension. *IEEE/ACM Transactions on Audio, Speech, and Language Processing*, 27(11):1664–1674.

Junru Zhou, Zuchao Li, and Hai Zhao. 2019. Parsing all: Syntax and semantics, dependencies and spans. *arXiv preprint arXiv:1908.11522*.

Junru Zhou and Hai Zhao. 2019. Head-driven phrase structure grammar parsing on penn treebank. In *Proceedings of the 57th Annual Meeting of the Association for Computational Linguistics*, pages 2396–2408.

ShanghaiTech at MRP 2019: Sequence-to-Graph Transduction with Second-Order Edge Inference for Cross-Framework Meaning Representation Parsing

Xinyu Wang, Yixian Liu, Zixia Jia, Chengyue Jiang, Kewei Tu

School of Information Science and Technology,
ShanghaiTech University, Shanghai, China
`{wangxy1,liuyx,jiazx,jiangchy,tukw}@shanghaitech.edu.cn`

Abstract

This paper presents the system used in our submission to the *CoNLL 2019 shared task: Cross-Framework Meaning Representation Parsing.* Our system is a graph-based parser which combines an extended pointer-generator network that generates nodes and a second-order mean field variational inference module that predicts edges. Our system achieved 1st and 2nd place for the DM and PSD frameworks respectively on the in-framework ranks and achieved 3rd place for the DM framework on the cross-framework ranks.

1 Introduction

The goal of the *Cross-Framework Meaning Representation Parsing* (MRP 2019, Oepen et al. (2019)) is learning to parse text to multiple formats of meaning representation with a uniform parsing system. The task combines five different frameworks of graph-based meaning representation. DELPH-IN MRS Bi-Lexical Dependencies (DM) (Ivanova et al., 2012) and Prague Semantic Dependencies (PSD) (Hajič et al., 2012; Miyao et al., 2014) first appeared in SemEval 2014 and 2015 shared task Semantic Dependency Parsing (SDP) (Oepen et al., 2014, 2015). Elementary Dependency Structures (EDS) (Oepen and Lønning, 2006) is the origin of DM Bi-Lexical Dependencies, which encodes English Resource Semantics (Flickinger et al., 2016) in a variable-free semantic dependency graph. Universal Conceptual Cognitive Annotation (UCCA) (Abend and Rappoport, 2013) targets a level of semantic granularity that abstracts away from syntactic paraphrases. Abstract Meaning Representation (AMR) (Banarescu et al., 2013) targets to abstract away from syntactic representations, which means that sentences have similar meaning should be assigned the same AMR graph. One of the main differences between these frameworks is their level of abstraction from the sentence. SDP is a bi-lexical dependency graph, where graph nodes correspond to tokens in the sentence. EDS and UCCA are general forms of anchored semantic graphs, in which the nodes are anchored to arbitrary spans of the sentence and the spans can have overlaps. AMR is an unanchored graph, which does not consider the correspondence between nodes and the sentence tokens. The shared task also provides a cross-framework metric which evaluates the similarity of graph components in all frameworks.

Previous work mostly focused on developing parsers that support only one or two frameworks while few work has explored cross-framework semantic parsing. Peng et al. (2017), Stanovsky and Dagan (2018) and Kurita and Søgaard (2019) proposed methods learning jointly on the three frameworks of SDP and Peng et al. (2018) further proposed to learn from different corpora. Hershcovich et al. (2018) converted UCCA, AMR, DM and UD (Universal Dependencies) into a unified DAG format and proposed a transition-based method for UCCA parsing.

In this paper, we present our system for MRP 2019. Our system is a graph-based method which combines an extended pointer-generator network introduced by Zhang et al. (2019) to generate nodes for EDS, UCCA and AMR graphs and a second-order mean field variational inference module introduced by Wang et al. (2019) to predict edges for all the frameworks. According to the official results, our system gets 94.88 F1 score in the cross-framework metric for DM, which is the 3rd place in the ranking. For in-framework metrics, our system gets 92.98 and 81.61 labeled F1 score for DM and PSD respectively, which are ranked 1st and 2nd in the ranking.

Proceedings of the Shared Task on Cross-Framework Meaning Representation Parsing at the 2019 CoNLL, pages 55–65
Hong Kong, November 3, 2019. ©2019 Association for Computational Linguistics
https://doi.org/10.18653/v1/K19-2005

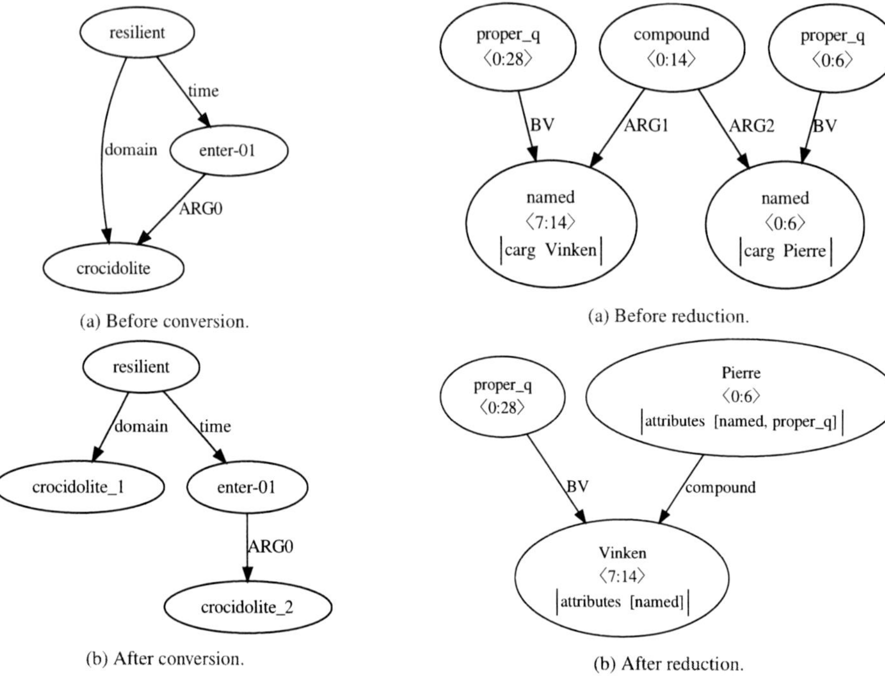

(a) Before conversion.

(b) After conversion.

Figure 1: An example of converting AMR graphs into tree structures. This is a sub-graph of sentence #20003002.

(a) Before reduction.

(b) After reduction.

Figure 2: An example of EDS reduction. This is a sub-graph of sentence #20001001.

2 Data Processing

In this section, we introduce our data pre-processing and post-processing in our system for all the frameworks. We use sentence tokenizations, POS tags and lemmas from the official companion data and named entity tags extracted by Illinois Named Entity Tagger (Ratinov and Roth, 2009) in the official 'white-list'. We follow Zhang et al. (2019) to convert each EDS, UCCA, and AMR graph to a tree through duplicating the nodes that have multiple edge entrances, An example is shown in Fig. 1. The node sequences for EDS, UCCA and AMR are decided by depth-first search that starts from the root node and sorts neighbouring nodes in alphanumerical order.

2.1 AMR Data Processing

Our data processing follows Zhang et al. (2019). In pre-processing, we remove the senses, wiki links and polarity attributes in AMR nodes, and replace the sub-graphs of special named entities, such as names, places, time, with anonymized words. The corresponding phrases in the sentences are also anonymized. A mapping from

NER tags to these entities is built to process the test data.

In post-processing, we generate the AMR sub-graphs from the anonymized words. Then we assign the senses, wiki links and polarity attributes with the method in Zhang et al. (2019).

2.2 EDS and UCCA Data Processing

In pre-processing we first clean the companion data to make sure the tokens in the companion data is consistent with those in the MRP input. We suppose anchors are continuous for each node, so we replace the anchors with the corresponding start and end token indices.

In EDS graphs, there are a lot of nodes without a direct mapping to individual surface tokens, which we call *type* 1 nodes. We call nodes with corresponding surface tokens *type* 2 nodes. We reduce *type* 1 nodes in two ways:

- If a node a of *type* 1 is connected to only one node b which is of *type* 2 and has the same anchor as a, we reduce node a into node b as a special *attribute* for the node.

- If a node a of *type* 1 is connected to exactly

two nodes b and c which are of *type* 2 and have a combined anchor range that matches the anchor of a. We reduce node a as an edge connecting b and c with the same label. The edge direction is decided by the labels of the edges connecting a to b and c. For example, if node a has two child nodes b and c, edge (a, c) has label $ARG2$ and edge (a, b) has label $ARG1$, then node a will be reduced to directed edge (b, c) with the label of node a.

An example of the reduction is shown in Fig. 2. This method reduces 4 nodes on average for each graph. We also look at nodes whose node label corresponds to a multi-word in the sentence For example, '_such+as' in an EDS graph corresponds to 'such as' in the sentence. In such case, if the phrase has a probability over 0.5 that maps to a single node, then all words in this phrase will be combined to a single token in the sentence.

In the post-processing, we recover reduced nodes by reversing the reduction precedure according to the node attributes and edge labels.

For UCCA, we label implicit nodes with special labels n_i, where i is the index that the implicit node appears in the node sequence.

3 System Description

In this section, we describe our model for the task. We first predict the nodes of the parse graph. For DM and PSD, there is a one-to-one mapping between sentence tokens and graph nodes. For EDS, UCCA and AMR, we apply an extended pointer-generator network (Zhang et al., 2019) for node prediction. Given predicted nodes, we then adopt the method of second-order mean field variational inference (Wang et al., 2019) for edge prediction. Figure 3 illustrates our system architecture.

3.1 Word Representation

Previous work found that various word representation could help improve parser performance. Many state-of-the-art parsers use POS tags and pre-trained GloVe (Pennington et al., 2014) embeddings as a part of the word representation. Dozat and Manning (2018) find that character-based LSTM and lemma embeddings can further improve the performance of semantic dependency parser. Zhang et al. (2019) use BERT (Devlin et al., 2019) embeddings for each token to improve the performance of AMR parsing. In our system,

we find that predicted named entity tags are helpful as well. The word representation o_i in our system is:

$$\mathbf{o}_i = [\mathbf{o}_i^w; \mathbf{o}_i^{\text{pos}}; \mathbf{o}_i^{\text{lemmas}}; \mathbf{o}_i^{pw}; \mathbf{o}_i^{bw}; \mathbf{o}_i^{\text{char}}; \mathbf{o}_i^{\text{ne}}]$$

where $\mathbf{o}_i^w$ is word embedding with random initialization, $\mathbf{o}_i^{pw}$ is pre-trained GloVe embedding and $\mathbf{o}_i^{bw}$ are BERT embedding through average pooling over subwords. $\mathbf{o}_i^{\text{pos}}$, $\mathbf{o}_i^{\text{lemmas}}$, $\mathbf{o}_i^{\text{char}}$, $\mathbf{o}_i^{\text{ne}}$ are XPOS, lemmas, character and NER embedding respectively. XPOS and lemmas are extracted from the official companion data.

3.2 Node Prediction

We use extended pointer-generator network (Zhang et al., 2019) for nodes prediction. Given a sentence with n words $\mathbf{w} = [w_1, w_2, ..., w_n]$, we predict a list of nodes $\mathbf{u} = [u_1, u_2, ..., u_m]$ sequentially and assign their corresponding indices $\mathbf{idx} = [idx_1, idx_2, ..., idx_m]$. The indices $\mathbf{idx}$ are used to track whether a copy of a previous generated nodes or a newly generated node.

$$P(\mathbf{u}) = \prod_{i=1}^{m} P(u_i \mid u_{<i}, idx_{<i}, \mathbf{w})$$

To encode the input sentence, we use a multi-layer BiLSTM fed with embeddings of the words:

$$R = \text{BiLSTM}(O) \tag{1}$$

where O represents $[\mathbf{o}_1, \ldots, \mathbf{o}_n]$, $\mathbf{o}_i$ is the concatenation different types of embeddings for w_i, and $R = [\mathbf{r}_1, \ldots, \mathbf{r}_n]$ represents the output from the BiLSTM.

For the decoder, at each time step t, we use an l-layer LSTM for generating hidden states z_t^l sequentially:

$$\mathbf{z}_t^l = f^l(\mathbf{z}_t^{l-1}, \mathbf{z}_{t-1}^l)$$

where f^l is the l-th layer of LSTM, $\mathbf{z}_0^l$ is the last hidden state r_n in Eq. 1. $\mathbf{z}_t^0$ is the concatenation of the label embedding of node u_{t-1} and attentional vector $\widetilde{\mathbf{z}}_{t-1}$. $\widetilde{\mathbf{z}}_t$ is defined by:

$$\mathbf{e}_{\text{src}}^t = \mathbf{W}_{satt}^\top \tanh(\mathbf{W}_{\text{src}} R + \mathbf{U}_{\text{src}} \mathbf{z}_t^l + \mathbf{b}_{\text{src}}) \tag{2}$$

$$\mathbf{a}_{\text{src}}^t = \text{softmax}(\mathbf{e}_{\text{src}}^t) \tag{3}$$

$$\mathbf{c}_t = \sum_i^n \mathbf{a}_{\text{src},i}^t \mathbf{r}_i$$

$$\widetilde{\mathbf{z}}_t = \tanh(\mathbf{W}_c[\mathbf{c}_t; \mathbf{z}_t^l] + \mathbf{b}_c) \tag{4}$$

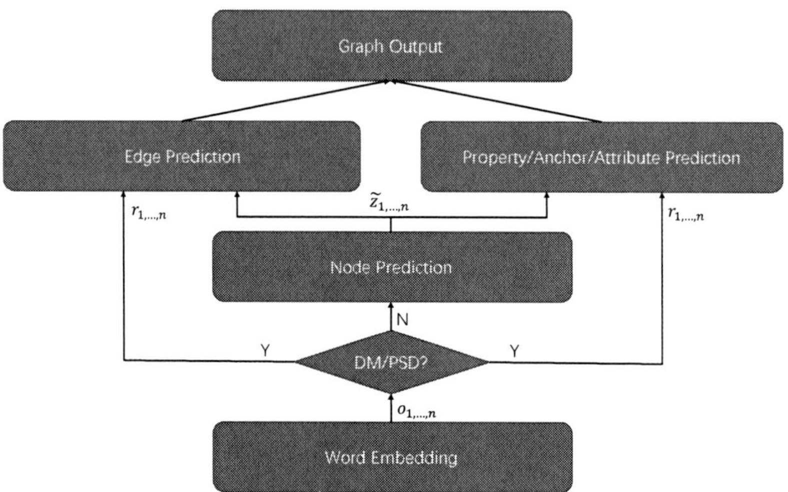

Figure 3: Illustration of our system architecture.

Where $\mathbf{a}_{\mathrm{src}}^{t}$ is the source attention distribution, and $\mathbf{c}_t$ is contextual vector of encoder hidden layers, $\mathbf{W}_{satt}$, $\mathbf{W}_{\mathrm{src}}$, $\mathbf{U}_{\mathrm{src}}$, $\mathbf{b}_{\mathrm{src}}$, $\mathbf{W}_c$, $\mathbf{b}_c$ are learnable parameters. The vocabulary distribution is given by:

$$P_{\mathrm{vocab}} = \mathrm{softmax}(\mathbf{W}_{\mathrm{vocab}}\widetilde{\mathbf{z}}_t + \mathbf{b}_{\mathrm{vocab}}) \quad (5)$$

where $\mathbf{W}_{\mathrm{vocab}}$ and $\mathbf{b}_{\mathrm{vocab}}$ are learnable parameters. The target attention distribution is defined similarly as Eq. 2 and 3:

$$\mathbf{e}_{\mathrm{tgt}}^{t} = \mathbf{W}_{tatt}^{\top}\tanh(\mathbf{W}_{\mathrm{tgt}}\widetilde{\mathbf{z}}_{1:t-1} + \mathbf{U}_{\mathrm{tgt}}\widetilde{\mathbf{z}}_t + \mathbf{b}_{\mathrm{tgt}}),$$
$$\mathbf{a}_{\mathrm{tgt}}^{t} = \mathrm{softmax}(\mathbf{e}_{\mathrm{tgt}}^{t}),$$

where $\mathbf{W}_{tatt}^{\top}$, $\mathbf{W}_{\mathrm{tgt}}$, $\mathbf{U}_{\mathrm{tgt}}$, $\mathbf{b}_{\mathrm{tgt}}$ are learnable parameters. Finally, at each time step, we need to decide which action should be taken. Possible actions include copying an existing node from previous nodes and generating a new node whose label is either from the vocabulary or a word from the source sentence. The corresponding probability of these three actions are p_{tgt}, p_{gen} and p_{src}:

$$[p_{\mathrm{tgt}}, p_{\mathrm{gen}}, p_{\mathrm{src}}] = \mathrm{softmax}(\mathbf{W}_{\mathrm{action}}\widetilde{\mathbf{z}}_t + \mathbf{b}_{\mathrm{action}})$$

where $p_{\mathrm{tgt}} + p_{\mathrm{gen}} + p_{\mathrm{src}} = 1$.

At time step t, if u_t is a copy of an existing nodes, then the probability $P^{(\mathrm{node})}(u_t)$ and the index idx_t is defined by:

$$P^{(\mathrm{node})}(u_t) = p_{\mathrm{tgt}} \sum_{i:u_i=u_t} \mathbf{a}_{\mathrm{tgt}}^{t}[i]$$
$$idx_t = idx_j$$

where idx_j is the copied node index. If u_t is a new node:

$$P^{(\mathrm{node})}(u_t) = p_{\mathrm{gen}}P_{\mathrm{vocab}}(u_t) + p_{\mathrm{src}} \sum_{i:w_i=u_t} \mathbf{a}_{\mathrm{src}}^{t}[i]$$
$$idx_t = t$$

3.3 Edge Prediction

We adopt the method presented in Wang et al. (2019) for edge prediction, which is based on second-order scoring and inference. Suppose that we have a sequence of vector representations of the predicted nodes $[\mathbf{r}'_1, \ldots, \mathbf{r}'_m]$, which can be the BiLSTM output $\mathbf{r}_i$ in Eq. 1 in the cases of DM and PSD, or the extended pointer-generator network output $\widetilde{\mathbf{z}}_i$ in Eq. 4 in the cases of EDS, UCCA and AMR. The edge prediction module is shown in Fig. 4.

To score first-order and second-order parts (i.e., edges and edge-pairs) in both edge-prediction and label-prediction, we apply the Biaffine function (Dozat and Manning, 2017, 2018) and Trilinear function (Wang et al., 2019) fed with node representations.

$$\mathrm{Biaff}(\mathbf{v}_1, \mathbf{v}_2) := \mathbf{v}_1^{\top}\mathbf{U}\mathbf{v}_2 + \mathbf{b}$$
$$\mathbf{g}_i := \mathbf{U}_i\mathbf{v}_i \quad i \in [1, 2, 3]$$
$$\mathrm{Trilin}(\mathbf{v}_1, \mathbf{v}_2, \mathbf{v}_3) := \sum_{i=1}^{d} \mathbf{g}_{1i} \circ \mathbf{g}_{2i} \circ \mathbf{g}_{3i} \quad (6)$$

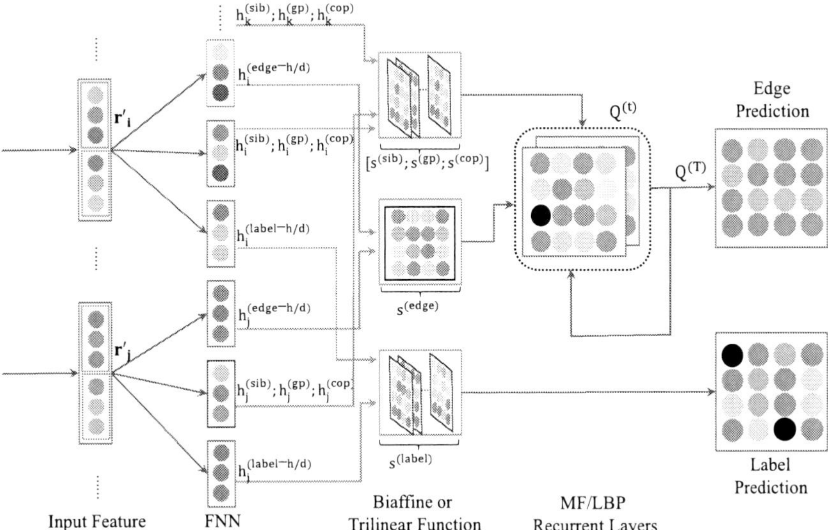

Figure 4: The structure of our edge prediction module. The figure is from Wang et al. (2019) with minor modifications.

where $\mathbf{U}_i$ is a $(d \times d)$-dimensional tensor, where d is hidden size and $\circ$ represents element-wise product. We consider three types of second-order parts: siblings (sib), co-parents (cop) and grandparents (gp) (Martins and Almeida, 2014). For a specific first-order and second-order *part*, we use single-layer FNNs to compute a *head* representation and a *dependent* representation for each word, as well as a *head_dep* representation which is used for grandparent parts:

$$\text{part} \in \{\text{edge}, \text{label}, \text{sib}, \text{cop}, \text{gp}\}$$
$$\mathbf{h}_i^{(\text{part-head})} = \text{FNN}^{(\text{part-head})}(\mathbf{r}'_i)$$
$$\mathbf{h}_i^{(\text{part-dep})} = \text{FNN}^{(\text{part-dep})}(\mathbf{r}'_i)$$
$$\mathbf{h}_i^{(\text{gp-head\_dep})} = \text{FNN}^{(\text{gp-head\_dep})}(\mathbf{r}'_i)$$

We then compute the part scores as follows:

$$s_{ij}^{(\text{edge})} = \text{Biaff}^{(\text{edge})}(\mathbf{h}_i^{(\text{edge-dep})}, \mathbf{h}_j^{(\text{edge-head})}) \quad (7)$$

$$\mathbf{s}_{ij}^{(\text{label})} = \text{Biaff}^{(\text{label})}(\mathbf{h}_i^{(\text{label-dep})}, \mathbf{h}_j^{(\text{label-head})}) \quad (8)$$

$$s_{ij,ik}^{(sib)} \equiv s_{ik,ij}^{(sib)} = \text{Trilin}^{(\text{sib})}(\mathbf{h}_i^{(\text{head})}, \mathbf{h}_j^{(\text{dep})}, \mathbf{h}_k^{(\text{dep})}) \quad (9)$$

$$s_{ij,kj}^{(cop)} \equiv s_{kj,ij}^{(cop)} = \text{Trilin}^{(\text{cop})}(\mathbf{h}_i^{(\text{head})}, \mathbf{h}_j^{(\text{dep})}, \mathbf{h}_k^{(\text{head})}) \quad (10)$$

$$s_{ij,jk}^{(gp)} = \text{Trilin}^{(\text{gp})}(\mathbf{h}_i^{(\text{head})}, \mathbf{h}_j^{(\text{head\_dep})}, \mathbf{h}_k^{(\text{dep})}) \quad (11)$$

In Eq. 7,8, the tensor $\mathbf{U}$ in the biaffine function is $(d \times 1 \times d)$-dimensional and $(d \times c)$-dimensional,

where c is the number of labels. We require $j < k$ in Eq. 9 and $i < k$ in Eq. 10.

In the label-prediction module, $s_{i,j}^{(\text{label})}$ is fed into a softmax layer that outputs the probability of each label for edge (i, j). In the edge-prediction module, we can view computing the edge probabilities as doing posterior inference on a Conditional Random Field (CRF). Each Boolean variable X_{ij} in the CRF indicates whether the directed edge (i, j) exists. We use Eq. 7 to define our unary potential ψ_u representing scores of an edge and Eqs. (9-11) to define our binary potential ψ_p. We define a unary potential $\phi_u(X_{ij})$ for each variable X_{ij}.

$$\phi_u(X_{ij}) = \begin{cases} \exp(s_{ij}^{(\text{edge})}) & X_{ij} = 1 \\ 1 & X_{ij} = 0 \end{cases}$$

For each pair of edges (i, j) and (k, l) that form a second-order part of a specific *type*, we define a binary potential $\phi_p(X_{ij}, X_{kl})$.

$$\phi_p(X_{ij}, X_{kl}) = \begin{cases} \exp(s_{ij,kl}^{(type)}) & X_{ij} = X_{kl} = 1 \\ 1 & \text{Otherwise} \end{cases}$$

Exact inference on this CRF is intractable. We use mean field variational inference to approximate a true posterior distribution with a factorized variational distribution and tries to iteratively minimize their KL divergence. We can derive the following iterative update equations of distribution

$Q_{ij}(X_{ij})$ for each edge (i, j).

$$\mathcal{F}_{ij}^{(t-1)} = \sum_{k \neq i,j} Q_{ik}^{(t-1)}(1)s_{ij,ik}^{(sib)} + Q_{kj}^{(t-1)}(1)s_{ij,kj}^{(cop)}$$
$$+ Q_{jk}^{(t-1)}(1)s_{ij,jk}^{(gp)} + Q_{ki}^{(t-1)}(1)s_{ki,ij}^{(gp)} \tag{12}$$
$$Q_{ij}^{(t)}(0) \propto 1$$
$$Q_{ij}^{(t)}(1) \propto \exp\{s_{ij}^{(\text{edge})} + \mathcal{F}_{ij}^{(t-1)}\}$$

The initial distribution $Q_{ij}^{(0)}(X_{ij})$ is set by normalizing the unary potential $\phi_u(X_{ij})$. We iteratively update the distributions for T steps and then output $Q_{ij}^{(T)}(X_{ij})$, where T is a hyperparameter. We can then predict the parse graph by including every edge $y_{ij}^{(\text{edge})}$ such that $Q_{ij}^{(T)}(1) > 0.5$. The edge labels $y_{ij}^{(\text{label})}$ are predicted by maximizing the label probabilities computed by the label-prediction module.

$$P(y_{ij}^{(\text{edge})}|\mathbf{w}) = \text{softmax}(Q_{ij}^{(T)}(X_{ij}))$$
$$P(y_{ij}^{(\text{label})}|\mathbf{w}) = \text{softmax}(\mathbf{s}_{ij}^{(\text{label})})$$

Note that the iterative updates in mean-field variational inference can be seen as a recurrent neural network that is parameterized by the potential functions. Therefore, the whole edge prediction module can be seen as an end-to-end neural network.

3.4 Other Predictions

The shared task also requires prediction of component pieces such as top nodes, node properties, node anchoring and edge attributes. In this section, we present our approaches to predicting these components.

Top Nodes

We add an extra *ROOT* node for each sentence to determine the top node through edge prediction for DM and PSD. For the other frameworks, we use the first predicted node as the top node.

Node Properties

Node properties vary among different frameworks. For DM and PSD, we need to predict the POS and frame for each node. As DM and PSD are bi-lexical semantic graphs, we directly use the prediction of XPOS from the official companion data. We use a single layer MLP fed with word features obtained in Eq. 1 for frame prediction. For EDS, the properties only contain 'carg' and the corresponding values are related to the surface string.

For example, the EDS sub-graph in Fig. 2 contains a node with label 'named' which has property 'carg' with a corresponding value 'Pierre'. The anchor of this node matches the token 'Pierre' in the sentence. We found that nodes with properties have limited types of node labels. Therefore, we exchange node labels and values for EDS nodes containing properties during training. We combine the node *attributes* and value predictions described in Section 2.2 together as a multi-label prediction task. We use a single layer MLP to predict node labels specially for nodes with properties. For each property value, we regard it as a node label and use the extended pointer-generator network described in Section 3.2 to predict it. Therefore, the probability of node property prediction is:

$$P_{prop} = \text{softmax}(\mathbf{W}_{\text{prop}}\widetilde{\mathbf{r}}_t' + \mathbf{b}_{\text{prop}}) \tag{13}$$

Node Anchoring

As DM and PSD contain only token level dependencies, we can decide a node anchor by the corresponding token. For the other frameworks, we use two biaffine functions to predict the 'start token' and 'end token' for each node and the final anchor range is decided by the start position of 'start token' and the end position of 'end token'. The biaffine function is fed by word features from the encoder RNN and node features from decoder RNN.

$$s_{ij}^{(\text{start/end})} = \text{Biaff}^{(\text{start/end})}(\mathbf{r}_i, \widetilde{\mathbf{z}}_j)$$
$$P_{\text{start/end},j} = \text{softmax}([s_{1j}, s_{2j}, \ldots, s_{nj}]) \tag{14}$$

where i ranges from 1 to n and j ranges from 1 to m.

Edge Attributes

Only UCCA requires prediction of edge attributes, which are the 'remote' attributes of edges. We create new edge labels by combining the original edge labels and edge attributes. In this way, edge attribute prediction is done by edge label prediction.

3.5 Learning

Given a gold graph $y^\star$, we use the cross entropy loss as learning objective:

$$\mathcal{L}^{(\text{edge})}(\theta) = -\sum_{i,j} \log(P_\theta(y_{ij}^{\star(\text{edge})}|\mathbf{w}))$$
$$\mathcal{L}^{(\text{label})}(\theta) = -\sum_{i,j} \mathbb{1}(y_{ij}^{\star(\text{edge})}) \log(P_\theta(y_{ij}^{\star(\text{label})}|\mathbf{w}))$$

	DM	PSD	EDS	UCCA	AMR
Ours-all	94.88	89.49	86.90	-	63.59
Best-all	**95.50**	**91.28**	**94.47**	**81.67**	**73.38**
Ours-lpps	94.28	85.22	87.49	-	66.82
Best-lpps	**94.96**	**88.46**	**92.82**	**82.61**	**73.11**

Table 1: Comparison of cross-framework F1 scores achieved by our system and best scores of other teams for each metric. *all* represents the F1 score over the full test set for each framework. *lpps* represents a 100-sentence sample from the little prince containing graphs over all the frameworks.

$$\mathcal{L}^{(\text{prop})}(\theta) = -\sum_{i,k} \log(P_\theta(y_{ik}^{\star(\text{prop})}|\mathbf{w}))$$

$$\mathcal{L}^{(\text{anchor})}(\theta) = -\sum_{i} \sum_{j \in \{\text{start},\text{end}\}} (\log(P_\theta(y_i^{\star(j)}|\mathbf{w})))$$

where θ is all the parameters of the model, $\mathbb{1}(\mathcal{X})$ is an indicator function of whether $\mathcal{X}$ exists in the graph, i, j range over all the nodes and k ranges over all possible *attributes* in the graph. The total loss is defined by:

$$\mathcal{L} = \lambda_1 \mathcal{L}^{(\text{edge})} + \lambda_2 \mathcal{L}^{(\text{label})} + \mathbb{1}(y^{\star(\text{prop})})\lambda_3 \mathcal{L}^{(\text{prop})} \\ + \mathbb{1}(y^{\star(\text{anchor})})\lambda_4 \mathcal{L}^{(\text{anchor})}$$

where $\lambda_{1,...,4}$ are hyperparameters. For DM and PSD, we tuned on λ_1, λ_2 and λ_3. For other frameworks, we set all of them to be 1.

4 Experiments and Results

4.1 Training

For DM, PSD and EDS, we used the same dataset split as previous approaches (Martins and Almeida, 2014; Du et al., 2015) with 33,964 sentence in the training set and 1,692 sentences in the development set. For each of the other frameworks, we randomly chose 5% to 10% of the training set as the development set. We additionally removed graphs with more than 60 nodes (or with input sentences longer than 60 words for DM and PSD). We trained our model for each framework separately and used Adam (Kingma and Ba, 2015) to optimize our system, annealing the learning rate by 0.5 for 10,000 steps. We trained the model for 100,000 iterations with a batch size of 6,000 tokens and terminated with 10,000 iterations without improvement on the development set.

4.2 Main Results

Due to an unexpected bug in UCCA anchor prediction, we failed to submit our UCCA prediction.

Our results are still competitive to those of the other teams and we get the 3rd place for the DM framework in the official metrics. The main result is shown in Table 1. Our system performs well on the DM framework with an F1 score only 0.4 percent F1 below the best score on DM. Note that our system does not learn to predict node labels for DM and PSD and simply uses lemmas from the companion data as node labels. We find that compared to gold lemmas from the original SDP dataset, lemmas from the companion data have only 71.4% accuracy. We believe that it is the main reason for the F1 score gap between our system and the best one on DM and PSD. A detailed comparison between each component will be discussed in Section 4.3. For PSD, EDS and AMR graph, our system ranks 6th, 5th and 7th among 13 teams.

4.3 Analysis

DM and PSD

Table 2 and 3 show detailed comparison for each evaluation component for DM and PSD. For DM, our system outperforms systems of the other teams on tops, properties and edges prediction and is competitive on anchors. For PSD, our system is also competitive on all the components except labels. There is a large gap in the performance of node label prediction between our system and the best one on both DM and PSD, we believe adding an MLP layer for label prediction would diminish this gap.

Table 4 shows the performance comparison on in-framework metrics for DM and PSD. For DM, our system outperforms the best of the other systems by 0.5 and 0.8 F1 scores on *all* and *lpps* test sets. For PSD, our system outperforms the best of the other systems by 0.4 F1 score for *lpps* and only 0.05 F1 score below the best score for *all*.

AMR

For AMR graph prediction, our node prediction module is based on Zhang et al. (2019), but our edge prediction module is based on the second-order method of Wang et al. (2019). To verify the effectiveness of second-order edge prediction, we compare the performances on the development set of our model and Zhang et al. (2019). The result is shown in Table 5. The result shows that our second-order edge prediction is useful not only on the SDP frameworks but also on the AMR framework.

	tops	labels	properties	anchors	edges	average
Ours-all	**93.68**	90.51	**95.16**	98.38	**92.32**	94.32
Best-all	93.23	**96.34**	94.93	**98.74**	92.08	**94.76**
Ours-lpps	**99.00**	87.26	**94.53**	**99.36**	**93.92**	94.03
Best-lpps	96.48	**94.82**	94.36	99.04	93.28	**94.64**

Table 2: Comparison of cross-framework F1 scores achieved by our system and best scores of the other teams for each evaluation component on DM. *average* is the micro-average among all components.

	tops	labels	properties	anchors	edges	average
Ours-all	95.68	84.79	91.83	97.66	**79.50**	88.77
Best-all	**95.83**	**94.68**	**92.38**	**98.35**	79.44	**90.76**
Ours-lpps	96.00	76.72	84.73	97.61	**79.80**	85.22
Best-lpps	**96.40**	**92.04**	**86.00**	**98.46**	79.18	**88.40**

Table 3: Comparison of cross-framework F1 scores achieved by our system and best scores of the other teams for each evaluation component on PSD.

	DM		PSD		Avg	
	all	lpps	all	lpps	all	lpps
Ours	**92.98**	**94.46**	81.61	**81.91**	**87.30**	**88.19**
Best	92.52	93.68	**81.66**	81.47	87.09	87.58

Table 4: Comparison of in-framework labeled F1 scores by our system and best scores over the other teams. Note that the *Best* scores are not only from a single system.

Model	Smatch
Zhang et al. (2019)	69.1
Ours	69.3

Table 5: Smatch F1 score on AMR development set. We compare the results without post-processing.

Set	MRP	Smatch
test	63.59	63.08
dev	72.03	71.55

Table 6: MRP and Smatch score on the development set and the test set.

From the official results on the test sets, we find it surprising that there is a huge gap between the test and development results on both the MRP and the Smatch (Cai and Knight, 2013) scores, as shown in Table 6. In future work, we will figure out the reason behind this problem.

EDS

For EDS, our parser ranks 5th. There are multiple details of our parser that can be improved. For example, our anchor prediction module described in Eq. 14 (ranking 4th in the task) may occasionally predict an end anchor positioned before a start anchor, which would be rejected by the evaluation system. This can be fixed by adding constraints.

UCCA

For UCCA, we failed to submit the result because of the same reversed start-end anchor predictions, which prevents us from obtaining an MRP score.

4.4 Ablation Study

BERT with Other Embeddings

We use BERT (Devlin et al., 2019) embedding in our model. We compared the performance of DM in the original SDP dataset with different subtoken pooling methods, and we also explored whether combining other embeddings such as pre-trained word embedding Glove (Pennington et al., 2014) and contextual embedding ELMo (Peters et al., 2018) will further improve the performance. The detailed results are shown in table 7. We found that Glove, lemma and character embeddings are helpful for DM and fine-tuning on the training set slightly improves the performance. ELMo embedding is also helpful but cannot outperform BERT embedding. However, the performance dropped when ELMo embedding and BERT embedding are combined. We speculate that the drop is caused by the conflict between the two types of contextual information. For subtoken pooling, we compared the performance of using first subtoken pooling and average pooling as token embedding. We found that average pooling is slightly better than

	LF1
Baseline	93.41
Base-fixed	94.17
Base-tuned	94.22
Base-fixed + Glove	94.45
Base-tuned + Glove	94.48
Large-fixed + Glove	94.62
Large-tuned + Glove	94.64
Large-fixed + Glove + Lemma	95.10
Large-fixed + Glove + Lemma + Char	95.22
ELMo + Large-fixed + Glove + Lemma	94.78
ELMo + Glove + Lemma + Char	95.06
BERT-First	95.22
BERT-Avg	95.28
BERT-Avg + dep-tree	95.30

Table 7: Comparing Labeled F1 scores of models with different types of embedding combinations on the development set of the gold DM dataset. *Baseline* represents the parser of Wang et al. (2019). *Base* represents the pre-trained BERT-Base uncased model and *Large* represents the pre-trained BERT-Large uncased model. *fixed* and *tuned* represents whether to fine-tune the BERT model. *BERT* in the last block represents the last embedding combination (Large-fixed + Glove + Lemma + Char) in the first block. *First* represents first subtoken pooling, *Avg* represents average pooling over subtokens. *dep-tree* represents adding dependency information into embeddings. For each case, we report the highest Labeled F1 score on the development set in our experiments.

	DM	PSD
basic	96.01	90.80
+lemma	96.09	90.79
+ner	96.07	90.80
+lemma & ner	**96.16**	**90.88**

Table 8: F1 score averaged over the labeled F1 score and the frame F1 score on the development sets of DM and PSD. *basic* represents our model with embeddings described in 3.1 except lemma and named entity embeddings.

first pooling. For syntactic information, we encode each head word and dependency label as embeddings and concatenate them together with other embeddings. The result shows that syntactic information as embeddings is not very helpful for the task. We will try other methods utilizing syntactic information in future work.

Lemma and Named Entity Tags

Dozat and Manning (2018) found that gold lemma embedding is helpful for semantic dependency parsing. However, in section 4.2, we note that the lemmas from the official companion data have only 71.4% accuracy compared to lemmas in gold SDP data, which makes lemma embeddings less helpful for parsing. We found that one of the difference is about the lemma annotations of entities, for example, lemmas of "Pierre Vinken" are "Pierre" and "Vinken" in the companion data while the lemmas are named-entity-like tags "Pierre" and "_generic_proper_ne" in the original SDP dataset. Based on this discovery, we experimented on the influence of named entity tags on parsing performance. We used Illinois Named Entity Tagger (Ratinov and Roth, 2009) in white list to predict named entity tags and compared the performance on the development sets of DM and PSD. The result is shown in table 8. We tuned the hyperparameters for all the embedding conditions in the table, and we found that adding lemma or named entity embeddings results in a slight improvement on DM but does not help on PSD. With both lemma and named entity embeddings, there is a further improvement on both DM and PSD, which shows the named entity tags are helpful for semantic dependency parsing. As a result, we apply named entity information in parsing other frameworks.

5 Conclusion

In this paper, we present our graph-based parsing system for MRP 2019, which combines two state-of-the-art methods for sequence to graph node generation and second-order edge inference. The result shows that our system performs well on the DM and PSD frameworks and achieves the best scores on the in-framework metrics. For future work, we will improve our system to achieve better performance on all these frameworks and explore cross-framework multi-task learning. Our code for DM and PSD is available at `https://github.com/wangxinyu0922/Second_Order_SDP`.

References

Omri Abend and Ari Rappoport. 2013. Universal conceptual cognitive annotation (UCCA). In *Proceedings of the 51st Annual Meeting of the Association* for Computational Linguistics (Volume 1: Long Papers), pages 228–238, Sofia, Bulgaria. Association for Computational Linguistics.

Laura Banarescu, Claire Bonial, Shu Cai, Madalina Georgescu, Kira Griffitt, Ulf Hermjakob, Kevin Knight, Philipp Koehn, Martha Palmer, and Nathan Schneider. 2013. Abstract meaning representation for sembanking. In *Proceedings of the 7th Linguistic Annotation Workshop and Interoperability with Discourse*, pages 178–186, Sofia, Bulgaria. Association for Computational Linguistics.

Shu Cai and Kevin Knight. 2013. Smatch: an evaluation metric for semantic feature structures. In *Proceedings of the 51st Annual Meeting of the Association for Computational Linguistics (Volume 2: Short Papers)*, pages 748–752, Sofia, Bulgaria. Association for Computational Linguistics.

Jacob Devlin, Ming-Wei Chang, Kenton Lee, and Kristina Toutanova. 2019. BERT: Pre-training of deep bidirectional transformers for language understanding. In *Proceedings of the 2019 Conference of the North American Chapter of the Association for Computational Linguistics: Human Language Technologies, Volume 1 (Long and Short Papers)*, pages 4171–4186, Minneapolis, Minnesota. Association for Computational Linguistics.

Timothy Dozat and Christopher D Manning. 2017. Deep biaffine attention for neural dependency parsing. In *International Conference on Learning Representations*.

Timothy Dozat and Christopher D. Manning. 2018. Simpler but more accurate semantic dependency parsing. In *Proceedings of the 56th Annual Meeting of the Association for Computational Linguistics (Volume 2: Short Papers)*, pages 484–490, Melbourne, Australia. Association for Computational Linguistics.

Yantao Du, Fan Zhang, Xun Zhang, Weiwei Sun, and Xiaojun Wan. 2015. Peking: Building semantic dependency graphs with a hybrid parser. In *Proceedings of the 9th international workshop on semantic evaluation (semeval 2015)*, pages 927–931.

Dan Flickinger, Emily M. Bender, and Woodley Packard. 2016. English resource semantics. In *Proceedings of the 2016 Conference of the North American Chapter of the Association for Computational Linguistics: Tutorial Abstracts*, pages 1–5, San Diego, California. Association for Computational Linguistics.

Jan Hajič, Eva Hajičová, Jarmila Panevová, Petr Sgall, Ondřej Bojar, Silvie Cinková, Eva Fučíková, Marie Mikulová, Petr Pajas, Jan Popelka, Jiří Semecký, Jana Šindlerová, Jan Štěpánek, Josef Toman, Zdeňka Urešová, and Zdeněk Žabokrtský. 2012. Announcing Prague Czech-English dependency treebank 2.0. In *Proceedings of the Eighth International Conference on Language Resources and Evaluation (LREC-2012)*, pages 3153–3160, Istanbul, Turkey. European Languages Resources Association (ELRA).

Daniel Hershcovich, Omri Abend, and Ari Rappoport. 2018. Multitask parsing across semantic representations. In *Proceedings of the 56th Annual Meeting of the Association for Computational Linguistics (Volume 1: Long Papers)*, pages 373–385, Melbourne, Australia. Association for Computational Linguistics.

Angelina Ivanova, Stephan Oepen, Lilja Øvrelid, and Dan Flickinger. 2012. Who did what to whom? A contrastive study of syntacto-semantic dependencies. In *Proceedings of the 6th Linguistic Annotation Workshop*, pages 2–11, Jeju, Republic of Korea.

Diederik P Kingma and Jimmy Ba. 2015. Adam: A method for stochastic optimization. In *International Conference on Learning Representations*.

Shuhei Kurita and Anders Søgaard. 2019. Multi-task semantic dependency parsing with policy gradient for learning easy-first strategies. In *Proceedings of the 57th Annual Meeting of the Association for Computational Linguistics*, pages 2420–2430, Florence, Italy. Association for Computational Linguistics.

André FT Martins and Mariana SC Almeida. 2014. Priberam: A turbo semantic parser with second order features. In *Proceedings of the 8th International Workshop on Semantic Evaluation (SemEval 2014)*, pages 471–476.

Yusuke Miyao, Stephan Oepen, and Daniel Zeman. 2014. In-house: An ensemble of pre-existing off-the-shelf parsers. In *Proceedings of the 8th International Workshop on Semantic Evaluation (SemEval 2014)*, pages 335–340, Dublin, Ireland. Association for Computational Linguistics.

Stephan Oepen, Omri Abend, Jan Hajič, Daniel Hershcovich, Marco Kuhlmann, Tim O'Gorman, Nianwen Xue, Jayeol Chun, Milan Straka, and Zdeňka Urešová. 2019. MRP 2019: Cross-framework Meaning Representation Parsing. In *Proceedings of the Shared Task on Cross-Framework Meaning Representation Parsing at the 2019 Conference on Natural Language Learning*, pages 1–27, Hong Kong, China.

Stephan Oepen, Marco Kuhlmann, Yusuke Miyao, Daniel Zeman, Silvie Cinková, Dan Flickinger, Jan Hajič, and Zdeňka Urešová. 2015. SemEval 2015 task 18: Broad-coverage semantic dependency parsing. In *Proceedings of the 9th International Workshop on Semantic Evaluation (SemEval 2015)*, pages 915–926, Denver, Colorado. Association for Computational Linguistics.

Stephan Oepen, Marco Kuhlmann, Yusuke Miyao, Daniel Zeman, Dan Flickinger, Jan Hajič, Angelina Ivanova, and Yi Zhang. 2014. SemEval 2014 task

8: Broad-coverage semantic dependency parsing. In *Proceedings of the 8th International Workshop on Semantic Evaluation (SemEval 2014)*, pages 63–72, Dublin, Ireland. Association for Computational Linguistics.

Stephan Oepen and Jan Tore Lønning. 2006. Discriminant-based MRS banking. In *Proceedings of the Fifth International Conference on Language Resources and Evaluation (LREC'06)*, Genoa, Italy. European Language Resources Association (ELRA).

Hao Peng, Sam Thomson, and Noah A. Smith. 2017. Deep multitask learning for semantic dependency parsing. In *Proceedings of the 55th Annual Meeting of the Association for Computational Linguistics (Volume 1: Long Papers)*, pages 2037–2048, Vancouver, Canada. Association for Computational Linguistics.

Hao Peng, Sam Thomson, Swabha Swayamdipta, and Noah A. Smith. 2018. Learning joint semantic parsers from disjoint data. In *Proceedings of the 2018 Conference of the North American Chapter of the Association for Computational Linguistics: Human Language Technologies, Volume 1 (Long Papers)*, pages 1492–1502, New Orleans, Louisiana. Association for Computational Linguistics.

Jeffrey Pennington, Richard Socher, and Christopher Manning. 2014. Glove: Global vectors for word representation. In *Proceedings of the 2014 conference on empirical methods in natural language processing (EMNLP)*, pages 1532–1543.

Matthew Peters, Mark Neumann, Mohit Iyyer, Matt Gardner, Christopher Clark, Kenton Lee, and Luke Zettlemoyer. 2018. Deep contextualized word representations. In *Proceedings of the 2018 Conference of the North American Chapter of the Association for Computational Linguistics: Human Language Technologies, Volume 1 (Long Papers)*, pages 2227–2237, New Orleans, Louisiana. Association for Computational Linguistics.

Lev Ratinov and Dan Roth. 2009. Design Challenges and Misconceptions in Named Entity Recognition. In *Proc. of the Conference on Computational Natural Language Learning (CoNLL)*.

Gabriel Stanovsky and Ido Dagan. 2018. Semantics as a foreign language. In *Proceedings of the 2018 Conference on Empirical Methods in Natural Language Processing*, pages 2412–2421, Brussels, Belgium. Association for Computational Linguistics.

Xinyu Wang, Jingxian Huang, and Kewei Tu. 2019. Second-order semantic dependency parsing with end-to-end neural networks. In *Proceedings of the 57th Annual Meeting of the Association for Computational Linguistics*, pages 4609–4618, Florence, Italy. Association for Computational Linguistics.

Sheng Zhang, Xutai Ma, Kevin Duh, and Benjamin Van Durme. 2019. AMR Parsing as Sequence-to-Graph Transduction. In *Proceedings of the 57th Annual Meeting of the Association for Computational Linguistics (Volume 1: Long Papers)*, Florence, Italy. Association for Computational Linguistics.

Saarland at MRP 2019:
Compositional parsing across all graphbanks

Lucia Donatelli, Meaghan Fowlie[*], Jonas Groschwitz, Alexander Koller,
Matthias Lindemann, Mario Mina, Pia Weißenhorn
Department of Language Science and Technology, Saarland University
[*] Department of Linguistics, Utrecht University
`{donatelli|jonasg|koller|mlinde|mariom|piaw}@coli.uni-saarland.de`
`m.fowlie@uu.nl`

Abstract

We describe the Saarland University submission to the shared task on Cross-Framework Meaning Representation Parsing (MRP) at the 2019 Conference on Computational Natural Language Learning (CoNLL).

1 Introduction

In this paper, we describe the semantic parser submitted by Saarland University to the MRP shared task (Oepen et al., 2019)[1]. This task consists in learning to accurately map English sentences to graph-based meaning representations across five different graphbanks.

There has been substantial previous work on graph parsing for each of the graphbanks in MRP, including DM and PSD (Peng et al., 2017; Dozat and Manning, 2018), EDS (Buys and Blunsom, 2017; Chen et al., 2018), AMR (Flanigan et al., 2014; Buys and Blunsom, 2017; Lyu and Titov; Zhang et al., 2019), and UCCA (Hershcovich et al., 2017, 2018; Jiang et al., 2019). One advantage of our parser is that it works accurately across all graphbanks at the same time.

Instead of learning to map directly from sentences to graphs, our parser learns to map sentences to *AM dependency trees*. Each AM dependency tree consists of a graph for the lexical meaning of each token in the sentence, along with a dependency tree that specifies the words that fill each semantic role of a given predicate. An AM dependency tree can be deterministically evaluated to a graph via the *AM Algebra* (Groschwitz et al., 2017). Thus, the parser compositionally maps sentences to graphs, with the AM dependency trees describing the compositional structure of the meaning representation. We will sketch the background on AM dependency trees in Section 2.

In earlier work, we showed how to accurately predict AM dependency trees for AMR using a neural dependency parser and supertagger (Groschwitz et al., 2018). We extended this parser from AMR to the DM, PAS, PSD, and EDS graphbanks and obtained state-of-the-art results across all of these graphbanks (Lindemann et al., 2019); we will call this system the *ACL-19 parser* throughout this paper. Earlier semantic parsers were only available for one or two families of closely related graphbanks; our system was the first to parse accurately across a range of different graphbanks. We took this parser as the starting point of our MRP submission; we explain the minor tweaks that were needed for the MRP flavors of DM, PSD, EDS, and AMR in Section 3.

The one MRP graphbank which was not directly supported by the ACL-19 parser is UCCA (Abend and Rappoport, 2013). We thus implemented heuristics for converting UCCA annotations into AM dependency graphs. Certain design decisions in UCCA made this more difficult than for the other graphbanks; we worked around some of these in preprocessing. We describe the details in Section 4.

We present detailed evaluation results in Section 5. We also describe a few post-deadline improvements, which bring our parser up to an MRP f-score of 71.6 on AMR and 70.1 on UCCA.

2 AM dependency parsing

We start by describing the ACL-19 parser (Lindemann et al., 2019). This parser is trained to map sentences into *AM dependency trees*, which are then deterministically evaluated to graphs in the *AM algebra*.

2.1 AM Algebra

The Apply-Modify Algebra (AM algebra; Groschwitz et al. (2017)) builds graphs from graph

---

[1] `http://mrp.nlpl.eu`

Proceedings of the Shared Task on Cross-Framework Meaning Representation Parsing at the 2019 CoNLL, pages 66–75
Hong Kong, November 3, 2019. ©2019 Association for Computational Linguistics
https://doi.org/10.18653/v1/K19-2006

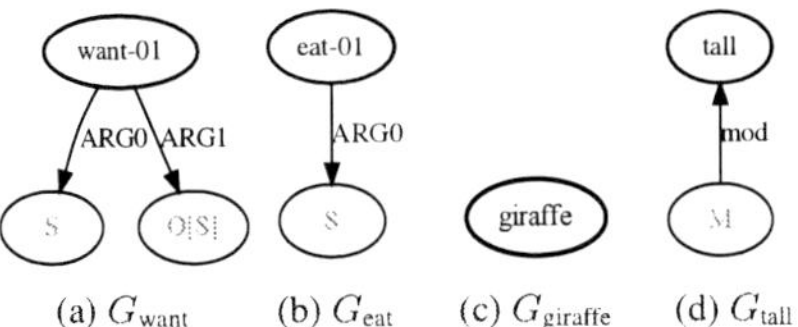

Figure 1: As-graphs (= supertags) for the words in the sentence "the tall giraffe wants to eat."

fragments called *annotated s-graphs*, or *as-graphs*. Figures 1a–1d show as-graphs from which the AMR in Fig. 3c for the sentence "the tall giraffe wants to eat" can be built. An as-graph is a labeled, directed graph, some of whose nodes have been marked as *sources*. Every as-graph used in AM dependency parsing has one special root source node, indicated with a bold outline. We mark the other sources with red labels (e.g. S and O); these are nodes at which the root source node of another as-graph will be inserted.

The AM algebra defines two operations for combining as-graphs: Apply, which combines a head with a semantic argument, and Modify, which combines a head with a modifier. Fig. 2a shows a term using these operations that evaluates to the AMR in Fig. 3c.

The result of the Apply-O operation APP_O $(G_{\text{want}}, G_{\text{eat}})$ is shown in Fig. 3a, where the root of the argument G_{eat} is inserted into the O-source of the head G_{want}. The annotation "[S]" at this O-source means that the O-argument must still have an S-source, as is the case for G_{eat}. When two graphs that share a source name are combined, the shared sources automatically merge, creating a re-entrancy. In our example this occurs for the S-source, creating a shared subject slot for G_{want} and G_{eat}.

Fig. 3b shows the result of the Modify-M operation MOD_M $(G_{\text{giraffe}}, G_{\text{tall}})$. The M-source of the modifier G_{tall} is merged with the root of the head G_{giraffe}, which has the effect of adding the modifier to G_{giraffe}; the operation leaves the root of G_{giraffe} where it was. Modify is defined only when it adds no new sources to the head.

Finally, the APP_S operation at the root of the term combines the two graphs we built so far, plugging the graph for "tall giraffe" into the S source of the combined want-eat graph. This yields the full graph in Fig. 3c. From a linguistic perspective, a term over the AM algebra serves as a compositional derivation (Montague, 1973) of the graph to which it evaluates.

For this last operation, too, a restriction applies: if a source has no annotation, like the S-source in Fig. 3a, the graph inserted there must have no remaining non-root sources (as is the case here). Thus, both Apply and Modify have restrictions on when they can be used. A term over the AM algebra that satisfies all these restrictions is called *well-typed*.

2.2 AM Dependency Parsing

Note that in a term over the AM algebra, such as in Fig. 2a, the root source of the resulting graph is always inherited from the left child; i.e. the left child is always the head. For example, after APP_O $(G_{\text{want}}, G_{\text{eat}})$, the head is still G_{want}. We can track the heads through the term, as indicated by the colors in the example term. This allows us to read terms over the AM algebra as *AM dependency trees* in the following manner. Each operation between two graphs is encoded as a dependency edge from the head to the argument (or modifier respectively), and the edge is labeled with the relevant operation. By aligning the graph fragments to the words in the sentence, we get a dependency tree over the sentence. As a result, the term in Fig. 2a can be unambiguously encoded as the dependency tree in Fig. 2b (Groschwitz et al., 2018).

We can now perform *AM dependency parsing* by training models for the following two tasks: (i) a supertagger to predict the as-graphs for the individual word tokens (such as G_{want}) and (ii) a dependency parser to predict the dependency tree. Together, these two components predict an AM dependency tree, which then evaluates to a graph in the AM algebra as explained above.

Both of these tasks can be performed by neural models with high accuracy. We train a BiLSTM to predict a supertag for each token and use the dependency parser of Kiperwasser and Goldberg (2016) to predict dependency trees. To ensure that we obtain well-typed AM dependency trees, we use the *fixed-tree decoder* algorithm of Groschwitz et al. (2018).

2.3 Decomposition

To train the neural supertagging and dependency models, we need AM dependency trees for the training set. However, the available graphbanks contain only sentences with their graph annotations. Thus we have to *decompose* the graphs in each graphbank into the corresponding AM dependency trees. We do this with handwritten heuristics, which we

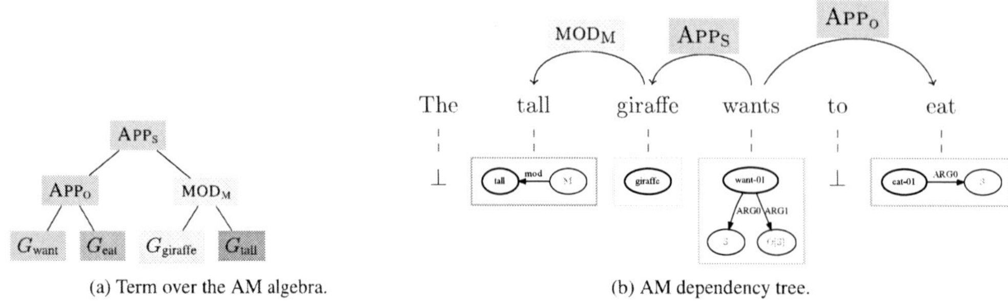

(a) Term over the AM algebra.

(b) AM dependency tree.

Figure 2: Compositional derivation of the example AMR graph in Fig. 3c.

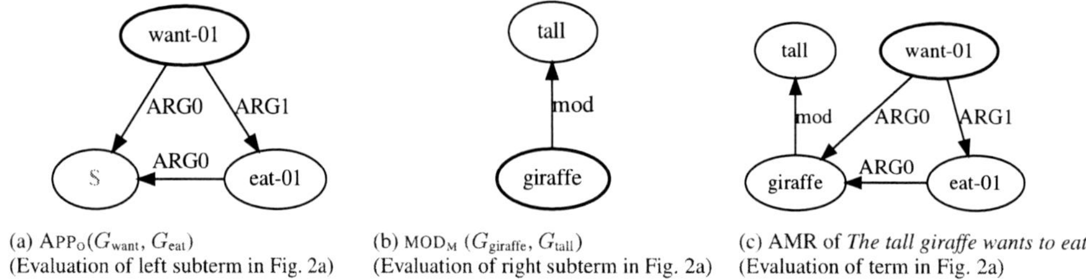

(a) APP_O(G_want, G_eat)
(Evaluation of left subterm in Fig. 2a)

(b) MOD_M (G_giraffe, G_tall)
(Evaluation of right subterm in Fig. 2a)

(c) AMR of *The tall giraffe wants to eat*
(Evaluation of term in Fig. 2a)

Figure 3: As-graphs to which the AM term in Fig. 2a and some of its subterms evaluate.

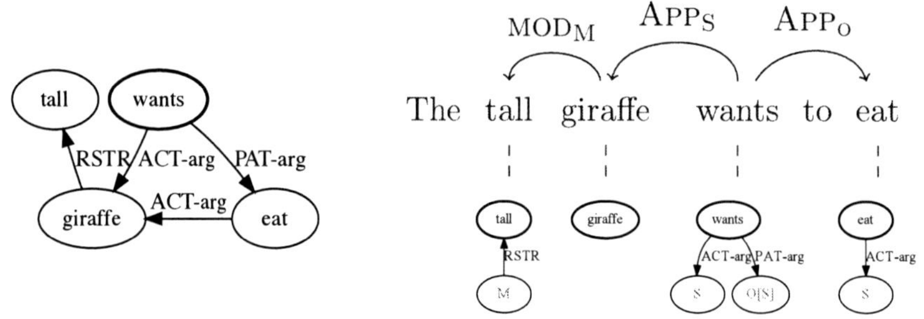

Figure 4: PSD graph (left) for *The tall giraffe wants to eat* and its AM dependency tree (right).

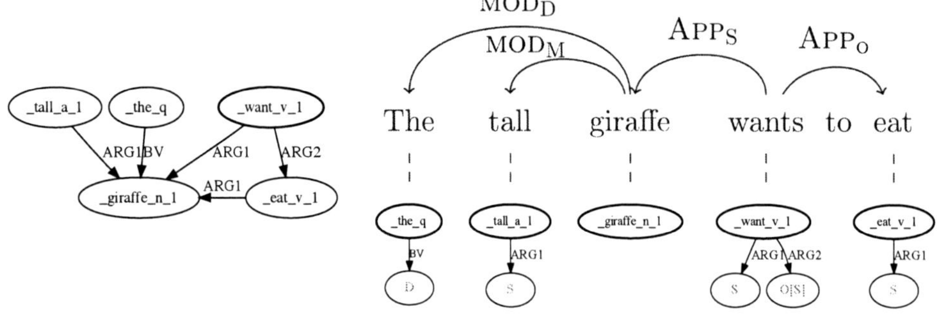

Figure 5: EDS graph (left) for *The tall giraffe wants to eat* and its AM dependency tree (right).

defined for AMR in Groschwitz et al. (2018) and for DM, PAS, PSD, and EDS in Lindemann et al. (2019). The decomposition heuristics perform the following three steps:

1. **align** graph nodes to words (not necessary for graphbanks with annotated alignments between tokens and nodes),

2. **group edges** with nodes, splitting the graph into disjoint aligned fragments,

3. **assign sources** and type annotations to the argument/modification slots of each graph fragment.

These steps define the supertags, and the dependency edges follow from there. Empirically, given an assignment of supertags to tokens, there is never more than one dependency tree which evaluates to the correct graph.

While the AM algebra was originally designed for AMR, the ACL-19 parser extends it to DM, PAS, PSD and EDS as well. In fact, as the AM algebra adds a layer of abstraction on top of the original graphs, using the same parser for all graphbanks becomes easy. Conceptually, we only need a different set of graph fragment supertags for each graphbank.

The decomposition heuristics for PSD and EDS are illustrated in Fig. 4 (PSD) and Fig. 5 (EDS), both for the same sentence "the tall giraffe wants to eat" whose AMR analysis we discussed in Fig. 2b. The examples show that structural differences in the graphbanks can lead to different AM dependencies: for example, the article "the" is part of the EDS graph but not of the PSD and AMR graphs. Overall, however, the AM dependency trees are much more uniform than the underlying graphs.

In Step 2, we group argument edges with the relevant head and modifying edges with the modifier. This yields consistent supertags: for example, "giraffe" can be assigned the same supertag regardless of whether and how many times it is modified. Our heuristics form these groups based only on the edge labels. For example, in AMR, DM and EDS, we group all 'ARGx' labels with their source node. In AMR, we group 'mod' edges with their target node (the modifier), and do the same with 'RSTR' edges in PSD.

The source names are loosely inspired by (deep) syntactic relations; for example, we use the source name S for the endpoints of 'ARG0' edges in AMR,

'ACT-arg' edges in PSD, and 'ARG1' edges in EDS, because these edge labels all correspond to "deep subjects". We also add variants of source assignments to account for e.g. passive. The source annotations are obtained by matching certain patterns in the final graph. For example, the [S] annotation in G_{want} in Figure 3 is added because of the triangle structure in the final graph. Details of these heuristics can be found in Lindemann et al. (2019).

3 Changes to the ACL-19 parser

For the DM, PSD, EDS, and AMR parts of the shared task, we used the ACL-19 parser with the following minor modifications.

3.1 Decomposition heuristics

We did not change any edge attachment or source naming heuristics, but focused on complying with the rules of the shared task and accommodating changes in the graphbanks.

EDS While the ACL-19 parser only dealt with connected EDS graphs, the training corpus of the shared task also contains disconnected graphs. We handle this in the same manner as we handle disconnected graphs in DM and PSD: by introducing an additional node that has a child in each of the disconnected components. This child is chosen as the node being anchored in the highest node in a UD dependency analysis. Along with this node, we introduce a corresponding additional artificial token to the end of the sentence.

Because our decomposition heuristics require a full alignment between tokens and nodes, but the EDS annotations can anchor arbitrary subgraphs in arbitrary substrings, we have to translate EDS anchorings into node-token alignments. We refine our method from the ACL-19 paper in two ways. First, we align *implicit conjunctions* to punctuation in their anchoring span, instead of their leftmost child. Second, we include a special treatment of comparisons in subordinated clauses, where a *subord* node is grouped with a *comp* node, even though they are not immediately connected. This is illustrated in Fig. 6. The ACL-19 heuristic would have tried to group *hard_a_for* and *subord* into one supertag, which makes it impossible to decompose the EDS graph into an AM dependency tree, because this supertag would have to have two root sources: *hard_a_for* for the modification with *comp_too*, and *subord* for the application to

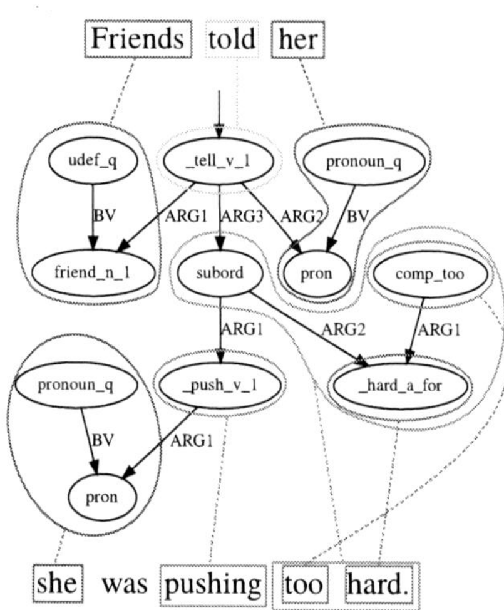

Figure 6: Anchored EDS graph for "Friends told her she was pushing too hard."

_tell_v_1. The revised heuristic instead groups *subord* and *comp_too* into one supertag, which then contains a source node into which *_hard_a_for* can be inserted via Apply.

AMR The aligner we developed for the ACL-19 parser makes non-trivial use of WordNet in order to link tokens to nodes with semantically related labels. Since WordNet was not on the white list of allowed resources, we had to replace it by ConceptNet (Speer et al., 2017). We found that this decreased the dev-set accuracy of our parser by more than a point, possibly because ConceptNet does not distinguish between word senses and thus offers a much larger variety of "hypernyms" than WordNet does.

3.2 Pre- and postprocessing

Unlike earlier versions of the graphbanks and their evaluation metrics, the MRP shared task makes a clear distinction between edges (which link two nodes) and attributes (which attach an atomic value to a node). For instance, information such as polarity and the parts of a named entity are represented as attributes in MRP-style AMR, and parsers are penalized for confusing edges with attributes.

Because our parser uses as-graphs internally, which have node and edge labels but no attributes, we encode attributes into as-graphs. For most graphbanks, we encode attribute information in the node labels and unpack them again in postprocessing. For AMR, we found a considerable amount of noise in the distinction of edges and attributes

in the data. We therefore chose to read attributes as edges and restore the distinction heuristically in postprocessing (see appendix).

EDS Since EDS nodes can be anchored in entire phrases but our parser only provides anchoring for tokens to subgraphs, we applied our ACL-19 heuristics to restore such non-trivial anchorings. Where this failed, we marked the node to be anchored in the entire sentence. The ACL-19 parser deleted unanchored subgraphs for evaluation with EDM (Dridan and Oepen, 2011).

AMR We fixed a postprocessing bug which occasionally resulted in invalid labels in the graph, originating from our procedure for handling rare words.

4 UCCA

For the shared task, we extended the AM dependency parser to UCCA. This was harder than expected. Unlike the other graphbanks, UCCA takes a phrase-structure-like perspective on semantic graphs, in which one terminal node can recursively be the head of several non-terminal nodes (see Fig. 7a). This introduces two challenges for our decomposition heuristic.

First, semantic arguments and modifiers can attach to nodes at any level of the "phrase structure". The graph in Fig. 7a predicates that "office" is an (A)rgument of "success"; these nodes only come together at the root of the UCCA graph. At the same time, the (F)unction word "a" modifies "success" at a lower level of the graph. The obvious decomposition heuristic, which would put the "success" leaf and all the nodes that dominate it into the same supertag, would fail because both of these nodes would have to be root sources, which is not allowed.

Second, under such a decomposition heuristic, the correct supertag for a given word depends on the circumstances. The unmodified word "office" should simply correspond to an as-graph with a single node labeled "office". However, in a sentence where "office" is modified, the correct as-graph consists of "office" with an extra parent node, which is linked to the "office" leaf node with a (C)enter edge (see Fig. 7a). Modifier edges can then attach to this new parent node. This increases lexical ambiguity for our parser, which now has to predict the correct supertag for a word from a larger class of possible supertags.

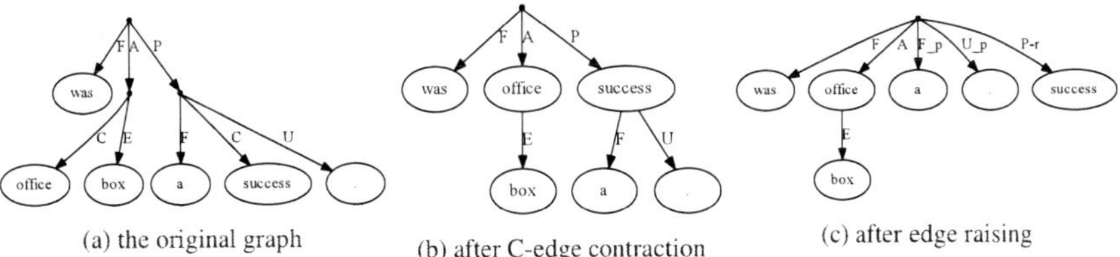

(a) the original graph   (b) after C-edge contraction   (c) after edge raising

Figure 7: Fragment of UCCA graph of the sentence *A Few Good Men was released in 1992 and was a box office success*

We address these issues in preprocessing, which we explain below. Edge attachment and source naming heuristics are in the appendix.

4.1 C-edge contraction

We tackle the second problem by contracting C-edges. Whenever we observe a C-edge in the training data, we delete the C-edge and replace its origin node (a nonterminal node) with the node to which the C-edge points (see Fig. 7b). As an exception, we do not contract C-edges for the conjuncts of a coordination, i.e. those C-edges that have a sister C-edge. This decreases the number of nonterminals in the UCCA graph, reduces lexical ambiguity, and increases the proportion of UCCA training graphs which we can decompose.

At test time, the parser predicts UCCA graphs with contracted C-edges, as in Fig. 7b. We uncontract these by creating an outgoing C-edge from all non-leaf nodes that have node labels, changing these nodes into nonterminal nodes. At uncontraction time, we keep the outgoing edges attached to the nonterminal node.

4.2 Edge raising

C-edge contraction is insufficient to completely solve the first problem. For instance, in Fig. 7b, the as-graph for "success" still has two nodes at which other graphs attach: the U and F edge attach to the "success" node with Modify operations, and the "was" node attaches to a non-terminal node with Modify as well. As above, this means that both "success" and this non-terminal node must be root-sources, which is not allowed.

In order to ensure that only one root-source node is required, we flatten the as-graph for "success" by raising the edges out of the lower node to the upper node, as illustrated in Fig. 7c. This means that all modifiers attach to the same node, which becomes the root-source. We train the semantic parser on these flattened UCCA graphs, and then lower the edges again in postprocessing.

Our objective when applying edge lowering on the graph is to redistribute the edges we had previously raised as they were before pre-processing. The initial idea was to make use of the edge labels and only allow lowering an edge from an upper to a lower node if they are connected by another edge with a specific label; however, we found instances where there were multiple outgoing edges with the same label, which resulted in an ambiguity regarding along which edge to lower. Thus, when we raised an edge from the lower node to the upper node, we also marked the edge that connects them with "-r" (for "raised"), and then lowered along the marked edge.

However, we encountered examples where edge lowering was still ambiguous. We found this to occur when edges were raised from multiple lower nodes to the same upper node, resulting in multiple outgoing edges of that upper node bearing the -r mark. Consequently, we had no way of determining which raised edge belonged to which lower node. To remedy this problem, we added a subindex on each of the raised edges indicating the edge over which we had raised the node (see Figure 7c for the subindices). This means for post-processing only lower a given edge to a node through another edge if the label of the former edge matched the subindex of the latter edge. For example, in Fig. 7c, we can only lower the edges with the labels U_p and F_p through another edge with the label P, which in this case implies that we can only lower these edges to the node "success". This procedure results in unambiguous lowering in most cases.

The edge raising and lowering procedure was *not* part of the submitted system. However, it is part of the improved system.

4.3 H-edge removal

An H-edge represents a scene evoked by a Process or State. These edges are normally outgoing edges of the top node in UCCA. If an H-edge appears in a given graph, it is either unique or accompanied by other H-edges representing multiple parallel scenes and an L-edge to link these scenes, i.e. from the top node there is a single outgoing H-edge in the former case and multiple outgoing H-edges as well as one or more L-edges in the latter. In order to simplify our decomposition heuristics, we remove the H-edge in former case and add it again in post-processing, and only include heuristics for the latter case, rather than distinguish between the two cases.

4.4 Remote edges

We found that removing remote edges drastically helps decomposability. Since this gives us more training data, we decided to remove them and thereby improved decomposability from 34% to 47% in the submitted system.

4.5 Node-token alignments

The UCCA annotation aligns the leaf nodes of the UCCA graph with the tokens in the string; our parser requires an alignment of *all* nodes with their corresponding tokens. We project the aligned tokens upwards from the leaf nodes using a simple set of head percolation rules (see appendix for details).

4.6 Tops

We mark nodes with no incoming edges as top nodes. In an improved version, when more than one top is found, rather than include all of them, we select an arbitrary one.

5 Evaluation

5.1 Experimental setup

We trained one single-task model per graphbank and made use of a concatenation of BERT (Devlin et al., 2019) and Elmo (Peters et al., 2018) embeddings, without any finetuning. We tweaked some hyperparameters of the neural network compared to the ACL-19 parser (see appendix for details).

For DM, PSD and EDS, we use the usual train/dev split. We take a random sample of 3% of all graphs as development data for AMR and 20% for UCCA since there is much less training data.

During parsing, we use the fixed-tree decoder described in Groschwitz et al. (2018) with the six highest-scoring supertags per token. Because the search for a well-typed AM dependency tree is NP-complete, we set a timeout for each graphbank; when the parsing time for a single sentence exceeds

a certain limit, we back off to a smaller number of supertags per token and restart parsing. We used a timeout of 30 minutes for DM, PSD and EDS, a timeout of 5 minutes for UCCA and 15 minutes for AMR. We ensured that every sentence was parsed using at least the highest scoring supertag.

In the ACL-19 parser, we used named entity tags as additional input to the neural network for all graphbanks. Here, we only do so for AMR, whose graphs contain very detailed named entity information. We use the Illinois Named Entity Tagger (Ratinov and Roth, 2009). We make use of the tokenization, POS tags and lemmas provided in the MRP companion data. Our code is publicly available at `https://github.com/coli-saar/am-parser`.

5.2 Results

Table 1 ("submitted") shows the official results of our parser in the shared task. Our parser achieved the highest accuracy on PSD and did very well on DM and EDS. It did much worse on AMR than we expected based on earlier results (Lindemann et al., 2019).

Table 2 shows a more detailed evaluation of the system on the development sets. First, we observe that not all graphs in the development sets can be decomposed by the heuristics described above. This is especially striking for EDS (which frequently requires graphs with multiple sources, see the discussion in Lindemann et al. (2019)) and UCCA, where the edge contraction and raising heuristics were still insufficient to decompose all graphs. The distinction between decomposable and non-decomposable graphs also has a clear effect on development f-score: the f-scores on the decomposable subset of each devset are noticeably higher than on the full devset.

Second, we report the accuracy of the two component parts of our parser: dependency parsing (reported as UAS and LAS) and supertagging (reported as 1-best and 6-best supertagging accuracy). It is noticeable that the errors in some graphbanks (e.g. PSD) are dominated by the supertagger, whereas others are hard for the dependency parser (e.g. UCCA). For most graphbanks, low supertagging accuracy goes together with a large supertag set, and low dependency accuracy with a large set of edge labels. For UCCA, accuracy is low across the board, which may be because the decomposable part of the UCCA training set is so small (47%).

	DM	PSD	EDS	UCCA	AMR	Average
Submitted	94.7	91.3	89.1	67.6	66.7	81.9
Improved	94.7	91.3	89.1	70.1	71.0	83.2
Improved + WordNet/Stanford	94.7	91.3	89.1	70.1	71.6	83.4

Table 1: Results of a single run on official test set (MRP cross-framework f-score).

	DM	PSD	EDS	UCCA	AMR	Average
F-score, complete	96.6	92.7	91.1	65.6	72.0	83.6
F-score, decomposable	96.9	92.8	92.0	74.6	73.5	86.0
Decomposability	93.2	97.2	82.0	48.6	91.3	82.5
UAS	95.4	95.7	94.6	74.7	75.2	87.1
LAS	94.6	91.8	93.4	68.1	69.2	83.4
Supertagging Accuracy (1-best)	96.6	88.6	93.9	74.5	75.2	85.8
Supertagging Accuracy (6-best)	99.8	98.8	99.2	94.2	94.2	97.2
Number supertags	424	1566	2739	298	4705	1946.4
Number edge labels	32	42	34	22	48	35.6

Table 2: Detailed dev set results of the submitted system. All rows except the first and third are based on the decomposable subsets. The last section contains statistics about the decomposed training set.

5.3 Improvements

After the shared task submission deadline, we implemented some further improvements.

AMR We fixed a bug in the post-processing of named entities, which improved the MRP f-score by 0.5 points on the dev set and by 4.3 points on the test set ("improved" in table 1).

We also analyzed the impact of switching out WordNet and the Stanford NER tagger for their whitelisted replacements, ConceptNet and the Illinois NER tagger. As Table 3 shows, the use of the whitelisted resources decreased the AMR devset accuracy by almost 1.5 points. This illustrates the impact of these low-level resources on the evaluation results. Interestingly, this translates only to an improvement of 0.6 points on the test set ("Improved + WordNet/Stanford" in table 1).

We leave an investigation why the magnitude of these improvements differs so much between dev set and test set for future work.

UCCA In contrast to the submitted version, we employed edge raising and lowering and used the improved version of the top handling (see 4.6). We also fixed a bug in the node-token alignments. Overall, this resulted in 85% of the training set being decomposable as opposed to 47% in the submitted system. The results are reported in row two

		Lexical database	
		WordNet	ConceptNet
NER tool	Stanford	73.9	72.7
	Illinois	73.7	72.5

Table 3: Comparison of MRP f-scores on our AMR development set for different NE recognizers and lexical databases, includes bugfix.

of table 1.

6 Conclusion

In this paper, we have described the Saarland University submission to the MRP shared task. Our system is mostly based on our compositional neural graph parser, which had already worked very well across all MRP graphbanks except for UCCA.

We found that extending the parser to UCCA was a challenge due to the radically different graph structures that UCCA uses. We aim to improve the accuracy of our parser on UCCA in future work.

One challenge our system faces is that nontrivial quantities of training data cannot be decomposed by the heuristics we used. It therefore wastes a lot of training data, especially for UCCA. In future work, we will look into better decomposition heuristics, and also into variants of the AM algebra which support multiple root-sources per as-graph.

Acknowledgments. We thank the MRP organizers for their efforts and their availability during the execution of the shared task. We thank Stephan Oepen for pointing out a bug in our AMR postprocessing in an early phase of the shared task. We are grateful to Antoine Venant and Weiwei Sun for discussions and to the anonymous reviewers for their comments.

References

Omri Abend and Ari Rappoport. 2013. Universal conceptual cognitive annotation (ucca). In *Proceedings of the 51st Annual Meeting of the Association for Computational Linguistics*.

Jan Buys and Phil Blunsom. 2017. Robust incremental neural semantic graph parsing. In *Proceedings of the 55th Annual Meeting of the Association for Computational Linguistics*.

Yufei Chen, Weiwei Sun, and Xiaojun Wan. 2018. Accurate SHRG-based semantic parsing. In *Proceedings of the ACL*, Melbourne, Australia.

Jacob Devlin, Ming-Wei Chang, Kenton Lee, and Kristina Toutanova. 2019. BERT: Pre-training of deep bidirectional transformers for language understanding. In *Proceedings of the 2019 Conference of the North American Chapter of the Association for Computational Linguistics: Human Language Technologies*.

Timothy Dozat and Christopher D. Manning. 2018. Simpler but more accurate semantic dependency parsing. In *Proceedings of the 56th Annual Meeting of the Association for Computational Linguistics*.

Rebecca Dridan and Stephan Oepen. 2011. Parser evaluation using elementary dependency matching. In *Proceedings of the 12th International Conference on Parsing Technologies*, pages 225–230.

Jeffrey Flanigan, Sam Thomson, Jaime Carbonell, Chris Dyer, and Noah A. Smith. 2014. A discriminative graph-based parser for the abstract meaning representation. In *Proceedings of the 52nd Annual Meeting of the Association for Computational Linguistics (Volume 1: Long Papers)*.

Jonas Groschwitz, Meaghan Fowlie, Mark Johnson, and Alexander Koller. 2017. A constrained graph algebra for semantic parsing with AMRs. In *Proceedings of the 12th International Conference on Computational Semantics (IWCS)*.

Jonas Groschwitz, Matthias Lindemann, Meaghan Fowlie, Mark Johnson, and Alexander Koller. 2018. AMR Dependency Parsing with a Typed Semantic Algebra. In *Proceedings of the ACL*.

Daniel Hershcovich, Omri Abend, and Ari Rappoport. 2017. A transition-based directed acyclic graph parser for UCCA. In *Proceedings of the ACL*, Vancouver, Canada.

Daniel Hershcovich, Omri Abend, and Ari Rappoport. 2018. Multitask parsing across semantic representations. In *Proceedings of the ACL*.

Wei Jiang, Zhenghua Li, Yu Zhang, and Min Zhang. 2019. HLT@SUDA at SemEval-2019 task 1: UCCA graph parsing as constituent tree parsing. In *Proceedings of the 13th International Workshop on Semantic Evaluation*, Minneapolis, Minnesota, USA.

Eliyahu Kiperwasser and Yoav Goldberg. 2016. Simple and Accurate Dependency Parsing Using Bidirectional LSTM Feature Representations. *Transactions of the Association for Computational Linguistics*, 4:313–327.

Matthias Lindemann, Jonas Groschwitz, and Alexander Koller. 2019. Compositional semantic parsing across graphbanks. In *Proceedings of the ACL*.

Chunchuan Lyu and Ivan Titov. AMR Parsing as Graph Prediction with Latent Alignment. In *Proceedings of the 56th Annual Meeting of the Association for Computational Linguistics*.

Richard Montague. 1973. The proper treatment of quantification in ordinary english. In *Approaches to natural language*, pages 221–242. Springer.

Stephan Oepen, Omri Abend, Jan Hajič, Daniel Hershcovich, Marco Kuhlmann, Tim O'Gorman, Nianwen Xue, Jayeol Chun, Milan Straka, and Zdeňka Urešová. 2019. MRP 2019: Cross-framework Meaning Representation Parsing. In *Proceedings of the Shared Task on Cross-Framework Meaning Representation Parsing at the 2019 Conference on Natural Language Learning*, pages 1–27, Hong Kong, China.

Hao Peng, Sam Thomson, and Noah A. Smith. 2017. Deep Multitask Learning for Semantic Dependency Parsing. In *Proceedings of the ACL*.

Matthew Peters, Mark Neumann, Mohit Iyyer, Matt Gardner, Christopher Clark, Kenton Lee, and Luke Zettlemoyer. 2018. Deep contextualized word representations. In *Proceedings of the 2018 Conference of the North American Chapter of the Association for Computational Linguistics: Human Language Technologies*.

Lev Ratinov and Dan Roth. 2009. Design challenges and misconceptions in named entity recognition. In *Proceedings of the Thirteenth Conference on Computational Natural Language Learning*, page 147–155.

Robyn Speer, Joshua Chin, and Catherine Havasi. 2017. Conceptnet 5.5: An open multilingual graph of general knowledge.

Sheng Zhang, Xutai Ma, Kevin Duh, and Benjamin Van Durme. 2019. AMR parsing as sequence-to-graph transduction. In *Proceedings of the 57th Annual Meeting of the Association for Computational Linguistics (ACL)*.

HIT-SCIR at MRP 2019:
A Unified Pipeline for Meaning Representation Parsing via Efficient Training and Effective Encoding

Wanxiang Che, Longxu Dou, Yang Xu, Yuxuan Wang, Yijia Liu, Ting Liu
Research Center for Social Computing and Information Retrieval
Harbin Institute of Technology, China
{car,lxdou,yxu,yxwang,yjliu,tliu}@ir.hit.edu.cn

Abstract

This paper describes our system (HIT-SCIR) for the CoNLL 2019 shared task: Cross-Framework Meaning Representation Parsing. We extended the basic transition-based parser with two improvements: a) **Efficient Training** by realizing stack LSTM parallel training; b) **Effective Encoding** via adopting deep contextualized word embeddings BERT (Devlin et al., 2019). Generally, we proposed a unified pipeline to meaning representation parsing, including framework-specific transition-based parsers, BERT-enhanced word representation, and post-processing. In the final evaluation, our system was ranked first according to ALL-F1 (86.2%) and especially ranked first in UCCA framework (81.67%).

1 Introduction

The goal of the CoNLL 2019 shared task (Oepen et al., 2019) is to develop a unified parsing system to process all five semantic graph banks.[1] For the first time, this task combines formally and linguistically different approaches to meaning representation in graph form in a uniform training and evaluation setup.

Recently, a lot of semantic graphbanks arise, which differ in the design of graphs (Kuhlmann and Oepen, 2016), or semantic scheme (Abend and Rappoport, 2017). More specifically, SDP (Oepen et al., 2015), including DM, PSD and PAS, treats the tokens as nodes and connect them with semantic relations; EDS (Flickinger et al., 2017) encodes MRS representations (Copestake et al., 1999) as graphs with the many-to-many relations between tokens and nodes; UCCA (Abend and Rappoport, 2013) represents semantic structures with the multi-layer framework; AMR (Banarescu

et al., 2013) represents the meaning of each word using a concept graph. Koller et al. (2019) classifies these frameworks into three flavors of semantic graphs, based on the degree of alignment between the tokens and the graph nodes. In DM and PSD, nodes are sub-set of surface tokens; in EDS and UCCA, graph nodes are explicitly aligned with the tokens; in AMR, the alignments are implicit.

Most semantic parsers are only designed for one or few specific graphbanks, due to the differences in annotation schemes. For example, the currently best parser for SDP is graph-based (Dozat and Manning, 2018), which assumes dependency graphs but cannot be directly applied to UCCA, EDS, and AMR, due the existence of concept node. Hershcovich et al. (2018) parses across different semantic graphbanks (UCCA, DM, AMR), but only works well on UCCA. The system of Buys and Blunsom (2017) is a good data-driven EDS parser, but does poorly on AMR. Lindemann et al. (2019) sets a new SOTA in DM, PAS, PSD, AMR and nearly SOTA in EDS, via representing each graph with the compositional tree structure (Groschwitz et al., 2017), but they do not expand this method to UCCA. Learning from multiple flavors of meaning representation in parallel has hardly been explored, and notable exceptions include the parsers of Peng et al. (2017, 2018); Hershcovich et al. (2018).

Therefore, the main challenge in cross-framework semantic parsing task is that diverse framework differs in the mapping way between surface string and graph nodes, which incurs the incompatibility among framework-specific parsers. To address that, we propose to use transition-based parser as our basic parser, since it's more flexible to realize the mapping (node generation and alignment) compared with graph-based parser, and we improve it from the two as-

---

[1] See http://mrp.nlpl.eu/ for further technical details, information on how to obtain the data, and official results.

Proceedings of the Shared Task on Cross-Framework Meaning Representation Parsing at the 2019 CoNLL, pages 76–85
Hong Kong, November 3, 2019. ©2019 Association for Computational Linguistics
https://doi.org/10.18653/v1/K19-2007

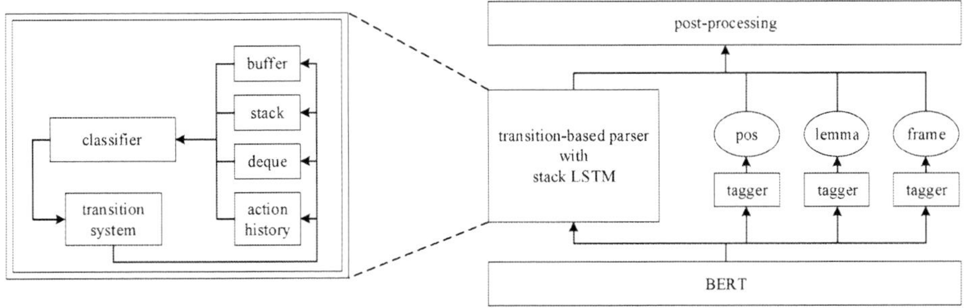

Figure 1: A unified pipeline for meaning representation parsing, including transition-based parser, BERT-enhanced word representation, and post-processing, along with the additional taggers for label the nodes with pos, frame and lemma.

pects: 1) **Efficient Training** Aligning the homogeneous operation in stack LSTM within a batch and then computing them simultaneously; 2) **Effective Encoding** Fine-tuning the parser with pretrained BERT (Devlin et al., 2019) embedding, which enrich the context information to make accurate local decisions, and global learning for exact search. Together with the post-processing, we developed a unified pipeline for meaning representation parsing.

Our contribution can be summarised as follows:

- We proposed a unified parsing framework for cross-framework semantic parsing.

- We designed a simple but efficient method to realize stack LSTM parallel training.

- We showed that semantic parsing task benefits a lot from adopting BERT.

- Our system was ranked first in CoNLL 2019 shared task among 16 teams upon ALL-F1.

2   System Architecture

Our system architecture is shown in Figure 1. In this section, we will first introduce the transition-based parser in Section 2.1, which is the central part of our system. Then, to speed up the training of stack LSTM at transition-based parser, we propose a simple method to do batch-training in Section 2.2. And we adopt BERT to extract the contextualized word representation in Section 2.3. At last, to label the nodes with pos, frame and lemma, we use additional tagger models to predict these in Section 2.4. The framework-specific transition system is presented in Section 3 and post-processing for each framework is discussed in Section 4.

2.1   Transition-based Parser

In order to design the unified transition-based parser, we refer to the following framework-specific parsers: Wang et al. (2018b) for DM and PSD, Hershcovich et al. (2017) for UCCA, Buys and Blunsom (2017) for EDS, Liu et al. (2018) for AMR. Those parsers differ in the design of transition system to generate oracle action sequence, but similar in modeling the parsing state.

A tuple (S, L, B, E, V) is used to represent parsing state, where S is a stack holding processed words, L is a list holding words popped out of S that will be pushed back in the future, and B is a buffer holding unprocessed words. E is a set of labeled dependency arcs. V is a set of graph nodes include concept nodes and surface tokens. The initial state is $([0], [\ ], [1, \cdots, n], [\ ], V)$, where V only contains surface tokens since the concept nodes would be generated during parsing. And the terminal state is $([0], [\ ], [\ ], E, V')$. We model the S, L, B and action history with stack LSTM, which supports PUSH and POP operation. [2]

Transition classifier takes the parsing state from multiple stack LSTM models as input at once, and outputs a action that maximizes the score. The score of a transition action a on state s is calculated as

$$p(a|s) = \frac{\exp\{g_a \cdot \text{STACK LSTM}(s) + b_a\}}{\sum_{a'} \exp\{g_{a'} \cdot \text{STACK LSTM}(s) + b_{a'}\}},$$

where STACK LSTM(s) encodes the state s into a vector, g_a and b_a are embedding vector, bias vector of action a respectively. The oracle transition action sequence is obtained through transition system, proposed in in Section 3.

---

[2] We encourage the reader to read Dyer et al. (2015) for more details.

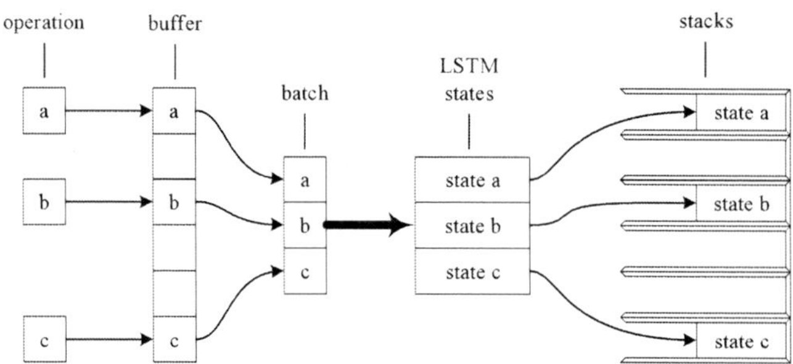

Figure 2: When some new INSERT operations come, the data to be inserted are pushed into corresponding buffers. They will be merged into a batch once batch-processing is triggered. After that, new LSTM states will be pushed to corresponding stacks.

2.2 Batch Training

Kiperwasser and Goldberg (2016) shows that batch training increases the gradient stability and speeds up the training. Delaying the backward to simulate mini-batch update is a simple way to realize batch training, but it fails to compute over data in parallel. To solve this, we propose a method of maintaining stack LSTM structure and using operation buffer.

stack LSTM The stack LSTM augments the conventional LSTM with a 'stack pointer'. And it supports the operation including: a) INSERT adds elements to the end of the sequence; b) POP moves the stack pointer to the previous element; c) QUERY returns the output vector where the stack pointer points. Among these three operation, POP and QUERY only manipulates the stack without complex computing, but INSERT performs lots of computing.

Batch Data in Operation-Level Like conventional LSTM can't form a batch inside a sequence due to the characteristics of sequential processing, stack LSTM can't either. Thus, we collect under-computed operations between different pieces of data to form a batch. In other words, we construct batch data on operation-level other than data-level in tradition. After collecting a batch of operation, we compute them simultaneously.

Operation Buffer To be more efficient, we adopt a buffer to collect operations and let it trigger the computing of those operations automatically (batch-processing), as shown in Figure 2. To ensure correctness, batch-processing will only be triggered when satisfy some conditions. More specifically, when a) operation INSERT comes and

there is already an INSERT in the buffer; b) operation POP or QUERY comes. To clarify, the depth of buffer per data is 1.

2.3 BERT-Enhance Word Representation

2.3.1 Deep Contextualized Word Representations

Neural parsers often use pretrained word embeddings as their primary input, i.e. word2vec (Mikolov et al., 2013) and GloVe (Pennington et al., 2014), which assign a single static representation to each word so that they cannot capture context-dependent meaning. By contrast, deep contextualized word representations, i.e. ELMo (Peters et al., 2018) and BERT (Devlin et al., 2019), encode words with respect to the context, which have been proven to be useful for many NLP tasks, achieving state-of-the-art performance in standard Natural Language Understanding (NLU) benchmarks, such as GLUE (Wang et al., 2018a). Che et al. (2018) adopted ELMo in CoNLL 2018 shared task (Zeman et al., 2018) and achieved first prize in terms of LAS metric. (Kondratyuk and Straka, 2019) exceeds the state-of-the-art in UD with fine-tuning model with BERT.

2.3.2 BERT

We adopt BERT in our model, which uses the language-modeling objective and trained on unannotated text for getting deep contextualized embeddings. BERT differs from ELMo in that it employs a bidirectional Transformer (Vaswani et al., 2017), which benefit from learning potential dependencies between words directly. For a token w_k in sentence S, BERT splits it to several pieces and use a sequence of WordPiece embedding (Wu et al., 2016) $s_{k,1}, s_{k,2}, ..., s_{k,piece\_num_k}$ instead of a single token embedding. Each $\mathbf{s}_{k,i}$ is passed to an L-layered BiTransformer, which is trained with a masked language modeling objective (i.e. randomly masking a percentage of input tokens and only predicting these masked tokens).

To encode the whole sentence, we extract the first piece $\mathbf{s}_{k,1}$ of each token w_k, with applying a scalar mix on all L layers of transformer, to represent the corresponding token w_k.

2.4 Tagger

Semantic graphs in all frameworks can be broken down into 'atomic' component pieces, i.e. tuples capturing (a) top nodes, (b) node labels, (c) node properties, (d) node anchoring, (e) unlabeled edges, (f) edge labels, and (g) edge attributes. Not all tuple types apply to all frameworks, however.[3] The released dataset and evaluation is annotated by MRP, which consists of the tuple including the graph component mentioned above.

Our transition-based parser can provide the edge information, while the other node information, such as pos, frame and lemma, require us to use additional tagger models to label the sentence sequence. The tagger we adopted is directly imported from AllenNLP library, which only models the dependency between node and label (emission score), not models the dependency between labels (transition score). The details about integrating and converting system output into MRP format will be introduced in Section 4.

3 Transition Systems

Building on previous work on parsing reentrancies, discontinuities, and non-terminal nodes, we define an extended set of transitions and features that supports the conjunction of these properties. To solve cross-arc problem, we use list-based arc-eager algorithm for DM, PSD, and EDS framework as Choi and McCallum (2013); Nivre (2003, 2008); for UCCA framework, we employ SWAP operation to generate cross-arc as Hershcovich et al. (2017).[4]

3.1 DM and PSD

We follow the work of (Wang et al., 2018b) to design transition system for DM and PSD.

---

[3]For further explanation, please visit the official website:http://mrp.nlpl.eu/index.php?page=5

[4] The transition sets for each framework have been introduced with table format in supplementary material.

- LEFT-EDGE$_X$ and RIGHT-EDGE$_X$ add an arc with label X between w_j and w_i, where w_i is the top elements of stack and w_j is the top elements of buffer. They are performed only when one of w_i and w_j is the head of the other.

- SHIFT is performed when no dependency exists between w_j and any word in S other than w_i, which pushes all words in list and w_j into stack S.

- REDUCE is performed only when w_i has head and is not the head or child of any word in buffer, which pops w_i out of stack.

- PASS is performed when neither SHIFT nor REDUCE can be performed, which moves w_i to the front of list.

- FINISH pops the root node and marks the state as terminal.

3.2 UCCA

We follow the work of (Hershcovich et al., 2017) to design transition system for UCCA.

- SHIFT and REDUCE operations are the same as DM and PSD. REDUCE pops the stack, to allow removing a node once all its edges have been created.

- NODE transition creates new non-terminal nodes. For every $X \in L$, NODE$_X$ creates a new node on the buffer as a parent of the first element on the stack, with an X labeled edge.

- LEFT-EDGE$_X$ and RIGHT-EDGE$_X$ create a new primary X-labeled edge between the first two elements on the stack, where the parent is the left or the right node, respectively.

- LEFT-REMOTE$_X$ and RIGHT-REMOTE$_X$ do not have this restriction, and the created edge is additionally marked as *remote*.

- SWAP pops the second node on the stack and adds it to the top of the buffer, as with the similarly named transition in previous work (Maier, 2015; Nivre, 2009).

- FINISH pops the root node and marks the state as terminal.

As a UCCA node may only have one incoming primary edge, EDGE transitions are disallowed if the child node already has an incoming primary edge. To support the prediction of multiple parents, node and edge transitions leave the stack unchanged, as in other work on transition-based dependency graph parsing (Sagae and Tsujii, 2008).

3.3 EDS

Based on the work of (Buys and Blunsom, 2017), we extended NODE-START$_L$ and NODE-END actions for generating concept node and realizing node alignment.

To clarify, w_i is the top element in stack and w_j is the top element in buffer. Moreover, w_i could only be concept node (stack and list only contain concept node), and w_j could be concept node or surface token.

- SHIFT and REDUCE operations are the same as DM and PSD.

- LEFT-EDGE$_X$ and RIGHT-EDGE$_X$ add an arc with label X between w_j and w_i. (w_j is the concept node)

- DROP pops w_j. Then push all elements in list into stack. (w_j is the surface token).

- REDUCE is performed only when w_i has head and is not the head or child of any node in buffer B, which pops w_i out of stack S.

- NODE-START$_X$ generates a new concept node with label X and set it's alignment starting from w_j. (w_j is the surface token)

- NODE-END set the alignment of w_i ending in w_j. (w_j is the surface token)

- PASS is performed when neither SHIFT nor REDUCE$_l$ can be performed, which moves w_i to the front of list .

- FINISH pops the root node and marks the state as terminal.

3.4 AMR

We extend the basic transition set to obtain the ability to generate graph nodes from the surface string, following previous work (Liu et al., 2018). There are 3 steps to parse graph nodes from the surface string in general. (a) Many concepts appear as phrases rather than single words, so we connect token spans on top of buffer to form special single tokens if needed using operation MERGE. (b) Then we use operation CONFIRM to convert a single token on buffer to a graph node(concept). In order to process entity concepts like *date-entity* better, operation ENTITY is a special form of CONFIRM which also generates property nodes of the entity concept. (c) The other concepts are not derived from surface string but previous concepts. If there is a concept node on top of buffer, operation NEW can be performed to parse this kind of concept nodes.

After solving the problem of parsing concept nodes from surface string, the basic transition set used in DM and PSD is able to predict edges between concept nodes.

- REDUCE and PASS operations are the same as DM and PSD.

- SHIFT, LEFT-EDGE$_X$ and RIGHT-EDGE$_X$ are similar to operations in DM and PSD, but they can be performed only when the top of buffer is a concept node.

- DROP operation pops the top of buffer when it is a token.

- MERGE operation connect the top two tokens in the buffer to a single token which is waiting for being converted to a concept node.

- CONFIRM$_X$ operation convert top of buffer to a concept node X if it is a token.

- ENTITY$_X$ operation does same things with CONFIRM$_X$ and then adds internal attributes of entity X, such as *year*, *month* and *day* of a *date-entity*.

- NEW$_X$ operation create a concept node labeled with X and push it to the buffer.

- FINISH pops the root node and marks the state as terminal.

4 Pre-processing and Post-processing

As discussed in 2.4, the official dataset is annotated with MRP format, while our system's input is a set of the triple (incoming arc, outgoing arc, arc label). Therefore, besides developing the transition system, we need to do: a) **Pre-processing:** Before training, we need to construct the input for our system based on MRP format graph; b) **Post-processing:** After prediction, we need to convert system's output into MRP format graph.

At first, all those framework construct triple input is basically the same, which using *directed edges*, *edge labels* and *node_id*. About *node anchor*, we directly derive the anchoring based on segmentation from companion data alignment with each sentence.[5]

While the other elements, such as *top nodes*, are a bit different among the frameworks. We will introduce these framework-specific work in the following.

4.1 DM and PSD

Node Properties Nodes in DM and PSD are labeled with lemmas and carry two additional properties that jointly determine the predicate sense, viz. pos and frame. We use two taggers to handle this problem.

Top Nodes At first, we construct an artifact node called ROOT. Then we add an edge (node, ROOT, ROOT) where the node is enumerated from top nodes.

Node Label We copy the lemmas from additional companion data and set it as node labels.

4.2 UCCA

Top Nodes There is only one top node in UCCA, which used to initialize the stack. Meanwhile, top node is the protect symbol of stack (never be popped out).

Edge Properties UCCA is the only framework with edge properties, used as a sign for remote edges. We treat remote edges the same as primary edge, except the edge label added with a special symbol, i.e. star(*).

Node Anchoring Refer to the original UCCA framework design, we link the the node in layer 0 to the surface token with edge label 'Terminal'. In post-processing, we combine surface token and layer 0 nodes via collapsing 'Terminal' edge to extract the alignment or anchor information.

4.3 EDS

Top Nodes The TOP operation will set the first concept node in buffer as top nodes.

Node Labels We train a tagger to handle this. Although there are many node labels exists, the result shows our system performs well on this.

Node Properties The only framework-specific property used on EDS nodes is carg (for constant argument), a string-valued parameter that is used with predicates(node label) like named or dofw, for proper names and the days of the week, respectively.

We write some rules to convert the surface token into properties value, such as converting million(token) to 1000000(value) when *card*(node label).

Node Anchoring We obtain alignment information through NODE_START and NODE_END operation,

4.4 AMR

Alignment There is no anchor between tokens from surface string and nodes from AMR graph. So we have to know which token aligns to which node, or we cannot train our model. Actually, finding alignment is a quite hard problem so that we could only get approximate solutions through heuristic searching. Although basic alignments have been contained in the companion data, we decide to use an enhanced rule-based aligner TAMR (Liu et al., 2018).

TAMR recalls more alignments by matching words and concepts from the view of semantic and morphological. (a) semantic match: Glove embedding represents words in some vector space. Considering a word and a concept striping off trailing number, we think them matching if their cosine similarity is small enough. (b) morphological match: Morphosemantic database in the Word-Net project provides links connecting noun and verb senses, which helps match words and concepts.

Top Nodes There is exact one top node in AMR. For the convenience of processing, we add a guard element to the stack and use operation LEFT-EDGE$_{ROOT}$ between guard element and concept nodes to predict top nodes.

Node Labels Node label appears as the name of each concept which is parameter of operation ENTITY, CONFIRM and NEW.

Node Properties This is the main part of post-processing. Since our model predicts everything

---

[5]Organizer released pre-tokenized, PoS-tagged, and lemmatized form for training and evaluation data, besides a sequence of 'raw' sentence string. You could download the sample companion data from `http://svn.nlpl.eu/mrp/2019/public/companion.tgz`

System	DM	PSD	EDS	UCCA	AMR	ALL-F1
HIT-SCIR	95.08 (2)	90.55(4)	90.75(2)	**81.67 (1)**	72.94 (2)	86.2
SJTU-NICT	**95.50 (1)**	91.19 (3)	89.90 (3)	77.80 (3)	71.97 (3)	85.3
Suda-Alibaba	92.26 (7)	85.56 (8)	**91.85 (1)**	78.43 (2)	71.72 (5)	84.0
Saarland	94.69 (4)	**91.28 (1)**	89.10 (4)	67.55 (6)	66.72 (6)	81.9
Hitachi	91.02 (8)	91.21 (2)	83.74 (6)	70.36 (5)	43.86 (8)	76.0
Amazon	93.26 (6)	89.98 (5)	-	-	**73.38 (1)**	-

Table 1: The top 5 evaluation results upon cross-framework metric ALL-F1. 95.08 (2) indicates HIT-SCIR system scores 95.08 F1 in DM framework, and it ranks 2nd in DM. Amazon achieves 1st in AMR. We only list the involved results they submitted.

Feature	DM		PSD		UCCA		EDS		AMR	
	LF1	MRP	LF1	MRP	LF1	MRP	EDM	MRP	SMATCH	MRP
GloVe	87.1	87.3	74.1	73.7	56.3	87.5	82.5	88.2	64.8	65.3
BERT(base)	94.3	90.5	83.6	76.7	64.3	92.8	87.6	91.5	71.0	71.4

Table 2: HIT-SCIR parser results on MRP split dataset with GloVe or BERT as pretrained word representation. MRP stands for cross-framework evaluation metric. LF1 stands for SDP Labeled F1 (Oepen et al., 2014) in DM/PSD, UCCA Labeled Dependency F1 (Hershcovich et al., 2019) in UCCA. And EDM (Dridan and Oepen, 2011) stands for Elementary Dependency Match in EDS. SMATCH (Cai and Knight, 2013) is an evaluation metric for semantic feature structures in AMR.

as nodes and edges, we need an extra procedure to recognize which nodes should be properties in the final result. Once recognized, node along with the corresponding edge will be converted to the property of its parent node, edge label for the key, and node label for the value.

We write some rules to perform the recognizing procedure. Rules come from 2 basic facts. (a) attribute node: Numbers, URLs, and other special tokens like '-'(value of 'polarity') should be values of properties. (b) constant relation: When an edge has a label like 'value', 'quant', 'op$_x$' and so on, it is usually a key to property. We treat it as property if there is an edge of constant relation connecting to an attribute node.

5 Experiments

In this section, we will show the basic model setup including BERT fine-tuning, and results including overall evaluation, training speed. More details about training, including model selection, hyperparameters and so on, are contained in supplementary material.

5.1 Model Setup

Our work uses the AllenNLP library built for the PyTorch framework. We split parameters into two groups, i.e., BERT parameters and the other parameters (base parameters). The two parameter groups differ in learning rate. For training we use Adam (Kingma and Ba, 2015). Code for our parser and model weights are available at `https://github.com/DreamerDeo/HIT-SCIR-CoNLL2019`.

Fine-Tuning BERT with Parser Based on Devlin et al. (2019), fine-tuning BERT with supervised downstream task will receive the most benefit. So we choose to fine-tune BERT model together with the original parser. In our preliminary study, gradual unfreezing and slanted triangular learning rate scheduler is essential for BERT fine-tuning model. More details are discussed in supplementary material.

5.2 Results

Overall Evaluation We list the evaluation results on Table 1, which is ranked by the cross-framework metric, named ALL-F1, attached with the result of specific framework. [6] In final submission, we only use the single model for prediction. In the follow-up experiments, we get further improvement via the ensemble model. The related results is listed in supplementary material.

Training Speed To explore the effect of batch-training methods which proposed in Section 2.2

---

[6]Evaluation results of CoNLL 2019 shared task are available at `http://bit.ly/cfmrp19`.

	Parser	Feature	DM		PAS		PSD	
			id F	ood F	id F	ood F	id F	ood F
Wang et al. (2018b)	T	word2vec	89.3	83.2	91.4	87.2	76.1	73.2
Dozat and Manning (2018)	G	GloVe+char	92.7	87.8	94.0	90.6	80.5	78.6
HIT-SCIR	T	GloVe+char	86.1	79.2	89.8	85.2	72.8	68.5
AllenNLP	G	GloVe+char	91.6	86.1	93.1	89.6	77.4	73.0
HIT-SCIR	T	BERT	92.9	89.2	94.4	92.4	81.6	81.0
AllenNLP	G	BERT	94.1	90.8	94.8	92.9	80.7	79.5

Table 3: Semantic parsing accuracies (id = in domain test set; ood = out of domain test set). G and T stand for graph-based parser and transition-based parser. We adopted BERT (base+cased) model here. AllenNLP refers to the graph-based parser (Dozat and Manning, 2018) re-implemented by AllenNLP.

in training process, we conduct several experiments through adjusting the batch-size. Since we have adopted two different ways to address the cross-arc problem: list-based (DM, PSD, EDS, AMR) and SWAP operation (UCCA), we try batch-training experiments on DM and UCCA respectively. The result is shown in Figure 3. 5.3x on DM and 2.7x on UCCA speedup could be reached approximately while increasing batch size. We use GloVe pretrained embedding instead of BERT to reduce memory cost and support a larger batch size in the speed test.

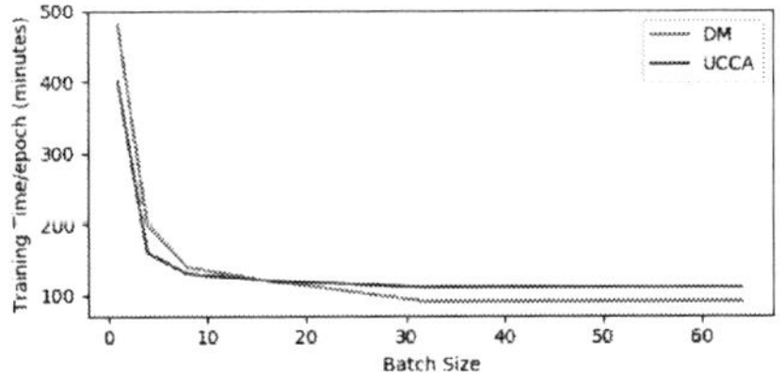

Figure 3: The training time per epoch, under different batch-size experiment setting, which indicates the efficient of batch-training methods we proposed in 2.2.

Improvement through BERT Our parser benefits a lot from BERT compared with GloVe as shown in Table 2. The improvement is more obvious in the out-of-domain evaluations, illustrating BERT's ability to transfer across domains.

6 Discussion

In recent years, graph-based parser holds the state-of-the-art in dependency parsing area due to its ability in the global decision, compared with transition-based parser. However, when we concatenated those models with BERT, we receive the similar performance, which shows that powerful representation could eliminate the gap between structure or parsing strategy.

Kulmizev et al. (2019) proposes that deep contextualized word representations are more effective at reducing errors in transition-based parsing than in graph-based parsing. Their experiments were all about dependency parsing (tree structure), and we found similar results in meaning representation parsing (graph structure), as shown in Table 3. It remains the future work to study this phenomenon with the theoretical analysis.

7 Conclusion and Future Work

Our system extends the basic transition-based parser with the following improvements: 1) adopting BERT for better word representation; 2) realizing batch-training for stack LSTM to speed up the training process. And we proposed a unified pipeline for meaning representation parsing, suitable for main stream graphbanks. In the final evaluation, we were ranked first place in CoNLL 2019 shared task according to ALL-F1 (86.2%) and especially ranked first in UCCA framework (81.67%).

Acknowledgments

We thank the reviewers for their insightful comments and the HIT-SCIR colleagues for the coordination on the machine usage. This work was supported by the National Natural Science Foundation of China (NSFC) via grant 61976072, 61632011 and 61772153.

References

Omri Abend and Ari Rappoport. 2013. Universal conceptual cognitive annotation (UCCA). In *ACL*.

Omri Abend and Ari Rappoport. 2017. The state of the art in semantic representation. In *ACL*.

Laura Banarescu, Claire Bonial, Shu Cai, Madalina Georgescu, Kira Griffitt, Ulf Hermjakob, Kevin Knight, Philipp Koehn, Martha Palmer, and Nathan Schneider. 2013. Abstract meaning representation for sembanking. In *LAWID*.

Jan Buys and Phil Blunsom. 2017. Robust incremental neural semantic graph parsing. In *ACL*.

Shu Cai and Kevin Knight. 2013. Smatch: an evaluation metric for semantic feature structures. In *ACL*.

Wanxiang Che, Yijia Liu, Yuxuan Wang, Bo Zheng, and Ting Liu. 2018. Towards better UD parsing: Deep contextualized word embeddings, ensemble, and treebank concatenation. In *CoNLL*.

Jinho D. Choi and Andrew McCallum. 2013. Transition-based dependency parsing with selectional branching. In *ACL*.

Ann Copestake, Dan Flickinger, Ivan A. Sag, and Carl Pollard. 1999. Minimal recursion semantics: an introduction.

Jacob Devlin, Ming-Wei Chang, Kenton Lee, and Kristina Toutanova. 2019. BERT: Pre-training of deep bidirectional transformers for language understanding. In *NAACL-HLT*.

Timothy Dozat and Christopher D. Manning. 2018. Simpler but more accurate semantic dependency parsing. In *ACL*.

Rebecca Dridan and Stephan Oepen. 2011. Parser evaluation using elementary dependency matching. In *ACL*.

Chris Dyer, Miguel Ballesteros, Wang Ling, Austin Matthews, and Noah A. Smith. 2015. Transition-based dependency parsing with stack long short-term memory. In *ACL and IJCNLP*.

Dan Flickinger, Jan Hajič, Angelina Ivanova, Marco Kuhlmann, Yusuke Miyao, Stephan Oepen, and Daniel Zeman. 2017. Open SDP 1.2.

Jonas Groschwitz, Meaghan Fowlie, Mark Johnson, and Alexander Koller. 2017. A constrained graph algebra for semantic parsing with AMRs. In *IWCS*.

Daniel Hershcovich, Omri Abend, and Ari Rappoport. 2017. A transition-based directed acyclic graph parser for UCCA. In *ACL*.

Daniel Hershcovich, Omri Abend, and Ari Rappoport. 2018. Multitask parsing across semantic representations. In *ACL*.

Daniel Hershcovich, Zohar Aizenbud, Leshem Choshen, Elior Sulem, Ari Rappoport, and Omri Abend. 2019. SemEval-2019 task 1: Cross-lingual semantic parsing with UCCA. In *IWSE*.

Diederik P. Kingma and Jimmy Ba. 2015. Adam: A method for stochastic optimization. In *ICLR*.

Eliyahu Kiperwasser and Yoav Goldberg. 2016. Simple and accurate dependency parsing using bidirectional LSTM feature representations. *TACL*.

Alexander Koller, Stephan Oepen, and Weiwei Sun. 2019. Graph-based meaning representations: Design and processing. In *ACL*.

Dan Kondratyuk and Milan Straka. 2019. 75 languages, 1 model: Parsing universal dependencies universally. In *EMNLP*.

Marco Kuhlmann and Stephan Oepen. 2016. Squibs: Towards a catalogue of linguistic graph Banks. *Computational Linguistics*.

Artur Kulmizev, Miryam de Lhoneux, Johannes Gontrum, Elena Fano, and Joakim Nivre. 2019. Deep contextualized word embeddings in transition-based and graph-based dependency parsing – a tale of two parsers revisited. In *EMNLP*.

Matthias Lindemann, Jonas Groschwitz, and Alexander Koller. 2019. Compositional semantic parsing across graphbanks. In *ACL*.

Yijia Liu, Wanxiang Che, Bo Zheng, Bing Qin, and Ting Liu. 2018. An AMR aligner tuned by transition-based parser. In *EMNLP*.

Wolfgang Maier. 2015. Discontinuous incremental shift-reduce parsing. In *ACL and IJCNLP*.

Tomas Mikolov, Kai Chen, Greg Corrado, and Jeffrey Dean. 2013. Efficient estimation of word representations in vector space. In *ICLR*.

Joakim Nivre. 2003. An efficient algorithm for projective dependency parsing. In *ICPT*.

Joakim Nivre. 2008. Algorithms for deterministic incremental dependency parsing. *Computational Linguistics*.

Joakim Nivre. 2009. Non-projective dependency parsing in expected linear time. In *ACL and AFNLP*.

Stephan Oepen, Omri Abend, Jan Hajič, Daniel Hershcovich, Marco Kuhlmann, Tim O'Gorman, Nianwen Xue, and Milan Straka. 2019. MRP 2019: Cross-framework Meaning Representation Parsing. In *CoNLL*.

Stephan Oepen, Marco Kuhlmann, Yusuke Miyao, Daniel Zeman, Silvie Cinková, Dan Flickinger, Jan Hajič, and Zdeňka Urešová. 2015. SemEval 2015 task 18: Broad-coverage semantic dependency parsing. In *SemEval*.

Stephan Oepen, Marco Kuhlmann, Yusuke Miyao, Daniel Zeman, Dan Flickinger, Jan Hajič, Angelina Ivanova, and Yi Zhang. 2014. SemEval 2014 task 8: Broad-coverage semantic dependency parsing. In *SemEval*.

Hao Peng, Sam Thomson, and Noah A. Smith. 2017. Deep multitask learning for semantic dependency parsing. In *ACL*.

Hao Peng, Sam Thomson, Swabha Swayamdipta, and Noah A. Smith. 2018. Learning joint semantic parsers from disjoint data. In *NAACL-HLT*.

Jeffrey Pennington, Richard Socher, and Christopher D. Manning. 2014. Glove: Global vectors for word representation. In *EMNLP*.

Matthew E Peters, Mark Neumann, Mohit Iyyer, Matt Gardner, Christopher Clark, Kenton Lee, and Luke Zettlemoyer. 2018. Deep contextualized word representations. In *NAACL-HLT*.

Kenji Sagae and Jun'ichi Tsujii. 2008. Shift-reduce dependency DAG parsing. In *Coling*.

Ashish Vaswani, Noam Shazeer, Niki Parmar, Jakob Uszkoreit, Llion Jones, Aidan N Gomez, Ł ukasz Kaiser, and Illia Polosukhin. 2017. Attention is all you need. In *NIPS*.

Alex Wang, Amanpreet Singh, Julian Michael, Felix Hill, Omer Levy, and Samuel Bowman. 2018a. GLUE: A multi-task benchmark and analysis platform for natural language understanding. In *EMNLP*.

Yuxuan Wang, Wanxiang Che, Jiang Guo, and Ting Liu. 2018b. A neural transition-based approach for semantic dependency graph parsing. In *AAAI*.

Yonghui Wu, Mike Schuster, Zhifeng Chen, Quoc V. Le, Mohammad Norouzi, Wolfgang Macherey, Maxim Krikun, Yuan Cao, Qin Gao, Klaus Macherey, Jeff Klingner, Apurva Shah, Melvin Johnson, Xiaobing Liu, ukasz Kaiser, Stephan Gouws, Yoshikiyo Kato, Taku Kudo, Hideto Kazawa, Keith Stevens, George Kurian, Nishant Patil, Wei Wang, Cliff Young, Jason Smith, Jason Riesa, Alex Rudnick, Oriol Vinyals, Greg Corrado, Macduff Hughes, and Jeffrey Dean. 2016. Google's neural machine translation system: Bridging the gap between human and machine translation. *CoRR*.

Daniel Zeman, Jan Hajič, Martin Popel, Martin Potthast, Milan Straka, Filip Ginter, Joakim Nivre, and Slav Petrov. 2018. CoNLL 2018 shared task: Multilingual parsing from raw text to universal dependencies. In *CoNLL*.

SJTU at MRP 2019: A Transition-Based Multi-Task Parser for Cross-Framework Meaning Representation Parsing

Hongxiao Bai[1,2,3]**, Hai Zhao**[1,2,3,*]
[1]Department of Computer Science and Engineering, Shanghai Jiao Tong University
[2]Key Laboratory of Shanghai Education Commission for Intelligent Interaction
and Cognitive Engineering, Shanghai Jiao Tong University, Shanghai, China
[3]MoE Key Lab of Artificial Intelligence, AI Institute, Shanghai Jiao Tong University
baippa@sjtu.edu.cn, zhaohai@cs.sjtu.edu.cn

Abstract

This paper describes the system of our team *SJTU* for our participation in the CoNLL 2019 Shared Task: Cross-Framework Meaning Representation Parsing. The goal of the task is to advance data-driven parsing into graph-structured representations of sentence meaning. This task includes five meaning representation frameworks: DM, PSD, EDS, UCCA, and AMR. These frameworks have different properties and structures. To tackle all the frameworks in one model, it is needed to find out the commonality of them. In our work, we define a set of the transition actions to once-for-all tackle all the frameworks and train a transition-based model to parse the meaning representation. The adopted multi-task model also can allow learning for one framework to benefit the others. In the final official evaluation of the shared task, our system achieves 42% F_1 unified MRP metric score.

1 Introduction

Semantic understanding of texts is very important in Natural Language Processing (NLP), in which, Meaning Representation Parsing (MRP) attracts attentions of many researchers. This task is to encode a sentence into a semantic graph, which usually is directed. Compared with dependency parsing (Ma and Zhao, 2012; Li et al., 2018a; Zhou and Zhao, 2019) or semantic role labeling (Zhao et al., 2009a,b; Li et al., 2018b; Guan et al., 2019), this task is much harder since its representation is a graph which may incorporate both syntactical and semantic information. These general graphs are more expressive and arguably more adequate target structures for sentence-level analysis beyond

shallow syntax and in particular for representations of the semantic structure. Many works have shown that these meaning representations are beneficial to other tasks such as machine translation and abstractive summarization. However, there are several types of meaning representations with different definitions, structures, and abstractions, which hinder the applications.

The CoNLL 2019 Shared Task (Oepen et al., 2019) combines formally and linguistically different meaning representation in graph form on a uniform training and evaluation setup for the first time. This task includes five MRP frameworks: DM, PSD, EDS, UCCA, and AMR. These frameworks have different anchoring types, i.e., the tightness of correspondence between graph nodes and sentence tokens with different abstractions. The nodes in DM and PSD are all the surface tokens in the sentences. In EDS and UCCA, the anchoring is flexible so that arbitrary parts of the sentence (e.g. sub-token or multi-token sequences) may be node anchors, as well as multiple nodes anchored to overlapping sub-strings. Further, AMR has even no anchoring but with the strongest expressive ability.

For each of these frameworks, the common methods for their parsing are transition-based method and graph-based method. The former parses sentences by making a sequence of transition actions according to the present state which usually consists of a stack, a buffer, and a processed edge set, while the latter gets nodes first and predicts the edges between these nodes.

In our system, we use the transition-based model to do the cross-framework meaning representation parsing, since we can define a set of transition actions and incorporate all the frameworks into our system, and the shared part of the model can learn from all the data from different frameworks. Our model is modified from

*Corresponding author. This paper was partially supported by National Key Research and Development Program of China (No. 2017YFB0304100) and Key Projects of National Natural Science Foundation of China (No. U1836222 and No. 61733011).

TUPA (Transition-based UCCA Parser) (Hersh-covich et al., 2017, 2018) in terms of neural networks, which is powerful in a lot of NLP tasks (Cai and Zhao, 2016; Zhang et al., 2016; Qin et al., 2016; Vaswani et al., 2017; Cai et al., 2017; Wang et al., 2017; Qin et al., 2017; Bai and Zhao, 2018; He et al., 2018; Cai et al., 2018; Zhang and Zhao, 2018; Zhang et al., 2018a,b; Zhu et al., 2018; Huang and Zhao, 2018; Li et al., 2018c; Wu et al., 2018; Zhang et al., 2019; Xiao et al., 2019). Neural networks can encode the texts into a dense representation. We put the parsing job of all the frameworks to one model and use a multi-task set-ting to jointly train the system. In the final official evaluation of the shared task, our system achieves $42\%F_1$ unified MRP metric score.

The rest of this paper is organized as follows. Section 2 introduces these frameworks. Section 3 shows our model. Section 4 gives the settings of our model and test results.

2 Framework Schemes

This shared task considers five meaning represen-tation frameworks. In this section, we briefly in-troduce these frameworks and figure out the traits of these frameworks.

2.1 DM and PSD

DELPH-IN MRS Bi-Lexical Dependen-cies (DM) (Ivanova et al., 2012) and Prague Semantic Dependencies (PSD) (Hajič et al., 2012; Miyao et al., 2014) use bi-lexical semantic dependencies to represent the meaning with different annotations. Graph nodes in DM and PSD correspond to surface tokens, and graphs are neither fully connected nor rooted trees, that is, some tokens from the underlying sentence remain structurally isolated, and for some nodes, there are multiple incoming edges.

2.2 EDS

Elementary Dependency Structures (EDS) (Oepen and Lønning, 2006) is a variable-free semantic de-pendency graph, where graph nodes correspond to logical predictions and edges to labeled argument positions. The variable-free feature makes these graphs quite similar to Abstract Meaning Repre-sentation (AMR). Nodes in EDS are in principle independent of surface lexical units, but for each node, there is an explicit and many-to-many an-choring onto sub-strings of the underlying sen-tence.

2.3 UCCA

Universal Conceptual Cognitive Annota-tion (UCCA) (Abend and Rappoport, 2013) targets to a more semantic way rather than only syntactically and can be extended to cross-linguistic settings. UCCA representations are directed acyclic graphs (DAGs), where termi-nal nodes correspond to the text tokens and non-terminal nodes to semantic units with more abstract meanings. Edges are labeled, indicating the role of a child in the relation. UCCA enable reentrancy to allow a node to participate in several semantic relations.

2.4 AMR

Abstract Meaning Representation (AMR) (Ba-narescu et al., 2013) tries to abstract out all the se-mantic information from the sentences. The AMR graphs are rooted directed graphs, in which both nodes and edges are labeled, and reentrancy is also allowed. AMR declines to make explicit how el-ements of the graph correspond to the surface ut-terance and the nodes are abstract. So similar to EDS, it is also needed to generate nodes from se-mantic information, but AMR is harder since even no anchor is available. AMR graphs quite gener-ally appear to be more abstractive compared to the other frameworks.

2.5 Framework Summary

	DM	PSD	EDS	UCCA	AMR
Node Labels	●	●	●	-	●
Node Properties	●	●	●	-	●
Node Anchoring	●	●	●	●	-
Generated Node	-	-	●	○	●
Edge Attributes	-	-	-	●	-

Table 1: Framework properties. Generated node means the nodes in the graph are not the superficial tokens and ○ means in UCCA they are empty non-terminal nodes.

These frameworks have different structures and different complexity. The graphs of these frame-works all have a top node or root node, and edges are all directed and labeled. Other properties are summarized in Table 1. By analyzing these prop-erties, we can design a transition set to accommo-date all these frameworks.

	Action	Current State	Resulting State	Description
1	Drop	$[\sigma|s_0, b_0|\beta, A]$	$[\sigma|s_0, \beta, A]$	drop the word that does not convey any semantics (the first element of the buffer)
2	New(c)	$[\sigma|s_0, b_0|\beta, A]$	$[\sigma|s_0, c|b_0|\beta, A]$	generate a new node c and push it into the buffer
3	Add	$[\sigma|s_0, b_0|\beta, A]$	$[\sigma|s_0, o|b_0|\beta, A]$	generate a non-terminal node for UCCA and push it into the buffer
4	Left(r)	$[\sigma|s_0, b_0|\beta, A]$	$[\sigma|s_0, b_0|\beta, A \cup s_0 \xleftarrow{r} b_0]$	make left-arc with label r (edge label)
5	Right(r)	$[\sigma|s_0, b_0|\beta, A]$	$[\sigma|s_0, b_0|\beta, A \cup s_0 \xrightarrow{r} b_0]$	make right-arc with label r (edge label)
6	Swap	$[\sigma|s_1|s_0, \beta, A]$	$[\sigma|s_0, s_1|\beta, A]$	swap the top two nodes in stack and then put the top one in the buffer
7	Shift	$[\sigma|s_0, b_0|\beta, A]$	$[\sigma|s_0|b_0, \beta, A]$	shift the first node of the buffer to the stack
8	Reduce	$[\sigma|s_0, b_0|\beta, A]$	$[\sigma, b_0|\beta, A]$	if the top node of the stack is processed, pop it from stack

Table 2: The transition system. σ is the stack and s_0 is the top element of the stack. β is the buffer and b_0 is the first element of the buffer. A is the set containing all processed edges. The $[\sigma|s_0, b_0|\beta, A]$ denotes one state of the transition procedure. For initialization, the σ and A are empty and β contains all tokens in the sentence (for AMR, only words that can be aligned to the graph are kept).

3 Model Description

For the joint learning task, we select a multi-task transition-based model. Following we will describe the transition set, the model, and the training/inference.

3.1 Transition Set

For a transition-based system, a transition action set is needed, and an oracle is also needed to generate gold-standard actions during training. We define the transition set to cover all meaning representation frameworks then these tasks can be learned consistently. Our transition system has a stack, a buffer, and a set of processed edges. Given a sentence consisting of a sequence of tokens $t_0, t_1, \cdots, t_n$, we put all these tokens to the buffer as initialization. During training, an oracle will generate a gold-standard action sequence, and during inference, the model will predict the action sequence and recover it to a graph. Table 2 summarizes all the actions. In these actions, actions 4, 5, 6, 7, 8 are used by all the frameworks, actions 1, 2 are used by EDS and AMR, action 3 is used by UCCA. If one action is not used by the framework, then the oracle will not generate this action for it, and during inference, the action is only selected from the legal actions for task-specified classifiers.

3.2 Model

Figure 1 depicts our model. $x_1, x_2, \cdots, x_i$ denotes the input tokens. Our model architecture

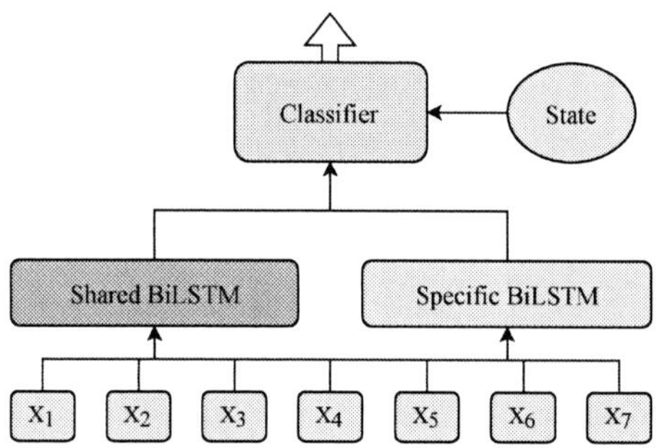

Figure 1: Model overview.

follows TUPA. The model uses a bi-directional LSTM (Hochreiter and Schmidhuber, 1997) to encode the sentence and a multi-layer perceptron (MLP) with a softmax layer for classification. Following Hershcovich et al. (2018), in the model, we have shared embedding components and a shared LSTM module, and for each framework, we have a task-specified LSTM module and a corresponding classifier. For each framework, the outputs of shared LSTM and task-specified LSTM are concatenated and fed into the task-specified classifier for action prediction. For the word embeddings, we use the pre-trained GloVe embeddings (Pennington et al., 2014) and the pre-trained BERT (Devlin et al., 2019). For each token, there are also embeddings for lemma, POS tag, and syntactic dependency label. These embeddings together with token embeddings and BERT outputs are concatenated and sent to the BiLSTMs as input. These embeddings and pre-trained models are tuned during training.

Besides the neural model, we also add hand-made features to the classifier. We use features representing the existing node labels related to the top four stack elements and the first three buffer elements. We also use the last three actions taken by the parser, and if there are less than three actions before, use zero embeddings instead. For all these features, we use vector embeddings to represent them, that is, node labels and transition actions are embedded to vectors. All these embeddings are initialized randomly. These features embeddings are concatenated as a feature vector for the state.

The final hidden state vectors of shared and specific BiLSTMs and the feature vector of the state are concatenated and fed as input to the action classifiers. The training is done with an oracle that yields the set of all optimal transitions at a given state. The actual transition performed in training is the one with the highest score given by the classifier, which is trained to maximize the sum of log-likelihoods of all optimal transitions at each step.

In addition to the main model, we also apply two classifiers for property prediction of DM and PSD. The classifier is an MLP and the input is the concatenated output vectors of each token from shared and specific BiLSTM since the nodes are one-to-one corresponding to the tokens in the sentence.

3.3 Training and Inference Procedures

The training and test data have companion data processed by UDPipe (Straka, 2018). For all the input sentences, we use the tokenization, lemma, POS tagging, dependency parsing, and anchor information results from UDPipe data. Then the anchors of the output graphs are directly obtained from the UDPipe data. For EDS and AMR, the anchors are derived from the first token in the buffer.

Since AMR has no anchoring between nodes and texts, so we use the alignments generated from JAMR (Flanigan et al., 2014) and the tokens and nodes which have no alignments are discarded. Then the oracle can generate an action sequence for AMR during training. We also do pre-process on AMR and EDS graphs by expanding the node properties of graphs in the two frameworks, that is, the property key is seen as edge label and property value is seen as node label. We collect these edge labels and convert these nodes and edges to properties. For DM and PSD, the *pos* node property is from *XPOS* in UDPipe data, and the *frame* property are predicted by additional classifiers. UCCA has edge attribute *remote* to reflect the reentrancy and we neglect the edge attribute in our transition system for convenience. So we add the attribute *remote* to the later predicted edges that link the used nodes. For node labels, we use the lemma corresponding to the token in the sentences as node label for DM and PSD, and we generate node label for EDS and AMR in the *New* action.

During training, an oracle is used to generate action sequences. We use a dynamic oracle which outputs a set of optimal transitions from a given state, and from the resulting state, the gold standard graph is still reachable. For example, for EDS and AMR, if the first element of the buffer is a token and it has aligned unprocessed nodes, then a node with small id is generated by the *New* and put to the buffer. For UCCA, if the top node in the stack connects to a non-terminal node which is not generated yet, then the *Add* this non-terminal node. If this token has no aligned nodes remaining, then the *Drop* is applied. If the top element of the stack and the first element of the buffer are nodes and the node in the buffer is the child of an unprocessed edge, then the *Right* action is applied. Similarly, we have the *Left* action. If the top element of the stack has no unprocessed edges, then the *Reduce* is applied. If the stack is empty and the buffer has elements, then the *Shift* is applied. If no other actions can be found, then we do the *Swap* action.

For inference, after the action sequence is predicted, we can generate a graph from this sequence. However, this graph may not conform to the graph rules of the respective framework. So we prune the generated graph. The pruning method includes: deleting the repeated nodes and edges, deleting the nodes containing empty labels of EDS and AMR, deleting the edges attached to the deleted nodes.

4 Experiments and Results

4.1 Data settings

Our system is trained and evaluated on the data provided by the shared task. The data size is shown in Table 5. We randomly sample out 3% of the training data in each framework as the development set. After the hyperparameters are de-

	tops	labels	properties	anchors	edges	attributes	all	rank	base all
all MRP	52.7	42.8	32.1	54.7	29.5	0.2	43.0	10	**45.3**
lpps MRP	60.2	44.3	24.9	56.0	30.8	0.1	45.1	10	**50.6**
all MRP DM	47.8	56.5	34.7	70.2	31.4	0.0	**43.2**	11	42.7
lpps MRP DM	61.2	55.8	33.1	70.4	27.9	0.0	**41.9**	11	39.5
all MRP PSD	48.4	60.7	39.0	72.8	23.4	0.0	47.6	11	**52.7**
lpps MRP PSD	53.3	60.6	40.5	72.7	24.8	0.0	48.8	11	**54.5**
all MRP EDS	32.6	53.1	52.8	64.8	40.5	0.0	53.2	8	**74.0**
lpps MRP EDS	43.2	53.6	40.0	67.8	43.2	0.0	55.3	8	**74.8**
all MRP UCCA	81.8	0.0	0.0	66.0	19.4	0.8	**32.7**	9	23.7
lpps MRP UCCA	75.6	0.0	0.0	69.3	23.4	0.7	35.3	9	**41.0**
all MRP AMR	53.2	43.8	34.1	0.0	33.0	0.0	**38.5**	9	33.8
lpps MRP AMR	67.7	51.4	10.8	0.0	34.8	0.0	**44.1**	9	43.4

Table 3: Test results. $F_1(\%)$ scores for tops, labels, properties, anchors, edges, attributes, and all unified score. MRP is the results of all frameworks and others are for specific frameworks. For the test data, "all" denotes all test data and "lpps" denotes the 100 sentences in *The Little Prince*. *base* denotes the results of TUPA baseline.

	labeled F	labeled M	labeled rank	unlabeled F	unlabeled M	unlabeled rank
all DM	37.9 (56.2)	1.7 (7.2)	11	41.6 (64.3)	1.8 (8.5)	12
lpps DM	33.5 (55.7)	0.0 (14.0)	11	37.8 (64.7)	0.0 (17.0)	12
all PSD	34.0 (50.1)	2.2 (8.6)	12	45.9 (66.0)	4.1 (22.0)	12
lpps PSD	35.9 (55.3)	0.0 (15.0)	12	45.7 (68.8)	0.0 (27.0)	12

Table 4: SDP results for DM and PSD. F denotes $F_1(\%)$ score and M denotes exact match score(%). The scores in the brackets are from TUPA baseline.

termined, we train our system on all the training data. The shared task also evaluates the system on the 100 annotated sentences from *The Little Prince* which denote as "lpps" in the Results section.

	Training	Test
DM	35,656	3359
PSD	35,656	3359
EDS	35,656	3359
UCCA	6,572	1131
AMR	56,240	1998

Table 5: Number of sentences of each framework in training set and test set.

4.2 Model Settings

We implement our model with PyTorch[1] and tuned on the development set. During inference, we use greedy decoding to get the action sequence. Table 6 shows the hyperparameter settings. The optimizer is Adam (Kingma and Ba, 2015). The dropout is applied to the embeddings, the outputs of BiLSTMs, and the outputs of the first MLP lay-

ers. If the length of one sentence is larger than the max length, then the exceeding tokens are discarded. Other features denote the node labels in the stack and buffer, and the previous actions introduced in Section 3.2.

4.3 Results

The evaluation is blindly conducted. The MRP score results are shown in Table 3. For framework specified metric, the SDP results for DM and PSD are reported in Table 4, the EDM results for EDS are reported in Table 7, and the SMATCH results for AMR are reported in Table 9. Table 3 also contains the comparison results with the TUPA baseline (Hershcovich and Arviv, 2019). For some of the frameworks, our model is better than the TUPA baseline.

4.4 Analysis

Though following the same model architecture and dynamic oracle of TUPA, we adopt a different transition set with a different feature set and setting. For example, UCCA only generates a node when an unprocessed edge is met and the node is on it, and UCCA has separate actions to predict

---

[1] https://pytorch.org/

Hyperparameter	Value
Max sentence length	100
GloVe embedding dim	300
BERT output dim	1024
Lemma embedding dim	200
POS-tag embedding dim	20
Dependency embedding dim	20
Other feature dim	10
BiLSTM layers	2
BiLSTM dim	300
MLP layers	2
MLP dim	50
Dropout	0.2
Optimizer	Adam
Learning rate	0.001
Adam β_1	0.9
Adam β_2	0.999

Table 6: Model hyperparameters.

	all	lpps
tops	28.8	40.5
names	50.6	52.8
arguments	34.7	35.5
properties	53.5	40.0
all	43.5 (65.6)	44.9 (66.0)
rank	8	8

Table 7: EDM $F_1(\%)$ results for EDS. The scores in the brackets are from TUPA baseline.

	all	lpps
labeled primary	4.7	5.6
labeled remote	0.6	1.6
labeled all	4.5 (22.4)	5.5 (28.4)
labeled rank	9	9
unlabeled primary	6.5	7.7
unlabeled remote	1.1	3.3
unlabeled all	6.3 (27.1)	7.5 (33.1)
unlabeled rank	9	9

Table 8: UCCA $F_1(\%)$ results. The scores in the brackets are from TUPA baseline.

	all	lpps
F_1	37.3 (32.8)	41.1 (41.1)
rank	9	9

Table 9: SMATCH $F_1(\%)$ results for AMR. SMATCH is the specific evaluation metric for AMR. The scores in the brackets are from TUPA baseline.

	Ours			TUPA		
	P	R	F	P	R	F
MRP	**46.0**	43.0	43.0	39.0	**57.0**	**45.3**
DM	**36.0**	53.0	**43.2**	31.0	**69.0**	42.7
PSD	**48.0**	48.0	47.6	45.0	**63.0**	**52.7**
EDS	**75.0**	41.0	53.2	74.0	**74.0**	**74.0**
UCCA	**31.0**	35.0	**32.7**	17.0	**38.0**	23.7
AMR	**40.0**	37.0	**38.5**	29.0	**41.0**	33.8

Table 10: Precision, Recall, and F_1 score comparisons on all MRP results.

node label, edge label, node property, and edge attribute. Whereas we have actions to generate nodes (*New* and *Add*) and the node or edge label is predicted when the node or the edge is generated. However, our set does not have actions for node properties and edge attributes, which has been introduced in Section 3.3. The motivation for designing our transition set is to use fewer actions to parse a sentence.

For the results, we find the MRP metric may be imperfect for every framework. For example, the MRP results for UCCA of ours and the baseline are comparative, whereas, for the UCCA task-specific metric, ours (Table 8) are much lower than TUPA. That is, a better MRP result may not reflect a better task-specific result. This is due to some items calculated by MRP that are not in UCCA graphs such as labels and properties, and the edge overlapping search methods are different. The gap comes from our transition set, which is not well suitable for UCCA, and this is mainly due to that

we generate non-terminal node separately whereas TUPA directly generates edges attached to the non-terminal nodes, and our method may even illegally connect two terminal nodes. Other frameworks have the same issue such as DM. These task-specific metrics pay more attention to edges and have a different overlapping search method compared with MRP metric, which is more similar to the AMR specific metric SMATCH.

Only for AMR, our MRP results and SMATCH results are both better, which may be due to the separate *New* action and expanding the properties as nodes.

In Table 10, we compare the precision, recall, and F_1 results for MRP metric, and we can find that though the F_1 scores are comparative, our precision scores are much higher than TUPA, whereas recall scores are much lower. That is, we can predict the elements in the graph more accurately, but our model misses too much nodes and edges. This is due to that the new node action and the separate property classifiers can bring better element prediction. Fewer actions also make the prediction more accurate. However, the design of the oracle and the training may have flaws, so some tokens are dropped and some edges are not predicted out, which makes the low recall. Our parser tends to predict a smaller graph, so for some frameworks which tend to have bigger graphs, such as PSD and EDS, the MRP results of our parser are worse.

5 Conclusion

In this paper, we describe our transition-based multi-task parsing system for the CoNLL 2019 Shared Task: Cross-Framework Meaning Representation Parsing. In our system, we integrate all the frameworks into one transition-based neural model using shared features, and we focus more on unified overall MRP metric results. The results of the blind test show that our system achieves 42% F_1 unified MRP metric score. Compared with baseline TUPA, our parser has higher precision but lower recall, for future work, we will optimize our transition set and oracle for better performance.

References

Omri Abend and Ari Rappoport. 2013. Universal conceptual cognitive annotation (UCCA). In *Proceedings of the 51st Annual Meeting of the Association for Computational Linguistics (ACL) (Volume 1: Long Papers)*, pages 228–238, Sofia, Bulgaria.

Hongxiao Bai and Hai Zhao. 2018. Deep enhanced representation for implicit discourse relation recognition. In *Proceedings of the 27th International Conference on Computational Linguistics (COLING)*, pages 571–583, Santa Fe, New Mexico, USA.

Laura Banarescu, Claire Bonial, Shu Cai, Madalina Georgescu, Kira Griffitt, Ulf Hermjakob, Kevin Knight, Philipp Koehn, Martha Palmer, and Nathan Schneider. 2013. Abstract meaning representation for sembanking. In *Proceedings of the 7th Linguistic Annotation Workshop and Interoperability with Discourse*, pages 178–186, Sofia, Bulgaria.

Deng Cai and Hai Zhao. 2016. Neural Word Segmentation Learning for Chinese. In *Proceedings of the 54th Annual Meeting of the Association for Computational Linguistics (ACL)*, pages 409–420, Berlin, Germany.

Deng Cai, Hai Zhao, Zhisong Zhang, Yuan Xin, Yongjian Wu, and Feiyue Huang. 2017. Fast and accurate neural word segmentation for Chinese. In *Proceedings of the 55th Annual Meeting of the Association for Computational Linguistics (ACL) (Volume 2: Short Papers)*, pages 608–615, Vancouver, Canada.

Jiaxun Cai, Shexia He, Zuchao Li, and Hai Zhao. 2018. A full end-to-end semantic role labeler, syntactic-agnostic over syntactic-aware? In *Proceedings of the 27th International Conference on Computational Linguistics (COLING)*, pages 2753–2765, Santa Fe, New Mexico, USA.

Jacob Devlin, Ming-Wei Chang, Kenton Lee, and Kristina Toutanova. 2019. BERT: Pre-training of deep bidirectional transformers for language understanding. In *Proceedings of the 2019 Conference of the North American Chapter of the Association for Computational Linguistics: Human Language Technologies (NAACL:HLT), Volume 1 (Long and Short Papers)*, pages 4171–4186, Minneapolis, Minnesota.

Jeffrey Flanigan, Sam Thomson, Jaime Carbonell, Chris Dyer, and Noah A. Smith. 2014. A discriminative graph-based parser for the abstract meaning representation. In *Proceedings of the 52nd Annual Meeting of the Association for Computational Linguistics (ACL) (Volume 1: Long Papers)*, pages 1426–1436, Baltimore, Maryland.

Chaoyu Guan, Yuhao Cheng, and Hai Zhao. 2019. Semantic role labeling with associated memory network. In *Proceedings of the 2019 Conference of the North American Chapter of the Association for Computational Linguistics: Human Language Technologies (NAACL:HLT), Volume 1 (Long and Short Papers)*, pages 3361–3371, Minneapolis, Minnesota.

Jan Hajič, Eva Hajičová, Jarmila Panevová, Petr Sgall, Ondřej Bojar, Silvie Cinková, Eva Fučíková, Marie Mikulová, Petr Pajas, Jan Popelka, Jiří Semecký, Jana Šindlerová, Jan Štěpánek, Josef Toman, Zdeňka Urešová, and Zdeněk Žabokrtský. 2012. Announcing Prague Czech-English dependency treebank 2.0. In *Proceedings of the Eighth International Conference on Language Resources and Evaluation (LREC-2012)*, pages 3153–3160, Istanbul, Turkey.

Shexia He, Zuchao Li, Hai Zhao, and Hongxiao Bai. 2018. Syntax for semantic role labeling, to be, or not to be. In *Proceedings of the 56th Annual Meeting of the Association for Computational Linguistics (ACL) (Volume 1: Long Papers)*, pages 2061–2071, Melbourne, Australia.

Daniel Hershcovich, Omri Abend, and Ari Rappoport. 2017. A transition-based directed acyclic graph parser for UCCA. In *Proceedings of the 55th Annual Meeting of the Association for Computational Linguistics (ACL) (Volume 1: Long Papers)*, pages 1127–1138, Vancouver, Canada.

Daniel Hershcovich, Omri Abend, and Ari Rappoport. 2018. Multitask parsing across semantic representations. In *Proceedings of the 56th Annual Meeting of the Association for Computational Linguistics (ACL) (Volume 1: Long Papers)*, pages 373–385, Melbourne, Australia.

Daniel Hershcovich and Ofir Arviv. 2019. TUPA at MRP 2019. A multi-task baseline system. In *Proceedings of the Shared Task on Cross-Framework Meaning Representation Parsing at the 2019 Conference on Natural Language Learning*, pages 27–38, Hong Kong, China.

Sepp Hochreiter and Jürgen Schmidhuber. 1997. Long Short-Term Memory. *Neural computation*, 9(8):1735–1780.

Yafang Huang and Hai Zhao. 2018. Chinese pinyin aided IME, input what you have not keystroked yet. In *Proceedings of the 2018 Conference on Empirical Methods in Natural Language Processing (EMNLP)*, pages 2923–2929, Brussels, Belgium.

Angelina Ivanova, Stephan Oepen, Lilja Øvrelid, and Dan Flickinger. 2012. Who did what to whom? a contrastive study of syntacto-semantic dependencies. In *Proceedings of the Sixth Linguistic Annotation Workshop*, pages 2–11, Jeju, Republic of Korea.

Diederik P Kingma and Jimmy Ba. 2015. Adam: A method for stochastic optimization. In *Proceedings of the International Conference on Learning Representations (ICLR)*, San Diego, CA.

Zuchao Li, Jiaxun Cai, Shexia He, and Hai Zhao. 2018a. Seq2seq dependency parsing. In *Proceedings of the 27th International Conference on Computational Linguistics (COLING)*, pages 3203–3214, Santa Fe, New Mexico, USA.

Zuchao Li, Shexia He, Jiaxun Cai, Zhuosheng Zhang, Hai Zhao, Gongshen Liu, Linlin Li, and Luo Si. 2018b. A unified syntax-aware framework for semantic role labeling. In *Proceedings of the 2018 Conference on Empirical Methods in Natural Language Processing (EMNLP)*, pages 2401–2411, Brussels, Belgium.

Zuchao Li, Shexia He, Zhuosheng Zhang, and Hai Zhao. 2018c. Joint learning of POS and dependencies for multilingual universal dependency parsing. In *Proceedings of the CoNLL 2018 Shared Task: Multilingual Parsing from Raw Text to Universal Dependencies*, pages 65–73, Brussels, Belgium.

Xuezhe Ma and Hai Zhao. 2012. Fourth-order dependency parsing. In *Proceedings of COLING 2012: Posters*, pages 785–796, Mumbai, India.

Yusuke Miyao, Stephan Oepen, and Daniel Zeman. 2014. In-house. An ensemble of pre-existing off-the-shelf parsers. In *Proceedings of the 8th International Workshop on Semantic Evaluation (SemEval 2014)*, pages 335–340, Dublin, Ireland.

Stephan Oepen, Omri Abend, Jan Hajič, Daniel Hershcovich, Marco Kuhlmann, Tim O'Gorman, and Nianwen Xue. 2019. MRP 2019. Cross-framework Meaning Representation Parsing. In *Proceedings of the Shared Task on Cross-Framework Meaning Representation Parsing at the 2019 Conference on Natural Language Learning*, pages 1–26, Hong Kong, China.

Stephan Oepen and Jan Tore Lønning. 2006. Discriminant-based MRS banking. In *Proceedings of the Fifth International Conference on Language Resources and Evaluation (LREC'06)*, Genoa, Italy.

Jeffrey Pennington, Richard Socher, and Christopher Manning. 2014. Glove: Global vectors for word representation. In *Proceedings of the 2014 Conference on Empirical Methods in Natural Language Processing (EMNLP)*, pages 1532–1543, Doha, Qatar.

Lianhui Qin, Zhisong Zhang, and Hai Zhao. 2016. A stacking gated neural architecture for implicit discourse relation classification. In *Proceedings of the 2016 Conference on Empirical Methods in Natural Language Processing (EMNLP)*, pages 2263–2270, Austin, Texas.

Lianhui Qin, Zhisong Zhang, Hai Zhao, Zhiting Hu, and Eric Xing. 2017. Adversarial connective-exploiting networks for implicit discourse relation classification. In *Proceedings of the 55th Annual Meeting of the Association for Computational Linguistics (ACL) (Volume 1: Long Papers)*, pages 1006–1017, Vancouver, Canada.

Milan Straka. 2018. UDPipe 2.0 prototype at CoNLL 2018 UD shared task. In *Proceedings of the CoNLL 2018 Shared Task: Multilingual Parsing from Raw Text to Universal Dependencies*, pages 197–207, Brussels, Belgium.

Ashish Vaswani, Noam Shazeer, Niki Parmar, Jakob Uszkoreit, Llion Jones, Aidan N Gomez, Łukasz Kaiser, and Illia Polosukhin. 2017. Attention is all you need. In *Advances in Neural Information Processing Systems (NIPS) 30*, pages 5998–6008.

Hao Wang, Hai Zhao, and Zhisong Zhang. 2017. A transition-based system for universal dependency parsing. In *Proceedings of the CoNLL 2017 Shared Task: Multilingual Parsing from Raw Text to Universal Dependencies*, pages 191–197, Vancouver, Canada.

Yingting Wu, Hai Zhao, and Jia-Jun Tong. 2018. Multilingual universal dependency parsing from raw text with low-resource language enhancement. In *Proceedings of the CoNLL 2018 Shared Task: Multilingual Parsing from Raw Text to Universal Dependencies*, pages 74–80, Brussels, Belgium.

Fengshun Xiao, Jiangtong Li, Hai Zhao, Rui Wang, and Kehai Chen. 2019. Lattice-based transformer encoder for neural machine translation. In *Proceedings of the 57th Annual Meeting of the Association for Computational Linguistics (ACL)*, pages 3090–3097, Florence, Italy.

Zhisong Zhang, Hai Zhao, and Lianhui Qin. 2016. Probabilistic graph-based dependency parsing with convolutional neural network. In *Proceedings of the 54th Annual Meeting of the Association for Computational Linguistics (ACL)*, pages 1382–1392, Berlin, Germany.

Zhuosheng Zhang, Yafang Huang, and Hai Zhao. 2018a. Subword-augmented embedding for cloze reading comprehension. In *Proceedings of the 27th International Conference on Computational Linguistics (COLING)*, pages 1802–1814, Santa Fe, New Mexico, USA.

Zhuosheng Zhang, Yafang Huang, and Hai Zhao. 2019. Open vocabulary learning for neural Chinese pinyin IME. In *Proceedings of the 57th Annual Meeting of the Association for Computational Linguistics (ACL)*, pages 1584–1594, Florence, Italy.

Zhuosheng Zhang, Jiangtong Li, Pengfei Zhu, Hai Zhao, and Gongshen Liu. 2018b. Modeling multi-turn conversation with deep utterance aggregation. In *Proceedings of the 27th International Conference on Computational Linguistics (COLING)*, pages 3740–3752, Santa Fe, New Mexico, USA.

Zhuosheng Zhang and Hai Zhao. 2018. One-shot learning for question-answering in Gaokao history challenge. In *Proceedings of the 27th International Conference on Computational Linguistics (COLING)*, pages 449–461, Santa Fe, New Mexico, USA.

Hai Zhao, Wenliang Chen, Jun'ichi Kazama, Kiyotaka Uchimoto, and Kentaro Torisawa. 2009a. Multilingual dependency learning: Exploiting rich features for tagging syntactic and semantic dependencies. In *Proceedings of the Thirteenth Conference on Computational Natural Language Learning (CoNLL 2009): Shared Task*, pages 61–66, Boulder, Colorado.

Hai Zhao, Wenliang Chen, and Chunyu Kit. 2009b. Semantic dependency parsing of NomBank and PropBank: An efficient integrated approach via a large-scale feature selection. In *Proceedings of the 2009 Conference on Empirical Methods in Natural Language Processing (EMNLP)*, pages 30–39, Singapore.

Junru Zhou and Hai Zhao. 2019. Head-driven phrase structure grammar parsing on Penn treebank. In *Proceedings of the 57th Annual Meeting of the Association for Computational Linguistics (ACL)*, pages 2396–2408, Florence, Italy.

Pengfei Zhu, Zhuosheng Zhang, Jiangtong Li, Yafang Huang, and Hai Zhao. 2018. Lingke: a fine-grained multi-turn chatbot for customer service. In *Proceedings of the 27th International Conference on Computational Linguistics (COLING): System Demonstrations*, pages 108–112, Santa Fe, New Mexico.

JBNU at MRP 2019: Multi-level Biaffine Attention for Semantic Dependency Parsing

Seung-Hoon Na[†], Jinwoo Min[†], Kwanghyeon Park[†], Jong-Hun Shin[‡] and Young-Kil Kim[‡]
[†]Computer Science and Engineering, Jeonbuk National University, South Korea
[‡]Electronics and Telecommunication Research Institute (ETRI), South Korea
nash@jbnu.ac.kr, jinwoomin4488@gmail.com, hpk23@naver.com,
{jhshin82,kimyk}@etri.re.kr

Abstract

This paper describes Jeonbuk National University (JBNU)'s system for the 2019 shared task on Cross-Framework Meaning Representation Parsing (*MRP 2019*) at the Conference on Computational Natural Language Learning. Of the five frameworks, we address only the DELPH-IN MRS Bi-Lexical Dependencies (DP), Prague Semantic Dependencies (PSD), and Universal Conceptual Cognitive Annotation (UCCA) frameworks. We propose a unified parsing model using *biaffine attention* (Dozat and Manning, 2017), consisting of 1) a *BERT-BiLSTM* encoder and 2) a biaffine attention decoder. First, the BERT-BiLSTM for sentence encoder uses BERT to compose a sentence's wordpieces into word-level embeddings and subsequently applies BiLSTM to word-level representations. Second, the biaffine attention decoder determines the scores for an edge's existence and its labels based on biaffine attention functions between *role*-dependent representations. We also present *multi-level* biaffine attention models by combining all the role-dependent representations that appear at multiple intermediate layers.

1 Introduction

Recent studies on meaning representation parsing (MRP) have focused on different semantic graph frameworks such as bilexical semantic dependency graphs (Peng et al., 2017; Wang et al., 2018; Peng et al., 2018; Dozat and Manning, 2018), universal conceptual cognitive annotation (Hershcovich et al., 2017, 2018), and abstract meaning representation (Wang and Xue; Guo and Lu; Song et al., 2019; Zhang et al., 2019). To jointly address various semantic graphs, the aim of the Cross-Framework MRP task (MRP 2019) at the 2019 Conference on Computational Natural Language Learning (CoNLL) is to develop semantic graph parsing across the following five

frameworks (Oepen et al., 2019): 1) **DM**: DELPH-IN MRS Bi-Lexical Dependencies (Ivanova et al., 2012), 2) **PSD**: Prague Semantic Dependencies (Hajič et al., 2012; Miyao et al., 2014), 3) **EDS**: Elementary Dependency Structures (Oepen and Lønning, 2006), 4) **UCCA**: Universal Conceptual Cognitive Annotation (Abend and Rappoport, 2013), and 5) **AMR**: Abstract Meaning Representation (Banarescu et al., 2013).

One of the main aims of MRP 2019 is to induce a unified parsing model for different semantic frameworks such that parsing models can be trained using multi-task learning or transfer learning. To enable multi-task learning, we explicitly make *shared* common components in a neural network architecture across different frameworks. For MRP 2019, we propose a unified neural model for the DM/PSD/UCCA frameworks based on the *biaffine attention* used in (Dozat and Manning, 2017, 2018; Zhang et al., 2019) by deploying the sentence encoder part as a "shared" component across these three frameworks. Our system consists of two main components:

1. **BERT-BiLSTM sentence encoder** (*shared across frameworks*): Given a sentence, the BERT encoder (Devlin et al., 2019) encodes to its wordpieces and the encoded word piece-level represenations are composed into word-level embeddings based on BiLSTM. Another BiLSTM layer is then applied to the resulting word-level embeddings to create the final sentence representations. We refer to this neural layer for encoding sentences as the *BERT-BiLSTM sentence encoder*. For multi-task learning, the BERT-BiLSTM sentence encoder is shared across all target frameworks.

2. **Biaffine attention decoder** (*framework-specific*): Role-dependent representations

Proceedings of the Shared Task on Cross-Framework Meaning Representation Parsing at the 2019 CoNLL, pages 95–103
Hong Kong, November 3, 2019. ©2019 Association for Computational Linguistics
https://doi.org/10.18653/v1/K19-2009

for each word are first induced from the sentence-level embeddings of the BERT-BiLSTM encoder using simple feed-forward layers. Biaffine attention is then performed on the resulting role-dependent representations to predict the existence of an edge and its labels. However, the biaffine attention decoder is not shared but separately trained for each framework. Thus, we have three different biaffine decoders corresponding to DM, PSD, and UCCA.

In addition, our system handles the following specific issues for UCCA parsing and node property prediction:

1. *UCCA parsing using biaffine attention* To handle UCCA formats using a biaffine attention model, we convert a UCCA graph to a bilexical framework using the `semstr` tool, which is based on the head rules of UCCA in (Hershcovich et al., 2017). [1] After the biaffine attention is performed, the parsed bilexical graph is converted back to the UCCA format.

2. *BiLSTM neural models for node property prediction*: In addition to predicting the existence and labels of an edge, the system is required to predict node properties (for DM and PSD). To handle node properties, we further develop *property-specific* BiLSTM-based neural models.[2] These property-specific neural components are designed in a framework-specific manner and are not shared across frameworks.

Furthermore, we present *multi-level* biaffine attention models, motivated by the multi-level architecture of FusionNet in the machine reading comprehension task (Huang et al., 2018).

The preliminary unofficial experiments using our own development seting show that multi-task learning is helpful in improving UCCA's performance, but it does not lead to improvement in performances on the DM and PSD frameworks.

---

[1] We first converted a UCCA MRP format to its xml format and then applied the converter (`semstr/convert.py`) in `semstr` to obtain its CoNLL format: https://github.com/danielhers/semstr

[2] The node properties required for DM and PSD are a POS tag and a *frame*. We prepared a BiLSTM neural model for predicting the frame information of a node only, whereas we used the companion data of MRP 2019 to predict POS tags.

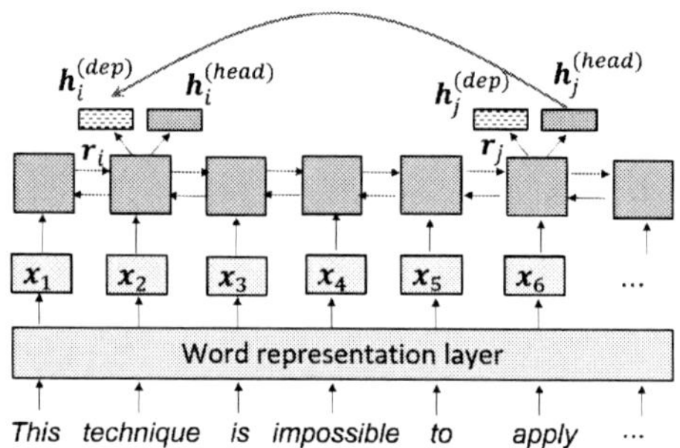

Figure 1: Biaffine attention for bilexical semantic dependency parsing based on word representation using BERT, Glove and POS embeddings.

The remainder of this paper is organized as follows: Section 2 presents our system architecture with details, Section 3 describes the detailed process for training biaffine attention models. Section 4 and 5 provide the preliminary experiment results and the official results at MRP 2019, respectively, and our concluding remarks and a description of future work are given in Section 6.

2 Model

Figure 1 shows the neural architecture based on biaffine attention for bilexical semantic dependency parsing. The neural architecture consists of two components: 1) the BERT-BiLSTM encoder and 2) the biaffine attention decoder. 1) In BERT-BiLSTM encoder, an input sentence is fed to a word representation layer using BERT, resulting in a sequence of word embedding vectors, which are then given to the BiLSTM layer to produce a sentence representation. 2) In biaffine attention, additional feed-forward layers are applied to obtain *role*-dependent representations for head and dependent roles, which are then forwarded to the biaffine attention.

2.1 Encoder: BERT-BiLSTM

2.1.1 Word representation layer using BERT

The word representation using BERT uses BiLSTM for composing to word-level embeddings from wordpiece-level embeddings, similar to (Zhang et al., 2019), which used the average pooling for composition. Specifically, suppose that an input sentence consists of n words, i.e., $x_1 \cdots x_n$. To obtain the word representation $\mathbf{x}_i$ for x_i, we use BERT from (Devlin et al., 2019), as shown in Figure 2. An input sentence is segmented into word-

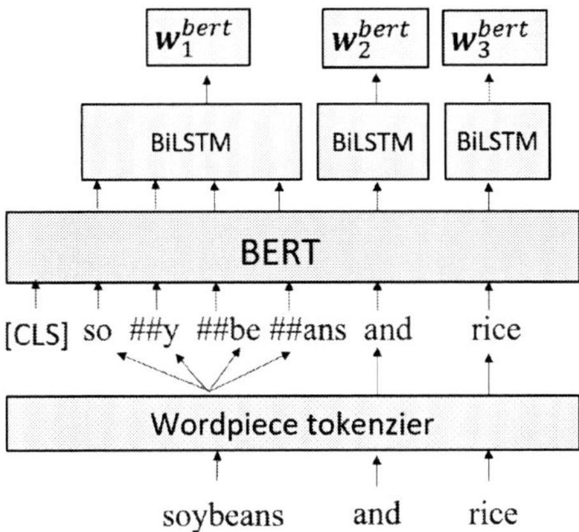

Figure 2: BERT Word embedding using Bi-LSTM.

pieces and they are fed to the BERT encoder. The resulting output from BERT, which consists of the word pieces in the i-th word are aggregated using BiLSTM, producing $\mathbf{w}_i^{bert}$, named *BERT word-level embedding*.[3]

The BERT word-level embedding is further combined with the pretrained GloVe word embedding of (Pennington et al., 2014) and part-of-speech (POS) tag embedding to produce the final word representation, as follows:

$$\mathbf{x}_i = \left[\mathbf{w}_i^{bert}; \mathbf{e}_i^{glove}; \mathbf{e}_i^{POS} \right]$$

where $\mathbf{e}_i^{glove}$ and $\mathbf{e}_i^{POS}$ denote the pretrained GloVe word embedding and the POS tag embedding for the i-th word, respectively.

2.1.2 BiLSTM sentence encoding layer

Once word representations are obtained, we further apply BiLSTM to $\mathbf{x}_1 \cdots \mathbf{x}_n$ to obtain the following initial hidden representation of the i-th word:

$$\mathbf{r}_i = BiLSTM_i \left(\mathbf{x}_1 \cdots \mathbf{x}_n \right)$$

where $BiLSTM_i$ refers to the i-th hidden representation obtained by applying BiLSTM to a given sequence.

2.2 Decoder: Biaffine attention

To formulate a decoder using biaffine attention, let $BiAff(x, y)$ be a biaffine function using the notations of (Dozat and Manning, 2018) and (Socher

---

et al., 2013) as follows:

$$BiAff_m(\mathbf{x}, \mathbf{y}) = \mathbf{x}^T \mathbf{U}^{[1:m]} \mathbf{y} + \mathbf{V} \begin{bmatrix} \mathbf{x} \\ \mathbf{y} \end{bmatrix} + \mathbf{b}$$

where $\mathbf{U}^{[1:k]} \in \mathbb{R}^{d \times d \times m}$ is a tensor, $\mathbf{x}^T \mathbf{U}^{[1:m]} \mathbf{y}$ produces vector $\mathbf{r} \in \mathbb{R}^k$, $\mathbf{V} \in \mathbb{R}^{m \times d}$ is a matrix and $\mathbf{b} \in \mathbb{R}^m$ is a vector for the bias term.

Our biaffine attention decoder is similar to that of (Dozat and Manning, 2018) and is formulated as follows:

$$
\begin{aligned}
FFN(\mathbf{x}) &= f(\mathbf{Ax} + \mathbf{b}) \\
\mathbf{h}_i^{(head)} &= FFN^{(head)}(\mathbf{r}_i) \\
\mathbf{h}_i^{(dep)} &= FFN^{(dep)}(\mathbf{r}_i) \\
\mathbf{h}_i^{(l\text{-}head)} &= FFN^{(l\text{-}head)}(\mathbf{r}_i) \\
\mathbf{h}_i^{(l\text{-}dep)} &= FFN^{(l\text{-}dep)}(\mathbf{r}_i) \\
s_{i,j}^{(edge)} &= BiAff_1^{(edge)}\left(\mathbf{h}_i^{(dep)}, \mathbf{h}_j^{(head)}\right) \\
\mathbf{s}_{i,j}^{(label)} &= BiAff_k^{(label)}\left(\mathbf{h}_i^{(l\text{-}dep)}, \mathbf{h}_j^{(l\text{-}head)}\right) \\
s_i^{(top)} &= FFN^{(top)}(\mathbf{r}_i) \quad (1)
\end{aligned}
$$

where k is the number of node labels, and f is the activation function used in the feed-forward layer FFN.[4]

In contrast to the setting of (Dozat and Manning, 2018), the top score $s_i^{(top)}$ is newly introduced in our model, where we exploit a simple feed-forward layer for predicting top nodes instead of using an attention method.

Using the score functions of Eq. (1), the prediction results for arcs, labels, and top nodes are formulated as follows:

$$
\begin{aligned}
y_{i,j}^{(edge)} &= \mathcal{I}\left(s_{i,j}^{edge} \geq 0\right) \\
y_{i,j}^{(label)} &= argmax\left\{\mathbf{s}_{i,j}^{(label)}\right\} \\
y_i^{(top)} &= \mathcal{I}\left(s_i^{(top)} \geq 0\right) \quad (2)
\end{aligned}
$$

where $\mathcal{I}(expr)$ is an indicator function which gives 1 if $expr$ is true and 0 otherwise.

2.3 Multi-level Biaffine attention

We also investigated a *multi-level* biaffine attention, whose information flow is described in Figure 3. Motivated by (Huang et al., 2018), we assume that multi-layer encoders gradually transform from a low-level word representation into a

---

[3] This aggregation is similar to the BiLSTM-based composition in (Ballesteros et al., 2015; Na et al., 2018) which uses characters as subtokens, whereas our aggregation uses word pieces as subtokens.

[4] In our submission, we used the identity function for f.

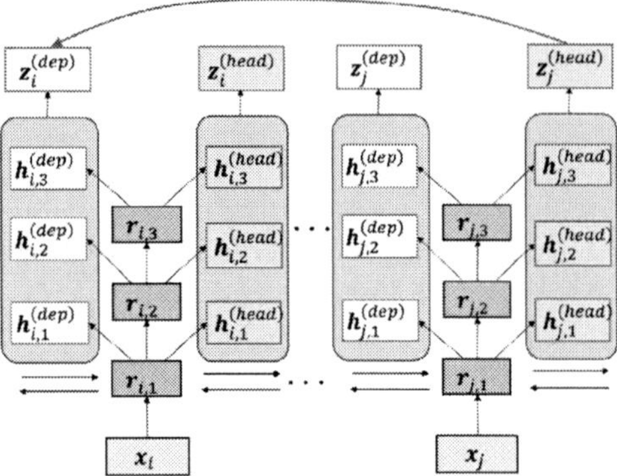

Figure 3: The neural architecture of multi-level biaffine attention. The hidden representations at three levels $\mathbf{h}_{i,k}^{(dep)}$ and $\mathbf{h}_{j,k}^{(head)}$ are composed to the final hidden representation $\mathbf{z}_i^{(dep)}$ and $\mathbf{z}_j^{(head)}$, respectively.

more abstract high-level representation. In the task of semantic graph parsing, predicting an arc and a label may be resolved not just by single-level representation but by the combination of various levels of representations; For example, predicting an arc between two *deep* semantic subgraphs (with high depths) may require more abstract representations for those graphs than the case of predicting an arc between two *shallow* semantic subgraphs (with low depths).

The multi-level biaffine attention is based on the *fusion* of all the *role*-dependent representations across levels.[5] This type of multi-level attention is different from deep biaffine attention of (Dozat and Manning, 2018), which uses only single role-dependent hidden representation at the final level.

To formulate the multi-level biaffine attention, we first apply deep BiLSTM encoder of L-levels to a list of word embeddings $\mathbf{x}_1, \cdots, \mathbf{x}_n$ as follows.

$$\mathbf{r}_{i,0} = \mathbf{x}_i$$
$$\mathbf{r}_{i,l} = BiLSTM_i\left(\mathbf{r}_{1,l-1}\cdots\mathbf{r}_{n,l-1}\right)$$

where $\mathbf{r}_{i,l}$ is the hidden representation of the BiLSTM at the l-th layer.

The role-dependent representation for each l-th layer is formulated as follows:

$$\mathbf{h}_{i,l}^{(head)} = FFN^{(head)}\left(\mathbf{r}_{i,l}\right)$$
$$\mathbf{h}_{i,l}^{(dep)} = FFN^{(dep)}\left(\mathbf{r}_{i,l}\right)$$

---

[5]A pair of syntactic roles in role-dependent representations are considered – head-dependent roles (or predicate-argument roles).

To aggregate all the role-dependent representations, we use the *fusion* function, denoted as $\mathbf{o} = fusion(\mathbf{x}, \mathbf{y})$, as defined in (Hu et al., 2018):

$$\tilde{\mathbf{x}} = gleu\left(\mathbf{W}_r\left[\mathbf{x}; \mathbf{y}; \mathbf{x} \odot \mathbf{y}; \mathbf{x} - \mathbf{y}\right]\right)$$
$$\mathbf{g} = \sigma\left(\mathbf{W}_g\left[\mathbf{x}; \mathbf{y}; \mathbf{x} \odot \mathbf{y}; \mathbf{x} - \mathbf{y}\right]\right)$$
$$\mathbf{o} = \mathbf{g} \odot \tilde{\mathbf{x}} + (1 - \mathbf{g}) \odot \mathbf{x}$$

where $\odot$ is element-wise multiplication. For notational simplicity, we further define $sfu(\mathbf{x}, \mathbf{y}, \mathbf{z})$, the fusion function that takes three arguments, as follows:

$$sfu\left(\mathbf{x}, \mathbf{y}, \mathbf{z}\right) = fusion\left(fusion\left(\mathbf{x}, \mathbf{y}\right), \mathbf{z}\right)$$

Applying the sfu function results in the compositional role-dependent representations $\mathbf{z}_i^{(head)}$ and $\mathbf{z}_i^{(dep)}$ at the i-th position. The multi-level biaffine attention is then defined on $\mathbf{z}_i^{(head)}$ and $\mathbf{z}_i^{(dep)}$ as follows:

$$\mathbf{z}_i^{(head)} = sfu^{(head)}\left(\mathbf{h}_{i,1}^{(head)}, \mathbf{h}_{i,2}^{(head)}, \mathbf{h}_{i,3}^{(head)}\right)$$
$$\mathbf{z}_i^{(dep)} = sfu^{(dep)}\left(\mathbf{h}_{i,1}^{(dep)}, \mathbf{h}_{i,2}^{(dep)}, \mathbf{h}_{i,3}^{(dep)}\right)$$
$$s_{i,j}^{(edge')} = BiAff_1^{(edge')}\left(\mathbf{z}_i^{(dep)}, \mathbf{z}_j^{(head)}\right) \quad (3)$$

Similar to the arc scores in Eq. (3), we straightforwardly define multi-level terms related to label scores such as $\mathbf{h}_{i,k}^{(l\text{-}dep)}$, $\mathbf{h}_{i,k}^{(l\text{-}head)}$, $\mathbf{z}_i^{(l\text{-}head)}$, and $\mathbf{z}_i^{(l\text{-}dep)}$.

2.4 Property prediction based on BiLSTM

To predict *frame* information, which is one of the node properties in DM and PSD, we use a simple BiLSTM architecture with a single output layer that generates a node property for each word.[6]

Different from the biaffine attention model, the property predictor does not use BERT but a simple word representation that consists of the pretrained GloVe and the POS tag embedding as follows:

$$\mathbf{x}_i^{(prop)} = \left[\mathbf{e}_i^{glove}; \mathbf{e}_i^{POS}\right]$$

For encoding a sentence, another BiLSTM is then applied to the sequence of word representations, as follows:

$$\mathbf{r}_i^{(prop)} = BiLSTM_i^{(prop)}\left(\mathbf{x}_1 \cdots \mathbf{x}_n\right)$$

---

[6]Here, words (or tokens) correspond to nodes in a semantic graph.

The output layer uses the following simple affine transformation:

$$\mathbf{s}_i^{(prop)} = FFN^{(prop)}\left(\mathbf{r}_i^{(prop)}\right) \qquad (4)$$

The loss function uses the cross entropy, which is formulated given a single training sentence as follows:

$$L^{(prop)} = \sum_i \log softmax_{g(i)}\left(\mathbf{s}_i^{(prop)}\right) \qquad (5)$$

where $g(i)$ is the gold property value of the i-th word and $softmax_k$ is the function of k-th element of softmax values.[7]

3 Training

3.1 Preprocessing

We use word tokens and their POS tags in the companion dataset provided by MRP 2019. To perform UCCA parsing using biaffine attention, conversion between UCCA and bilexical formats is required. For the conversion, we use the `semstr` tool, which is based on the head rules defined in (Hershcovich et al., 2017).

3.2 Multi-task learning on a single framework

In each semantic graph framework, the biaffine attention models consist of three subtasks — edge detection, edge labeling, and top node prediction. We jointly train the neural components of all the subtasks for each framework in the multi-task learning setting using the following combined loss function:

$$L = \lambda_1 L^{(edge)} + \lambda_2 L^{(label)} + \lambda_3 L^{(top)} \qquad (6)$$

where $L^{(edge)}$, $L^{(label)}$, and $L^{(top)}$ are the loss functions for edge detection, edge labeling, and top node prediction, respectively, and λ_i is the weight for each loss function.

However, the property predictor of Section 2.4 is not jointly trained on a single framework because its neural components can be shared in any component in the biaffine attention models.

---

[7]We allow a NULL value to be a gold property value. Given this setting, the values of $g(i)$ are mostly NULL in the frame property of PSD.

GloVe	
source	840B
dim	300
BERT layer	
source	BERT-Base-cased
dim	784
Word embedding layer: BiLSTM	
hidden_size	384
num_layers	1
Sentence encoder: BiLSTM	
hidden_size	600
num_layers	3
(Multi-level) Biaffine decoder	
hidden_size	600
Property predictor	
BiLSTM_hidden_size	600
BiLSTM_num_layers	3
output_vocab_size(DM)	474
output_vocab_size(PSD)	5474
Adam optimizer	
learning_rate	0.001
weight_decay_rate	3e-9
Adam β_1	0.0
Adam β_2	0.95
BERT Adam optimizer	
learning_rate	2e-5
weight_decay_rate	0.01
Adam β_1	0.9
Adam β_2	0.999
Loss for multi-task learning of Eq. (6)	
λ_1	0.025
λ_2	0.975
λ_3	1.0
batch_size	16

Table 1: Hyper-parameter settings

3.3 Multi-task learning across frameworks

To enable multi-task learning across frameworks, we share the BERT-BiLSTM encoder as a common neural component across three frameworks and use framework-specific models for the biaffine attention decoder. Our approach to multi-task learning is similar to that of SHARED1 of (Peng et al., 2017).

In multi-task learning, we alternate training examples for each framework using the framework-specific loss function of Eq. (6) such that, over each epoch, all the training examples across the three frameworks are fairly fed without bias to a specific framework.

3.4 Hyperparameters

We used Adam optimizer (Kingma and Ba, 2015) to train our biaffine attention models. Table 1 summarizes the hyper-parameters used for training these models

Framework	Train	Dev
DM	32091	3565
PSD	32091	3565
UCCA	5915	656

Table 2: Statistics of dataset used in the preliminary experiment

4 Unofficial Results: Preliminary Experiment

In this section, we present the preliminary experimental results, which compare variants of our models. To perform the preliminary experiment, we randomly split the MRP 2019 dataset into training and development sets. Table 2 shows the statistics of training and development sets for the three frameworks.

The evaluation measures are unlabeled dependency F1 scores (**UF**), labeled dependency F1 scores (**LF**), and top node prediction accuracy (**Top**). We report the evaluation metrics for the development sets.

4.1 Experimental results

We evaluated the following four biaffine attention methods:

1. **Biaffine**: This model is the baseline biaffine attention model based on the BiLSTM sentence encoder without using BERT.

2. **BERT+Biaffine**: This model uses the BERT-BiLSTM encoder of Section 2.1 and the biaffine attention model of Section 2.2.

3. **BERT+Multi-level Biaffine**: This model uses BERT-BiLSTM encoder of Section 2.1 and uses the multi-level attention method of Section 2.3.

4. **BERT+Biaffine+MTL**: This model is the same as BERT+Biaffine but uses the multi-task learning across frameworks described in Section 3.3.

Table 3 shows the UF, LF, and Top on the three semantic graph frameworks, comparing the four variants of biaffine attention models. BERT+Biaffine performs better than Biaffine, in particular, obtaining the increases of about 5% for UF and LF on the UCCA framework. However, BERT+Multi-level Biaffine does not achieve any

further improvements with respect to Biaffine, often yielding weak performances similar to that of the BERT-Biaffine model on the PSD and UCCA frameworks.

BERT+Biaffine+MTL only achieves small improvements on UCCA framework whereas no improvements on DM and PSD frameworks can be observed. A statistically insignificant improvement for multi-task learning in BERT+Biaffine+MTL was similarly reported in the results of SHARED1 in (Peng et al., 2017). These results imply that instead of naively using the shared encoder only, other advanced multi-task learning approaches such as placing task-specific encoding, as detailed in (Peng et al., 2017), need to be considered.

5 Official Results

Given the preliminary results, we chose the basic biaffine model "BERT+Biaffine" of Table 3 for the final submission to MRP 2019. The official results using BERT+Biaffine are summarized in Tables 4 and 5, which compare the results of ERG (Oepen and Flickinger, 2019) and TUPA (Hershcovich and Arviv, 2019) which were provided by the task organizer. Table 4 shows the performances of the *MRP metrics* on the three frameworks, whereas Table 5 presents the performances of *task-specific metrics* using the SDM metrics (Oepen et al., 2014) and UCCA metric (Hershcovich et al., 2019). The SDM metrics use the unlabeled dependency precision/recall/F1 (UP/UR/UF), the labeled dependency precision/recall/F1 (LP/LR/LF), and the unlabeled/labeled exact matches (UM/LM). The UCCA metrics use the unlabeled and labeled arc precision/recall/F1 for primary, remote and all types of arcs.[8]

Overall, our system shows better performances over the baseline TUPA's system, except for the results of UCCA metrics. Comparing to ERG which is the top-performing system in MRP metric on DM, our biaffine system shows slightly improved performance over ERG in terms of UF of the SDP metric. Comparing to the published MRP metrics of the best system (i.e. MRP all metric), the performances of our system are about 1.5 *percentage point* (p.p.) lower on DM framework, about 3.4

---

[8]Our system ranked fifth for framework-specific LF on DM and PSD, ranked eighth on UCCA, first for framework-specific UF using the 100-sentence LPPS sub-set, and second for LF on the PSD framework.

method	DM			PSD			UCCA		
	Top	UF	LF	Top	UF	LF	Top	UF	LF
Biaffine	93.67	92.08	90.86	95.97	90.50	78.21	72.60	69.67	65.17
BERT+Biaffine	95.06	93.85	93.00	96.89	92.30	80.24	77.09	74.85	70.15
BERT+Multi-level Biaffine	95.09	93.86	93.02	96.76	91.95	79.76	78.12	74.42	69.81
BERT+Biaffine+MTL	N/A	93.66	92.73	N/A	92.13	79.63	N/A	75.40	70.59

Table 3: Unofficial results of Top, UF, and LF metrics on the three frameworks (DM, PSD, and UCCA), comparing variants of biaffine attention models.

p.p. lower on PSD framework, and about 31 p.p. lower on UCCA framework.

6 Summary and Conclusion

In this paper, we presented the Jeonbuk National University's system based on unified biaffine attention models for DM, PSD, and UCCA frameworks for the MRP 2019 task. We investigated the extensions of the original biaffine models using multi-level biaffine attention and multi-task learning. The preliminary experiment results show that the use of multi-level models and multi-task learning had no effect on MRP performances under our current settings. The statistically insignificant results of multi-task learning imply that there may be some necessary conditions beyond the default setting to meet before multi-task learning with parameter sharing is effective. In this direction, we plan to explore why multi-task learning is not effective in our current experiment, try to postulate reasonable hypothesis that will help clarifying the effect of multi-task learning, and further examine other advanced multi-task learning including the approaches of (Peng et al., 2017). In addition, we would like to examine alternative fusion functions for multi-level affine attention.

Acknowledgments

This work was supported by Institute of Information & communications Technology Planning & Evaluation (IITP) grant funded by the Korea government(MSIT) (R7119-16-1001, Core technology development of the real-time simultaneous speech translation based on knowledge enhancement)

References

Omri Abend and Ari Rappoport. 2013. Universal conceptual cognitive annotation (UCCA). In *Proceedings of the 51st Annual Meeting of the Association for Computational Linguistics*, ACL '13, pages 228–238. Association for Computational Linguistics.

Miguel Ballesteros, Chris Dyer, and Noah A. Smith. 2015. Improved transition-based parsing by modeling characters instead of words with lstms. In *Proceedings of the 2015 Conference on Empirical Methods in Natural Language Processing (EMNLP '15)*, pages 349–359.

Laura Banarescu, Claire Bonial, Shu Cai, Madalina Georgescu, Kira Griffitt, Ulf Hermjakob, Kevin Knight, Philipp Koehn, Martha Palmer, and Nathan Schneider. 2013. Abstract meaning representation for sembanking. In *Proceedings of the 7th Linguistic Annotation Workshop and Interoperability with Discourse*.

Jacob Devlin, Ming-Wei Chang, Kenton Lee, and Kristina Toutanova. 2019. BERT: Pre-training of deep bidirectional transformers for language understanding. In *Proceedings of the 2019 Conference of the North American Chapter of the Association for Computational Linguistics: Human Language Technologies*, NAACL-HLT '19, pages 4171–4186.

Timothy Dozat and Christopher D. Manning. 2017. Deep biaffine attention for neural dependency parsing. In *5th International Conference on Learning Representations*, ICLR '17.

Timothy Dozat and Christopher D. Manning. 2018. Simpler but more accurate semantic dependency parsing. In *Proceedings of the 56th Annual Meeting of the Association for Computational Linguistics*, ACL'18, pages 484–490.

Zhijiang Guo and Wei Lu. Better transition-based AMR parsing with a refined search space. In *Proceedings of the 2018 Conference on Empirical Methods in Natural Language Processing*, EMNLP '18.

Jan Hajič, Eva Hajičová, Jarmila Panevová, Petr Sgall, Ondřej Bojar, Silvie Cinková, Eva Fučíková, Marie Mikulová, Petr Pajas, Jan Popelka, Jiří Semecký, Jana Šindlerová, Jan Štěpánek, Josef Toman, Zdeňka Urešová, and Zdeněk Žabokrtský. 2012. Announcing Prague Czech-English dependency treebank 2.0. In *Proceedings of the Eighth International Conference on Language Resources and Evaluation (LREC-2012)*, LREC-2012, pages 3153–3160.

Daniel Hershcovich, Omri Abend, and Ari Rappoport. 2017. A transition-based directed acyclic graph parser for UCCA. In *Proceedings of the 55th Annual Meeting of the Association for Computational Linguistics*, ACL'17, pages 1127–1138.

method		tops			labels			properties			anchors			edges			all		
		P	R	F	P	R	F	P	R	F	P	R	F	P	R	F	P	R	F
ERG	all	0.92	0.92	0.92	0.99	0.99	0.99	0.96	0.96	0.96	0.99	0.99	0.99	0.91	0.91	0.91	0.96	0.96	0.9608
	lpps	0.95	0.95	0.95	0.99	0.99	0.99	0.98	0.98	0.98	0.99	1.00	0.99	0.93	0.93	0.93	0.97	0.97	0.9731
TUPA	all	0.53	0.51	0.52	0.40	0.75	0.52	0.22	0.66	0.33	0.85	0.83	0.84	0.24	0.54	0.33	0.31	0.69	0.4270
	lpps	0.74	0.67	0.71	0.35	0.73	0.48	0.19	0.64	0.29	0.85	0.84	0.85	0.21	0.56	0.31	0.28	0.68	0.3946
BERT+Biaffine	all	0.92	0.92	0.92	0.91	0.90	0.90	0.91	0.95	0.94	0.95	0.99	0.98	0.99	0.92	0.91	0.94	0.94	0.9401
	lpps	0.96	0.96	0.96	0.88	0.88	0.88	0.91	0.92	0.91	0.98	0.98	0.98	0.93	0.92	0.92	0.92	0.92	0.9240

(a) The official results of MRP metrics on the DM framework

method		tops			labels			properties			anchors			edges			all		
		P	R	F	P	R	F	P	R	F	P	R	F	P	R	F	P	R	F
TUPA	all	0.58	0.46	0.51	0.56	0.77	0.65	0.34	0.57	0.42	0.82	0.80	0.80	0.27	0.39	0.32	0.45	0.63	0.5265
	lpps	0.62	0.53	0.57	0.58	0.77	0.66	0.31	0.60	0.41	0.82	0.81	0.81	0.30	0.42	0.35	0.47	0.65	0.5453
BERT+Biaffine	all	0.96	0.96	0.96	0.86	0.85	0.86	0.88	0.88	0.88	0.99	0.98	0.99	0.79	0.78	0.78	0.88	0.88	0.88
	lpps	0.96	0.96	0.96	0.77	0.77	0.77	0.78	0.95	0.86	0.98	0.98	0.98	0.79	0.79	0.79	0.84	0.88	0.8568

(b) The official results of MRP metrics on the PSD framework

method		tops			anchors			edges			attributes			all		
		P	R	F	P	R	F	P	R	F	P	R	F	P	R	F
TUPA	all	0.87	0.83	0.8492	0.90	0.52	0.6574	0.08	0.29	0.1299	0.10	0.08	0.0907	0.17	0.38	0.2365
	lpps	0.90	0.88	0.8889	0.93	0.67	0.7776	0.19	0.42	0.2645	0.28	0.14	0.1832	0.34	0.52	0.4104
BERT+Biaffine	all	0.91	0.91	0.9142	0.77	0.80	0.7833	0.33	0.28	0.3026	0.19	0.11	0.1405	0.53	0.49	0.5069
	lpps	0.91	0.91	0.9100	0.90	0.92	0.9126	0.47	0.42	0.4411	0.13	0.07	0.0882	0.66	0.62	0.6365

(c) The official results of MRP metrics on the UCCA framework

Table 4: The official results of MRP metrics on the three frameworks (DM, PSD, and UCCA), comparing ERG (Oepen and Flickinger, 2019), TUPA (Hershcovich and Arviv, 2019), and our system (BERT+Biaffine).

method		labeled				unlabeled			
		LP	LR	LF	LM	UP	UR	UF	UM
ERG	all	0.91	0.91	0.9121	0.5144	0.92	0.92	0.9204	0.5374
	lpps	0.93	0.93	0.9295	0.6900	0.93	0.94	0.9348	0.7200
TUPA	all	0.51	0.62	0.5623	0.0723	0.63	0.66	0.6430	0.0848
	lpps	0.50	0.63	0.5571	0.1400	0.62	0.67	0.6468	0.1700
BERT+Biaffine	all	0.92	0.90	0.9119	0.3998	0.93	0.92	0.9233	0.4329
	lpps	0.93	0.92	0.9265	0.5700	0.95	0.94	0.9413	0.6100

(a) The official results of SDP metrics on the DM framework

method		labeled				unlabeled			
		LP	LR	LF	LM	UP	UR	UF	UM
TUPA	all	0.47	0.53	0.5012	0.0863	0.65	0.67	0.6599	0.2200
	lpps	0.52	0.59	0.5533	0.1500	0.67	0.71	0.6876	0.2700
BERT+Biaffine	all	0.80	0.80	0.7998	0.1920	0.92	0.91	0.9164	0.4519
	lpps	0.82	0.81	0.8147	0.2800	0.93	0.93	0.9272	0.5500

(b) The official results of SDP metrics on the PSD framework

method		labeled									unlabeled								
		primary			remote			all			primary			remote			all		
		P	R	F	P	R	F	P	R	F	P	R	F	P	R	F	P	R	F
TUPA	all	0.30	0.19	0.23	0.08	0.06	0.07	0.28	0.19	0.22	0.37	0.23	0.28	0.09	0.06	0.07	0.35	0.22	0.27
	lpps	0.33	0.26	0.29	0.21	0.10	0.14	0.32	0.25	0.28	0.38	0.31	0.34	0.23	0.10	0.14	0.38	0.30	0.33
BERT+Biaffine	all	0.19	0.17	0.18	0.13	0.08	0.10	0.19	0.17	0.18	0.23	0.20	0.21	0.13	0.08	0.10	0.22	0.20	0.21
	lpps	0.35	0.32	0.34	0.04	0.02	0.03	0.34	0.31	0.33	0.41	0.39	0.40	0.04	0.02	0.03	0.40	0.37	0.38

(c) The official results of UCCA metrics on the UCCA framework

Table 5: The official results of task-specific metrics on the three frameworks, comparing ERG (Oepen and Flickinger, 2019), TUPA (Hershcovich and Arviv, 2019), and our system (BERT+Biaffine).

Daniel Hershcovich, Omri Abend, and Ari Rappoport. 2018. Multitask parsing across semantic representations. In *Proceedings of the 56th Annual Meeting of the Association for Computational Linguistics*, pages 373–385.

Daniel Hershcovich, Zohar Aizenbud, Leshem Choshen, Elior Sulem, Ari Rappoport, and Omri Abend. 2019. SemEval-2019 task 1: Cross-lingual semantic parsing with UCCA. In *Proceedings of the 13th International Workshop on Semantic Evaluation*.

Daniel Hershcovich and Ofir Arviv. 2019. TUPA at MRP 2019: A multi-task baseline system. In *Proceedings of the Shared Task on Cross-Framework Meaning Representation Parsing at the 2019 Conference on Natural Language Learning*, pages 27 – 38, Hong Kong, China.

Minghao Hu, Yuxing Peng, Zhen Huang, Xipeng Qiu, Furu Wei, and Ming Zhou. 2018. Reinforced mnemonic reader for machine reading comprehension. In *Proceedings of the Twenty-Seventh International Joint Conference on Artificial Intelligence*, IJCAI '18, pages 4099–4106.

Hsin-Yuan Huang, Chenguang Zhu, Yelong Shen, and Weizhu Chen. 2018. Fusionnet: Fusing via fully-aware attention with application to machine comprehension. In *International Conference on Learning Representations*.

Angelina Ivanova, Stephan Oepen, Lilja Øvrelid, and Dan Flickinger. 2012. Who did what to whom?: A contrastive study of syntacto-semantic dependencies. In *Proceedings of the Sixth Linguistic Annotation Workshop*, LAW VI '12, pages 2–11.

Diederick P Kingma and Jimmy Ba. 2015. Adam: A method for stochastic optimization. In *International Conference on Learning Representations*, ICLR '13.

Yusuke Miyao, Stephan Oepen, and Daniel Zeman. 2014. In-house: An ensemble of pre-existing off-the-shelf parsers. In *Proceedings of the 8th International Workshop on Semantic Evaluation*, SemEval 2014.

Seung Hoon Na, Jianri Li, Jong hoon Shin, and Kangil Kim. 2018. Transition-based Korean dependency parsing using hybrid word representations of syllables and morphemes with LSTMs. *ACM Transactions on Asian and Low-Resource Language Information Processing (TALLIP)*, 18(2).

Stephan Oepen, Omri Abend, Jan Hajič, Daniel Hershcovich, Marco Kuhlmann, Tim O'Gorman, Nianwen Xue, and Milan Straka. 2019. MRP 2019: Cross-framework Meaning Representation Parsing. In *Proceedings of the Shared Task on Cross-Framework Meaning Representation Parsing at the 2019 Conference on Natural Language Learning*, pages 1 – 26, Hong Kong, China.

Stephan Oepen and Dan Flickinger. 2019. The ERG at MRP 2019: Radically compositional semantic dependencies. In *Proceedings of the Shared Task on Cross-Framework Meaning Representation Parsing at the 2019 Conference on Natural Language Learning*, pages 39 – 43, Hong Kong, China.

Stephan Oepen, Marco Kuhlmann, Yusuke Miyao, Daniel Zeman, Dan Flickinger, Jan Hajič, Angelina Ivanova, and Yi Zhang. 2014. SemEval 2014 task 8: Broad-coverage semantic dependency parsing. In *Proceedings of the 8th International Workshop on Semantic Evaluation (SemEval 2014)*, pages 63–72.

Stephan Oepen and Jan Tore Lønning. 2006. Discriminant-based MRS banking. In *Proceedings of the Fifth International Conference on Language Resources and Evaluation*, LREC'06.

Hao Peng, Sam Thomson, and Noah A. Smith. 2017. Deep multitask learning for semantic dependency parsing. In *Proceedings of the 55th Annual Meeting of the Association for Computational Linguistics*, ACL '17, pages 2037–2048.

Hao Peng, Sam Thomson, Swabha Swayamdipta, and Noah A. Smith. 2018. Learning joint semantic parsers from disjoint data. In *Proceedings of the 2018 Conference of the North American Chapter of the Association for Computational Linguistics: Human Language Technologies*, NAACL '18, pages 1492–1502.

Jeffrey Pennington, Richard Socher, and Christopher Manning. 2014. Glove: Global vectors for word representation. In *Proceedings of the 2014 Conference on Empirical Methods in Natural Language Processing (EMNLP)*, pages 1532–1543, Doha, Qatar. Association for Computational Linguistics.

Richard Socher, Danqi Chen, Christopher D. Manning, and Andrew Y. Ng. 2013. Reasoning with neural tensor networks for knowledge base completion. In *Proceedings of the 26th International Conference on Neural Information Processing Systems - Volume 1*, NIPS'13, pages 926–934.

Linfeng Song, Daniel Gildea, Yue Zhang, Zhiguo Wang, and Jinsong Su. 2019. Semantic neural machine translation using AMR. *Transactions of the Association for Computational Linguistics*, 7:19–31.

Chuan Wang and Nianwen Xue. Getting the most out of AMR parsing. In *Proceedings of the 2017 Conference on Empirical Methods in Natural Language Processing*, EMNLP '17.

Yuxuan Wang, Wanxiang Che, Jiang Guo, and Ting Liu. 2018. A neural transition-based approach for semantic dependency graph parsing. In *Proceedings of the Thirty-Second AAAI Conference on Artificial Intelligence*, AAAI '18, pages 5561–5568.

Sheng Zhang, Xutai Ma, Kevin Duh, and Benjamin Van Durme. 2019. AMR parsing as sequence-to-graph transduction. In *Proceedings of the 57th Annual Meeting of the Association for Computational Linguistics*, ACL '19, pages 80–94.

CUHK at MRP 2019: Transition-Based Parser with Cross-Framework Variable-Arity Resolve Action

Sunny Lai[1,4], Chun Hei Lo[2], Kwong Sak Leung[1,4] and Yee Leung[3,4]
[1]Department of Computer Science and Engineering
[2]Department of Systems Engineering and Engineering
[3]Department of Geography and Resource Management
[4]Institute of Future Cities
The Chinese University of Hong Kong, Shatin, N.T., Hong Kong
`{slai, ksleung}@cse.cuhk.edu.hk,`
`chlo@se.cuhk.edu.hk, yeeleung@cuhk.edu.hk`

Abstract

This paper describes our system (RE-SOLVER) submitted to the CoNLL 2019 shared task on Cross-Framework Meaning Representation Parsing (MRP). Our system implements a transition-based parser with a directed acyclic graph (DAG) to tree preprocessor and a novel cross-framework variable-arity resolve action that generalizes over five different representations. Although we ranked low in the competition, we have shown the current limitations and potentials of including variable-arity action in MRP and concluded with directions for improvements in the future.

1 Introduction

This paper describes our submission[1] to the CoNLL 2019 shared task on Cross-Framework Meaning Representation Parsing (Oepen et al., 2019). The task requires participants to develop a unified system for parsing sentences under five different meaning representation frameworks, which are DELPH-IN MRS (DM; (Ivanova et al., 2012)), Prague Semantic Dependencies (PSD; (Hajic et al., 2012; Miyao et al., 2014)), Elementary Dependency Structures (EDS; (Oepen and Lønning, 2006)), Universal Conceptual Cognitive Annotation (UCCA; (Abend and Rappoport, 2013)) and Abstract Meaning Representation (AMR; (Banarescu et al., 2013)). Given a sentence together with its companion data (e.g. morpho-syntactic parse results) as input, the parser system should generate five graphs according to each frameworks' rules.

Transition-based approaches have been shown useful in parsing a spectrum of semantic graphs, including bi-lexical dependency graphs (flavor 0, e.g. DM, PSD), general anchored semantic graphs (flavor 1, e.g. EDS, UCCA), and unanchored semantic graphs (flavor 2, e.g. AMR). Previous transition-based parsing systems define a set of constant-arity transition actions[2] and these systems learn to select the best action at each state. Constant-arity parser actions work well for tackling individual tasks, but may not generalize well across representations because:

- The graph representation details are different across frameworks. i.e. the edge directions and labels are different when comparing figure 2a and 2c but they describe the same dependency in terms of semantics. The parser will have to learn two actions separately (LEFT-EDGE and RIGHT-EDGE) as the actions have different semantics depending on the framework used.

- Parsing actions can be unique for specific frameworks defined by different authors (Table 1). i.e. Action NODE(X) in UCCA creates a new node without node label, which may not be a suitable action for other frameworks.

As the primary focus of the task is about developing a robust model that unifies the learning process across different semantic graph banks, we develop our system following the traditional transition-based approach, while adding a DAG-to-Tree preprocessor and a set of cross-representation variable-arity actions in an attempt to tackle these two generalization problems. By converting graphs of all five frameworks to a common tree structure using the DAG-to-Tree prepro-

---

[1]Our submission is open-sourced in GitHub: https://github.com/Yermouth/mrp2019

[2]For instance, in basic arc-standard transition system (Nivre, 2008), SHIFT takes one node as argument and RE-DUCE takes two. The number of arguments (arity) for the action is constant and will not change depending on the word being parsed.

Proceedings of the Shared Task on Cross-Framework Meaning Representation Parsing at the 2019 CoNLL, pages 104–113
Hong Kong, November 3, 2019. ©2019 Association for Computational Linguistics
https://doi.org/10.18653/v1/K19-2010

MRP	F	Actions	Author
PSD	0	LEFT-REDUCE(L), RIGHT-SHIFT(L), NO-SHIFT, NO-REDUCE, LEFT-PASS(L), RIGHT-PASS(L), NO-PASS	(Wang et al., 2018)
UCCA	1	SHIFT, REDUCE, **NODE(X)**, LEFT-EDGE(X), RIGHT-EDGE(X), LEFT-REMOTE(X), RIGHT-REMOTE(X), SWAP, FINISH	(Hershcovich et al., 2017)
AMR	2	SHIFT, REDUCE, RIGHT-LABEL(R), LEFT-LABEL(R), SWAP, MERGE, PRED(N), **ENTITY(L)**, GEN(N)	(Guo and Lu, 2018)
*	*	SHIFT, IGNORE, RESOLVE	This paper

Table 1: Transition-based parsing actions defined by different authors.

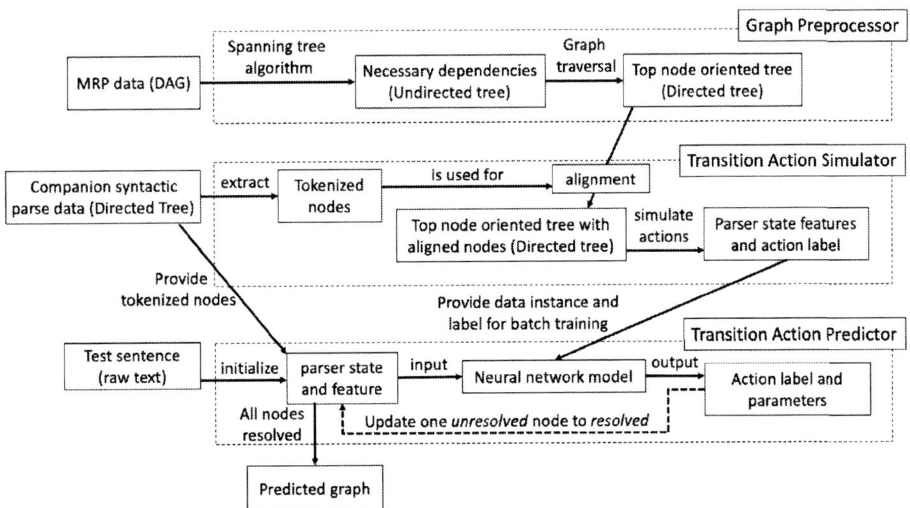

Figure 1: System pipeline diagram.

cessor, we can describe the tree generation process using three common high-level actions — SHIFT, IGNORE and RESOLVE.

The three actions in our system are most similar to the actions defined in the non-binary bottom-up shift-reduce constituent parsing strategy of Fernández-González and Gómez-Rodríguez (2018). SHIFT and IGNORE both have an arity of one. Unlike standard binary RE-DUCE action which handles the relationship between two nodes at a time, RESOLVE is a cross-framework variable-arity action that can reduce multiple nodes and resolve their dependency simultaneously. We introduce the RESOLVE action so that there is no need to include additional binarization of the dependencies and reduce the number of transitions as mentioned by Fernández-González and Gómez-Rodríguez. It is also more natural to consider the dependency of multiple nodes jointly as meaning representations like semantic frames usually involve multiple arguments.

The main difference between RESOLVER and the strategy of Fernández-González and Gómez-Rodríguez is that their strategy handles only constituent parsing problem while RESOLVER can handle cross-framework parsing problem. Our cross-framework RESOLVE action can be customized by generating framework-specific subgraphs.

Our submission ranked 13th overall in the post-evaluation period of the shared task. Although we ranked low in the task, we have experimented with adding variable-arity actions to the transition-based parsing approach and investigated its downsides. We studied why variable-arity transition actions are hard to learn and propose future directions for improving the system to predict variable-arity transition actions more accurately.

The rest of the paper is organized as follows: Section 2 describes the our system architecture. Section 3 details the model training steps. We analyze and discuss the result in Section 4 and conclude our work in Section 5.

2 System Architecture

Our system pipeline (Figure 1) is divided into three main components — DAG-to-Tree preprocessor, transition action simulator, and transition action predictor. First, we preprocess the meaning representation data and align it with the companion syntactic parse data to generate a top-node oriented tree structure. Then, we generate the transition actions required to reproduce the tree structure and extract the features involved in each action state. Finally, we train the neural network model to predict the correct actions.

2.1 DAG-to-Tree Preprocessor

Although the five frameworks differ in terms of the nodes and edges used, they are essentially conveying similar semantic messages. In an attempt to tackle the first generalization problem, our DAG-to-Tree preprocessor focuses on transforming the five frameworks into a common tree representation.

Our preprocessor converts directed acyclic graphs (DAGs) to top-node oriented tree structures. As the top-node of a sentence represents the most important message or word, they are similar amongst the five representations for the same sentence. Therefore, we can transform the five representations to a similar tree structure, where the root of the tree is the top-node.

As there are mature and standardized systems and algorithms for tackling tree-structured syntactic parsing, tree approximations schemes for transforming semantic dependency graphs to trees have been proposed (Schluter et al., 2014; Agić et al., 2015). While most of the proposed schemes are lossy, heuristics are applied to reduce information loss. For instance, the graph *packing* scheme (Schluter et al., 2014) use a set of 99.6%-reversible graph transformations to secure graph information, and the graph *deletion* scheme (Agić et al., 2015) remove minimum number of edges (worst case 5.7%) from undirected cycles in digraph to generate tree approximation.

2.1.1 Tree Approximation

Following the *deletion* scheme, we run an algorithm based on Kruskal's spanning tree algorithm (Kruskal, 1956) to select the edges for forming an undirected tree, and determine the edge direction of the edges in the tree by traversing the graph from top-node to every child recursively. The lat-ter part is intuitive as the edge direction is unique (anti-arborescence) once the root of the undirected tree is fixed. As for graphs with more than one top node, we find the common ancestor of these top nodes and keep the graph if the ancestor is the root of the tree.

As for the undirected tree generation process, we first sort the nodes according to their appearance in the sentence, and assign the nodes with its appearance index in ascending order (i.e. Node anchored to the first word in the sentence have appearance index 1).

Then we extract the appearance index of the source node and the target node for each edge, and sort the edge in ascending order first by the maximum appearance index involved, and then by the minimum appearance index regardless of the edge direction (i.e. An edge with appearance indexes 1 and 3 will be placed in front of an edge with indexes 1 and 5).

Finally, we initialize meaning representation nodes as forest in a graph, and add the sorted edge one by one to the graph if the edge connects to two different trees. After traversing the resulting graph from top-node, a set of edges accompanied with its direction is obtained and we refer to these edges as major edges (e.g. primary edges in UCCA). Other edges not in the major edge set are considered as minor edges. Minor edges can exist in PSD and UCCA, where one node can have multiple parents. For instance, nodes in UCCA can have a non-remote edge (major edge) with label "C" and a remote edge with label "A". For EDS specifically, edges that involve quantifiers are considered as minor edges at the moment to facilitate alignment.

In figure 2, 2a, 2c and 2e are the original meaning representation graphs and 2b, 2d, 2f are the top-node oriented trees created by using only the major edges after preprocessing. All three frameworks have the same top-node *"_cost_v_1"*.

Edge directions between the node *"page"* and its children are changed in figure 2b as *"cost"* is the top-node and traverse to node *"page"* before reaching nodes *"a"*, *"full"*, *"color"* and *"in"*.

Figure 2d is the same as 2c as the original graph is a tree and the edges' direction follow the traversal order from top-node.

As for figure 2f, minor edges including the edge with label *"BV"* from node *"udef_q"* to node *"_dollar_n_1"* are dropped in the current prepro-

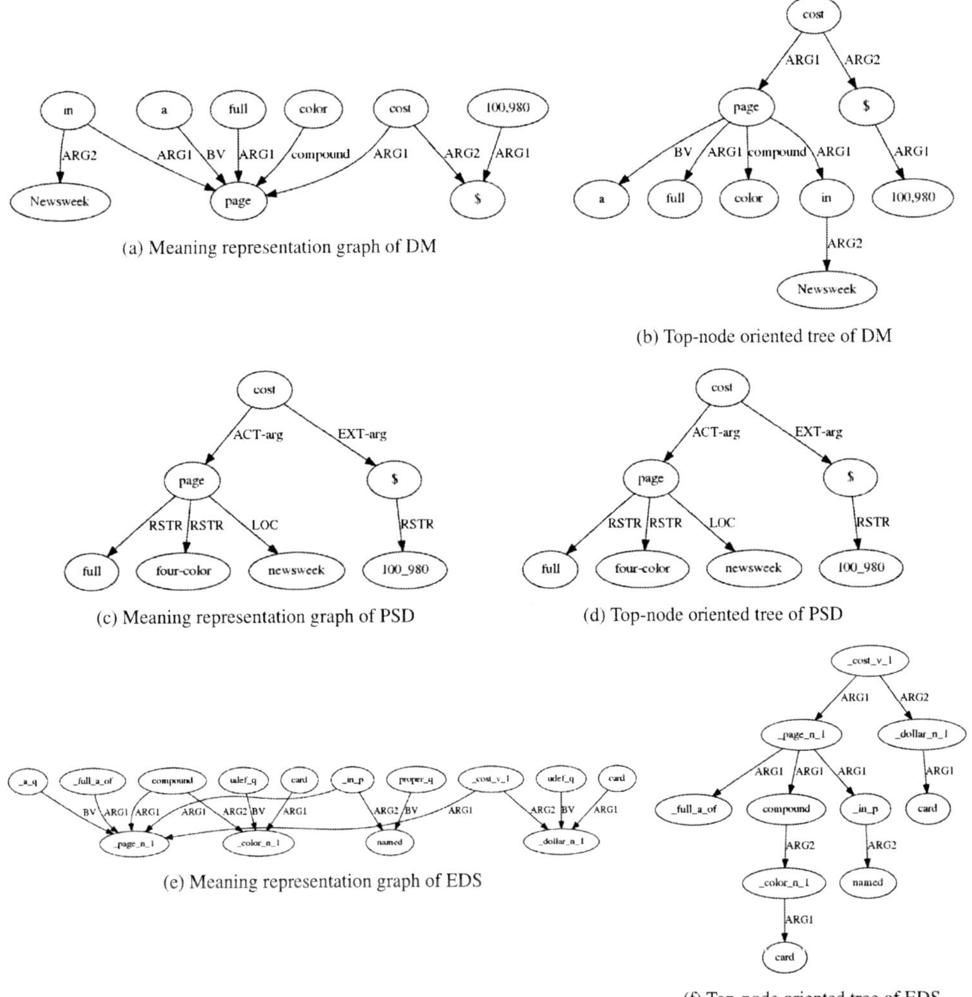

(a) Meaning representation graph of DM

(b) Top-node oriented tree of DM

(c) Meaning representation graph of PSD

(d) Top-node oriented tree of PSD

(e) Meaning representation graph of EDS

(f) Top-node oriented tree of EDS

Figure 2: Meaning representation graphs of DM, PSD and EDS frameworks, accompanied with their top-node oriented tree after applying the DAG-to-Tree preprocessor for the sentence *"A full, four-color page in Newsweek will cost $100,980."*.

cessing procedures.

After these conversions, by comparing figure 2a, 2c, 2e with 2b, 2d, 2f, we can easily observe that the dependencies for the top-node oriented trees for are more unified as they are aligned with the top-node and its dependencies from the tree root. Despite the difference between DM, PSD and EDS in handling specific words (i.e. *"a"* is kept in DM and dropped in PSD), the general dependency structure is now more similar (i.e. all framework express that node *"page"* and *"$"* are necessary for resolving the complete semantics of

the top-node *"cost"*).

2.1.2 Limitation

Limitations of the top-node oriented tree representation are apparent. The current representation sacrifices minor edges to retain the cross framework tree structure using the major edges. In this paper, we adopt the graph *deletion* scheme and mainly focus on tackling major edges that are common amongst the five frameworks. We leave minor edges and the use of graph *packing* scheme as future work.

2.2 Transition Action Simulator

To solve the second generalization problem, we define three actions: SHIFT, IGNORE and RE-SOLVE as the high-level actions in our action set which is common amongst the five frameworks. The tokenized nodes provided by the morpho-syntactic parse tree are the basic units for applying the actions. We initialize the parser state with a queue that stores all the tokenized nodes and an empty stack that stores the processed tokenized nodes.

2.2.1 Shift and Ignore

SHIFT and IGNORE are two constant-arity actions identical for all representations, and both apply directly to the first tokenized nodes in the queue. While both actions pop the first tokenized node from the token queue, SHIFT pushes the popped node to the stack and sets its state to <u>unresolved</u>, while IGNORE omits the popped node and move on to the next tokenized node in the queue. This action is required as the tokenization method of the syntactic parse is different from that of the MRP. Tokenized nodes in the syntactic parse can be ignored by the representation, for instance, verbs like "is" are omitted by DM, while it is preserved in PSD. From our observation, whether the word is ignored or not depends on only itself but not its neighbor nodes, so we can apply the action directly to the queue without considering the state of the stack.

2.2.2 Resolve

RESOLVE is a variable-arity and representation-customizable action. This action is similar to LEFT-REDUCE and RIGHT-REDUCE, but instead of reducing only 2 nodes at each time, RESOLVE can reduce an arbitrary number of nodes in one single action. We required our system to learn the dependencies of multiple nodes jointly in order to determine frame information in a holistic manner.

This action is mainly parameterized by n (arity), the number of nodes from the top of the stack to be reduced (n is a strictly positive integer). The first n nodes must include one and only one *unresolved* node (i.e. the most recently pushed *unresolved* node in the stack). After an *unresolved* node is resolved, it is pushed into the stack. As we have obtained a top-node oriented tree representation from the DAG-to-Tree preprocessor, the dependencies of each node of the tree are defined explicitly and RESOLVE is applied when an *un-*

resolved node's children are all *resolved*. For instance, in Figure 2(b), the top-node of the graph is *"cost"* and its dependencies is *"page"* and *"$"*. To RESOLVE the node *"cost"*, we need to first RE-SOLVE both *"page"* and *"$"*, which further depends on their own children. The number of reduced node n in this case is 3 (2 resolved nodes *"page"* and *"$"* plus 1 unresolved node *"cost"*).[3] If a node is a leaf node, n in this case would be 1 as only one node is involved.

After selecting n nodes from the stack, the RE-SOLVE action build the edges between the *resolved* nodes and the *unresolved* ones, and give node label and properties for the *unresolved* node. Finally, the resolved node is pushed back to the stack.

2.3 Alignment

Aligning a sentence S to a graph $G = \langle V, E \rangle$ of meaning representation gives a mapping between the tokens of S and V. Formally, given a parse tree of S with tokenized nodes $\langle N_0, N_1, \ldots, N_n \rangle$, with each N_i containing $\langle a_{start}, a_{end} \rangle$ of S: pair of from-to sub-string indices, pos: part of speech tag, and $lemma$: lemmatized form, we aim to produce an alignment $V = \langle M_0, M_1, \ldots, M_m \rangle$, where each node object M_i contains $\langle a_{start}, a_{end} \rangle$: pair of from-to sub-string indices to S, pos: part of speech tag, $frame$: semantic frame (optional) and $label$: node label (Figure 3).

As the alignment of the tokenized nodes in the companion parse to the nodes in the meaning representation graph is not given, we devised alignment strategies for the respective framework using anchors and parse information. For DM and PSD, an oracle look-ahead algorithm is designed, where the alignment is conducted as guided by a set of heuristic rules manually derived from the train data. For each sentence, the alignment process proceeds by scanning tokenized nodes of the parse tree from left to right, one at a time. Each node is either ignored or aligned to one node of the meaning representations.

For DM, as white-listed resources are provided, we allow more aggressive grouping and prediction on semantic frames. Generally, $M_j.pos$ and $M_j.label$ will be copied directly from the corresponding $N_i.pos$ and $N_i.lemma$ respectively, with a few exceptions handled the other ways; and $M_j.frame$ are predicted using a simple count-based approach with train data. Multi-word ex-

---

[3] This corresponds to the last RESOLVE action in Table 1

Action	n	Stack	Tokenized Node Queue	RESOLVE Details
		[]	[A, full, ...]	
SHIFT		[A]	[full, , ...]	
RESOLVE	1	[**a**]	[full, , ...]	Leaf node
SHIFT		[a, full]	[,, four-color, ...]	
RESOLVE	1	[a, **full**]	[,, four-color, ...]	Leaf node
IGNORE		[a, full]	[four-color, page, ...]	
SHIFT		[a, full, four-color]	[page, in, ...]	
RESOLVE	1	[a, full, **color**]	[page, in, ...]	Leaf node
SHIFT		[a, full, color, page]	[in, Newsweek, ...]	
SHIFT		[a, full, color, page, in]	[Newsweek, will, ...]	
SHIFT		[a, full, color, page, in, Newsweek]	[will, cost, ...]	
RESOLVE	1	[a, full, color, page, in, **Newsweek**]	[will, cost, ...]	Leaf node
RESOLVE	2	[a, full, color, page, **in**]	[will, cost, ...]	in $\xrightarrow{\text{ARG2}}$ Newsweek
RESOLVE	5	[**page**]	[will, cost, ...]	page $\xrightarrow{\text{BV}}$ a, page $\xrightarrow{\text{ARG1}}$ full page $\xrightarrow{\text{compound}}$ color, page $\xrightarrow{\text{ARG1}}$ in
IGNORE		[page]	[cost, $, ...]	
SHIFT		[page, cost]	[$, 100,980]	
SHIFT		[page, cost, $]	[100,980]	
SHIFT		[page, cost, $, 100,980]	[]	
RESOLVE	1	[page, cost, $, **100,980**]	[]	Leaf node
RESOLVE	2	[page, cost, **$**]	[]	$ $\xrightarrow{\text{ARG1}}$ 100,980
RESOLVE	3	[**cost**]	[]	cost $\xrightarrow{\text{ARG1}}$ page, cost $\xrightarrow{\text{ARG2}}$ $

Initial tokenized nodes queue: [A, full, ,, four-color, page, in, Newsweek, will, cost, $, 100,980]

Table 2: Actions required to generate the Figure 2(b) graph for the sentence *"A full, four-color page in Newsweek will cost $100,980."*. The column n indicates the number of nodes to be resolved. When $n = 1$, the resolved node is a leaf node. When $n > 1$, the column RESOLVE details shows the edge involved in the RESOLVE process. Resolved nodes are in normal font. Unresolved nodes are underlined, and the nodes to be resolved in each action are denoted in boldface. The number of RESOLVE in the actions is the same as the number of nodes in the top-node oriented tree. The two IGNORE actions ignore the tokenized nodes *","* and *"will"* respectively.

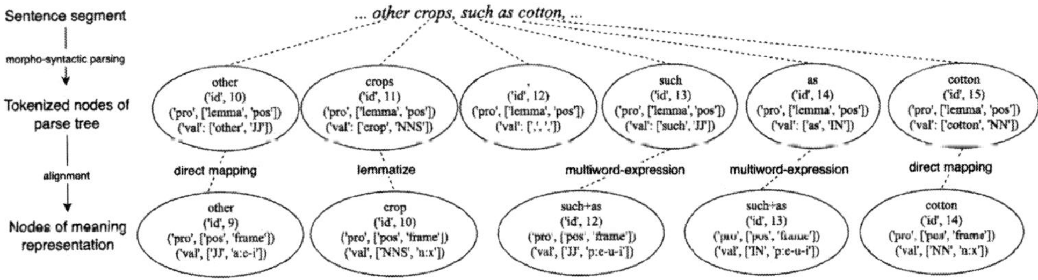

Figure 3: Example of alignment of nodes of DM meaning representation.

pressions (MWE) are also accounted for during the alignment through a greedy look-ahead mechanism, i.e. searching for MWE in S that appeared in train data or the SDP 2016 data (Oepen et al., 2016), which is one of the white-listed resources for the task. Figure 3 illustrates the alignment process from tokenized nodes to nodes of DM representation: MWE *"such as"* is handled with heuristics to produce two nodes; *"crops"* is lemmatized as the label of the produced node; Frames are copied except for punctuation *","*, which is ignored. Details of the alignment process are provided in the supplementary material.

For PSD, only frames that appeared in train data were inferred. Similar to the approach for DM, alignment is generally done by copying $M_j.pos$ and $M_j.label$ from the corresponding $N_i.pos$ and $N_i.lemma$ respectively; and $M_j.frame$ are predicted only for verbs using the same count-based approach as for DM. Multi-word expressions are also accounted for during the alignment process through a greedy look-ahead mechanism. PSD also includes the use of non-lexical nodes for abstract concepts (e.g. *#perspron* for personal pronoun), and they are aligned to N_i first, if possible, followed by lexical nodes.

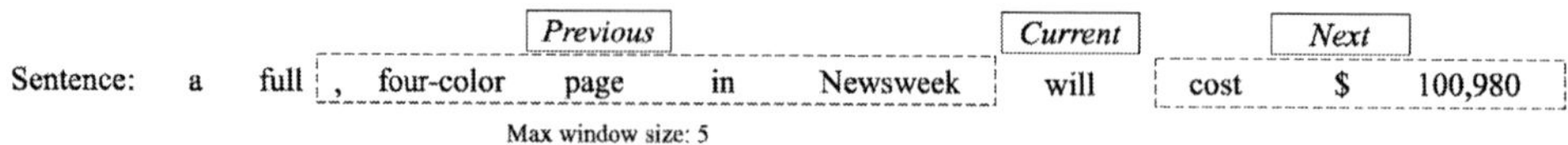

(a) Original sentence with current node, nodes before the current node (previous) and nodes after the current node (Next) annotated.

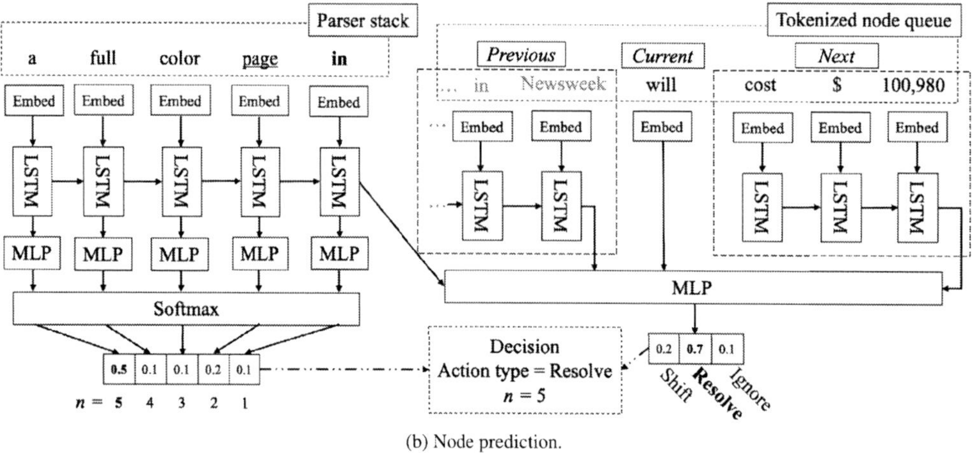

(b) Node prediction.

Figure 4: Neural network architecture diagram of Action type prediction.

For both DM and PSD, given the tokens, frame predictions are done by a simple count-based method, i.e. we choose the most-occurred frame as in the train data given each token; if no such token is found in train data, we choose the first frame from the frame inventories of DM and PSD (white-listed resources) for the corresponding token or lemma. More robust statistical methods for frame prediction are left for future work.

For EDS and UCCA, we use exact matching policy to match the anchors of the tokenized with the graph nodes. If one tokenized node is mapped to multiple graph nodes, we drop the whole graph in the current system. For AMR, we use the JAMR (Flanigan et al., 2014) alignment provided in the companion data to align the unanchored nodes to the tokenized nodes.

2.4 Neural Network Model

To determine the correct action for a particular parser state, we use two neural network models to first decide what action should be taken, and determine the framework details if the action is RE-SOLVE.

2.4.1 Action Type Prediction

Figure 4 describes the neural network architecture for predicting the actions. The nodes in the parser stack and tokenized node queue are first mapped to feature embeddings. The feature embedding of each node is created by concatenating the GloVe (Pennington et al., 2014) word embedding together with three randomly initialized embeddings for the features *word lemma*, *upos* and *xpos* provided by the syntactic parse. Then, we use LSTM (Hochreiter and Schmidhuber, 1997) layers to encode three nodes sequences: (1) nodes in the parser stack, (2) nodes before the current node and (3) nodes after the current node. For sequence (2) and (3) we limit the size of the sequence to be 5. We concatenate the hidden state at the last time step of the three sequences with the current node's feature embedding and feed it to a multilayer perceptron (MLP) to predict the action type. As we need n, the number of nodes to be reduced for the reduce action, we use the hidden states for every time step of sequence (1) and pass them to the same MLP, and then the softmax layer to predict the value of n. We choose the action type and n with the greatest probability to execute. If RESOLVE is to be executed, we extract the first n nodes from the parser stack, and proceed with the RESOLVE prediction.

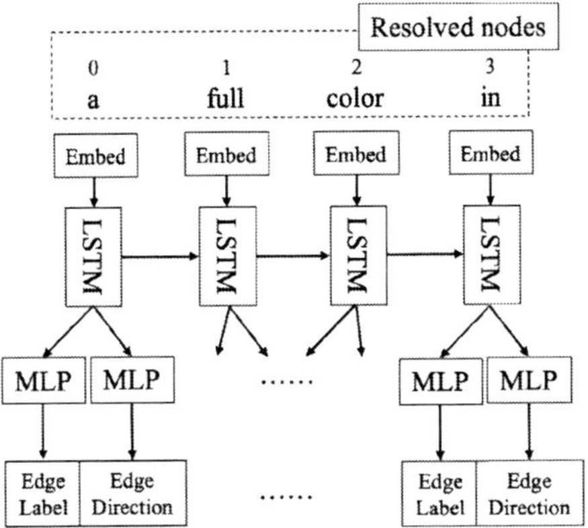

(a) Edge predictions when $n > 1$.

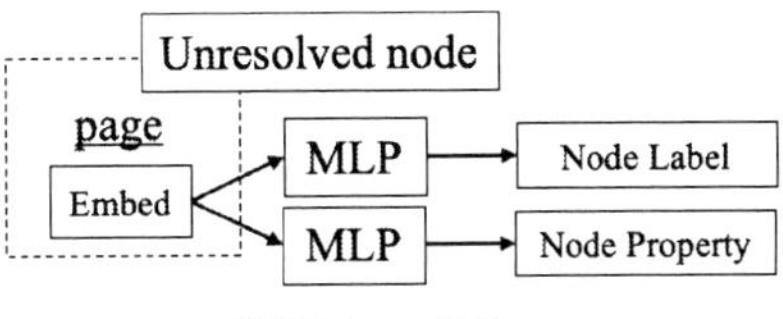

(b) Node prediction.

Figure 5: Neural network architecture diagram of RE-SOLVE prediction.

2.4.2 Resolve Prediction

Figure 5 pictures the neural network architecture for predicting the label and properties of the nodes and edges in the RESOLVE process. If a leaf node is to be resolved ($n = 1$), then no edge is involved. we use the feature embedding of the unresolved node as input, and pass it to feature specific MLP for predicting the node label and properties. If more than one node is involved ($n > 1$), then we, in addition, predict the edge information by passing the feature embedding to an LSTM layer, followed by feature-specific MLPs for predicting edge label and directions.

2.4.3 Multi-Task Learning

To enable multi-task learning, we use the same neural network model for parsing all five frameworks. We shared the parameters of word embeddings and LSTM layers across frameworks, and separate the MLP parameters for each framework.

3 Training

3.1 Data

We use the official dataset as the development set to train our system. We use the DAG-to-Tree preprocessor and action simulator to generate action snapshots of the parser state features (parser stack and tokenized node queue) and action labels for each action applied, acting as the data instances for training the neural network model. A total of 169,780 MRP-parse data pairs are given, for which we generate 2,434,026 action snapshots as training data instances. Our system is required to predict the MRP graphs for 13,206 unseen sentences.

3.2 Implementation Details

Our system is packaged as an AllenNLP library (Gardner et al., 2017), which comprises DAG-to-Tree preprocessors, dataset readers, training instance iterators, neural network models and MRP graph predictors. The neural network model is implemented using Pytorch and support training with either CPU or single GPU setting. Time required for each procedure is summarized in table 3.

Procedures	Required Time (hour)
Run DAG-to-Tree preprocessor and action simulator using training data	10
Use AllenNLP data reader to read data instances	1.5
Train the neural network model (single GPU setting)	30 in total (2 per epoch)
Predict the MRP graph of testing data	8
Total	49.5

Table 3: Running time for each procedure.

3.3 Batch training

As each graph is broken down into training instances for each action and the size of the instances is large, batch training is necessary to speed up the training process. We group the data instance into mini-batch of size 100 by their prediction type (whether it is action type prediction or resolve prediction), meaning representation framework, and the length of the stack and queue to facilitate batch training. Both training batches and training instances in the same framework batch are shuffled in each epoch.

4 Results and Discussion

4.1 Official Results

According to the results announced, we ranked 13th overall in the post-evaluation period of the shared task. We compared the results of our system with a similar transition-based parser TUPA (Hershcovich and Arviv, 2019) in Table 4. Our

Submissions	tops			labels			properties			anchors			edges		
	P	R	F	P	R	F	P	R	F	P	R	F	P	R	F
TUPA(multi)	0.67	0.57	0.616	0.40	0.55	0.457	0.29	0.42	0.327	0.68	0.60	0.626	0.30	0.45	0.347
RESOLVER	0.51	0.50	0.502	0.34	0.40	0.365	0.29	0.35	0.317	0.55	0.59	0.568	0.10	0.10	0.095

Submissions	attributes			all		
	P	R	F	P	R	F
TUPA(multi)	0.06	0.03	0.037	0.39	0.57	0.453
RESOLVER	0.00	0.00	0.00	0.36	0.41	0.378

Table 4: Final results of our system compared with the transition based parser TUPA. All scores are calculated according to the MRP metric.

system performs slightly worse than TUPA in general, while we performed much worse in the edges component.

4.2 Discussion

We analyze our system and investigate three reasons for causing the low performance.

- Variable-arity actions are hard to learn. Our system predicts the action type with accuracy around 0.8 across frameworks, but cannot predict the number of nodes, i.e. n, to be reduced well (less than 0.35). As the number of training instances with $n = 1$ is much larger than that of $n > 1$, we believe the unbalanced number of training examples can be a hindrance for learning to predict n correctly.

- Information loss happens when converting graphs to tree structures. As we are using the DAG-to-Tree preprocessor to convert graphs to top-node oriented trees using major edges, we ignore minor edges in the current model and loss features for predicting the action and chances for predicting them. Moreover, we cannot find direct and empirical proof of why this top-node oriented tree conversion can help the parsing process.

- Model design can still be improved. There are numerous variations including neural network architecture, hyperparameters, action set, feature set, etc, that our team can experiment with under the variable-arity transition action and top-node oriented tree paradigm. More time is required to test if this is a valid approach to tackle the parsing problem in general.

5 Conclusion

We present RESOLVER, the first transition-based parser with top-node oriented DAG-to-Tree preprocessor and variable-arity actions to the best of our knowledge. We aim to create a generalized representation and parsing steps of the five graphs. We discuss the benefits and limitations of adding variable-arity actions, and we will continue to work on our system to show the practical usefulness of allowing variable-arity transition actions in transition-based meaning representation parsers.

References

Omri Abend and Ari Rappoport. 2013. Universal conceptual cognitive annotation (ucca). In *Proceedings of the 51st Annual Meeting of the Association for Computational Linguistics (Volume 1: Long Papers)*, pages 228–238.

Željko Agić, Alexander Koller, and Stephan Oepen. 2015. Semantic dependency graph parsing using tree approximations. In *Proceedings of the 11th International Conference on Computational Semantics*, pages 217–227.

Laura Banarescu, Claire Bonial, Shu Cai, Madalina Georgescu, Kira Griffitt, Ulf Hermjakob, Kevin Knight, Philipp Koehn, Martha Palmer, and Nathan Schneider. 2013. Abstract meaning representation for sembanking. In *Proceedings of the 7th Linguistic Annotation Workshop and Interoperability with Discourse*, pages 178–186.

Daniel Fernández-González and Carlos Gómez-Rodríguez. 2018. Faster shift-reduce constituent parsing with a non-binary, bottom-up strategy. *arXiv preprint arXiv:1804.07961*.

Jeffrey Flanigan, Sam Thomson, Jaime Carbonell, Chris Dyer, and Noah A Smith. 2014. A discriminative graph-based parser for the abstract meaning representation. In *Proceedings of the 52nd Annual Meeting of the Association for Computational Linguistics (Volume 1: Long Papers)*, pages 1426–1436.

Matt Gardner, Joel Grus, Mark Neumann, Oyvind Tafjord, Pradeep Dasigi, Nelson F. Liu, Matthew Peters, Michael Schmitz, and Luke S. Zettlemoyer. 2017. Allennlp: A deep semantic natural language processing platform.

Zhijiang Guo and Wei Lu. 2018. Better transition-based amr parsing with a refined search space. In *Proceedings of the 2018 Conference on Empirical Methods in Natural Language Processing*, pages 1712–1722.

Jan Hajic, Eva Hajicová, Jarmila Panevová, Petr Sgall, Ondrej Bojar, Silvie Cinková, Eva Fucíková, Marie Mikulová, Petr Pajas, Jan Popelka, et al. 2012. Announcing prague czech-english dependency treebank 2.0. In *LREC*, pages 3153–3160.

Daniel Hershcovich, Omri Abend, and Ari Rappoport. 2017. A transition-based directed acyclic graph parser for ucca. *arXiv preprint arXiv:1704.00552*.

Daniel Hershcovich and Ofir Arviv. 2019. TUPA at MRP 2019: A multi-task baseline system. In *Proceedings of the Shared Task on Cross-Framework Meaning Representation Parsing at the 2019 Conference on Natural Language Learning*, pages 28 – 39, Hong Kong, China.

Sepp Hochreiter and Jürgen Schmidhuber. 1997. Long short-term memory. *Neural computation*, 9(8):1735–1780.

Angelina Ivanova, Stephan Oepen, Lilja Øvrelid, and Dan Flickinger. 2012. Who did what to whom?: A contrastive study of syntacto-semantic dependencies. In *Proceedings of the sixth linguistic annotation workshop*, pages 2–11. Association for Computational Linguistics.

Joseph B Kruskal. 1956. On the shortest spanning subtree of a graph and the traveling salesman problem. *Proceedings of the American Mathematical society*, 7(1):48–50.

Yusuke Miyao, Stephan Oepen, and Daniel Zeman. 2014. In-house: An ensemble of pre-existing off-the-shelf parsers. In *Proceedings of the 8th International Workshop on Semantic Evaluation (SemEval 2014)*, pages 335–340.

Joakim Nivre. 2008. Algorithms for deterministic incremental dependency parsing. *Computational Linguistics*, 34(4):513–553.

Stephan Oepen, Omri Abend, Jan Hajič, Daniel Hershcovich, Marco Kuhlmann, Tim O'Gorman, Nianwen Xue, Jayeol Chun, Milan Straka, and Zdeňka Urešová. 2019. MRP 2019: Cross-framework Meaning Representation Parsing. In *Proceedings of the Shared Task on Cross-Framework Meaning Representation Parsing at the 2019 Conference on Natural Language Learning*, pages 1 – 27, Hong Kong, China.

Stephan Oepen, Marco Kuhlmann, Yusuke Miyao, Daniel Zeman, Silvie Cinková, Dan Flickinger, Jan Hajic, Angelina Ivanova, and Zdenka Uresova. 2016. Towards comparability of linguistic graph banks for semantic parsing. In *Proceedings of the Tenth International Conference on Language Resources and Evaluation (LREC 2016)*, pages 3991–3995.

Stephan Oepen and Jan Tore Lønning. 2006. Discriminant-based mrs banking. In *LREC*, pages 1250–1255.

Jeffrey Pennington, Richard Socher, and Christopher Manning. 2014. Glove: Global vectors for word representation. In *Proceedings of the 2014 conference on empirical methods in natural language processing (EMNLP)*, pages 1532–1543.

Natalie Schluter, Anders Søgaard, Jakob Elming, Dirk Hovy, Barbara Plank, Hector Martinez Alonso, Anders Johanssen, and Sigrid Klerke. 2014. Copenhagen-malmö: Tree approximations of semantic parsing problems. In *Proceedings of the 8th International Workshop on Semantic Evaluation (SemEval 2014)*, pages 213–217.

Yuxuan Wang, Wanxiang Che, Jiang Guo, and Ting Liu. 2018. A neural transition-based approach for semantic dependency graph parsing. In *Thirty-Second AAAI Conference on Artificial Intelligence*.

Hitachi at MRP 2019: Unified Encoder-to-Biaffine Network for Cross-Framework Meaning Representation Parsing

Yuta Koreeda*, Gaku Morio*, Terufumi Morishita*, Hiroaki Ozaki*, and Kohsuke Yanai
Hitachi, Ltd.
Research & Development Group
Kokubunji, Tokyo, Japan
{yuta.koreeda.pb, gaku.morio.vn, terufumi.morishita.wp,
hiroaki.ozaki.yu, kohsuke.yanai.cs}@hitachi.com

Abstract

This paper describes the proposed system of the *Hitachi* team for the Cross-Framework Meaning Representation Parsing (MRP 2019) shared task. In this shared task, the participating systems were asked to predict nodes, edges and their attributes for five frameworks, each with different order of "abstraction" from input tokens. We proposed a unified encoder-to-biaffine network for all five frameworks, which effectively incorporates a shared encoder to extract rich input features, decoder networks to generate anchorless nodes in UCCA and AMR, and biaffine networks to predict edges. Our system was ranked fifth with the macro-averaged MRP F1 score of 0.7604, and outperformed the baseline unified transition-based MRP. Furthermore, post-evaluation experiments showed that we can boost the performance of the proposed system by incorporating multi-task learning, whereas the baseline could not. These imply efficacy of incorporating the biaffine network to the shared architecture for MRP and that learning heterogeneous meaning representations at once can boost the system performance.

1 Introduction

This paper describes the proposed system of the *Hitachi* team for the CoNLL 2019 Cross-Framework Meaning Representation Parsing (MRP 2019) shared task. The goal of the task was to design a system that predicts sentence-level graph-based meaning representations in five frameworks, each with its specific linguistic assumptions. The task was formulated as prediction of nodes, edges and their attributes from an input sentence (see Oepen et al. (2019) for details). The target frameworks were (1) DELPH-IN MRS Bi-Lexical Dependencies (DM; Flickinger, 2000;

Ivanova et al., 2012), (2) Prague Semantic Dependencies (PSD; Hajič et al., 2012; Miyao et al., 2014), (3) Elementary Dependency Structures (EDS; Oepen and Lønning, 2006), (4) Universal Conceptual Cognitive Annotation framework (UCCA; Abend and Rappoport, 2013; Hershcovich et al., 2017), and (5) Abstract Meaning Representation (AMR; Banarescu et al., 2013).

In this work, we propose to unify graph predictions in all frameworks with a single encoder-to-biaffine network. This objective was derived from our expectation that it would be advantageous if a single neural network can deal with all the frameworks, because it allows all frameworks to benefit from architectural enhancements and it opens up possibility to perform multi-task learning to boost overall system performance. We argue that it is non-trivial to formulate different kinds of graph predictions as a single machine learning problem, since each framework has different order of "abstraction" from input tokens. Moreover, such formulation has hardly been explored, with few exceptions including unified transition-based MRP (Hershcovich et al., 2018), to which we empirically show the superiority of our system (Section 9). We also present a multi-task variant of such system, which did not make it to the task deadline.

Our *non*-multi-task system obtained the fifth position in the formal evaluation. We also evaluated the multi-task setup after the formal run, showing multi-task learning can yield an improvement in the performance. This result implies learning heterogeneous meaning representations at once can boost the system performance.

2 Overview of the Proposed System

The key challenge in unifying graph predictions with a single encoder-to-biaffine network lays in

---

* Contributed equally.

Proceedings of the Shared Task on Cross-Framework Meaning Representation Parsing at the 2019 CoNLL, pages 114–126
Hong Kong, November 3, 2019. ©2019 Association for Computational Linguistics
https://doi.org/10.18653/v1/K19-2011

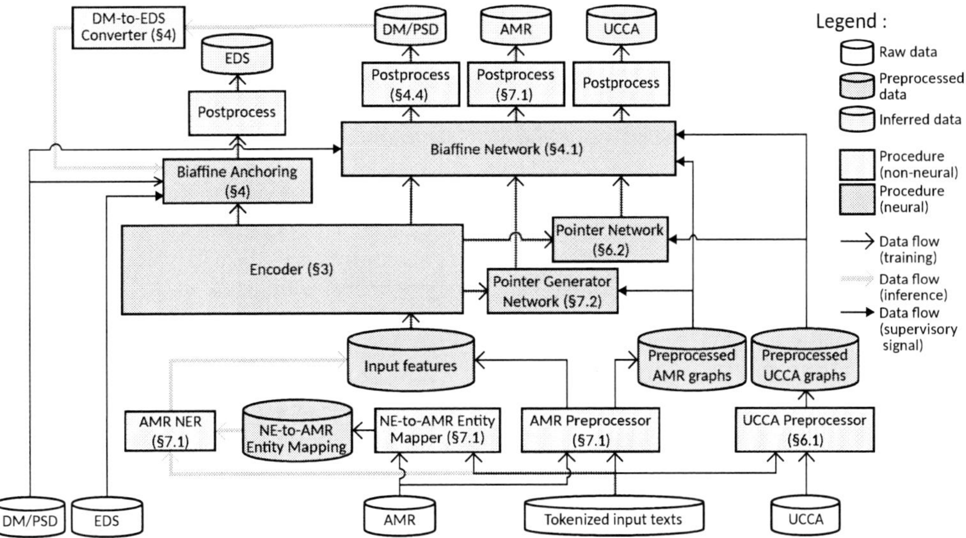

Figure 1: The overview of the proposed unified encoder-to-biaffine network for cross-framework meaning representation parsing.

complementation of nodes, because the biaffine network can narrow down the node candidates but cannot generate new ones. Our strategy is that we start from input tokens, generate missing nodes (nodes that do not have anchors to the input tokens) and finally predict edges with the biaffine network (Figure 1). More concretely, the shared encoder (Section 3.2) fuses together rich input features for each token including features extracted from pretrained language models, which are then fed to bidirectional long short-term memories (biLSTMs; Hochreiter and Schmidhuber, 1997; Schuster and Paliwal, 1997) to obtain task-independent contextualized token representations. The contextualized representations are fed to biaffine networks (Dozat and Manning, 2018) to predict graphs for each framework along with the following framework-specific procedures:

DM and PSD Contextualized representations are fed to biaffine network to predict edges and their labels. They are also used to predict the node property `frame` (Section 4).

EDS The predicted DM graphs are converted to nodes and edges of EDS graphs. Contextualized representations are used to predict node anchors (Section 5).

UCCA Nodes in training data are serialized and aligned with input tokens. Contextualized representations are fed to a pointer network to gen-

erate non-terminal nodes, and to a biaffine network to predict edges and labels (Section 6).

AMR Contextualized representations are fed to pointer-generator network to generate nodes. Hidden states of the network are fed to a biaffine network to predict edges and their labels (Section 7).

All models are trained end-to-end using mini-batch stochastic gradient decent with backpropagation (see Appendix A.1 for the details).

3 Shared Encoder

3.1 Feature Extraction

Following work by Dozat and Manning (2018) and Zhang et al. (2019), we propose to incorporate multiple types of token representations to provide rich input features for each token. Specifically, the proposed system combines surface, lemma, part-of-speech (POS) tags, named entity label, GloVe (Pennington et al., 2014) embedding, ELMo (Peters et al., 2018) embedding and BERT (Devlin et al., 2019) embedding as input features . The following descriptions explain how we acquire each input representations:

Surface and lemma We use the lower-cased node labels and the `lemma` properties from the companion data, respectively. Surfaces and lemmas that appear less than four times are replaced by a special <UNK> token. We also map

numerical expressions[1] to a special <NUM> token.

POS tags We use Universal POS tags and English
specific POS tags from node properties `upos`
and `xpos` in the companion data, respectively.

Named entity label Named entity (NE) recognition is applied to the input text (see Section 7.1).

GloVe We use 300-dimensional GloVe (Pennington et al., 2014) pretrained on Common Crawl[2]
which are kept fixed during the training. Surfaces that do not appear in the pretrained GloVe
are mapped to a special <UNK> token which is
set to a vector whose values are randomly drawn
from normal distribution with standard deviation of $1/\sqrt{\text{dimension of a GloVe vector}}$.

ELMo We use the pretrained "original" ELMo[3].
Following Peters et al. (2018), we "mix" different layers of ELMo for each token;

$$\tilde{s}_j = \operatorname*{softmax}_j(s_j) = \frac{\exp(s_j)}{\sum_k \exp(s_k)},$$

$$\mathbf{h}^{ELMo} = \sum_{j=0}^{N^{ELMo}-1} \tilde{s}_j \mathbf{h}_j^{ELMo},$$

where $\mathbf{h}_j^{ELMo}$ $(0 \leq j < N^{ELMo})$ is the hidden
state of the j-th layer of ELMo, $\mathbf{h}_0^{ELMo}$ is the
features from character-level CNN of ELMo,
and s_j are trainable parameters. $\mathbf{h}_j^{ELMo}$ are
fixed in the training by truncating backpropagation to $\mathbf{h}_j^{ELMo}$.

BERT We use the pretrained BERT-Large, Uncased (Original)[4]. Since BERT takes subword
units as input, a BERT embedding for a token is
generated as the average of its subword BERT
embeddings as in Zhang et al. (2019).

The surface, lemma, POS tags and NE label of
a token are each embedded as a vector. The vectors are randomly initialized and updated during
training. To allow prediction of the top nodes for
DM, PSD and UCCA, a special <ROOT> token

is prepended to each input sequence. For GloVe,
ELMo and BERT, the <ROOT> is also embedded in the similar manner as other tokens with
<ROOT> as the surface for the token. A multi-
layered perceptron (MLP) is applied to each of
GloVe, ELMo and BERT embeddings.

To prevent the model from overrelying only
on certain types of features, we randomly drop a
group of features, where the groups are (i) lemma,
(ii) POS tags and (iii) the rest. All features in the
same group are randomly dropped simultaneously
but independently from other groups.

All seven features are then concatenated to form
input token representation $\mathbf{h}_i^0$ (where $0 \leq i < L_{in}$
is the index of the token).

3.2 Obtaining Contextualized Token Representation

The input token representations $\mathbf{h}_i^0$ are fed to the
multi-layered biLSTM with N layers to obtain the
contextualized token representations.

$$\overrightarrow{\mathbf{h}}_i^l = \overrightarrow{\text{LSTM}}(\mathbf{h}_i^{l-1}, \overrightarrow{\mathbf{h}}_{i-1}^l, \overrightarrow{\mathbf{c}}_{i-1}^l),$$

$$\overleftarrow{\mathbf{h}}_i^l = \overleftarrow{\text{LSTM}}(\mathbf{h}_i^{l-1}, \overleftarrow{\mathbf{h}}_{i+1}^l, \overleftarrow{\mathbf{c}}_{i+1}^l),$$

$$\mathbf{h}_i^l = \left[\overrightarrow{\mathbf{h}}_i^l; \overleftarrow{\mathbf{h}}_i^l\right],$$

where $\mathbf{h}_i^l$ and $\mathbf{c}_i^l$ $(0 < l \leq N)$ are the hidden states
and the cell states of the l-th layer LSTM for i-th
token.

4 DM and PSD-specific Procedures

4.1 Biaffine Classifier

DM and PSD are Flavor (0) frameworks whose
nodes have one-to-one correspondence to tokens.
We utilize biaffine networks to filter nodes, and to
predict edges, edge labels and node attributes. For
each framework $\text{fw} \in \{\text{dm}, \text{psd}\}$, probability that
there exists an edge (i, j) from the i-th node to the
j-th node $y_{\text{fw},i,j}^{\text{edge}}$ is calculated for all pairs of nodes
$(0 \leq i, j < L_{in})$.

$$\mathbf{h}_{\text{fw},i}^{\text{edge\_from}} = \text{MLP}^{\text{edge\_from}}(\mathbf{h}_i^N),$$

$$\mathbf{h}_{\text{fw},i}^{\text{edge\_to}} = \text{MLP}^{\text{edge\_to}}(\mathbf{h}_i^N),$$

$$y_{\text{fw},i,j}^{\text{edge}} = \sigma\left(\text{Biaff}_{\text{fw}}^{\text{edge}}\left(\mathbf{h}_{\text{fw},i}^{\text{edge\_from}}, \mathbf{h}_{\text{fw},j}^{\text{edge\_to}}\right)\right), \tag{1}$$

where σ is an element-wise sigmoid function. Biaffine operation $\text{Biaff}^{\text{edge}}$ is defined as:

$$\text{Biaff}_{\text{fw}}^{\text{edge}}(\mathbf{x}, \mathbf{y}) = \mathbf{x}^\top \mathbf{U}_{\text{fw}}^{\text{edge}} \mathbf{y} + \mathbf{W}_{\text{fw}}^{\text{edge}}[\mathbf{x}; \mathbf{y}] + b_{\text{fw}}^{\text{edge}},$$

---

[1] Surfaces or lemmas that can successfully be converted to numerics with `float` operation on Python 3.6

[2] `http://nlp.stanford.edu/data/glove.840B.300d.zip`

[3] `https://s3-us-west-2.amazonaws.com/allennlp/models/elmo/2x4096_512_2048cnn_2xhighway/elmo_2x4096_512_2048cnn_2xhighway_weights.hdf5` and `elmo_2x4096_512_2048cnn_2xhighway_options.json`.

[4] `https://s3.amazonaws.com/models.huggingface.co/bert/bert-large-uncased-pytorch_model.bin`, which is converted from the whitelisted BERT model in `https://github.com/google-research/bert`

where $\mathbf{U}_{\text{fw}}^{\text{edge}}$, $\mathbf{W}_{\text{fw}}^{\text{edge}}$ and $b_{\text{fw}}^{\text{edge}}$ are model parameters. Probability of an edge (i, j) being the c-th edge label $y_{\text{fw},i,j,c}^{\text{label}}$ is calculated for all pairs of nodes.

$$
\begin{aligned}
\mathbf{h}_{\text{fw},i}^{\text{label\_from}} &= \text{MLP}^{\text{label\_from}}(\mathbf{h}_i^N), \\
\mathbf{h}_{\text{fw},i}^{\text{label\_to}} &= \text{MLP}^{\text{label\_to}}(\mathbf{h}_i^N), \\
t_{\text{fw},i,j,c}^{\text{label}} &= \text{Biaff}_{\text{fw},c}^{\text{label}}\left(\mathbf{h}_{\text{fw},i}^{\text{label\_from}}, \mathbf{h}_{\text{fw},j}^{\text{label\_to}}\right), \\
y_{\text{fw},i,j,c}^{\text{label}} &= \operatorname*{softmax}_c\left(t_{\text{fw},i,j,c}^{\text{label}}\right).
\end{aligned}
\tag{2}
$$

Another form of biaffine operation for the edge label prediction $\text{Biaff}_{\text{fw},c}^{\text{label}}$ is defined as:

$$
\text{Biaff}_{\text{fw},c}^{\text{label}}(\mathbf{x},\mathbf{y}) = \mathbf{x}^\top \mathbf{U}_{\text{fw},c}^{\text{label}}\mathbf{y} + \mathbf{W}_{\text{fw},c}^{\text{label}}\mathbf{y},
$$

where $\mathbf{U}_{\text{fw},c}^{\text{label}}$ and $\mathbf{W}_{\text{fw},c}^{\text{label}}$ are model parameters.

A candidate edge (i, j) whose edge probability $y_{\text{fw},i,j}^{\text{edge}}$ $(0 < i, j)$ exceeds 0.5 is adopted as a valid edge. Edge label with the highest probability $\arg\max_c y_{\text{fw},i,j,c}$ is selected for each valid edge (i, j). A candidate top node j whose edge probability $y_{\text{fw},0,j}^{\text{edge}}$ $(0 < j)$ exceeds 0.5 is adopted as a top node, allowing multiple tops. Non-top nodes with no incoming or outgoing edge are discarded and remaining nodes are adopted as the predicted nodes.

4.2 DM Frame Classifier

A DM node property `frame` consists of a frame type and frame arguments; e.g. `named:x-c` indicates the frame type is "named entity" with two possible arguments x and c. The proposed system utilizes the contextualized features to predict the frame types and arguments separately.

Probability of the i-th node being c-th frame type $y_{\text{dm},i,c}^{\text{frame\_type}}$ is predicted by applying MLP to the contextualized features:

$$
\begin{aligned}
t_{\text{dm},i,c}^{\text{frame\_type}} &= \text{MLP}_c^{\text{frame\_type}}(\mathbf{h}_i^N), \\
y_{\text{dm},i,c}^{\text{frame\_type}} &= \operatorname*{softmax}_c\left(t_{\text{dm},i,c}^{\text{frame\_type}}\right).
\end{aligned}
$$

The number of arguments for a frame is not fixed and the first argument can be trivially inferred from the frame type. Thus, we predict from the second to the fifth arguments for each node. Probability of j-th argument being c-th frame type $y_{\text{dm},i,j,c}^{\text{frame\_arg}}$ is also predicted by applying MLP to the contextualized features:

$$
\begin{aligned}
t_{\text{dm},i,j,c}^{\text{frame\_arg}} &= \text{MLP}_{j,c}^{\text{frame\_arg}}(\mathbf{h}_i^N), \\
y_{\text{dm},i,j,c}^{\text{frame\_arg}} &= \operatorname*{softmax}_c\left(t_{\text{dm},i,j,c}^{\text{frame\_arg},j}\right).
\end{aligned}
$$

4.3 Training Objective

DM and PSD are trained jointly in a multi-task learning setting but independently from other frameworks. The loss for the edge prediction $\ell_{\text{fw}}^{\text{edge}}$ is cross entropy between the predicted edge $y_{i,j}^{\text{edge}}$ and the corresponding ground truth label. A top node j is treated as an edge $(0, j)$ and is trained along with the edge prediction. The loss for the edge label prediction $\ell_{\text{fw}}^{\text{label}}$ is cross entropy between the predicted edge label $y_{i,j,c}^{\text{label}}$ and ground truth label. The loss for the frame prediction $\ell_{\text{dm}}^{\text{frame}}$ is the sum of the frame type prediction loss $\ell_{\text{dm}}^{\text{frame\_type}}$ and the frame arguments prediction loss $\ell_{\text{dm}}^{\text{frame\_arg}}$, both of which are cross entropy loss between the prediction and the corresponding ground truth label. Final multi-task loss is defined as:

$$
\begin{aligned}
\ell_{\text{sdp}} =& \lambda^{\text{label}}\left(\ell_{\text{dm}}^{\text{label}} + \ell_{\text{psd}}^{\text{label}} + \lambda^{\text{frame}}\ell_{\text{dm}}^{\text{frame}}\right) \\
& + \left(1 - \lambda^{\text{label}}\right)\left(\ell_{\text{dm}}^{\text{edge}} + \ell_{\text{psd}}^{\text{edge}}\right).
\end{aligned}
\tag{3}
$$

4.4 Postprocessing

We reconstruct node property `frame` from the predicted frame types and arguments using external resources. For DM, we filter out pairs of predicted frame type and arguments that do not appear in ERG SEM-I[5] or the training dataset (e.g. a word "parse" has only two possible frames `n:x` and `v:e-i-p`). Then, we select a frame with the highest *empirically scaled likelihood* which is calculated by scaling predicted joint probability $y_{\text{dm},i,c}^{\text{frame\_type}} \prod_j y_{\text{dm},i,j,c'}^{\text{frame\_arg}}$ proportionally to the frame frequency in the corpus.

For PSD, we use CzEngVallex[6], which contains frequency and the required arguments of each frame, to reconstruct frames. We identify the frame type of a token from its lemma and POS tag. Then, candidate frames are filtered using the required arguments (extracted by stripping `-suffix` from connected edges) and the most frequent frame is chosen as the node frame.

Token lemma is used for the node label, except for the special node labels in PSD (e.g. `#Bracket` and `#PersPron`) that are looked-up from a hand-crafted dictionary using the surface and POS tag as a key.

---

[5] `http://svn.delph-in.net/erg/tags/1214/etc`

[6] `http://hdl.handle.net/11234/1-1512`

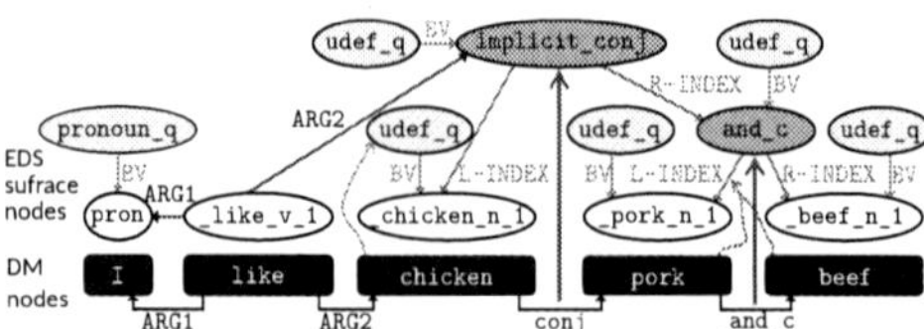

Figure 2: Generation of abstract nodes and their edges from *I like chicken, pork and beef.*

5   EDS-specific Procedure

DM graphs are constructed by lossy conversion from EDS graphs, both of which are derived from English Resource Semantics (ERS; Flickinger et al., 2014). Making use of such relationship, we developed heuristic inverse conversion from DM to EDS graphs by carefully studying EDS-to-DM conversion rules described in the ERG SEM-I corpus. Specifically, our system generates EDS in three steps; the system (i) convert all DM nodes to EDS surface nodes[7] with simple rules, (ii) generate abstract nodes, and (iii) predict anchors for the abstract nodes.

We explain the generation of abstract nodes (ii) in details using an example in Figure 2:

1. Some abstract nodes (e.g. _and_c) and their node labels are generated with rules.
2. Presence of an abstract node on a node or an edge is detected with rules (e.g. _and_c implies presence of _q node) or with binary logistic regression (e.g. udef_q on _chicken_n_1).
3. The system predicts labels of the nodes generated in 2 using multi-class logistic regression.
4. The system predicts labels of edges from/to the generated nodes using multi-class logistic regression.

POS tags, predicted DM frames and edge labels of adjacent nodes are used as features for the logistic regression.

We employ another neural network that utilize the contextualized features from the encoder to predict the anchors for the generated abstract nodes (iii). For each abstract node (indexed i), let $\mathcal{T}_i$ be a subset of token indices $\mathcal{S} \equiv \{0, \ldots, L_{in} - 1\}$ each of which is selected as a DM node and the corresponding EDS surface node has the abstract node i as an ancestor. First, we create an

---

[7]For ease of explanation, we adopt a definition that "the EDS surface nodes are the nodes that appear in DM and the abstract nodes are those that do not" which results in slight inconsistence with the original definition.

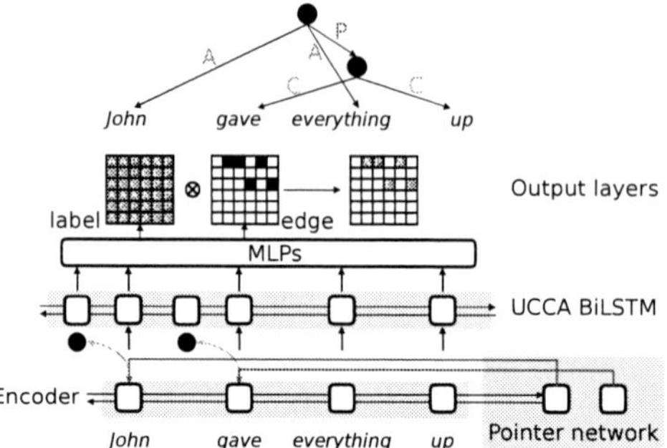

Figure 3: Illustration of UCCA parsing with pointer network and biaffine classifier.

input feature $x_{i,j}^{\text{eds}}$ ($j \in \mathcal{S}$) which is set as the label of node i if $j \in \mathcal{T}_i$ or <UNK> otherwise. Then, we embed $x_{i,j}^{\text{eds}}$ to obtain trainable vector $\mathbf{e}_{i,j}^{\text{eds}}$ and feed them to a biLSTM to obtain a contextualized representation $\boldsymbol{h}_{i,j}^{\text{eds}}$. Finally, we predict a span in input tokens $[\text{argmax}_j y_{i,j}^{\text{eds\_from}}, \text{argmax}_j y_{i,j}^{\text{eds\_to}}]$ for the i-th abstract node,

$$y_{i,j}^{\text{eds\_from}} = \underset{j}{\text{softmax}} \left((\mathbf{h}_{i,j}^{\text{eds}})^\top \cdot \text{MLP}^{\text{eds\_from}}(\mathbf{h}_j^N) \right),$$

$$y_{i,j}^{\text{eds\_to}} = \underset{j}{\text{softmax}} \left((\mathbf{h}_{i,j}^{\text{eds}})^\top \cdot \text{MLP}^{\text{eds\_to}}(\mathbf{h}_j^N) \right).$$

The loss for the anchor prediction ℓ_{eds} is the sum of cross entropy between the predicted span $(y_{i,j}^{\text{eds\_from}}, y_{i,j}^{\text{eds\_to}})$ and the corresponding ground truth span.

6   UCCA-specific Procedure

A UCCA graph consists of terminal nodes which represent words, non-terminal nodes which represent internal structure, and labeled edges (e.g., participant (A), center (C), linker (L), process (P) and punctuation (U)) which represent connections between the nodes. Motivated by the recent advances in constituency parsing, we predict spans of each terminal nodes at once without using any complicated mechanism as seen in transition-based (Hershcovich and Arviv, 2019) and greedy bottom-up (Yu and Sagae, 2019) systems. Our proposed UCCA parser (Figure 3) consists of (i) a pointer network (Vinyals et al., 2015) which generates non-terminal nodes from the contextualized token representations of the encoder, (ii) an additional biLSTM that encodes context of both the terminal and generated non-terminal nodes, and (iii) a biaffine network which predicts edges.

6.1 Preprocessing

We treat the generation of non-terminal nodes as a "pointing" problem. Specifically, the system has to point the starting position of a span which has terminal or non-terminal children. For example, upper part of Figure 3 shows a graph with two non-terminal nodes •. The right non-terminal node has a span of *gave everything up*, and our system points at the starting position of the span *gave*. By taking such strategy, we can serialize the graph in a consistent, straightforward manner; i.e. by inserting the non-terminal nodes to the left of the corresponding span.

The system also has to predict an anchor of a proper noun or a compound expression to merge constituent tokens into a single node. For example, *no feathers in stock!!!!* is tokenized as *"(no), (feathers), (in), (stock), (!), (!), (!), (!)"* according to the companion data, but the UCCA parser is expected to output *"(no), (feathers), (in), (stock), (!!!!)"*. To solve the problem, we formulate the mergence of tokens as edge prediction; e.g. we assume that there exist virtual edges CT from leftmost constituent token to each subsequent token within a compound expression:

and CT is predicted by the system along with the other edges. There still exists tokenization discrepancy between the companion data and the graphs from EWT and Wiki. The graphs with such discrepancy are simply discarded from the training data.

6.2 Generating Non-terminal Nodes with Pointer Network

Our system generates non-terminal nodes by pointing where to insert non-terminal nodes as described in Section 6.1. To point a terminal node, we employ a pointer network, which is a decoder that uses attention mechanism to produce probability distribution over the input tokens. Given hidden states of the encoder $\mathbf{h}_j^N$, hidden states of the decoder are initialized by the last states of the shared encoder:

$$\mathbf{h}_{-1}^{\text{ucca\_dec}} = \left[\overrightarrow{\mathbf{h}}_{L_{in}}^{N-K:N}; \overleftarrow{\mathbf{h}}_0^{N-K:N} \right],$$

$$\mathbf{c}_{-1}^{\text{ucca\_dec}} = \left[\overrightarrow{\mathbf{c}}_{L_{in}}^{N-K:N}; \overleftarrow{\mathbf{c}}_0^{N-K:N} \right],$$

where K is the stacking number of the biLSTMs in the shared encoder. We then obtain the hidden states of the decoder $\mathbf{h}_i^{\text{ucca\_dec}}$ as:

$$\mathbf{h}_i^{\text{ucca\_dec}} = \text{LSTM}_{\text{dec}}(\mathbf{x}_i^{\text{ucca\_dec}}, \mathbf{h}_{i-1}^{\text{ucca\_dec}}, \mathbf{c}_{i-1}^{\text{ucca\_dec}}).$$

Attention distribution $\tilde{a}_{i,j}$ over the input tokens is calculated as:

$$a_{i,j} = \mathbf{v}^\top \tanh\left(\mathbf{W}^{\text{ucca\_dec}}[\mathbf{h}_i^{\text{ucca\_dec}}; \mathbf{h}_j^N]\right),$$

$$\tilde{a}_{i,j} = \operatorname*{softmax}_j(a_{i,j}),$$

where $\mathbf{W}^{\text{ucca\_dec}}$ and $\mathbf{v}$ are parameters of the pointer network. The successive input to the decoder $\mathbf{x}_{i+1}^{\text{ucca\_dec}}$ is the encoder states of the pointed token $\mathbf{h}_{\operatorname{argmax}_j \tilde{a}_{i,j}}^N$. $\mathbf{x}_i^{\text{ucca\_dec}}$ is chosen from the gold $\tilde{a}_{i,j}$ when training.

The decoder terminates its generation when it finally points the <ROOT>. We obtain new hidden states $\mathbf{h}_i^{\text{ucca\_ptr}}$ ($0 \leq i \leq L_{\text{ucca}}$) by inserting pointer representations $\mathbf{h}^\bullet$ before the pointed token. For example, *John gave everything up* (discussed above) will have hidden states

$$\left(\mathbf{h}_{<\text{ROOT}>}^N, \mathbf{h}^\bullet, \mathbf{h}_{\text{John}}^N, \mathbf{h}^\bullet, \mathbf{h}_{\text{gave}}^N, \mathbf{h}_{\text{everything}}^N, \mathbf{h}_{\text{up}}^N\right).$$

The pointer representation is defined as $\mathbf{h}^\bullet = \text{MLP}_\bullet(\mathbf{r})$, where $\mathbf{r}$ is a randomly initialized constant vector.

We note that the generated non-terminal nodes $\mathbf{h}^\bullet$ lack positional information because all $\mathbf{h}^\bullet$ have the same values. To remedy this problem, a positional encoding Vaswani et al. (2017) is concatenated to each of $\mathbf{h}_i^{\text{ucca\_ptr}}$ to obtain position-aware $\mathbf{h}_i^{\text{ucca\_ptr}'}$. Furthermore, we feed $\mathbf{h}_i^{\text{ucca\_ptr}'}$ to an additional biLSTM and obtain $\mathbf{h}_i^{\text{ucca}}$ in order to further encode the order information.

6.3 Edge Prediction with Biaffine Network

Now that we have contextualized representations for all candidate terminal and non-terminal nodes, the system can simply predict the edges and their labels in the exact same way as Flavor (0) graphs (Section 4.1). Following Equation (1) and Equation (2), we obtain probabilities if there exists an edge (i, j), $y_{\text{ucca},i,j}^{\text{edge}}$, and its label being c, $y_{\text{ucca},i,j,c}^{\text{label}}$, with the input being $\mathbf{h}_i^{\text{ucca}}$ instead of $\mathbf{h}_i^N$. We treat the remote edges[8] independently but in the same way as the primary edges to predict $y_{\text{ucca},i,j}^{\text{remote}}$.

The loss for the edge prediction $\ell_{\text{ucca}}^{\text{edge}}$, the edge label prediction $\ell_{\text{ucca}}^{\text{label}}$, the remote edge prediction

---

[8] Edges for implicit relations and arguments. They were annotated as unlabeled edges each with an attribute `remote` in MRP.

$\ell_{\text{ucca}}^{\text{remote}}$ and the pointer prediction $\ell_{\text{ucca}}^{\text{dec}}$ are defined as cross entropy between the prediction $y_{\text{ucca},i,j}^{\text{edge}}$, $y_{\text{ucca},i,j,c}^{\text{label}}$, $y_{\text{ucca},i,j}^{\text{remote}}$ and $\tilde{a}_{i,j}$ with the corresponding ground truth labels, respectively. Thus, we arrive at the multi-task objective defined as:

$$\ell_{\text{ucca}} = \lambda_{\text{ucca}}^{\text{edge}} \ell_{\text{ucca}}^{\text{edge}} + \lambda_{\text{ucca}}^{\text{label}} \ell_{\text{ucca}}^{\text{label}} + \lambda_{\text{ucca}}^{\text{remote}} \ell_{\text{ucca}}^{\text{remote}} + \lambda_{\text{ucca}}^{\text{dec}} \ell_{\text{ucca}}^{\text{dec}}.$$

7 AMR-specific Procedures

Because AMR graphs do not have clear alignment between input tokens and nodes, the nodes have to be identified in prior to predicting edges. Following Zhang et al. (2019), we incorporate a pointer-generator network (i.e. a decoder with copy mechanisms) for the node generation and a biaffine network for the edge prediction. There are two key preconditions in using a pointer-generator network; i.e. (i) node labels and input tokens share fair amount of vocabulary to allow copying a node from input tokens, and (ii) graphs are serialized in a consistent, straightforward manner for it to be easily predicted by sequence generation. To this end, we apply preprocessing to raw AMR graphs, train model to generate preprocessed graphs, and reconstruct final AMR graphs with postprocessing.

7.1 Preprocessing

We modify the input tokens and the node labels to account for the precondition (i). A node labeled with `.*-entity` or a subgraph connected with `name` edge is replaced with a node whose label is an anonymized entity label such as `PERSON.0` (Konstas et al., 2017). Then, for each entity node, a corresponding span of tokens is identified by rules similar to Flanigan et al. (2014); i.e. a span of tokens with the longest common prefix between the token surfaces and the node attribute (e.g. for `date-entity` whose attribute `month` is `11`, we search for "November" and "Nov" in the token surfaces). Unlike Zhang et al. (2019) which has replaced input token surfaces with anonymized entity labels, we add them as an additional input feature as described in Section 3.1 to avoid hurting the performance of other frameworks. At the prediction, we first identify NE tags in input tokens with Illinois NER tagger (Ratinov and Roth, 2009). Then we map them to anonymized entity labels with frequency-based mapping constructed from the training dataset.

For non-entity nodes, we strip sense indices (e.g. `-01`) from node labels (Lyu and Titov, 2018), which will then share fair amount of vocabulary with the input token lemmas. Nodes with labels that still do not appear as lemmas after preprocessing are subject to normal generation from decoder vocabulary.

Directly serializing an AMR graph, which is a directed acyclic graph (DAG), may result in a complex conversion, which do not fulfill the precondition (ii). Therefore, we convert DAG to a spanning tree by replicating nodes with reentrancies (i.e. nodes with more than one incoming edge) for each incoming edge and serialize the graph with simple pre-order traversal over the tree.

7.2 Extended Pointer-Generator Network

We employ an extended pointer-generator network. It automatically switches between three generation strategies; i.e. (1) *source-side copy*, (2) *decoder-side copy* that copies nodes that have been already generated, and (3) normal generation from decoder vocabulary. More formally, it uses attention mechanism to calculate probability distribution $\mathbf{p}_i$ over input tokens, generated nodes and node vocabulary. Given contextualized token representation of the encoder $H_i^{\text{enc}} = \{\mathbf{h}_0^l, \ldots, \mathbf{h}_{L_{in}-1}^l\}$, we obtain hidden states of the decoder $\mathbf{h}_i^{\text{amr}}$ and $\mathbf{p}_i$ as:

$$\mathbf{h}_i^{\text{amr}}, \mathbf{p}_i = \text{Decoder}_{\text{amr}}(\mathbf{h}_i^{\text{enc'}}, \mathbf{h}_{i-1}^{\text{amr}}, \mathbf{p}_{i-1}, H_N^{\text{enc}}),$$
$$\mathbf{h}_i^{\text{enc'}} = \text{Encoder}_{\text{amr}}(\mathbf{p}_i, \mathbf{h}_0^{\text{amr}} \ldots \mathbf{h}_{i-1}^{\text{amr}}, H_0^{\text{enc}}),$$
$$\mathbf{h}_0^{\text{enc'}}, \mathbf{h}_{-1}^{\text{amr}} = \text{MLP}_{\text{amr}}\left(\left[\overrightarrow{\mathbf{h}}_{L_{in}}^N ; \overleftarrow{\mathbf{h}}_0^N ; \overrightarrow{\mathbf{c}}_{L_{in}}^N ; \overleftarrow{\mathbf{c}}_0^N \right] \right).$$

$\text{Encoder}_{\text{amr}}$ treats a node as if it is a token, and utilizes the encoder (Section 3) with shared model parameters to obtain representation of $(i-1)$-th generated nodes $h_i^{\text{enc'}}$. Concretely, $\text{Encoder}_{\text{amr}}$ combines lemma (corresponds to the node label), POS tags (only when copied from a token) and GloVe (from the node label) of a node, embeds each of them to a feature vector using the encoder and concatenates feature vectors to obtain $h_i^{\text{enc'}}$.

7.3 Edge Prediction with Biaffine Network

Now that we have representations $\mathbf{h}_i^{\text{amr}}$ for all nodes, the system can simply predict the edges and their labels in the same way as Flavor (0) graphs (Section 4.1). Following Equation (1) and Equation (2), we obtain probabilities that there exists an

Table 1: MRP F1 scores for the formal run (shown as "score/rank")

Team	Mean	DM	PSD	EDS	UCCA	AMR
HIT-SCIR	.8620/1	.9508/2	.9055/4	.9075/2	.8167/1	.7294/2
SJTU-NICT	.8527/2	.9550/1	.9119/3	.8990/3	.7780/3	.7197/3
SUDA-Alibaba	.8396/3	.9226/7	.8556/8	.9185/1	.7843/2	.7172/5
Saarland	.8187/4	.9469/4	.9128/1	.8910/4	.6755/6	.6672/6
Hitachi (ours)	**.7604/5**	**.9102/8**	**.9121/2**	**.8374/6**	**.7036/5**	**.4386/8**
ÚFAL MRPipe	.7474/6	.8495/9	.7627/9	.6745/7	.7322/4	.7183/4
ShanghaiTech	.6697/7	.9488/3	.8949/6	.8690/5	-	.6359/7
Amazon	.5132/8	.9326/6	.8998/5	-	-	.7338/1
JBNU	.4652/9	.9401/5	.8788/7	-	.5069/7	-
SJTU	.4303/10	.4315/11	.4761/11	.5321/8	.3266/9	.3851/9
ÚFAL-Oslo	.3442/11	.8051/10	.6092/10	.3064/9	-	-
HKUST	.2450/12	.3699/12	.3529/12	-	.5021/8	-
Bocharov	.0655/13	-	-	-	-	.3273/10
TUPA[†] single	.5770	.5554	.5176	.8100	.2756	.4473
TUPA[†] multi	.4534	.4270	.5265	.7395	.2365	.3375

[†] baseline (Hershcovich and Arviv, 2019)

edge (i, j), $y^{\text{edge}}_{\text{amr},i,j}$, and its label being c, $y^{\text{label}}_{\text{amr},i,j,c}$, with the input being $\mathbf{h}^{\text{amr}}_i$ instead of $\mathbf{h}^N_i$. Note that we do not predict the top nodes for AMR, because the first generated node is always the top node in our formalism.

The loss for the edge prediction $\ell^{\text{edge}}_{\text{amr}}$, the edge label prediction $\ell^{\text{label}}_{\text{amr}}$, and the decoder prediction $\ell^{\text{dec}}_{\text{amr}}$ are cross entropy between the prediction $y^{\text{edge}}_{\text{amr},i,j}$, $y^{\text{label}}_{\text{amr},i,j,c}$ and $\mathbf{p}_i$ with the corresponding ground truth labels, respectively. Thus, we arrive at the multi-task loss for AMR defined as:

$$\ell_{\text{amr}} = \lambda^{\text{biaf}}_{\text{amr}} \left(\lambda^{\text{label}}_{\text{amr}} \ell^{\text{label}}_{\text{amr}} + (1 - \lambda^{\text{label}}_{\text{amr}}) \ell^{\text{edge}}_{\text{amr}} \right) + \lambda^{\text{cov}}_{\text{amr}} \ell^{\text{cov}}_{\text{amr}} + (1 - \lambda^{\text{biaf}}_{\text{amr}} - \lambda^{\text{cov}}_{\text{amr}}) \ell^{\text{dec}}_{\text{amr}},$$

where $\ell^{\text{cov}}_{\text{amr}}$ is coverage loss (Zhang et al., 2019).

For node prediction, we adopt beam search with search width of five. For edge prediction, we apply Chu-Liu-Edmonds algorithm to find the maximum spanning tree. Postprocessing, which includes inverse transformation of the preprocessing, is applied to reconstruct final AMR graphs.

8 Multi-task Variant

We developed multi-task variant after the formal run. Multi-task variant is trained to minimize following multi-task loss,

$$\ell_{mt} = \lambda^{\text{biaf}} \left(\lambda^{\text{label}} \left(\sum_{\text{fw}} \ell^{\text{label}}_{\text{fw}} + \lambda^{\text{frame}} \ell^{\text{frame}}_{\text{dm}} \right) \right.$$
$$\left. + (1 - \lambda^{\text{label}}) \sum_{\text{fw}} \ell^{\text{edge}}_{\text{fw}} \right) + \lambda^{\text{cov}}_{\text{amr}} \ell^{\text{cov}}_{\text{amr}}$$
$$+ \sum_{\text{tw} \in \{\text{ucca},\text{amr}\}} \lambda^{\text{dec}}_{\text{fw}} \ell^{\text{dec}}_{\text{fw}} + \lambda^{\text{remote}}_{\text{ucca}} \ell^{\text{remote}}_{\text{ucca}}.$$
$$(4)$$

All training data is simply merged and losses for frameworks that are missing in an input data are set to zero. For example, if an input sentence has reference graphs for DM, PSD and AMR, losses for UCCA ($\ell^{\text{label}}_{\text{ucca}}$, $\ell^{\text{edge}}_{\text{ucca}}$, $\ell^{\text{dec}}_{\text{ucca}}$ and $\ell^{\text{remote}}_{\text{ucca}}$) are set to zero and sum of other losses are used to update the model parameters. Then, the training data (sentences) are shuffled at the start of each epoch and are fed sequentially to update the model parameters as in normal mini-batch training. No under-/over-sampling was done to scale the losses of frameworks, each with different number of reference graphs, but we instead applied early stopping for each framework separately (see Appendix A for the details). For EDS, we do not train EDS anchor prediction jointly even in multi-task setting but apply transfer learning; the encoder of the EDS anchor prediction network is initialized from trained multi-task model.

We also experimented with a *fine-tuned* multi-task variant. For each target framework, we take the multi-task variant as a pretrained model (whose training data also includes the target framework) and train the model on the target framework independently to the other frameworks (except for DM and PSD, which are always trained together).

9 Experiments

9.1 Method

Experiments were carried out on the evaluation split of the dataset. We applied hyperparameter tuning and ensembling to our system, which are detailed in Appendix A along with other training details. BERT was excluded for the formal run since it did not make it to the task deadline.

We experimented with enhanced models with BERT after the formal run. For these models, we adopted the best hyperparameters chosen by the submitted model without re-running the hyperparameter tuning.

All models were implemented using Chainer (Tokui et al., 2015; Akiba et al., 2017).

9.2 Results

The official results are shown in Table 1 and Table 2. Our system obtained macro-averaged MRP F1 score of 0.7604 and was ranked fifth amongst all submissions. Our system outperformed conventional unified architecture for MRP (TUPA baselines; Hershcovich and Arviv, 2019) in all frameworks but AMR. This indicates the efficacy

Table 2: MRP and framework specific scores (shown as "score/rank"). Gray background indicates that it is the score on LPPS subset.

Framework	MRP							Framework specific[†]
	Tops	Labels	Properties	Anchors	Edges	Attributes	All	
All	0.8929/3	0.6409/6	0.5186/9	0.7547/5	0.6958/5	0.0418/7	0.7604/5	-
	0.9167/3	0.6238/6	0.3743/9	0.7602/6	0.7025/5	0.0340/7	0.7618/5	-
DM	0.9219/6	0.9107/6	0.8649/9	0.9909/4	0.9190/5	-	0.9102/9	0.9189/5
	0.9505/5	0.8818/8	0.8367/10	0.9862/6	0.9245/5	-	0.8939/9	0.9272/4
PSD	0.9538/5	0.9494/3	0.9118/7	0.9896/5	0.7948/5	-	0.9121/2	0.8085/4
	0.9515/5	0.9204/2	0.8366/8	0.9820/6	0.7846/4	-	0.8840/2	0.8075/4
EDS	0.7319/9	0.8225/7	0.5851/7	0.8694/6	0.8497/7	-	0.8374/7	0.7826/7
	0.8515/7	0.7763/7	0.0670/9	0.8737/7	0.8427/7	-	0.8110/7	0.7571/7
UCCA	0.9965/2	-	-	0.9238/6	0.5588/6	0.2092/7	0.7036/6	0.4277/6
	0.9900/2	-	-	0.9593/7	0.6050/6	0.1698/7	0.7498/6	0.5024/6
AMR	0.8604/3	0.5221/8	0.2314/9	-	0.3568/8	-	0.4386/8	0.4254/8
	0.8400/4	0.5404/8	0.1311/9	-	0.3558/8	-	0.4701/8	0.4530/8

[†] DM/PSD: SDP labeled F1, EDS: EDM all F1, UCCA:UCCA labeled all F1, AMR: SMATCH F1

Table 3: MRP F1 scores for the variants of the proposed system (shown as "score/rank" where the rank is calculated by assuming that it was the submitted model).

Variant	Average	DM	PSD	EDS	UCCA	AMR
SFL	0.7575/5	0.9071/9	0.9064/3	0.8339/7	0.7014/6	0.4386/8
SFL(ensemble)[†]	0.7604/5	0.9102/9	0.9121/2	0.8374/7	0.7036/6	0.4386/8
BERT+SFL(NT)	0.7450/6	0.9038/9	0.9069/3	0.8301/7	0.6945/6	0.3896/8
BERT+MTL(NT)	0.7144/6	0.8726/9	0.8791/7	0.7987/7	0.6422/6	0.3794/9
BERT+MTL+FT(NT)	0.7507/5	0.9045/9	0.9054/4	0.8304/7	0.7126/6	0.4008/8

SFL: single-framework learning, MTL: multi-task learning, FT: fine-tuning, ensemble: with ensembles, NT: random seed is not tuned, [†] formal run

of using the biaffine network as a shared architecture for MRP.

Our system obtained relatively better (second) position in PSD. This was due to relatively good performance on the node label prediction where we carefully constructed postprocessing rule for special nodes' labels (Section 4.4) instead of just using lemmas.

Our system obtained significantly worse result in AMR (difference of 0.2952 MRP F1 score to the best performing system), even though our system incorporates the state-of-the-art AMR parser (Zhang et al., 2019). One reason is that Zhang et al. (2019) was obtaining a large score boost from the Wikification task, which was not part of the MRP 2019 shared task. Another reason could be that we may have missed out important implementation details for the pointer-generator network, since the implementation of Zhang et al. (2019) was not yet released at the time of our system development.

Table 3 shows the performance of other variants of the proposed system. The single-framework learning variant (SFL) without BERT (SFL) performed better than SFL with BERT (BERT+SFL(NT)), which suggests that impact of hyperparameter tuning was larger than that of incorporating BERT. The multi-task learning variant (MTL) with fine-tuning (BERT+MTL+FT(NT)) outperformed the SFL in the comparable condition (BERT+SFL(NT)). This result implies learning heterogeneous meaning representations at once can boost the system performance.

10 Conclusions

In this paper, we described our proposed system for the CoNLL 2019 Cross-Framework Meaning Representation Parsing (MRP 2019) shared task. Our system was the unified encoder-to-biaffine network for all five frameworks. The system was ranked fifth in the formal run of the task, and outperformed the baseline unified transition-based MRP. Furthermore, post-evaluation experiments showed that we can boost the performance of the proposed system by incorporating multi-task learning. These imply efficacy of incorporating the biaffine network to the shared architecture for MRP and that learning heterogeneous meaning representations at once can boost the system performance.

While our architecture successfully unified graph predictions in the five frameworks, it is nontrivial to extend the architecture to another framework. It is because there could be a more suitable node generation scheme for a different framework and naively applying the pointer network for partial nodes complementation (or extended pointer-generator network for full nodes generation) may result in a poor performance. Thus, it is our future work to design a more universal method for the node generation.

References

Omri Abend and Ari Rappoport. 2013. Universal conceptual cognitive annotation (UCCA). In *Proceedings of the 51st Annual Meeting of the Association for Computational Linguistics*.

Takuya Akiba, Keisuke Fukuda, and Shuji Suzuki. 2017. ChainerMN: Scalable Distributed Deep Learning Framework. In *Proceedings of Workshop on ML Systems in The 31st Annual Conference on Neural Information Processing Systems*.

Laura Banarescu, Claire Bonial, Shu Cai, Madalina Georgescu, Kira Griffitt, Ulf Hermjakob, Kevin Knight, Philipp Koehn, Martha Palmer, and Nathan Schneider. 2013. Abstract meaning representation for sembanking. In *Proceedings of the 7th Linguistic Annotation Workshop and Interoperability with Discourse*.

Jacob Devlin, Ming-Wei Chang, Kenton Lee, and Kristina Toutanova. 2019. BERT: Pre-training of deep bidirectional transformers for language understanding. In *Proceedings of the 2019 Conference of the North American Chapter of the Association for Computational Linguistics: Human Language Technologies*.

Timothy Dozat and Christopher D. Manning. 2018. Simpler but More Accurate Semantic Dependency Parsing. In *Proceedings of the 56th Annual Meeting of the Association for Computational Linguistics*.

Jeffrey Flanigan, Sam Thomson, Jaime Carbonell, Chris Dyer, and Noah A. Smith. 2014. A discriminative graph-based parser for the abstract meaning representation. In *Proceedings of the 52nd Annual Meeting of the Association for Computational Linguistics*.

Dan Flickinger. 2000. On building a more efficient grammar by exploiting types. *Natural Language Engineering*, 6(1):15–28.

Dan Flickinger, Emily M. Bender, and Stephan Oepen. 2014. Towards an encyclopedia of compositional semantics: Documenting the interface of the English resource grammar. In *Proceedings of the Ninth International Conference on Language Resources and Evaluation*.

Jan Hajič, Eva Hajičová, Jarmila Panevová, Petr Sgall, Ondřej Bojar, Silvie Cinková, Eva Fučíková, Marie Mikulová, Petr Pajas, Jan Popelka, Jiří Semecký, Jana Šindlerová, Jan Štěpánek, Josef Toman, Zdeňka Urešová, and Zdeněk Žabokrtský. 2012. Announcing Prague Czech-English dependency treebank 2.0. In *Proceedings of the Eighth International Conference on Language Resources and Evaluation*.

Daniel Hershcovich, Omri Abend, and Ari Rappoport. 2017. A transition-based directed acyclic graph parser for UCCA. In *Proceedings of the 55th Annual Meeting of the Association for Computational Linguistics*.

Daniel Hershcovich, Omri Abend, and Ari Rappoport. 2018. Multitask parsing across semantic representations. In *Proceedings of the 56th Annual Meeting of the Association for Computational Linguistics*.

Daniel Hershcovich and Ofir Arviv. 2019. TUPA at MRP 2019: A multi-task baseline system. In *Proceedings of the Shared Task on Cross-Framework Meaning Representation Parsing at the 2019 Conference on Natural Language Learning*.

Sepp Hochreiter and Jürgen Schmidhuber. 1997. Long Short-Term Memory. *Neural Computation*, 9(8):1735–1780.

Angelina Ivanova, Stephan Oepen, Lilja Øvrelid, and Dan Flickinger. 2012. Who did what to whom? a contrastive study of syntaco-semantic dependencies. In *Proceedings of the Sixth Linguistic Annotation Workshop*.

Diederik Kingma and Jimmy Ba. 2014. Adam: A Method for Stochastic Optimization. In *the Third International Conference on Learning Representations*.

Ioannis Konstas, Srinivasan Iyer, Mark Yatskar, Yejin Choi, and Luke Zettlemoyer. 2017. Neural AMR: Sequence-to-sequence models for parsing and generation. In *Proceedings of the 55th Annual Meeting of the Association for Computational Linguistics*.

Chunchuan Lyu and Ivan Titov. 2018. AMR parsing as graph prediction with latent alignment. In *Proceedings of the 56th Annual Meeting of the Association for Computational Linguistics*.

Yusuke Miyao, Stephan Oepen, and Daniel Zeman. 2014. In-house: An ensemble of pre-existing off-the-shelf parsers. In *Proceedings of the 8th International Workshop on Semantic Evaluation*.

Stephan Oepen, Omri Abend, Jan Hajič, Daniel Hershcovich, Marco Kuhlmann, Tim O'Gorman, Nianwen Xue, Jayeol Chun, Milan Straka, and Zdeňka Urešová. 2019. MRP 2019: Cross-framework Meaning Representation Parsing. In *Proceedings of the Shared Task on Cross-Framework Meaning Representation Parsing at the 2019 Conference on Natural Language Learning*.

Stephan Oepen, Marco Kuhlmann, Yusuke Miyao, Daniel Zeman, Dan Flickinger, Jan Hajič, Angelina Ivanova, and Yi Zhang. 2014. SemEval 2014 task 8: Broad-coverage semantic dependency parsing. In *Proceedings of the 8th International Workshop on Semantic Evaluation*.

Stephan Oepen and Jan Tore Lønning. 2006. Discriminant-based MRS banking. In *Proceedings of the Fifth International Conference on Language Resources and Evaluation*.

Jeffrey Pennington, Richard Socher, and Christopher Manning. 2014. Glove: Global vectors for word representation. In *Proceedings of the 2014 Conference on Empirical Methods in Natural Language Processing*.

Matthew Peters, Mark Neumann, Mohit Iyyer, Matt Gardner, Christopher Clark, Kenton Lee, and Luke Zettlemoyer. 2018. Deep Contextualized Word Representations. In *Proceedings of the 2018 Conference of the North American Chapter of the Association for Computational Linguistics: Human Language Technologies*.

Lev Ratinov and Dan Roth. 2009. Design challenges and misconceptions in named entity recognition. In *Proceedings of the Thirteenth Conference on Computational Natural Language Learning*.

Mike Schuster and Kuldip K Paliwal. 1997. Bidirectional recurrent neural networks. *IEEE Transactions on Signal Processing*, 45(11):2673–2681.

Nitish Srivastava, Geoffrey Hinton, Alex Krizhevsky, Ilya Sutskever, and Ruslan Salakhutdinov. 2014. Dropout: A simple way to prevent neural networks from overfitting. *Journal of Machine Learning Research*, 15:1929–1958.

Seiya Tokui, Kenta Oono, Shohei Hido, and Justin Clayton. 2015. Chainer: a next-generation open source framework for deep learning. In *Proceedings of Workshop on Machine Learning Systems in The 29th Annual Conference on Neural Information Processing Systems*.

Ashish Vaswani, Noam Shazeer, Niki Parmar, Jakob Uszkoreit, Llion Jones, Aidan N Gomez, Ł ukasz Kaiser, and Illia Polosukhin. 2017. Attention is all you need. In I. Guyon, U. V. Luxburg, S. Bengio, H. Wallach, R. Fergus, S. Vishwanathan, and R. Garnett, editors, *Advances in Neural Information Processing Systems 30*, pages 5998–6008. Curran Associates, Inc.

Oriol Vinyals, Meire Fortunato, and Navdeep Jaitly. 2015. Pointer networks. In C. Cortes, N. D. Lawrence, D. D. Lee, M. Sugiyama, and R. Garnett, editors, *Advances in Neural Information Processing Systems 28*, pages 2692–2700. Curran Associates, Inc.

Dian Yu and Kenji Sagae. 2019. UC Davis at SemEval-2019 task 1: DAG semantic parsing with attention-based decoder. In *Proceedings of the 13th International Workshop on Semantic Evaluation*.

Sheng Zhang, Xutai Ma, Kevin Duh, and Benjamin Van Durme. 2019. AMR parsing as sequence-to-graph transduction. In *Proceedings of the 57th Annual Meeting of the Association for Computational Linguistics*. Association for Computational Linguistics.

A Training Details

We split dataset into training dataset which was used to update model parameters, validation dataset (i) which was used for early stopping, and validation dataset (ii) which was used for hyperparameter tuning and construction of ensembles. For AMR and UCCA, we selected sentences that appear in more than one framework to populate the training dataset, and extracted 500 (300) and 1500 (700) data from the rest as validation dataset (i) and (ii) for AMR (UCCA), respectively. For DM, PSD and EDS, we selected data that appear in AMR or UCCA to populate the training dataset, and extracted 500 and 1500 data from the rest as validation dataset (i) and (ii), respectively.

A.1 Model Training

All models are trained using mini-batch stochastic gradient decent with backpropagation. We use Adam optimizer (Kingma and Ba, 2014) with gradient clipping.

For the non-multi-task variant, early stopping is applied for each framework with SDP labeled dependency F1 score (Oepen et al., 2014) (for DM, PSD and UCCA) or validation loss (for EDS and AMR) as the objective. Note that early stopping is applied separately to each framework for the joint training of DM and PSD. Concretely, for the joint training of DM and PSD, we train the model with respect to the joint loss ℓ_{sdp} in Equation (3) but we use a model at a training epoch whose DM-specific (or PSD-specific) SDP labeled dependency F1 score is highest for DM (or PSD) prediction.

For the multi-task variants, we employ a slightly different strategy for early stopping. For the multi-task variant without fine-tuning, we apply early stopping separately to each framework with respect to the framework-specific validation loss. For example, we train the multi-task model with respect to ℓ_{mtl} in Equation (4) but we use a model at a training epoch whose PSD-specific validation loss $\lambda^{\text{label}}\ell_{\text{psd}}^{\text{label}} + \left(1 - \lambda^{\text{label}}\right)\ell_{\text{psd}}^{\text{edge}}$ is lowest for PSD prediction. For each framework in the fine-tuned multi-task variant, we adopt the multi-task pretrained model at a training epoch whose framework-specific validation loss is lowest and fine-tune on the model in the same manner as the non-multi-task variant. Note that, for DM and PSD, which are fine-tuned together even in the fine-tuned multi-task variant, we adopt the multi-task pretrained model at a training epoch whose multi-task validation loss ℓ_{mtl} is lowest.

Dropout (Srivastava et al., 2014) is applied to (a) the input to each layer of the shared encoder, (b) the input to the biaffine networks, and (c) the input to each layer of the UCCA and AMR decoders.

A.2 Hyperparameter Tuning

We random searched subset of hyperparameters for DM, PSD, UCCA and AMR. See Table 4 for hyperparameter search space and the list of hyperparameters chosen by the best performing model in each framework. We tried 20 hyperparameter sets for DM/PSD, 50 for UCCA, and 25 for AMR.

We did not tune the hyperparameters of the multi-task variants. We adopted the best hyperparameters chosen in the non-multi-task variants (Table 4) and hand-tuned the hyperparameters by examining learning curves over few runs. For the fine-tuning, we adopted the best hyperparameters chosen in the non-multi-task variants (Table 4). See Table 5 for the list of hyperparameters used in the multi-task variants.

A.3 Ensembling

We formed ensembles from the models trained in the hyperparameter tuning. Models are added to the ensemble in descending order of MRP F1 score on validation dataset (II) until MRP F1 score of the ensemble no longer improves.

For DM and PSD, we simply averaged edge predictions $y_{\text{fw},i,j}^{\text{edge}}$ and label predictions $y_{\text{fw},i,j,c}^{\text{label}}$, respectively. On the other hand, the simple average ensembling cannot be applied to UCCA, because number of nodes maybe distinct to each model due to the non-terminal node generation. Hence, we propose to use a two-step *voting ensemble* for UCCA; for each input sentence, (1) the most popular pointer sequence is chosen, and (2) edge and label predictions from the models that outputted the chosen sequence are averaged in the same way as DM and PSD.

For EDS, we do not explicitly use ensemble learning, but utilize DM graphs from ensembled DM models to reconstruct EDS graphs. For AMR, we do not use ensembles.

Table 4: List of hyperparameters. Multiple values indicates that the hyperparameter was tuned within that values. Subscript d (DM), p (PSD), u (UCCA) and a (AMR) denotes the hyperparameter chosen by the best performing model on validation dataset. $\mathcal{U}(a, b)$ is a uniform distribution in $[a, b]$.

Hyperparameter	Value or search space
Common	
Word embedding dimension	100
Lemma embedding dimension	100
POS embedding dimension	100
NE embedding dimension	100
GloVe MLP hidden size	125
ELMo MLP hidden size	512
Word drop probability	0.1_{dpua}, 0.2, 0.4
POS drop probability	0.1_{du}, 0.2_{a}, 0.4_{p}
Lemma drop probability	0.1_{p}, 0.2_{da}, 0.4_{u}
# of layers in encoder	2_{pu}, 3_{da}
Encoder LSTM hidden size	256, 512_{dpua}
Encoder dropout rate	0.1_{a}, 0.25_{d}, 0.5_{pu}
Biaffine input dropout	0.2_{pua}, 0.45_{d}
Edge prediction dropout	0.25_{dpua}, 0.4
Learning rate	$10^{\mathcal{U}(-3.32, -2.92)}$ $\rightarrow 0.000858_{\text{d}}$, 0.000675_{p}, 0.00117_{u}, 0.00059_{a}
Adam (β_1, β_2)[†]	$(0.9, 0.999)_{\text{dp}}$, $(0, 0.95)_{\text{ua}}$
DM/PSD	
Edge MLP hidden size	600
Edge label MLP hidden size	600
Frame prediction MLP hidden size	600
Frame prediction dropout	0.2, 0.55_{dp}
Edge label prediction dropout	0.33_{d}, 0.5_{p}
Loss coefficient $\lambda_{\text{fw}}^{\text{label}}$	$\mathcal{U}(0.02, 0.03)$ $\rightarrow 0.0210_{\text{d}}$, 0.0242_{p}
Loss coefficient $\lambda_{\text{fw}}^{\text{frame}}$	0.5
# of epochs	50
Batch size	64
UCCA	
Edge MLP hidden size	400, 500_{u}, 600
Edge label MLP hidden size	400_{u}, 500, 600
Edge label prediction dropout	0.25_{u}, 0.33
Decoder dropout	0.5
Loss coefficient $\lambda_{\text{ucca}}^{\text{edge}}$	0.3
Loss coefficient $\lambda_{\text{ucca}}^{\text{label}}$	0.3
Loss coefficient $\lambda_{\text{ucca}}^{\text{remote}}$	0.2
Loss coefficient $\lambda_{\text{ucca}}^{\text{dec}}$	0.2
# of epochs	40
Batch size	100
AMR	
Edge MLP hidden size	600
Edge label MLP hidden size	600
Edge label prediction dropout	0.33_{a}, 0.5
Decoder type[‡]	deep small$_{\text{a}}$, shallow wide
Decoder dropout	0.25, 0.33_{a}, 0.5
Loss coefficient $\lambda_{\text{amr}}^{\text{label}}$	$\mathcal{U}(0.1, 0.5) \rightarrow 0.395_{\text{a}}$
Loss coefficient $\lambda_{\text{amr}}^{\text{cov}}$	$\mathcal{U}(0.2, 0.4) \rightarrow 0.339_{\text{a}}$
Loss coefficient $\lambda_{\text{amr}}^{\text{gen}}$	$\mathcal{U}(0.2, 0.4) \rightarrow 0.271_{\text{a}}$
# of epochs	50
Batch size	64

[†] Commonly used setting and the setting used in Dozat and Manning (2018).

[‡] "deep small" is three-layered LSTM with hidden size of 512 and "shallow wide" is two-layered LSTM with hidden size of 1024.

Table 5: Hyperparameters for the multi-task variants

Hyperparameter	Value
Model architecture	
Word embedding dimension	100
Lemma embedding dimension	100
POS embedding dimension	100
NE embedding dimension	100
GloVe MLP hidden size	125
ELMo MLP hidden size	512
# of layers in encoder	3
Encoder LSTM hidden size	512
Edge MLP hidden size	600
Edge label MLP hidden size	600
Frame prediction MLP hidden size	600
AMR decoder type[†]	deep small
Training conditions	
Multi-task (pre)training	
Word drop probability	0.2
POS drop probability	0.2
Lemma drop probability	0.2
Encoder dropout rate	0.5
Biaffine input dropout	0.45
Edge prediction dropout	0.25
Edge label prediction dropout	0.33
Learning rate	0.00006
Adam (β_1, β_2)[†]	(0.9, 0.999)
Loss coefficient λ^{biaf}	1.0
Loss coefficient λ^{label}	0.15
Loss coefficient λ^{frame}	0.5
Loss coefficient $\lambda_{\text{ucca}}^{\text{remote}}$	0.5
Loss coefficient $\lambda_{\text{ucca}}^{\text{dec}}$	0.08
Loss coefficient $\lambda_{\text{amr}}^{\text{dec}}$	1.2
Loss coefficient $\lambda_{\text{amr}}^{\text{cov}}$	1.0
# of epochs	60
Batch size	128
DM/PSD fine-tuning	
Word drop probability	0.1
POS drop probability	0.2
Lemma drop probability	0.2
Encoder dropout rate	0.25
Biaffine input dropout	0.45
Edge prediction dropout	0.25
Learning rate	0.001[‡]
Adam (β_1, β_2)[†]	$(0, 0.95)$[‡]
Frame prediction dropout	0.55
Edge label prediction dropout	0.33
Loss coefficient $\lambda_{\text{fw}}^{\text{label}}$	0.025
Loss coefficient $\lambda_{\text{fw}}^{\text{frame}}$	0.5
# of epochs	50
Batch size	64
UCCA fine-tuning	
Word drop probability	0.1
POS drop probability	0.1
Lemma drop probability	0.4
Encoder dropout rate	0.5
Biaffine input dropout	0.2
Edge prediction dropout	0.25
Learning rate	0.00117
Adam (β_1, β_2)[†]	(0, 0.95)
Edge label prediction dropout	0.25
Decoder dropout	0.5
Loss coefficient $\lambda_{\text{ucca}}^{\text{edge}}$	0.3
Loss coefficient $\lambda_{\text{ucca}}^{\text{label}}$	0.3
Loss coefficient $\lambda_{\text{ucca}}^{\text{remote}}$	0.2
Loss coefficient $\lambda_{\text{ucca}}^{\text{dec}}$	0.2
# of epochs	40
Batch size	100
AMR fine-tuning	
Word drop probability	0.1
POS drop probability	0.2
Lemma drop probability	0.2
Encoder dropout rate	0.1
Biaffine input dropout	0.2
Edge prediction dropout	0.25
Learning rate	0.00059
Adam (β_1, β_2)[†]	(0, 0.95)
Edge label prediction dropout	0.33
Decoder dropout	0.33
Loss coefficient $\lambda_{\text{amr}}^{\text{label}}$	0.395
Loss coefficient $\lambda_{\text{amr}}^{\text{cov}}$	0.339
Loss coefficient $\lambda_{\text{amr}}^{\text{gen}}$	0.271
# of epochs	50
Batch size	64

[†] See Table 4.

[‡] These are bugs. They should have been different values according to Table 4.

ÚFAL MRPipe at MRP 2019:
UDPipe Goes Semantic in the Meaning Representation Parsing Shared Task

Milan Straka and **Jana Straková**

Charles University
Faculty of Mathematics and Physics
Institute of Formal and Applied Linguistics
{straka,strakova}@ufal.mff.cuni.cz

Abstract

We present a system description of our contribution to the CoNLL 2019 shared task, Cross-Framework Meaning Representation Parsing (MRP 2019). The proposed architecture is our first attempt towards a semantic parsing extension of the UDPipe 2.0, a lemmatization, POS tagging and dependency parsing pipeline.

For the MRP 2019, which features five formally and linguistically different approaches to meaning representation (DM, PSD, EDS, UCCA and AMR), we propose a uniform, language and framework agnostic graph-to-graph neural network architecture. Without any knowledge about the graph structure, and specifically without any linguistically or framework motivated features, our system implicitly models the meaning representation graphs.

After fixing a human error (we used earlier incorrect version of provided test set analyses), our submission would score third in the competition evaluation. The source code of our system is available at https://github.com/ufal/mrpipe-conll2019.

1 Introduction

The goal of the CoNLL 2019 shared task, Cross-Framework Meaning Representation Parsing (MRP 2019; Oepen et al., 2019) is to parse a raw, unprocessed sentence into its corresponding graph-structured meaning representation.

The MRP 2019 features five formally and linguistically different approaches to meaning representation with varying degree of linguistic and structural complexity:

- **DM:** DELPH-IN MRS Bi Lexical Dependencies (Ivanova et al., 2012),
- **PSD:** Prague Semantic Dependencies (Hajič et al., 2012; Miyao et al., 2014),

- **EDS:** Elementary Dependency Structures (Oepen and Lønning, 2006),
- **UCCA:** Universal Conceptual Cognitive Annotation (Abend and Rappoport, 2013),
- **AMR:** Abstract Meaning Representation (Banarescu et al., 2013).

In line with the shared task objective to advance uniform meaning representation parsing across distinct semantic graph frameworks, we propose a uniform, language and structure agnostic graph-to-graph neural network architecture which models semantic representation from input sequences. The system is an extension of the UDPipe 2.0, a tagging, lemmatization and syntactic tool (Straka, 2018; Straka et al., 2019).

Our contributions are the following:

- We propose a uniform semantic graph parsing architecture, which accommodates simple directed cyclic graphs, independently on the underlying semantic formalism.

- Our method does not use linguistic information such as structural constraints, dictionaries, predicate banks or lexical databases.

- We added a new extension to UDPipe 2.0, a lemmatization, POS tagging and dependency parsing tool. The semantic extension parses semantic graphs from the raw token input, making use of the POS and lemmas (but not syntax) from the existing UDPipe 2.0.

- As an improvement over UDPipe 2.0, we use the "frozen" contextualized embeddings on the input (BERT; Devlin et al., 2019) in the same way as Straka et al. (2019).

After fixing a human error (we used earlier incorrect version of provided test set analyses), our submission would score third in the competition evaluation.

Proceedings of the Shared Task on Cross-Framework Meaning Representation Parsing at the 2019 CoNLL, pages 127–137
Hong Kong, November 3, 2019. ©2019 Association for Computational Linguistics
https://doi.org/10.18653/v1/K19-2012

2   Related Work

Numerous parsers have been proposed for parsing semantic formalisms, including the systems participating in recent semantic parsing shared tasks SemEval 2016 and SemEval 2017 (May, 2016; May and Priyadarshi, 2017) featuring AMR; and SemEval 2019 (Hershcovich et al., 2019) featuring UCCA. However, proposals of general, formalism independent semantic parsers are scarce in the literature.

Hershcovich et al. (2018) propose a general transition-based parser for directed, acyclic graphs, able to parse multiple conceptually and formally different schemes. TUPA is a transition-based top-down shift-reduce parser, while ours, although also based on transitions/operations, models the graph as a sequence of layered, iterative graph-like operations, rather (but not necessarily) in a bottom-up fashion. Consequently, our architecture allows parsing cyclic graphs and is not restricted to single-rooted graphs. Also, we do not enforce any task-specific constraints, such as restriction on number of parents in UCCA or number of children given by PropBank in AMR and we completely rely on the neural network to implicitly infer such framework-specific features.

3   Methods

3.1   Uniform Graph Model

The five shared task semantic formalisms differ notably in specific formal and linguistic assumptions, but from a higher-level view, they universally represent the full-sentence semantic analyses with directed, possibly cyclic graphs. Universally, the semantic units are represented with graph nodes and the semantic relationships with graph edges.

To accommodate these semantic structures, we model them as directed simple graphs $G = (V, E)$, where V is a set of nodes and $E \subseteq \{(x, y) \mid (x, y) \in V^2, x \neq y\}$ is a set of directed edges.[1]

One of the most fundamental differences between the five featured MRP 2019 frameworks lies apparently in the relationship between the graph structure (graph nodes) and the input surface word forms (tokens). In the MRP 2019, this relationship is called *anchoring* and its degree varies from

a tight connection between graph nodes being directly corresponding to surface tokens in *Flavor 0* frameworks (DM and PSD) through more relaxed relationship *Flavor 1* (EDS and UCCA) in which arbitrary parts of the sentence can be represented in the semantic graph, to a completely *unanchored* semantic graph of *Flavor 2* in the AMR framework.

To alleviate the need for a framework-specific handling of the anchoring, we broaden our understanding of the semantic graph: We consider the tokens as nodes and the anchors (connections from the graph nodes to tokens) as regular edges, thus the anchors are naturally learned jointly with the graph without an explicit knowledge of the underlying semantic formalism.

In order to represent anchors as regular edges in the graph, the input tokenization needs to be consistent with the annotated anchors: each anchor must match one or multiple input tokens. In order to achieve the exact anchor-token(s) match, we created a simple tokenizer. The tokenizer is uniform for all frameworks with a slight change to capture UCCA's fine-grained anchoring; see Figure 1 for the pseudocode.[2]

Furthermore, to represent anchors as edges, the anchors have to be annotated in the data, which is not the case for AMR. We therefore utilize externally generated anchoring from the JAMR tool (Flanigan et al., 2016).[3]

3.2   Graph-to-graph Parser

We propose a general graph-to-graph parser which models the graph meaning representation as a sequence of layered group transformations from input from input sequence to meaning graphs. A schematic overview of our architecture is presented in Figure 2.

Having reduced the task to a graph-to-graph transformation modeling, we iteratively build the graph from its initial state (a set of isolated nodes – tokens) by alternating between two layer-wise transformations:

1. **AddNodes**: The first operation creates new nodes and connects them to already existing

---

[1]Specifically, our graphs are directed and allow cycles. Furthermore, they are *simple* graphs, not *multigraphs*.

[2]Instead of generating tokens consistent with the anchors, the anchoring edges could be allowed to refer only to a part of a token (for example by having two attributes *first anchored token character* and *last anchored token character*), which is an approach we plan to adopt in the future.

[3]We plan to model the anchors jointly using an attention mechanism (Zhang et al., 2019a).

1. Any single non-space character
2a. UCCA: `\w+[$]?`
2b. other: `\w(\w-[^-\s]|&|/|'S\w|'[A-RT-Z]|[.](?=.*\w)\w|\d)*[$]?;`
    `\d+-\d+; \d+,\d+; \d+,\d+,\d+`
3. `--+; `+; '+; [.]+; !+`
4. `n't;'s;'d;'m;'re;'ve;'ll`
5. Split the following word into two tokens: `would|n't; could|n't; ca|n't; is|n't; are|n't; ai|n't; was|n't; were|n't; do|n't; does|n't; did|n't; should|n't; have|n't; has|n't; had|n't; wo|n't; might|n't; need|n't; can|not; wan|na; got|ta`

Figure 1: Tokenizer pseudocode as a sequence of regular expressions. Expressions with higher number override previous ones.

nodes. Specifically, for each already existing node we decide whether to a) create a new node and connect it as a parent, b) create a new node and connect it as a child, c) do nothing. When a new node is created, its label and all its properties are generated too. Intuitively, anchors are modeled in the first step from the initial set of individual nodes (tokens) and in the next steps, higher-layer nodes are modeled. As a special case, **AddNodes** is relatively simple for the Flavor 0 frameworks (DM and PSD): zero or one node is created for every token in the first and only **AddNodes** iteration. This is illustrated in Table 1, which shows node coverage after performing a fixed number of **AddNodes** iterations, reaching 100% after one **AddNodes** iteration in DM and PSD.

2. **AddEdges**: The second operation creates edges between the new nodes and any other existing nodes (both old and new) using a classifier for each pair of nodes. Any number of edges can be connected to a newly created node.

At the end of each iteration, the created nodes and edges are frozen and the computation moves to its next iteration. We describe the crucial part of the graph modeling, **token**, **node** and **edge representation**, in Section 3.4.

An example of a graph step by step build-up is shown in Figure 2.

In contrast to purely sequential series of single transitions, such as adding a new edge in one step, adding new nodes and edges in a layer-wise fashion improves runtime performance and might avoid error accumulation by performing many independent decisions. On the other hand, we assume that creating nodes from a single existing one might be problematic, especially if the graph has constituency structure.

3.2.1 Creating AddNodes Operations

For training, a sequence of the **AddNodes** operations must be created. For this purpose, we define an ordering of the graph nodes which guides the graph traversal. The initial order of the isolated graph nodes set (tokens) is left to right, the first token being the first to be visited. The other graph nodes' ordering is then induced by the order of creation.

Given a training graph, we then generate a sequence of **AddNodes** operations. In every iteration, we traverse all existing nodes in the graph in the above defined order and for each node, we consider all its not-yet-created neighbors, from which we choose the one which is "in the lowest layer". This is motivated by our intention to build the graph in a bottom-up fashion. Specifically, we choose such a node which has the smallest number of token descendants (based on the assumption that nodes in the lower levels tend to govern less descendants than the nodes in the higher levels), and if there are several such nodes, the one where the token descendant indices are smallest in the ordering. Finally, we favour creating parents to creating children, and if a node can be created as a parent, we never create it as a child.

As a special case, the first iteration always traverses the set of isolated nodes (tokens) and connects their immediate parents with the anchor-defined edges. For DM and PSD frameworks, this is the first and only iteration of the **AddNodes** operations.

The number of required iterations to generate all nodes and construct complete graphs is presented in Table 1. Performing three iterations is enough to cover more than 99% of nodes in all frameworks, but EDS and AMR frameworks sometimes require more than 10 iterations to generate a full graph.

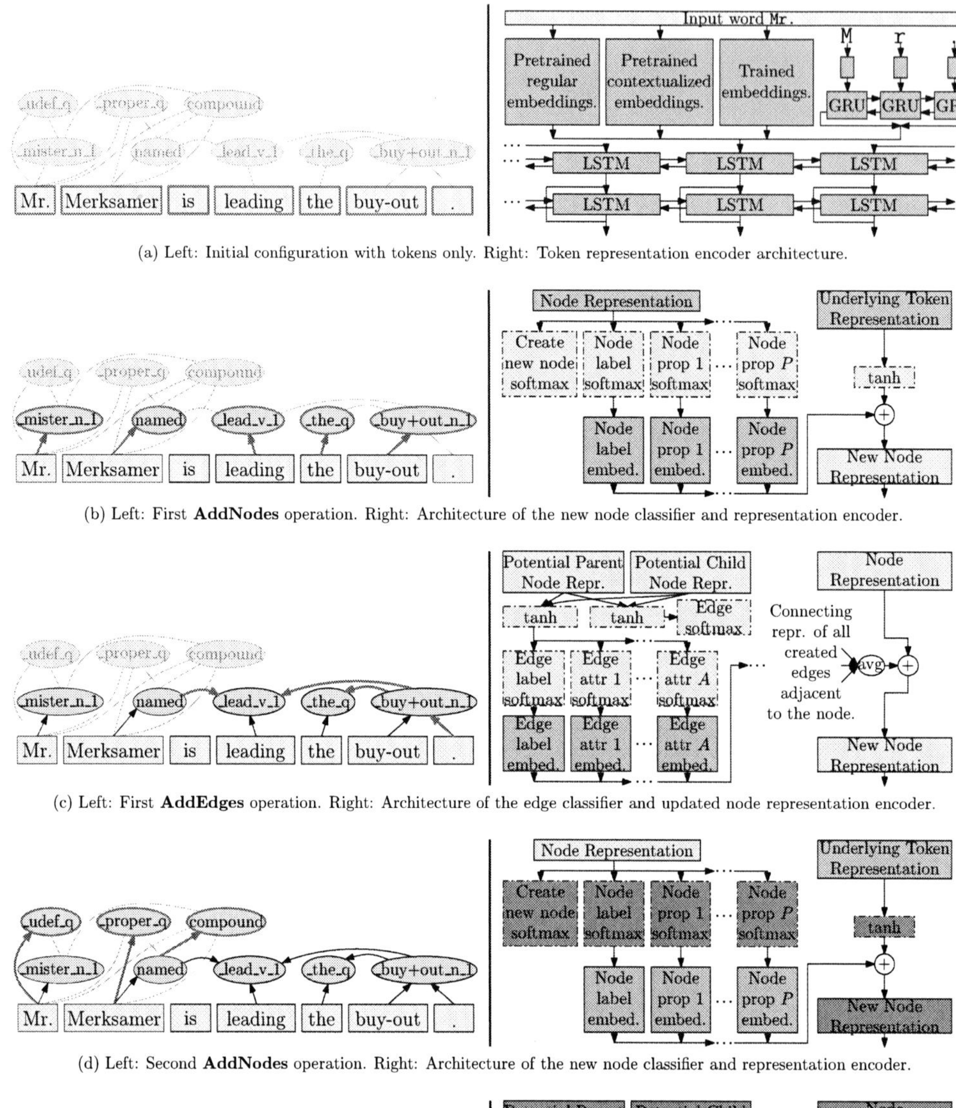

(a) Left: Initial configuration with tokens only. Right: Token representation encoder architecture.

(b) Left: First **AddNodes** operation. Right: Architecture of the new node classifier and representation encoder.

(c) Left: First **AddEdges** operation. Right: Architecture of the edge classifier and updated node representation encoder.

(d) Left: Second **AddNodes** operation. Right: Architecture of the new node classifier and representation encoder.

(e) Left: Second **AddEdges** operation. Right: Architecture of the edge classifier and updated node representation encoder.

Figure 2: Our graph-to-graph architecture schematic overview and an example of semantic graph build-up for the sentence *"Mr. Merksamer is leading the buy-out."* from the EDS framework (Oepen and Lønning, 2006). Note that the weights for all classification layers and for all displayed fully connected layers (displayed with dashed border) are different for every iteration of **AddNodes/AddEdges** operations.

Framework		Iterations									
		1	2	3	4	5	6	7	8	9	10
DM	Nodes	100.00%									
	Graphs	100.00%									
PSD	Nodes	100.00%									
	Graphs	100.00%									
EDS	Nodes	69.18%	97.18%	99.31%	99.64%	99.90%	99.95%	99.97%	99.99%	100.00%	100.00%
	Graphs	2.15%	59.31%	91.68%	93.09%	98.84%	99.46%	99.55%	99.87%	99.99%	99.99%
UCCA	Nodes	69.63%	97.57%	99.87%	99.97%	100.00%	100.00%				
	Graphs	0.00%	43.72%	97.29%	99.19%	99.92%	100.00%				
AMR	Nodes	78.23%	96.15%	99.01%	99.69%	99.88%	99.94%	99.96%	99.97%	99.98%	99.99%
	Graphs	19.73%	74.58%	93.48%	98.18%	99.49%	99.86%	99.94%	99.96%	99.97%	99.98%

Table 1: Coverage of training graphs after a fixed number of the layer-wise iterations. Rows labeled "Nodes" show percentage of covered nodes. Rows labeled "Graphs" show percentage of complete graphs.

During inference, we currently perform a fixed number of iterations of **AddNodes** and **AddEdges** operations; we use one iteration for DM and PSD, two iterations for UCCA and AMR, and three iterations for EDS. Alternatively, we could allow a dynamic number of iterations, stopping when **AddNodes** generates no new nodes.

3.3 Node Labels and Properties Encoding

Besides the graph structure, node labels and properties must also be modeled. For some node labels or properties, it might be beneficial to generate them relatively to a token. For example, when creating a lemma *look* from a token *looked*, it might be easier to generate it as a rule *remove the last two token characters* instead of generating *look* directly. Such approach was taken by UDPipe lemmatizer (Straka et al., 2019), which produced the best results in lemmatization in Task 2 of the SIG-MORPHON 2019 Shared Task.

We adopt this approach, and generate all node labels and properties using a simple classification into a collection of rules. Each rule can either generate an independent value (which we call *absolute encoding*) or it describes how a value should be created from a token (which we call *relative encoding*). For detailed description of the relative encoding rules, please refer to Straka et al. (2019). In short, the lemmas in UDPipe are generated by classifying into a set of character edit scripts performed on the prefix and suffix. First, a common root is found between the input and the output (word form and lemma). If there is no common character, the lemma is considered irregular and an *absolute encoding* is used. Otherwise, the shortest edit script is computed for the prefix and suffix.

In our setting, however, we need to extend the UDPipe approach in two directions. First,

Framework	Property	Absolutely encoded values	Relatively encoded values
DM	label	26 907	**1 086**
	pos	**38**	356
	frame	**468**	2613
PSD	label	32 284	**774**
	pos	**42**	314
	frame	**5 294**	8 868
EDS	label	15 905	**4 339**
	carg	13 667	**427**
UCCA	—	—	—
AMR	label	14 554	**6 278**
	op1	7 377	**1 402**
	op2	3 673	**545**
	op3	1 149	**242**
	op4	482	**113**
	op5	245	**56**
	ARG1	48	**30**
	ARG2	127	**68**
	ARG3	22	**20**
	quant	885	**603**
	value	861	**590**
	time	**110**	111
	year	153	**58**
	li	56	**40**
	mod	79	**33**
	day	**31**	57
	month	**14**	17
	…	…	…

Table 2: Cardinality of absolute and relative encoded node properties in all frameworks. The chosen encoding is displayed in **bold**.

some properties like *pos* should never be relatively encoded. Therefore, during data loading, we consider both allowing and disallowing relative encoding, and choose the approach yielding the smaller number of classes. As Table 2 indicates, even such a simple heuristic seems satisfactory.

Second, compared to lemmatization, where the lemma and the original form are single words, in our setting both the property and the anchored tokens can be a sequence of words (e.g., "Pierre

Vinken"). We overcome this issue by encoding each word of a property independently, and for every property word, we choose a subsequence of anchoring tokens which yields the shortest relative encoding.

3.4 Graph Representation

Token Encoder. The input representation is a sequence of tokens encoded as a concatenation of word and character-level word vectors:

- trainable word embeddings (WE),
- character-level word embeddings (CLE): bidirectional GRUs in line with Ling et al. (2015). We represent every Unicode character with a vector of dimension 256, and concatenate GRU output for forward and reversed word characters. The character-level word embeddings are trained together with the network.
- pre-trained FastText word embeddings of dimension 300 (Mikolov et al., 2018),[4]
- pre-trained ("frozen") contextual BERT embeddings of dimension 768 (Devlin et al., 2019).[5] We average the last four layers of the BERT model and we produce a word embedding for a token as an average of the corresponding BERT subword embeddings.

  Contextualized embeddings have recently been shown to improve performance of many NLP tasks, see for example Straka et al. (2019) in the context of UDPipe and POS tagging, lemmatization and dependency parsing. Therefore, we expected that utilization of BERT embeddings would improve results considerably, which was the case, as demonstrated in Section 4.1.

Furthermore, the input tokens could be processed by a POS tagger, lemmatizer, dependency parser or a named entity recognizer. If such analyses are available, they can be used as additional embeddings of input tokens. Specifically, we utilize the POS tags and lemmas provided in the shared task. We did not experiment with dependency parses, which we plan to do in the future. Furthermore, we tried utilizing the Illinois Named Entity Tagger (Ratinov and Roth, 2009), but it did not improve our results.

---

[4] `https://fasttext.cc/docs/en/english-vectors.html`

[5] We use the `Base English Uncased` model from `https://github.com/google-research/bert`.

All available embeddings for a token are concatenated and processed with two bidirectional LSTM layers with residual connections.

Node Encoder. A node is represented by a concatenation of these features:

- the (transitively) attaching token representation (every node has exactly one token which generated it using the **AddNodes** operations), transformed by a dense layer followed by tanh nonlinearity; every **AddNodes** iteration has its own dense layer weights,
- the node *label* and *properties* embeddings,
- an average of edge representations of all connected edges.

A natural extension would be to represent all node's descendants instead of the one token generating this node through a sequence of **AddNodes**, because the current implementation seems to generate suboptimal representations in later iterations. We leave a proper way of propagating all information through the graph as our future work.

Edge Representation. An edge is represented by a sum of its *label* and *attributes* embeddings.

3.5 Decoders

In the **AddNodes** operation, we employ the following classification decoders, each utilizing the node representation and consisting of a fully connected layer followed by a softmax activation:

- decide among three possibilities, whether to a) add a node as a parent, b) add a node as a child, or c) do nothing;
- generate node label;
- for each property, generate its value (or a special class NONE).

During training, we sum the losses of the decoders, apart from the situation when no new node is created, in which case we ignore the label and properties losses.

In the **AddEdges** operation, we consider all edges to and from the newly created nodes. Utilizing all suitable pairs of nodes, we decide for each pair separately whether to add an edge or not.

Although biaffine attention seems to be the preferred architecture for dependency parsing recently (Zeman et al., 2018), in our experiments it performed poorly when we used it for deciding whether to add an edge between any pair of nodes individually. Our hypothesis is that the range of the biaffine attention output is changing rapidly.

That is not an issue when the outputs "compete" with each other in a softmax layer, but is problematic when we compare each with a fixed threshold.

Consequently, we utilized a Bahdanau-like attention (Bahdanau et al., 2014) instead. Specifically, we pass potential parent and child nodes' representations through a pair of fully connected layers with the same output dimensionality, sum the results, apply a tanh nonlinearity, and attach a binary classifier (a fully connected layer with two outputs and a softmax activation) indicating whether the edge should be added.[6]

In order to predict edge label and attributes, we repeat the same attention process (pass potential parent and child nodes' representation through a different pair of fully connected layers, sum and tanh), and attach classifiers for edge labels and as many edge attributes as present in the data.

Lastly, in order to predict *top* nodes, we employ a sigmoid binary classifier processing the final node representations.

Finally, every iteration of **AddNodes** and **AddEdges** operations has invidiual set of weights for all layers described in this section.

3.6 Training

We implemented the described architecture using TensorFlow 2.0 beta (Agrawal et al., 2019). The eager evaluation allowed us to construct inputs to **AddNodes** and **AddEdges** for every batch specifically, so we could easily handle dynamic graphs.

We trained the network using a lazy variant of Adam optimizer (Kingma and Ba, 2014)[7] with $\beta_2 = 0.98$, for 10 epochs with a learning rate of 10^{-3} and for 5 additional epochs with a learning rate 10^{-4} (the difference being UCCA which used 15 and 10 epochs, respectively, because of considerably smaller training data). We utilized a batch size of 64 graphs.[8] The training time on a single GPU was 1-4 hours for DM, PSD, EDS and UCCA, and 10 hours for AMR.

For replicability, we also describe the used hyperparameters in detail. The only differences among the frameworks were:

- slightly different tokenizer for UCCA (Fig 1),

- larger number of training epochs for UCCA,
- number of layer-wise iterations: 1, 1, 3, 2, 2 for DM, PSD, EDS, UCCA and AMR, respectively.

In the encoder, we utilized trainable embeddings of dimension 512, and trainable character-level embeddings using character embeddings of size 256 and a single layer of bidirectional GRUs with 256 units. We processed token embeddings using two layers of bidirectional LSTMs with residual connections and a dimension of 768. The node representations also had dimensionality 768, as did node label and properties embeddings. We employed dropout with rate 0.3 before and after every LSTM layer and on all node representations, and utilized also word dropout (zeroing the whole WE for a given word) with a rate of 0.2. In the **AddEdges** operation, all attention layers have a dimensionality of 1024.

3.7 Data Preprocessing

We created two train/dev splits from the training data provided by the organizers: Firstly, a 90%/10% train/dev split was used to train the model and tune the hyperparameters of the competition entry. For the ablation experiments in the post-competition phase, we later tried a 99%/1% train/dev split, which improved the results only marginally, as shown in Section 4.1.

We further used the provided morphological annotations and the JAMR anchoring for the AMR framework (Flanigan et al., 2016).

4 Results

We present the overall results of our system in Table 3. Please note that our official shared task submission contained an error – test data companion analyses had been updated during the evaluation phase, but we used the original incorrect ones for DM, PSD and EDS frameworks. The error was discovered only after the official deadline, at which point we sent a bugfix submission using the same trained models, the only difference being the utilization of the correct test data analyses during prediction. We present both these submissions in the Table 3, but refer only to the bugfix submission from now on.

The overall results of our system using the official MRP metric are present in Table 3. All reported scores are macro-averaged F1 scores of all

---

[6]We always add an edge generated in the **AddNodes** operation independently on the prediction for that edge in the **AddEdges** operation.

[7]`tf.contrib.opt.lazyadamoptimizer`

[8]Because we trained on a 8GB GPU, we actually needed to process two batches of size 32 and only then perform parameter update using summed gradients.

System	Tops		Labels		Properties		Anchors		Edges		Attributes		All	
Original ST submission	75.12%	6	63.99%	7	56.53%	6	69.53%	6	62.17%	7	7.85%	4	74.74%	6
Bugfix ST submission	81.47%	6	**73.06%**	**1**	**69.95%**	**1**	77.23%	3	73.89%	5	7.87%	4	83.96%	3
99% training data	80.59%	6	**73.06%**	**1**	**70.18%**	**1**	77.35%	3	74.27%	5	7.96%	4	84.14%	3
No BERT embeddings	70.50%	8	70.71%	4	67.01%	4	76.02%	4	65.02%	6	5.30%	6	78.99%	5
Ensemble	81.13%	6	**73.39%**	**1**	**70.82%**	**1**	77.57%	3	75.85%	4	8.28%	3	85.05%	3
HIT-SCIR (Che et al., 2019)	*90.41%*	*2*	*70.85%*	*3*	***69.86%***	***1***	*77.61%*	*2*	***79.37%***	***1***	***12.40%***	***1***	***86.20%***	***1***
SJTU–NICT (Li et al., 2019)	***91.50%***	***1***	*71.24%*	*2*	*68.73%*	*2*	***77.62%***	***1***	*77.74%*	*2*	*9.40%*	*2*	*85.27%*	*2*
SUDA–Alibaba (Zhang et al., 2019b)	*86.01%*	*5*	*69.50%*	*4*	*68.24%*	*3*	*77.11%*	*3*	*76.85%*	*3*	*8.16%*	*3*	*83.96%*	*3*
Saarland (Donatelli et al., 2019)	*86.70%*	*4*	***71.33%***	***1***	*61.11%*	*5*	*75.08%*	*5*	*75.01%*	*4*	—		*81.87%*	*4*

Table 3: Overall results, macro-averaged on all frameworks. We present F1 scores and ranks compared to official ST submissions. Results with rank 1 are typeset in **bold**, best results in each column have gray background.

five frameworks. The results for individual frameworks are presented in Table 4.

Our bugfix submission would score third in in the macro-averaged *all* metric. Overall, our system reaches high accuracy in node *labels* and *properties* prediction, ranking first in both of them. These predictions employ the relative encoding extended from UDPipe and demonstrate its effectiveness.

The weakest points of our system are the *top* nodes prediction and *edges* prediction. We hypothesise that the lower performance of the **AddEdges** operation could be improved by better node representation (i.e., including all dependent tokens of a node, not only the one token generating the node) and by a better edge prediction architecture (i.e., global decision over edge connection in the context of all graph nodes instead of considering only the current node pair).

Framework-wise, our system would achieve ranks 5, 4, 4, 4 and 4 on DM, PSD, EDS, UCCA and AMR, respectively, showing relatively balanced performance. The largest absolute performance gap of our system occurs on UCCA, where we reach 8 percent points lower score than the best system, which is supposedly caused by the fact that there are no *labels* and *properties* which our system excels in predicting, and also by the constituency structure of the UCCA graphs which we represent poorly.

4.1 Ablation Experiments

Given that our submission utilized only 90% of the available training data, we also evaluated a variant employing 99% of the training data, keeping the last 1% for error detection. However, as Tables 3 and 4 show, the results are nearly identical.

In order to asses the BERT embeddings effect, we further evaluated a version of our system with-

out them. The macro-averaged *all* performance without BERT embeddings is substantially lower, 79% compared to 84%. Generally all metrics decrease without BERT embeddings, showing that contextual embeddings help "everywhere".

Lastly, we evaluated performance of an 5-model ensemble. Each model was trained using 99% of the training data and utilized different random initialization. The system performance increased by more than 1 percent point. Although the overall rank of the ensemble is unchanged, the rank on individual frameworks increased from 5 to 2 on DM, from 4 to 1 on PSD, 4 to 3 on EDS and 4 to 2 on AMR. As with the non-ensemble system, the weakest point of our solution are the *edge* predictions, which rank 8, 7, 6, 4 and 3 on DM, PSD, EDS, UCCA and AMR, respectively.

5 Conclusions

We introduced a uniform graph-to-graph architecture for parsing into semantic graphs. The model implicitly learns the linguistic information and the graph structure without the need for any specific hand-crafted or structural knowledge and is suitable for any directed graph, including graphs with cycles. In contrast to a transition-based system, we build the graph in a layer-wise fashion, with operations joined in groups.

Acknowledgments

The work described herein has been supported by OP VVV VI LINDAT/CLARIN project (CZ.02.1.01/0.0/0.0/16_013/0001781) and it has been supported and has been using language resources developed by the LINDAT/CLARIN project (LM2015071) of the Ministry of Education, Youth and Sports of the Czech Republic.

We thank the anonymous reviewers for their insightful comments.

System	Tops	Labels	Properties	Anchors	Edges	Attributes	All
Bugfix ST submission	87.39% 8	**97.29%** **1**	94.50% 5	99.02% 6	88.32% 8	—	94.66% 5
99% training data	88.36% 8	**97.38%** **1**	94.57% 5	99.04% 6	88.47% 8	—	94.75% 4
No BERT embeddings	80.70% 9	96.24% 2	92.19% 7	98.45% 8	80.06% 10	—	91.75% 8
Ensemble	89.06% 7	**97.51%** **1**	94.86% 4	99.12% 3	89.72% 8	—	95.17% 2
HIT-SCIR (Che et al., 2019)	92.65% 3	93.00% 4	95.33% 3	**99.28%** **1**	92.54% 2	—	95.08% 2
SJTU–NICT (Li et al., 2019)	93.26% 2	94.89% 3	95.49% 2	99.27% 2	92.39% 3	—	**95.50%** **1**
SUDA–Alibaba (Zhang et al., 2019b)	91.13% 6	90.27% 8	91.51% 7	98.16% 8	89.84% 7	—	92.26% 7
Saarland (Donatelli et al., 2019)	85.87% 8	**96.82%** **1**	93.55% 5	99.05% 5	90.95% 6	—	94.69% 4

(a) DM framework

System	Tops	Labels	Properties	Anchors	Edges	Attributes	All
Bugfix ST submission	94.48% 6	**95.94%** **1**	92.61% 2	99.00% 4	76.06% 7	—	90.96% 4
99% training data	86.49% 9	**96.05%** **1**	92.70% 2	99.00% 3	76.37% 7	—	90.89% 4
No BERT embeddings	67.57% 12	95.14% 3	90.72% 7	98.47% 8	68.22% 10	—	87.58% 8
Ensemble	87.35% 8	**96.19%** **1**	93.04% 2	99.02% 3	78.20% 7	—	**91.51%** **1**
HIT-SCIR (Che et al., 2019)	96.03% 3	89.30% 5	**93.10%** **1**	**99.12%** **1**	79.65% 3	—	90.55% 4
SJTU–NICT (Li et al., 2019)	**96.30%** **1**	93.14% 4	91.57% 5	99.11% 2	**80.27%** **1**	—	91.19% 3
SUDA–Alibaba (Zhang et al., 2019b)	86.55% 8	84.51% 8	85.03% 8	97.51% 8	75.22% 7	—	85.56% 8
Saarland (Donatelli et al., 2019)	93.50% 6	95.21% 2	92.20% 4	99.00% 3	78.32% 6	—	**91.28%** **1**

(b) PSD framework

System	Tops	Labels	Properties	Anchors	Edges	Attributes	All
Bugfix ST submission	82.82% 6	89.99% 3	**91.21%** **1**	92.67% 4	84.76% 7	—	89.12% 4
99% training data	83.79% 6	90.19% 3	**91.19%** **1**	92.88% 4	85.09% 6	—	89.37% 4
No BERT embeddings	73.91% 8	84.52% 5	85.76% 3	89.08% 5	76.73% 7	—	83.43% 7
Ensemble	84.59% 6	90.86% 2	**92.00%** **1**	93.52% 3	86.55% 6	—	90.29% 3
HIT-SCIR (Che et al., 2019)	85.23% 5	89.45% 3	89.54% 2	94.29% 2	88.77% 3	—	90.75% 2
SJTU–NICT (Li et al., 2019)	87.72% 3	89.42% 4	77.53% 4	93.37% 3	87.82% 4	—	89.90% 3
SUDA–Alibaba (Zhang et al., 2019b)	89.94% 2	**91.20%** **1**	**89.72%** **1**	**94.86%** **1**	89.66% 2	—	**91.85%** **1**
Saarland (Donatelli et al., 2019)	86.31% 4	90.61% 2	78.99% 3	86.55% 6	**90.96%** **1**	—	89.10% 4

(c) EDS framework

System	Tops	Labels	Properties	Anchors	Edges	Attributes	All
Bugfix ST submission	62.51% 9	—	—	95.44% 2	59.45% 4	39.35% 4	73.24% 4
99% training data	63.53% 9	—	—	95.80% 2	60.51% 4	39.81% 4	73.95% 4
No BERT embeddings	59.40% 10	—	—	94.11% 5	48.70% 8	26.52% 6	66.90% 7
Ensemble	63.28% 9	—	—	96.19% 2	62.14% 4	41.39% 3	75.22% 4
HIT-SCIR (Che et al., 2019)	**100.00%** **1**	—	—	95.36% 3	**72.66%** **1**	**61.98%** **1**	**81.67%** **1**
SJTU–NICT (Li et al., 2019)	95.31% 5	—	—	**96.36%** **1**	65.56% 3	47.00% 2	77.80% 3
SUDA–Alibaba (Zhang et al., 2019b)	99.56% 3	—	—	95.02% 4	67.74% 2	40.80% 3	78.43% 2
Saarland (Donatelli et al., 2019)	80.95% 8	—	—	90.81% 6	52.66% 6	—	67.55% 6

(d) UCCA framework

System	Tops	Labels	Properties	Anchors	Edges	Attributes	All
Bugfix ST submission	80.17% 6	82.09% 4	71.44% 5	—	60.83% 6	—	71.83% 4
99% training data	80.77% 6	81.69% 4	72.45% 4	—	60.93% 6	—	71.73% 5
No BERT embeddings	70.91% 8	77.67% 6	66.36% 6	—	51.39% 8	—	65.29% 7
Ensemble	81.39% 6	82.40% 3	74.21% 4	—	62.65% 3	—	**73.03%** **2**
HIT-SCIR (Che et al., 2019)	78.15% 7	**82.51%** **2**	71.33% 5	—	**63.21%** **2**	—	72.94% 2
SJTU–NICT (Li et al., 2019)	84.88% 4	78.78% 5	**79.08%** **1**	—	62.64% 3	—	71.97% 3
SUDA–Alibaba (Zhang et al., 2019b)	62.86% 9	81.53% 4	74.96% 3	—	61.78% 5	—	71.72% 5
Saarland (Donatelli et al., 2019)	**86.89%** **1**	74.02% 6	40.79% 7	—	62.16% 4	—	66.72% 6

(e) AMR framework

Table 4: Results on individual frameworks. We present F1 scores and ranks compared to official ST submissions. Results with rank 1 are typeset in **bold**, best results in each column have gray background .

References

Omri Abend and Ari Rappoport. 2013. Universal conceptual cognitive annotation (UCCA). In *Proceedings of the 51st Annual Meeting of the Association for Computational Linguistics (Volume 1: Long Papers)*, pages 228–238, Sofia, Bulgaria. Association for Computational Linguistics.

Akshay Agrawal, Akshay Naresh Modi, Alexandre Passos, Allen Lavoie, Ashish Agarwal, Asim Shankar, Igor Ganichev, Josh Levenberg, Mingsheng Hong, Rajat Monga, and Shanqing Cai. 2019. TensorFlow Eager: A Multi-Stage, Python-Embedded DSL for Machine Learning. *arXiv e-prints*, page arXiv:1903.01855.

Dzmitry Bahdanau, Kyunghyun Cho, and Yoshua Bengio. 2014. Neural machine translation by jointly learning to align and translate. *CoRR*, abs/1409.0473.

Laura Banarescu, Claire Bonial, Shu Cai, Madalina Georgescu, Kira Griffitt, Ulf Hermjakob, Kevin Knight, Philipp Koehn, Martha Palmer, and Nathan Schneider. 2013. Abstract meaning representation for sembanking. In *Proceedings of the 7th Linguistic Annotation Workshop and Interoperability with Discourse*, pages 178–186, Sofia, Bulgaria. Association for Computational Linguistics.

Wanxiang Che, Longxu Dou, Yang Xu, Yuxuan Wang, Yijia Liu, and Ting Liu. 2019. HIT-SCIR at MRP 2019: A unified pipeline for meaning representation parsing via efficient training and effective encoding. In *Proceedings of the Shared Task on Cross-Framework Meaning Representation Parsing at the 2019 Conference on Natural Language Learning*, pages 76 – 85, Hong Kong, China.

Jacob Devlin, Ming-Wei Chang, Kenton Lee, and Kristina Toutanova. 2019. BERT: Pre-training of deep bidirectional transformers for language understanding. In *Proceedings of the 2019 Conference of the North American Chapter of the Association for Computational Linguistics: Human Language Technologies, Volume 1 (Long and Short Papers)*, pages 4171–4186, Minneapolis, Minnesota. Association for Computational Linguistics.

Lucia Donatelli, Meaghan Fowlie, Jonas Groschwitz, Alexander Koller, Matthias Lindemann, Mario Mina, and Pia Weienhorn. 2019. Saarland at MRP 2019: Compositional parsing across all graphbanks. In *Proceedings of the Shared Task on Cross-Framework Meaning Representation Parsing at the 2019 Conference on Natural Language Learning*, pages 66 – 75, Hong Kong, China.

Jeffrey Flanigan, Chris Dyer, Noah A. Smith, and Jaime Carbonell. 2016. CMU at SemEval-2016 task 8: Graph-based AMR parsing with infinite ramp loss. In *Proceedings of the 10th International Workshop on Semantic Evaluation (SemEval-2016)*, pages 1202–1206, San Diego, California. Association for Computational Linguistics.

Jan Hajič, Eva Hajičová, Jarmila Panevová, Petr Sgall, Ondřej Bojar, Silvie Cinková, Eva Fučíková, Marie Mikulová, Petr Pajas, Jan Popelka, Jiří Semecký, Jana Šindlerová, Jan Štěpánek, Josef Toman, Zdeňka Urešová, and Zdeněk Žabokrtský. 2012. Announcing Prague Czech-English dependency treebank 2.0. In *Proceedings of the Eighth International Conference on Language Resources and Evaluation (LREC-2012)*, pages 3153–3160, Istanbul, Turkey. European Languages Resources Association (ELRA).

Daniel Hershcovich, Omri Abend, and Ari Rappoport. 2018. Multitask parsing across semantic representations. In *Proceedings of the 56th Annual Meeting of the Association for Computational Linguistics (Volume 1: Long Papers)*, pages 373–385, Melbourne, Australia. Association for Computational Linguistics.

Daniel Hershcovich, Zohar Aizenbud, Leshem Choshen, Elior Sulem, Ari Rappoport, and Omri Abend. 2019. SemEval-2019 task 1: Cross-lingual semantic parsing with UCCA. In *Proceedings of the 13th International Workshop on Semantic Evaluation*, pages 1–10, Minneapolis, Minnesota, USA. Association for Computational Linguistics.

Angelina Ivanova, Stephan Oepen, Lilja Øvrelid, and Dan Flickinger. 2012. Who did what to whom?: A contrastive study of syntacto-semantic dependencies. In *Proceedings of the Sixth Linguistic Annotation Workshop*, LAW VI '12, pages 2–11, Stroudsburg, PA, USA. Association for Computational Linguistics.

Diederik Kingma and Jimmy Ba. 2014. Adam: A Method for Stochastic Optimization. *International Conference on Learning Representations*.

Zuchao Li, Hai Zhao, Zhuosheng Zhang, Rui Wang, Masao Utiyama, and Eiichiro Sumita. 2019. SJTU–NICT at MRP 2019: Multi-task learning for end-to-end uniform semantic graph parsing. In *Proceedings of the Shared Task on Cross-Framework Meaning Representation Parsing at the 2019 Conference on Natural Language Learning*, pages 45 – 54, Hong Kong, China.

Wang Ling, Tiago Luís, Luís Marujo, Ramón Fernandez Astudillo, Silvio Amir, Chris Dyer, Alan W. Black, and Isabel Trancoso. 2015. Finding function in form: Compositional character models for open vocabulary word representation. *CoRR*.

Jonathan May. 2016. SemEval-2016 task 8: Meaning representation parsing. In *Proceedings of the 10th International Workshop on Semantic Evaluation, SemEval@NAACL-HLT 2016, San Diego, CA, USA, June 16-17, 2016*, pages 1063–1073. The Association for Computer Linguistics.

Jonathan May and Jay Priyadarshi. 2017. SemEval-2017 task 9: Abstract meaning representation parsing and generation. In *Proceedings of the*

11th International Workshop on Semantic Evaluation (SemEval-2017), pages 536–545, Vancouver, Canada. Association for Computational Linguistics.

Tomas Mikolov, Edouard Grave, Piotr Bojanowski, Christian Puhrsch, and Armand Joulin. 2018. Advances in Pre-Training Distributed Word Representations. In *Proceedings of the International Conference on Language Resources and Evaluation (LREC 2018)*.

Yusuke Miyao, Stephan Oepen, and Daniel Zeman. 2014. In-House. An ensemble of pre-existing off-the-shelf parsers. In *Proceedings of the 8th International Workshop on Semantic Evaluation*, page 63 – 72, Dublin, Ireland.

Stephan Oepen, Omri Abend, Jan Hajič, Daniel Hershcovich, Marco Kuhlmann, Tim O'Gorman, Nianwen Xue, Jayeol Chun, Milan Straka, and Zdeňka Urešová. 2019. MRP 2019: Cross-framework Meaning Representation Parsing. In *Proceedings of the Shared Task on Cross-Framework Meaning Representation Parsing at the 2019 Conference on Natural Language Learning*, pages 1 – 27, Hong Kong, China.

Stephan Oepen and Jan Tore Lønning. 2006. Discriminant-based MRS banking. In *Proceedings of the Fifth International Conference on Language Resources and Evaluation (LREC'06)*, Genoa, Italy. European Language Resources Association (ELRA).

Lev Ratinov and Dan Roth. 2009. Design Challenges and Misconceptions in Named Entity Recognition. In *Proc. of the Conference on Computational Natural Language Learning (CoNLL)*.

Milan Straka. 2018. UDPipe 2.0 Prototype at CoNLL 2018 UD Shared Task. In *Proceedings of CoNLL 2018: The SIGNLL Conference on Computational Natural Language Learning*, pages 197–207, Stroudsburg, PA, USA. Association for Computational Linguistics.

Milan Straka, Jana Straková, and Jan Hajic. 2019. UDPipe at SIGMORPHON 2019: Contextualized Embeddings, Regularization with Morphological Categories, Corpora Merging. In *Proceedings of the 16th Workshop on Computational Research in Phonetics, Phonology, and Morphology*, pages 95–103, Florence, Italy. Association for Computational Linguistics.

Milan Straka, Jana Straková, and Jan Hajič. 2019. Evaluating Contextualized Embeddings on 54 Languages in POS Tagging, Lemmatization and Dependency Parsing. *arXiv e-prints*, page arXiv:1908.07448.

Daniel Zeman, Jan Hajič, Martin Popel, Martin Potthast, Milan Straka, Filip Ginter, Joakim Nivre, and Slav Petrov. 2018. CoNLL 2018 Shared Task: Multilingual Parsing from Raw Text to Universal Dependencies. In *Proceedings of the CoNLL 2018 Shared Task: Multilingual Parsing from Raw Text to Universal Dependencies*, pages 1–20, Brussels, Belgium. Association for Computational Linguistics.

Sheng Zhang, Xutai Ma, Kevin Duh, and Benjamin Van Durme. 2019a. AMR parsing as sequence-to-graph transduction. In *Proceedings of the 57th Annual Meeting of the Association for Computational Linguistics*, pages 80–94, Florence, Italy. Association for Computational Linguistics.

Yue Zhang, Wei Jiang, Qingrong Xia, Junjie Cao, Rui Wang, Zhenghua Li, and Min Zhang. 2019b. Suda–alibaba at MRP 2019: Graph-based models with BERT. In *Proceedings of the Shared Task on Cross-Framework Meaning Representation Parsing at the 2019 Conference on Natural Language Learning*, pages 149 – 157, Hong Kong, China.

Amazon at MRP 2019: Parsing Meaning Representations with Lexical and Phrasal Anchoring

Jie Cao[†][*], Yi Zhang[‡], Adel Youssef[‡], Vivek Srikumar[†]

[†]School of Computing, University of Utah

[‡]AWS AI, Amazon

{jcao, svivek}@cs.utah.edu, {yizhngn, adel}@amazon.com

Abstract

This paper describes the system submission of our team *Amazon* to the shared task on Cross Framework Meaning Representation Parsing (MRP) at the 2019 Conference for Computational Language Learning (CoNLL). Via extensive analysis of implicit alignments in AMR, we recategorize five meaning representations (MRs) into two classes: Lexical-Anchoring and Phrasal-Anchoring. Then we propose a unified graph-based parsing framework for the lexical-anchoring MRs, and a phrase-structure parsing for one of the phrasal-anchoring MRs, UCCA. Our system submission ranked 1st in the AMR subtask, and later improvements shows promising results on other frameworks as well.

1 Introduction

The design and implementation of broad-coverage and linguistically motivated meaning representation frameworks for natural language is attracting growing attention in recent years. With the advent of deep neural network-based machine learning techniques, we have made significant progress to automatically parse sentences intro structured meaning representation (Oepen et al., 2014, 2015; May, 2016; Hershcovich et al., 2019). Moreover, the differences between various representation frameworks has a significant impact on the design and performance of the parsing systems.

Due to the abstract nature of semantics, there is a diverse set of meaning representation frameworks in the literature (Abend and Rappoport, 2017). In some application scenario, tasks-specific formal representations such as database queries and arithmetic formula have also been proposed. However, primarily the study in computational semantics focuses on frameworks that are theoretically grounded on formal semantic theories, and sometimes also with assumptions on underlying syntactic structures.

Anchoring is crucial in graph-based meaning representation parsing. Training a statistical parser typically starts with a conjectured alignment between tokens/spans and the semantic graph nodes to help to factorize the supervision of graph structure into nodes and edges. In our paper, with evidence from previous research on AMR alignments (Pourdamghani et al., 2014; Flanigan et al., 2014; Wang and Xue, 2017; Chen and Palmer, 2017; Szubert et al., 2018; Lyu and Titov, 2018), we propose a uniform handling of three meaning representations from `Flavor-0` (DM, PSD) and `Flavor-2` (AMR) into a new group referred to as the **lexical-anchoring** MRs. It supports both explicit and implicit anchoring of semantic concepts to tokens. The other two meaning representations from `Flavor-1` (EDS, UCCA) is referred to the group of **phrasal-anchoring** MRs where the semantic concepts are anchored to phrases as well.

To support the simplified taxonomy, we named our parser as LAPA (Lexical-Anchoring and Phrasal-Anchoring)[1]. We proposed a graph-based parsing framework with a latent-alignment mechanism to support both explicit and implicit lexicon anchoring. According to official evaluation results, our submission for this group ranked 1st in the AMR subtask, 6th on PSD, and 7th on DM respectively, among 16 participating teams. For phrasal-anchoring, we proposed a CKY-based constituent tree parsing algorithm to resolve the anchor in UCCA, and our post-evaluation submission ranked 5th on UCCA subtask.

2 Anchoring in Meaning Representation

The 2019 Conference on Computational Language Learning (CoNLL) hosted a shared task on

---

[*]Work done when Jie Cao was an intern at AWS AI

[1]The code is available online at https://github.com/utahnlp/lapa-mrp

Proceedings of the Shared Task on Cross-Framework Meaning Representation Parsing at the 2019 CoNLL, pages 138–148

Hong Kong, November 3, 2019. ©2019 Association for Computational Linguistics

https://doi.org/10.18653/v1/K19-2013

Cross-Framework Meaning Representation Parsing (MRP 2019, Oepen et al., 2019), which encourage participants in building a parser for five different meaning representations in three distinct flavors. `Flavor-0` includes the DELPH-IN MRS Bi-lexical Dependencies (DM, Ivanova et al., 2012) and Prague Semantic Dependencies (PSD, Hajic et al., 2012; Miyao et al., 2014). Both frameworks under this representation have a syntactic backbone that is (either natively or by-proxy) based on bi-lexical dependency structures. As a result, the semantic concepts in these meaning representations can be anchored to the individual lexical units of the sentence. `Flavor-1` includes Elementary Dependency Structures (EDS, Oepen and Lønning, 2006) and Universal Conceptual Cognitive Annotation framework (UCCA, Abend and Rappoport, 2013), which shows an explicit, many-to-many anchoring of semantic concepts onto sub-strings of the underlying sentence. Finally, `Flavor-2` includes Abstract Meaning Representation (AMR, Banarescu et al., 2013), which is designed to abstract the meaning representation away from its surface token. But it leaves open the question of how these are derived. Previous studies have shown that the nodes in AMR graphs are predominantly aligned with the surface lexical units, although explicit anchoring is absent from the AMR representation. In this section, we review the related work supporting the claim of the implicit anchoring in AMR is actually lexical-anchoring, which can be merged into `Flavor-0` when we consider the parsing methods on it.

2.1 Implicit Anchoring in AMR

AMR tries to abstract the meaning representation away from the surface token. The absense of explicit anchoring can present difficulties for parsing. In this section, by extensive analysis on previous work AMR alignments, we show that AMR nodes can be implicitly aligned to the leixical tokens in a sentence.

AMR-to-String Alignments A straightforward solution to find the missing anchoring in an AMR Graph is to align it with a sentence; We denote it as AMR-to-String alignment.

ISI alignments (Pourdamghani et al., 2014) first linearizes the AMR graph into a sequence, and then use IBM word alignment model (Brown et al., 1993) to align the linearized sequence of concepts and relations with tokens in the sentence. According to the AMR annotation guidelines and error analysis of ISI aligner, some of the nodes or relations are evoked by subwords, e.g., the whole graph fragment `(p/possible-01 :polarity -)` is evoked by word "impossible", where the subword `"im-"` actually evoked the relation polarity and concept `"-"`; On the other side, sometimes concepts are evoked by multiple words, e.g., named entities, `(c/city :name (n/name :op1 "New":op2 "York"))`, which also happens in explict anchoring of DM and PSD. Hence, aligning and parsing with recategorized graph fragments are a natural solution in aligners and parsers. JAMR aligner (Flanigan et al., 2014) uses a set of rules to greedily align single tokens, special entities and a set of multiple word expression to AMR graph fragments, which is widely used in previous AMR parsers (*e.g.* Flanigan et al., 2014; Wang et al., 2015; Artzi et al., 2015; Pust et al., 2015; Peng et al., 2015; Konstas et al., 2017; Wang and Xue, 2017).

Other AMR-to-String Alignments exists, such as the extended HMM-based aligner. To consider more structure info in the linearized AMR concepts, Wang and Xue (2017) proposed a Hidden Markov Model (HMM)-based alignment method with a novel graph distance. All of them report over 90% F-score on their own hand-aligned datasets, which shows that AMR-to-String alignments are almost token-level anchoring.

AMR-to-Dependency Alignments Chen and Palmer (2017) first tries to align an AMR graph with a syntactic dependency tree. Szubert et al. (2018) conducted further analysis on dependency tree and AMR interface. It showed 97% of AMR edges can be evoked by words or the syntactic dependency edges between words. Those nodes in the dependency graph are anchored to each lexical token in the original sentence. Hence, this observation indirectly shows that AMR nodes can be aligned to the lexical tokens in the sentence.

Both AMR-to-String and AMR-to-dependency alignments shows that AMR nodes, including recategorized AMR graph fragements, do have implicit lexical anchoring. Based on this, Lyu and Titov (2018) propose to treat token-node alignments as discrete and exclusive alignment matrix and learn the latent alignment jointly with parsing. Recently, attention-based seq2graph model also

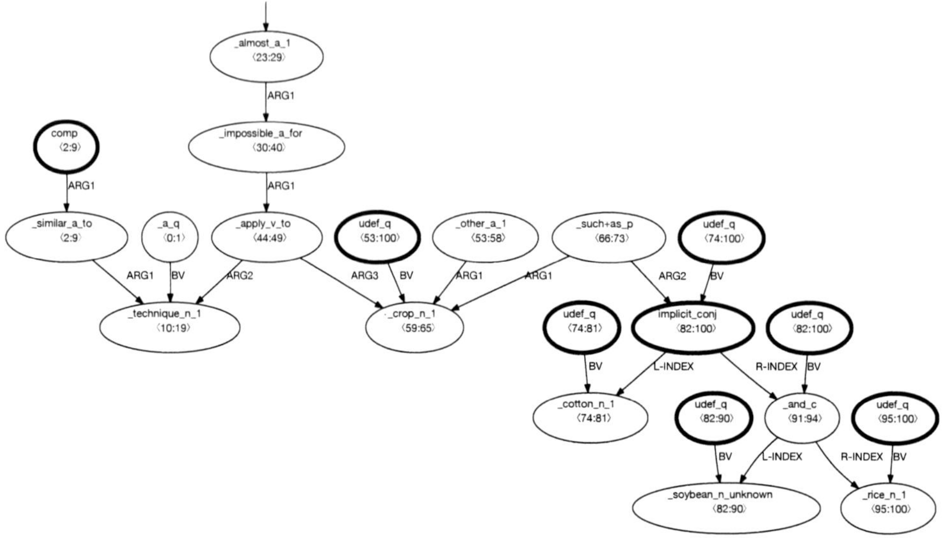

Figure 1: Phrasal-anchoring in EDS[wsj#0209013], for the sentence "A similar technique is almost impossible to apply to other crops, such as cotton, soybeans and rice.". Bold nodes are similar to the non-terminal nodes in UCCA, which are anchored multiple tokens, thus overlapping with the anchors of other nodes.

achieved the state-of-the-art accuracy on AMR parsing (Zhang et al., 2019). However, whether the attention weights can be explained as AMR alignments needs more investigation in future.

2.2 Taxonomy of Anchroing

Given the above analysis on implicit alignments in AMR, in this section, we further discuss the taxonomy of anchoring of the five meaning representations in this shared task.

Lexical-Anchoring According to the bi-lexical dependency structures of DM and PSD, and implicit lexical token anchoring on AMR, the nodes/-categorized graph fragments of DM, PSD, and AMR are anchored to surface lexical units in an explicit or implicit way. Especially, those lexical units do not overlap with each other, and most of them are just single tokens, multiple word expression, or named entities. In other words, when parsing a sentence into DM, PSD, AMR graphs, tokens in the original sentence can be merged by looking up a lexicon dict when preprocessing and then may be considered as a single token for aligning or parsing.

Phrasal-Anchoring However, different from the lexical anchoring without overlapping, nodes

in EDS and UCCA may align to larger overlapped word spans which involves syntactic or semantic pharsal structure. Nodes in UCCA do not have node labels or node properties, but all the nodes are anchored to the spans of the underlying sentence. Furthermore, the nodes in UCCA are linked into a hierarchical structure, with edges going between parent and child nodes. With certain exceptions (e.g. remote edges), the majority of the UCCA graphs are tree-like structures. According to the position as well as the anchoring style, nodes in UCCA can be classified into the following two types:

1. **Terminal nodes** are the leaf semantic concepts anchored to individual lexical units in the sentence

2. **Non-terminal nodes** are usually anchored to a span with more than one lexical units, thus usually overlapped with the anchoring of terminal nodes.

The similar classification of anchoring nodes also applies to the nodes in EDS, although they do not regularly form a recursive tree like UCCA. As the running example in Figure 1, most of the nodes belongs to terminal nodes, which can be explicitly anchored to a single token in the original sentence. However, those bold non-teriminal nodes are anchored to a large span of words. For example, the node `"undef_q"` with span `<53:100>` is aligned to the whole substring starting from "other crops" to the end; The abstract node with label `imp_conj` are corresponding to the whole coordinate structure between `soybeans and rice`.

In summary, by treating AMR as an implicitly lexically anchored MR, we propose a simplified taxonomy for parsing the five meaning representation in this shared task.

- `Lexical-anchoring`: DM, PSD, AMR

- `Phrasal-anchoring`: EDS, UCCA

3 Model

For the two groups of meaning representations defined in Section 2, in this section, we propose two parsing framework: a graph-based parsing framework with latent alignment for lexically anchored MRs, and a minimal span-based CKY parser for one of the phrasally anchored MRs, UCCA.[2]

3.1 Graph-based Parsing Framework with Latent Alignment

Before formulating the graph-based model into a probabilistic model as Equation 1, we denote some notations: C, R are sets of concepts (nodes) and relations (edges) in the graph, and w is a sequence of tokens. $a \in \mathbb{Z}^m$ as the alignment matrix, each a_i is the index of aligned token where ith node aligned to. When modeling the negative log likelihood loss (NLL), with independence assumption between each node and edge, we decompose it into node- and edge-identification pipelines.

$$
\begin{aligned}
&NLL(P(C, R \mid w)) \\
&= -\log(P(C, R \mid w)) \\
&= -\log(\sum_a P(a)P(C, R \mid w, a)) \\
&= -\log\left(\sum_a P(a)P(R \mid w, a, c)P(c \mid w, a)\right) \\
&= -\log\left(\sum_a P(a)\prod_i^m P(c_i \mid h_{a_i}) \right. \\
&\quad \left. \cdot \prod_{i,j=1}^m P(r_{ij} \mid h_{a_i}, c_i, h_{a_j}, c_j)\right)
\end{aligned}
$$

(1)

---

[2]After the CKY parser gets the related phrasal spans, graph-based parser can also be used to predict the relations between nodes.

In DM, PSD, and AMR, every token will only be aligned once. Hence, we train a joint model to maximize the above probability for both node identification $P(c_i \mid h_{a_i})$ and edge identification $P(r_{ij} \mid h_{a_i}, c_i, h_{a_j}, c_j)$, and we need to marginalize out the discrete alignment variable a.

3.1.1 Alignment Model

The above model can support both explicit alignments for DM, PSD, and implicit alignments for AMR.

Explicit Alignments For DM, PSD, with explicit alignments $a*$, we can use $P(a^*) = 1.0$ and other alignments $P(a|a \neq a^*) = 0.0$

Implicit Alignments For AMR, without gold alignments, one requires to compute all the valid alignments and then condition the node- and edge-identification methods on the alignments.

$$
\begin{aligned}
&\log(P(C, R \mid w)) \geq \\
&E_Q[\log(P_\theta(c \mid w, a)P_\Phi(R \mid w, a, c))] \\
&\quad - D_{KL}(Q_\Psi(a \mid c, R, w) \| P(a))
\end{aligned}
$$

(2)

However, it is computationally intractable to enumerate all alignments. We estimate posterior alignments model Q as Equation 3, please refer to Lyu and Titov (2018) for more details.

- Applying variational inference to reduce it into Evidence Lower Bound (ELBO, Kingma and Welling, 2013)

- The denominator Z_Ψ in Q can be estimated by Perturb-and-Max(MAP) (Papandreou and Yuille, 2011)

$$
Q_\Psi(a \mid c, R, w) = \frac{\exp(\sum_{i=1}^n \phi(g_i, h_{a_i}))}{Z_\Psi(c, w)}
$$

(3)

Where $\phi(g_i, h_{a_i})$ score each alignment link between node i and the corresponding words, g_i is node encoding, and h_{a_i} is encoding for the aligned token.

- Discrete `argmax` of a permutation can be estimated by Gumbel-Softmax Sinkhorn Networks (Mena et al., 2018; Lyu and Titov, 2018)

3.1.2 Node Identification

Node Identification predicts a concept c given a word. A concept can be either *NULL* (when there is no semantic node anchoring to that word, e.g.,

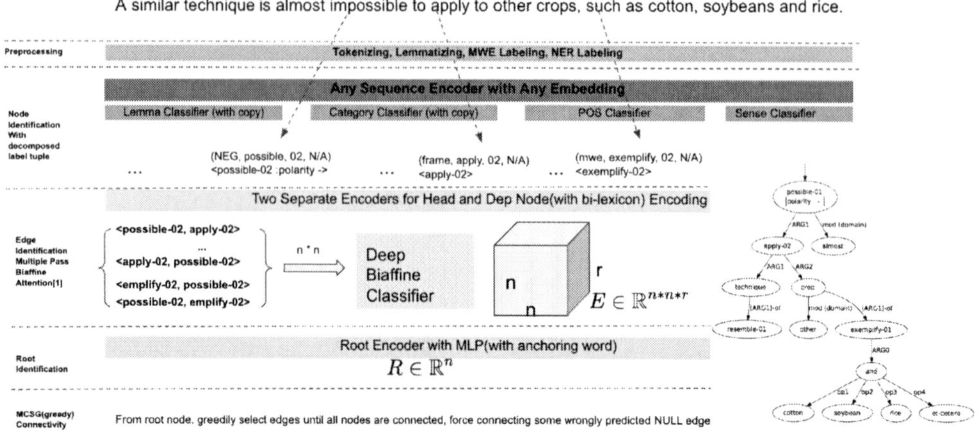

Figure 2: Architecture of graph-based model and inference, for running exmaple [wsj#0209013]

the word is dropped), or a node label (e.g., lemma, sense, POS, name value in AMR, frame value in PSD), or other node properties. One challenge in node identification is the data sparsity issue. Many of the labels are from open sets derived from the input token, e.g., its lemma. Moreover, some labels are constrained by a deterministic label set given the word. Hence, we designed a copy mechanism (Luong et al., 2014) in our neural network architecture to decide whether to copying deterministic label given a word or estimate a classification probability from a fixed label set.

3.1.3 Edge Identification

By assuming the independence of each edge, we model the edges probabilites independently. Given two nodes and their underlying tokens, we predict the edge label as the semantic relation between the two concepts with a bi-affine classifier (Dozat and Manning, 2016).

3.1.4 Inference

In our two-stage graph-based parsing, after nodes are identified, edge identification only output a probility distribution over all the relations between identified nodes. However, we need to an inference algorithm to search for the maximum spanning connected graph from all the relations. We use Flanigan et al. (MSCG, 2014) to greedily select the most valuable edges from the identified nodes and their relations connecting them. As shown in Figure 2, an input sentence goes through preprocessing, node identification, edge identification, root identification, and MCSG to generate a final connected graph as structured output.

3.2 Minimal Span-based CKY Parsing Framework

Let us now see our phrasal-anchoring parser for UCCA. We introduce the transformation we used to reduce UCCA parsing into a consituent parsing task, and finally introduce the detailed CKY model for the constituent parsing.

3.2.1 Graph-to-CT Transformation

We propose to transform a graph into a constituent tree structure for parsing, which is also used in recent work (Jiang et al., 2019). Figure 3 shows an example of transforming a UCCA graph into a constituent tree. The primary transformation assigns the original label of an edge to its child node. Then to make it compatible with parsers for standard PennTree Bank format, we add some auxiliary nodes such as special non-terminal nodes, TOP, HEAD, and special terminal nodes TOKEN and MWE. We remove all the "remote" annotation in UCCA since the constituent tree structure does not support reentrance. A fully compatible transformation should support both graph-to-tree and tree-to-graph transformation.

In our case, due to time constraints, we remove those remote edges and reentrance edges during training. Besides that, we also noticed that for multi-word expressions, the children of a parent node might not be in a continuous span (i.e., discontinuous constituent), which is also not supported by our constituent tree parser. Hence, when training the tree parser, by reattaching the discontinuous tokens to its nearest continuous parent nodes, we force every sub span are continuous in the transformed trees. We leave the postprocessing to recover those discontinuous as future work.

For inference, given an input sentence, we first use the trained constituent tree parsing model to parse it into a tree, and then we transform a tree back into a directed graph by assigning the edge label as its child's node label, and deleting those auxiliary labels, adding anchors to every remaining node.

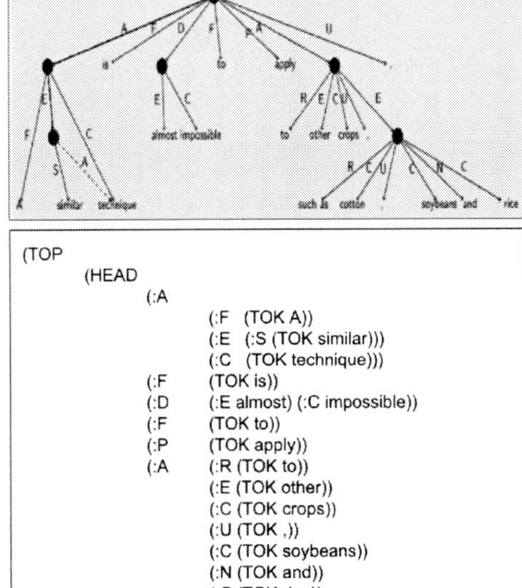

```
(TOP
    (HEAD
        (:A
                        (:F   (TOK A))
                        (:E   (:S (TOK similar)))
                        (:C   (TOK technique)))
            (:F     (TOK is))
            (:D     (:E almost) (:C impossible))
            (:F     (TOK to))
            (:P     (TOK apply))
            (:A     (:R (TOK to))
                    (:E (TOK other))
                    (:C (TOK crops))
                    (:U (TOK ,))
                    (:C (TOK soybeans))
                    (:N (TOK and))
                    (:C (TOK rice))
            (:U     (TOK .))
        )
    )
)
```

Figure 3: UCCA to Constituent Tree Transformation for [wsj#0209013]

3.2.2 CKY Parsing and Span Encoding

After transforming the UCCA graph into a constituent tree, we reduce the UCCA parsing into a constituent tree parsing problem. Similar to the previous work on UCCA constituent tree parsing (Jiang et al., 2019), we use a minimal span-based CKY parser for constituent tree parsing. The intuition is to use dynamic programming to recursively split the span of a sentence recursively, as shown in Figure 3. The entire sentence can be splitted from top to bottom until each span is a single unsplittable tokens. For each node, we also need to assign a label. Two simplified assumptions are made when predicting the hole tree given a sentence. However, different with previous work,

we use 8-layers with 8 heads transformer encoder, which shows better performance than LSTM in Kitaev and Klein (2018).

Tree Factorization In the graph-to-tree transformation, we move the edge label to its child node. By assuming the labels for each node are independent, we factorize the tree structure prediction as independent span-label prediction as Equation 4. However, this assumption does not hold for UCCA. Please see more error analysis in §4.4

$$T^* = \arg\max_T s(T)$$
$$s(T) = \sum_{(i,j,l) \in T} s(i,j,l) \tag{4}$$

CKY Parsing By assuming the label prediction is independent of the splitting point, we can further factorize the whole tree as the following dynamic programming in Equation 5.

$$s_{\text{best}}(i, i+1) = \max_l s(i, i+1, l)$$
$$s_{\text{best}}(i, j) = \max_l s(i, j, l)$$
$$+ \max_k [s_{\text{best}}(i, k) + s_{\text{best}}(k, j)] \tag{5}$$

Span Encoding For each span (i, j), we represent the span encoding vector $v_{(i,j)} = [\vec{y_j} - \vec{y_i}] \oplus [\overleftarrow{y_{j+1}} - \overleftarrow{y_{i+1}}]$. $\oplus$ denotes vector concatenation. Assuming a bidirectional sentence encoder, we use the forward and backward encodings $\vec{y_i}$ and $\overleftarrow{y_i}$ of i_{th} word. Following the previous work, and we also use the loss augmented inference training. More details about the network architecture are in the Section 4.2

3.3 Summary of Implementation

We summarize our implementation for five meaning representations as Table 1. As we mentioned in the previous sections, we use latent-alignment graph-based parsing for lexical anchoring MRs (DM, PSD, AMR), and use CKY-based constituent parsing phrasal anchoring in MRs (UCCA, EDS). This section gives information about various decision for our models.

Top The first row "Top" shows the numbers of root nodes in the graph. We can see that for PSD, 11.56% of graphs with more than 1 top nodes. In our system, we only predict one top node with a N (N is size of identified nodes) way classifier, and

	Lexicon Anchoring			Phrase Anchoring	
	DM	PSD	AMR	EDS	UCCA
Top	1	≥ 1 (11.56%)	1	1	1
Node Label	Lemma	Lemma(*)	Lemma(*) + NeType(143+)	_lemma(*)_semi_sense	N/A
Node Properties	POS semi(160*)_args(25)	POS wordid_sense(25)	constant values polarity, Named entity	carg: constant value	N/A N/A
Edge Label	(45)	(91)	(94+)	(45)	(15)
Edge Properties	N/A	N/A	N/A	N/A	"remote"
Connectivity	True	True	True	True	True
Training Data	35656	35656	57885	35656	6485
Test Data	3269	3269	1998	3269	1131

Table 1: Detailed classifiers in our model, round bracket means the number of ouput classes of our classify, * means copy mechanism is used in our classifier. At the end of shared task, EDS are not fully supported to get an official results, we leave it as our future work.

then fix this with a post-processing strategy. When our model predicts one node as the top node, and if we find additional coordination nodes with it, we add the coordination node also as the top node.

Node Except for UCCA, all other four MRs have labeled nodes, the row "Node Label" shows the templates of a node label. For DM and PSD, the node label is usually the lemma of its underlying token. But the lemma is neither the same as one in the given companion data nor the predicted by Stanford Lemma Annotators. One common challenge for predicting the node labels is the open label set problem. Usually, the lemma is one of the morphology derivations of the original word. But the derivation rule is not easy to create manually. In our experiment, we found that handcrafted rules for lemma prediction only works worse than classification with copy mechanism, except for DM.

For AMR and EDS, there are other components in the node labels beyond the lemma. Especially, the node label for AMR also contains more than 143 fine-grained named entity types; for EDS, it uses the full SEM-I entry as its node label, which requires extra classifiers for predicting the corresponding sense. In addition to the node label, the properties of the label also need to be predicted. Among them, node properties of DM are from the SEMI sense and arguments handler, while for PSD, senses are constrained the senses in the predefined the vallex lexicon.

Edge Edge predication is another challenge in our task because of its large label set (from 45 to 94) as shown in row "Edge Label", the round bracket means the number of output classes of our classifiers. For Lexical anchoring MRs, edges are usually connected between two tokens, while phrasal anchoring needs extra effort to figure out the corresponding span with that node. For example, in UCCA parsing, To predict edge labels, we first predicted the node spans, and then node labels based that span, and finally we transform back the node label into edge label.

Connectivity Beside the local label classification for nodes and edges, there are other global structure constraints for all five MRs: All the nodes and edges should eventually form a connected graph. For lexical anchoring, we use MSCG algorithm to find the maximum connected graph greedily; For phrasal anchoring, we use dynamic programming to decoding the constituent tree then deterministically transforming back to a connected UCCA Graph [3]

4 Experiments and Results

4.1 Dataset and Evaluation

For DM, PSD, EDS, we split the training set by taking WSJ section (00-19) as training, and section 20 as dev set. For other datasets, when developing and parameter tuning, we use splits with a ratio of 25:1:1. In our submitted model, we did not use multitask learning for training. Following the unified MRP metrics in the shared tasks, we train our model based on the development set and finally evaluate on the private test set. For more details of the metrics, please refer to the summarization of the MRP 2019 task (Oepen et al., 2019),

4.2 Model Setup

For lexical-anchoring model setup, our network mainly consists of node and edge prediction model. For AMR, DM, and PSD, they all use one layer Bi-directional LSTM for input sentence encoder, and two layers Bi-directional LSTM for head or dependent node encoder in the bi-affine classifier. For every sentence encoder, it takes a sequence of word embedding as input (We use 300 dimension Glove here), and then their output will pass a softmax layer to predicting output distribution. For the latent AMR model, to model the posterior alignment, we use another Bi-LSTM for node sequence encoding. For phrasal-anchoring model setup, we follow the original model set up in Kitaev and Klein (2018), and we use 8-layers 8-headers transformer with position encoding to encode the input sentence.

For all sentence encoders, we also use the character-level CNN model as character-level embedding without any pre-trained deep contextualized embedding model. Equipping our model with Bert or multi-task learning is promising to get further improvement. We leave this as our future work.

Our models are trained with Adam (Kingma and Ba, 2014), using a batch size 64 for a graph-based model, and 250 for CKY-based model. Hyperparameters were tuned on the development set, based on labeled F1 between two graphs. We exploit early-stopping to avoid over-fitting.

4.3 Results

At the time of official evaluation, we submitted three lexical anchoring parser, and then we submitted another phrasal-anchoring model for UCCA parsing during post-evaluation stage, and we leave EDS parsing as future work. The following sections are the official results and error breakdowns for lexical-anchoring and phrasal-anchoring respectively.

Official Results on Lexical Anchoring Table 2 shows the official results for our lexical-anchoring models on AMR, DM, PSD. By using our latent alignment based AMR parser, our system ranked top 1 in the AMR subtask, and outperformed the top 5 models in large margin. Our parser on PSD ranked 6, but only 0.02% worse then the top 5 model. However, official results on DM and PSD shows that there is still around 2.5 points performance gap between our model and the top 1 model.

Official Results on Phrasal Anchoring Table 3 shows that our span-based CKY model for UCCA

MR	Ours (P/R/F1)	Top 1/3/5 (F1)
AMR(1)	**75/71/73.38**	**73.38/71.97/71.72**
PSD(6)	89/89/**88.75**	90.76/89.91/**88.77**
DM(7)	93/92/92.14	94.76/94.32/93.74

Table 2: Official results overview on unified MRP metric, we selected the performance from top 1/3/5 system(s) for comparison

can achieve 74.00 F1 score on official test set, and ranked 5th. When adding ELMo (Peters et al., 2018) into our model, it can further improve almost 3 points on it.

MR	Ours (P/R/F1)	Top 1/3/5 (F1)
UCCA(5)	80.83/73.42/**76.94**	81.67/77.80/73.22
EDS	N/A	94.47/90.75/89.10

Table 3: Official results overview on unified MRP metric, we selected the performance from top 1/3/5 system(s) for comparison. It shows our UCCA model for post-evluation can rank 5th

4.4 Error Breakdown

Table 4, 5, 6 and 7 shows the detailed error breakdown of AMR, DM, PSD and UCCA respectively. Each column in the table shows the F1 score of each subcomponent in a graph: top nodes, node lables, node properties, node anchors, edge labels, and overall F1 score. No anchors for AMR, and no node label and propertis for UCCA. We show the results of MRP metric on two datasets. "all" denotes all the examples for that specific MR, while lpps are a set of 100 sentences from The Little Prince, and annotated in all five meaning representations. To better understand the performance, we also reported the official results from two baseline models TUPA (Hershcovich and Arviv, 2019) and ERG (Oepen and Flickinger, 2019).

	data	tops	labels	prop	edges	all
TUPA	all	63.95	57.20	22.31	36.41	44.73
single	lpps	71.96	55.52	26.42	36.38	47.04
TUPA	all	61.30	39.80	27.70	27.35	33.75
multi	lpps	72.63	50.11	20.25	33.12	43.38
Ours(1)	all	65.92	82.86	**77.26**	63.57	**73.38**
	lpps	72.00	78.71	58.93	63.96	71.11
Top 2	all	78.15	82.51	71.33	63.21	72.94
	lpps	83.00	76.24	51.79	60.43	69.03

Table 4: Our parser on AMR ranked 1st. This table shows the error breakdown when comparing to the baseline TUPA model and top 2 (Che et al., 2019) in official results

	data	tops	labels	prop	anchors	edges	all
ERG	all	91.83	98.22	95.25	98.82	90.76	95.65
	lpps	95.00	97.32	97.75	99.46	92.71	97.03
Top 1	all	93.23	94.14	94.83	98.40	91.55	94.76
	lpps	96.48	91.85	94.36	99.04	93.28	94.64
Ours(7)	all	70.95	93.96	92.13	97.25	86.45	92.14
	lpps	84.00	90.55	91.91	97.96	87.24	91.82

Table 5: Our parser on DM ranked 7th. This table shows the error breakdown when comparing to the model ranked Top 1 (Li et al., 2019) in official results

	data	tops	labels	prop	anchors	edges	all
Top 1	all	93.45	94.68	91.78	98.35	77.79	90.76
	lpps	93.33	91.73	84.37	98.40	77.63	88.34
Ours(6)	all	82.01	94.18	91.28	96.94	72.40	88.75
	lpps	85.85	90.48	82.63	95.97	73.60	85.83

Table 6: Our parser on PSD ranked 6th. This table shows the error breakdown when comparing to the model ranked top 1 (Donatelli et al., 2019) in official results

4.4.1 Error Analysis on Lexical-Anchoring

As shown in Table 4, our AMR parser is good at predicting node properties and consistently perform better than other models in all subcomponent, except for top prediction. Node properties in AMR are usually named entities, negation, and some other quantity entities. In our system, we recategorize the graph fragments into a single node, which helps for both alignments and structured inference for those special graph fragments. We see that all our 3 models perform almost as good as the top 1 model of each subtask on node label prediction, but they perform worse on top and edge prediction. It indicates that our bi-affine relation classifier are main bottleneck to improve. Moreover, we found the performance gap between node labels and node anchors are almost consistent, it indicates that improving our model on predicting `NULL` nodes may further improve node label prediction as well. Moreover, we believe that multi-task learning and pre-trained deep models such as BERT (Devlin et al., 2018) may also boost the performance of our paser in future.

4.4.2 Error Analysis on Phrasal-Anchoring

According to Table 7, our model with ELMo works slightly better than the top 1 model on anchors prediction. It means our model is good at predicting the nodes in UCCA and we belive that it is also helpful for prediction phrasal anchoring nodes in EDS.

However, when predicting the edge and edge

	data	tops	anchors	edge	attr	all
TUPA single	all	78.73	69.17	16.96	15.18	27.56
	lpps	86.03	76.26	28.32	24.00	40.06
TUPA multi	all	84.92	65.74	12.99	9.07	23.65
	lpps	88.89	77.76	26.45	18.32	41.04
(Che et al., 2019)	all	1.00	95.36	72.66	61.98	81.67
	lpps	1.00	96.99	73.08	48.37	82.61
Ours(*5)	all	98.85	94.92	60.17	0.00	**74.00**
	lpps	96.00	96.75	60.20	0.00	75.17
Ours + ELMo	all	99.38	95.70	64.88	0.00	**76.94**
	lpps	98.00	96.84	66.63	0.00	78.77

Table 7: Our UCCA parser in post-evaluation ranked 5th according to the original official evaluation results. This table shows the error breakdown when comparing to the model ranked top 1 (Che et al., 2019) in official results. * denotes the ranking of post-evaluation results

attributes, our model performs 7-8 points worse than the top 1 model. In UCCA, an edge label means the relation between a parent nodes and its children. In our UCCA transformation, we assign edge label as the node label of its child and then predict with only child span encoding. Thus it actually misses important information from the parent node. Hence, in future, more improvement can be done to use both child and parent span encoding for label prediction, or even using another span-based bi-affine classifier for edge prediction, or remote edge recovering.

5 Conclusion

In summary, by analyzing the AMR alignments, we show that implicit AMR anchoring is actually lexical-anchoring based. Thus we propose to regroup five meaning representations as two groups: lexical-anchoring and phrasal-anchoring. For lexical anchoring, we suggest to parse DM, PSD, and AMR in a unified latent-alignment based parsing framework. Our submission ranked top 1 in AMR sub-task, ranked 6th and 7th in PSD and DM tasks. For phrasal anchoring, by reducing UCCA graph into a constituent tree-like structure, and then use the span-based CKY parsing to parse their tree structure, our method would rank 5th in the original official evaluation results.

Acknowledgments

The authors wish to thank the anonymous reviewers and members of the Amazon LEX team for their valuable feedback.

References

Omri Abend and Ari Rappoport. 2013. Universal conceptual cognitive annotation (ucca). In *Proceedings of the 51st Annual Meeting of the Association for Computational Linguistics (Volume 1: Long Papers)*, pages 228–238.

Omri Abend and Ari Rappoport. 2017. The state of the art in semantic representation. In *Proceedings of the 55th Annual Meeting of the Association for Computational Linguistics (Volume 1: Long Papers)*, pages 77–89.

Yoav Artzi, Kenton Lee, and Luke Zettlemoyer. 2015. Broad-coverage CCG Semantic Parsing with AMR. *EMNLP*.

Laura Banarescu, Claire Bonial, Shu Cai, Madalina Georgescu, Kira Griffitt, Ulf Hermjakob, Kevin Knight, Philipp Koehn, Martha Palmer, and Nathan Schneider. 2013. Abstract Meaning Representation for Sembanking. *LAW@ACL*.

Peter F Brown, Vincent J Della Pietra, Stephen A Della Pietra, and Robert L Mercer. 1993. The mathematics of statistical machine translation: Parameter estimation. *Computational linguistics*, 19(2):263–311.

Wanxiang Che, Longxu Dou, Yang Xu, Yuxuan Wang, Yijia Liu, and Ting Liu. 2019. HIT-SCIR at MRP 2019: A unified pipeline for meaning representation parsing via efficient training and effective encoding. In *Proceedings of the Shared Task on Cross-Framework Meaning Representation Parsing at the 2019 Conference on Natural Language Learning*, pages 76–85, Hong Kong, China.

Wei-Te Chen and Martha Palmer. 2017. Unsupervised amr-dependency parse alignment. In *Proceedings of the 15th Conference of the European Chapter of the Association for Computational Linguistics: Volume 1, Long Papers*, volume 1, pages 558–567.

Jacob Devlin, Ming-Wei Chang, Kenton Lee, and Kristina Toutanova. 2018. Bert: Pre-training of deep bidirectional transformers for language understanding. *arXiv preprint arXiv:1810.04805*.

Lucia Donatelli, Meaghan Fowlie, Jonas Groschwitz, Alexander Koller, Matthias Lindemann, Mario Mina, and Pia Weienhorn. 2019. Saarland at MRP 2019: Compositional parsing across all graphbanks. In *Proceedings of the Shared Task on Cross-Framework Meaning Representation Parsing at the 2019 Conference on Natural Language Learning*, pages 66–75, Hong Kong, China.

Timothy Dozat and Christopher D Manning. 2016. Deep biaffine attention for neural dependency parsing. *ICLR*.

Jeffrey Flanigan, Sam Thomson, Jaime G Carbonell, Chris Dyer, and Noah A Smith. 2014. A Discriminative Graph-Based Parser for the Abstract Meaning Representation. *ACL*.

Jan Hajic, Eva Hajicová, Jarmila Panevová, Petr Sgall, Ondrej Bojar, Silvie Cinková, Eva Fucíková, Marie Mikulová, Petr Pajas, Jan Popelka, et al. 2012. Announcing prague czech-english dependency treebank 2.0. In *LREC*, pages 3153–3160.

Daniel Hershcovich, Zohar Aizenbud, Leshem Choshen, Elior Sulem, Ari Rappoport, and Omri Abend. 2019. SemEval-2019 task 1: Cross-lingual semantic parsing with UCCA. In *Proceedings of the 13th International Workshop on Semantic Evaluation*, pages 1–10, Minneapolis, Minnesota, USA. Association for Computational Linguistics.

Daniel Hershcovich and Ofir Arviv. 2019. TUPA at MRP 2019: A multi-task baseline system. In *Proceedings of the Shared Task on Cross-Framework Meaning Representation Parsing at the 2019 Conference on Natural Language Learning*, pages 28–39, Hong Kong, China.

Angelina Ivanova, Stephan Oepen, Lilja Øvrelid, and Dan Flickinger. 2012. Who did what to whom?: A contrastive study of syntacto-semantic dependencies. In *Proceedings of the sixth linguistic annotation workshop*, pages 2–11. Association for Computational Linguistics.

Wei Jiang, Yu Zhang, Zhenghua Li, and Min Zhang. 2019. Hlt@ suda at semeval 2019 task 1: Ucca graph parsing as constituent tree parsing. *arXiv preprint arXiv:1903.04153*.

Diederik P Kingma and Jimmy Ba. 2014. Adam: A method for stochastic optimization. *arXiv preprint arXiv:1412.6980*.

Diederik P Kingma and Max Welling. 2013. Autoencoding variational bayes. *ICLR*.

Nikita Kitaev and Dan Klein. 2018. Constituency parsing with a self-attentive encoder. *arXiv preprint arXiv:1805.01052*.

Ioannis Konstas, Srinivasan Iyer, Mark Yatskar, Yejin Choi, and Luke Zettlemoyer. 2017. Neural AMR: Sequence-to-Sequence Models for Parsing and Generation.

Zuchao Li, Hai Zhao, Zhuosheng Zhang, Rui Wang, Masao Utiyama, and Eiichiro Sumita. 2019. SJTU-NICT at MRP 2019: Multi-task learning for end-to-end uniform semantic graph parsing. In *Proceedings of the Shared Task on Cross-Framework Meaning Representation Parsing at the 2019 Conference on Natural Language Learning*, pages 45–54, Hong Kong, China.

Minh-Thang Luong, Ilya Sutskever, Quoc V Le, Oriol Vinyals, and Wojciech Zaremba. 2014. Addressing the rare word problem in neural machine translation. *IJCNLP*.

Chunchuan Lyu and Ivan Titov. 2018. Amr parsing as graph prediction with latent alignment. *ACL*.

J May. 2016. SemEval-2016 Task 8: Meaning Representation Parsing. In *Proceedings of SemEval*, pages 1063–1073, Stroudsburg, PA, USA. Association for Computational Linguistics.

Gonzalo Mena, David Belanger, Scott Linderman, and Jasper Snoek. 2018. Learning latent permutations with gumbel-sinkhorn networks. *arXiv preprint arXiv:1802.08665*.

Yusuke Miyao, Stephan Oepen, and Daniel Zeman. 2014. In-house: An ensemble of pre-existing off-the-shelf parsers. In *Proceedings of the 8th International Workshop on Semantic Evaluation (SemEval 2014)*, pages 335–340.

Stephan Oepen, Omri Abend, Jan Hajič, Daniel Hershcovich, Marco Kuhlmann, Tim O'Gorman, Nianwen Xue, Jayeol Chun, Milan Straka, and Zdeňka Urešová. 2019. MRP 2019: Cross-framework Meaning Representation Parsing. In *Proceedings of the Shared Task on Cross-Framework Meaning Representation Parsing at the 2019 Conference on Natural Language Learning*, pages 1 – 27, Hong Kong, China.

Stephan Oepen and Dan Flickinger. 2019. The ERG at MRP 2019: Radically compositional semantic dependencies. In *Proceedings of the Shared Task on Cross-Framework Meaning Representation Parsing at the 2019 Conference on Natural Language Learning*, pages 40 – 44, Hong Kong, China.

Stephan Oepen, Marco Kuhlmann, Yusuke Miyao, Daniel Zeman, Silvie Cinková, Dan Flickinger, Jan Hajič, and Zdeňka Urešová. 2015. SemEval 2015 Task 18. Broad-coverage semantic dependency parsing. In *Proceedings of the 9th International Workshop on Semantic Evaluation*, page 915 – 926, Bolder, CO, USA.

Stephan Oepen, Marco Kuhlmann, Yusuke Miyao, Daniel Zeman, Dan Flickinger, Jan Hajič, Angelina Ivanova, and Yi Zhang. 2014. SemEval 2014 Task 8. Broad-coverage semantic dependency parsing. In *Proceedings of the 8th International Workshop on Semantic Evaluation*, page 63 – 72, Dublin, Ireland.

Stephan Oepen and Jan Tore Lønning. 2006. Discriminant-based mrs banking. In *LREC*, pages 1250–1255.

George Papandreou and Alan Yuille. 2011. Perturb-and-map random fields: Using discrete optimization to learn and sample from energy models–iccv 2011 paper supplementary material–.

Xiaochang Peng, Linfeng Song, and Daniel Gildea. 2015. A Synchronous Hyperedge Replacement Grammar based approach for AMR parsing. In *Proceedings of the Nineteenth Conference on Computational Natural Language Learning*, pages 32–41, Stroudsburg, PA, USA. Association for Computational Linguistics.

Matthew E Peters, Mark Neumann, Mohit Iyyer, Matt Gardner, Christopher Clark, Kenton Lee, and Luke Zettlemoyer. 2018. Deep contextualized word representations. *arXiv preprint arXiv:1802.05365*.

Nima Pourdamghani, Yang Gao, Ulf Hermjakob, and Kevin Knight. 2014. Aligning English Strings with Abstract Meaning Representation Graphs. In *Proceedings of the 2014 Conference on Empirical Methods in Natural Language Processing (EMNLP)*, pages 425–429, Stroudsburg, PA, USA. Association for Computational Linguistics.

Michael Pust, Ulf Hermjakob, Kevin Knight, Daniel Marcu, and Jonathan May. 2015. Using Syntax-Based Machine Translation to Parse English into Abstract Meaning Representation. *arXiv.org*.

Ida Szubert, Adam Lopez, and Nathan Schneider. 2018. A structured syntax-semantics interface for english-amr alignment. In *Proceedings of the 2018 Conference of the North American Chapter of the Association for Computational Linguistics: Human Language Technologies, Volume 1 (Long Papers)*, pages 1169–1180.

Chuan Wang and Nianwen Xue. 2017. Getting the most out of amr parsing. In *Proceedings of the 2017 conference on empirical methods in natural language processing*, pages 1257–1268.

Chuan Wang, Nianwen Xue, and Sameer Pradhan. 2015. Boosting Transition-based AMR Parsing with Refined Actions and Auxiliary Analyzers. *Proceedings of the 53rd Annual Meeting of the Association for Computational Linguistics and the 7th International Joint Conference on Natural Language Processing (Volume 2: Short Papers)*, pages 1–6.

Sheng Zhang, Xutai Ma, Kevin Duh, and Benjamin Van Durme. 2019. AMR Parsing as Sequence-to-Graph Transduction. In *Proceedings of the 57th Annual Meeting of the Association for Computational Linguistics (Volume 1: Long Papers)*, Florence, Italy. Association for Computational Linguistics.

SUDA–Alibaba at MRP 2019: Graph-Based Models with BERT

Yue Zhang[1], Wei Jiang[2], Qingrong Xia[2], Junjie Cao[1], Rui Wang[1], Zhenghua Li[2*], Min Zhang[2]

[1] Alibaba Group, China

[2] School of Computer Science and Technology, Soochow University, China

{shiyu.zy, junjie.junjiecao, masi.wr}@alibaba-inc.com

wjiang0501@stu.suda.edu.cn, kirosummer.nlp@gmail.com

{zhli13, minzhang}@suda.edu.cn

Abstract

In this paper, we describe our participating systems in the shared task on Cross-Framework Meaning Representation Parsing (MRP) at the 2019 Conference for Computational Language Learning (CoNLL). The task includes five frameworks for graph-based meaning representations, i.e., DM, PSD, EDS, UCCA, and AMR. One common characteristic of our systems is that we employ graph-based methods instead of transition-based methods when predicting edges between nodes. For SDP, we jointly perform edge prediction, frame tagging, and POS tagging via multi-task learning (MTL). For UCCA, we also jointly model a constituent tree parsing and a remote edge recovery task. For both EDS and AMR, we produce nodes first and edges second in a pipeline fashion. External resources like BERT are found helpful for all frameworks except AMR. Our final submission ranks the third on the overall MRP evaluation metric, the first on EDS and the second on UCCA.

1 Introduction

Cross-Framework Meaning Representation Parsing (MRP) at CoNLL 2019 contains five different graph-based semantic representations, including DM, PSD, EDS, UCCA and AMR. The shared task releases training and testing data for all five frameworks. For different frameworks, organizers design different evaluation criteria and provide standard evaluation scripts. Details about the five semantic formalisms and evaluation criteria are given in the MRP shared task homepage[1] and the overview paper (Oepen et al., 2019). In the following, we give a brief introduction of each framework and followed by our corresponding approaches.

Semantic Dependency Parsing (SDP) aims to parse the predicate-argument relationships for all words in the input sentence, leading to bilexical semantic dependency graphs (Oepen et al., 2014, 2015, 2016). This shared task focuses on two different formal types of SDP representations, i.e., DELPH-IN MRS Bi-Lexical Dependencies (abbr. as DM, Ivanova et al., 2012) and Prague Semantic Dependencies (abbr. as PSD, Hajič et al., 2012; Miyao et al., 2014). They are both classified as Flavor 0 representations in the sense that every node in the graph must anchor to one and only one token unit, and vice verse. Compared with syntactic dependency trees, some nodes in an SDP graph may have no incoming edges and some may have multiple ones. Borrowing the idea of Dozat and Manning (2018), we encode the input word sequence with BiLSTMs and predict the edges and labels between words with two MLPs. We also predict the POS tag and frame of each word jointly under the MTL framework.

Universal Conceptual Cognitive Annotation (UCCA) is a multi-layer linguistic framework (Flavor 1) firstly proposed by Abend and Rappoport (2013). In UCCA graphs, input words are leaf (or terminal) nodes. One non-terminal node governs one or more nodes, which may be discontinuous; and one node can have multiple governing (parent) nodes through multiple edges, consisting of a single primary edge and other remote edges. Relationships between nodes are given by edge labels. The primary edges form a tree structure, whereas the remote edges introduce reentrancy, forming directed acyclic graphs (DAGs).[2] We directly adopt the previous graph-based UCCA parser proposed by Jiang et al. (2019), treating UCCA graph parsing as constituent parsing and remote edge recovery under the MTL framework.

---

*Corresponding author

[1] http://mrp.nlpl.eu/index.php?page=1

[2] The full UCCA scheme also has implicit nodes and linkage relations, which are excluded in the shared task.

Proceedings of the Shared Task on Cross-Framework Meaning Representation Parsing at the 2019 CoNLL, pages 149–157
Hong Kong, November 3, 2019. ©2019 Association for Computational Linguistics
https://doi.org/10.18653/v1/K19-2014

Elementary Dependency Structure (EDS) is a graph-structured semantic representation formalism (Flavor 1) proposed by Oepen and Lønning (2006). Buys and Blunsom (2017) introduce a neural encoder-decoder transition-based model to obtain the EDS graph. They use external knowledge to generate nodes[3]. Chen et al. (2018) introduce a novel SHRG (Synchronous Hyperedge Replacement Grammar) extraction algorithm which requires a syntactic tree and alignments between conceptual edges and surface strings. Such alignment information is not provided in the shared task and seems difficult for us to induce due to time limitation. Therefore, we divide the EDS task into two-stage task: node prediction and edge prediction, and treat both as sequence labeling. To tackle with the explicit, many-to-many relationship between nodes and sub-strings of the underlying sentence (via anchoring), we introduce a similar method used in dependency SRL (semantic role labeling) to produce nodes. For the edge prediction, the widely-used Biaffine model is used.

Abstract meaning representation (AMR), proposed by Banarescu et al. (2013), is a broad-coverage sentence-level semantic formalism (Flavor 2) to encode the meaning of natural language sentences. AMR can be regarded as a rooted labeled directed acyclic graph. Nodes in AMR graphs represent concepts, and labeled directed edges are relations between the concepts. Due to the time limitation and the complexity of the AMR parsing problem, we directly employ the state-of-the-art parser of Lyu and Titov (2018), which treats AMR parsing as a graph prediction problem.

Methodology Summarization. Our participating systems can be characterized in the following aspects:

- **Graph-Based.** All our methods for the five frameworks belong to graph-based methods in the sense that we directly predict edges among nodes, instead of using a transition system. In particular, the constituent parser for UCCA is also graph-based.

- **Joint Model.** We simplify our architecture and use less training steps by jointly modeling subtasks whenever it is possible. This is achieved by sharing the encoder component

---

[3]Their knowledge sources ERG 1214 (http://svn.delph-in.net/erg/tags/1214) are not in the white list of this shared task.

under the MTL framework and it is adopted by the DM, PSD, and UCCA models. For both EDS and AMR, we first produce nodes and then predict edges in a pipeline architecture. We have not attempted to jointly solve multiple semantic frameworks via MTL yet.

- **BERT.** We observe that using BERT as our extra inputs is effective for all the models, except AMR. It is also interesting that BERT-large does not produce more improvements over BERT-base based our preliminary experiments.

Our final submission ranks the third on the overall evaluation metric, the first on EDS and the second on UCCA. In the following, We introduce our methods in detail in Section 2, and present the experimental results in Section 3, and finally conclude our paper in Section 4.

2 Methods

2.1 SDP

We construct our SDP parser based on the ideas of Dozat and Manning (2017) and Dozat and Manning (2018). Note that lemmas, POS tags and frames are also included in the MRP evaluation metrics, so our method is a bit different from Dozat and Manning (2018).

Edge Prediction. Our basic edge prediction model is similar to the Dozat and Manning (2017) and Dozat and Manning (2018). The input words are first mapped into a dense vector composed by pretrained word embeddings and character-level features.

$$\mathbf{x}_i = \mathbf{e}_i^{word} \oplus \mathbf{e}_i^{char}$$

where $\mathbf{e}_i^{char}$ is extracted by the bidirectional character-level LSTM (Lample et al., 2016). They are then fed into a multilayer bidirectional word-level LSTM to get contextualized representations. Finally, two modules are applied to predict edges. One is to predict whether or not a directed edge exists between two words (keeping the edges between pairs of words with positive scores); and the other is to predict the most probable label for each potential edge (choosing the label with maximum score). Each of them has two seperate MLPs for head and dependent representations and a biaffine layer for scoring. The training loss is the sum of sigmoid cross-entropy loss for edges and softmax

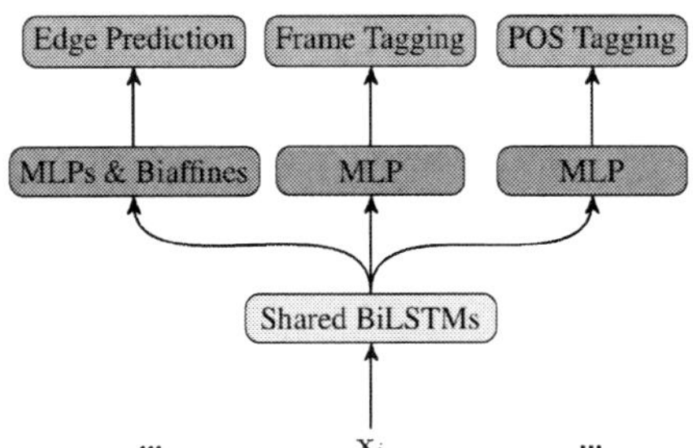

Figure 1: The framework of our SDP Parser.

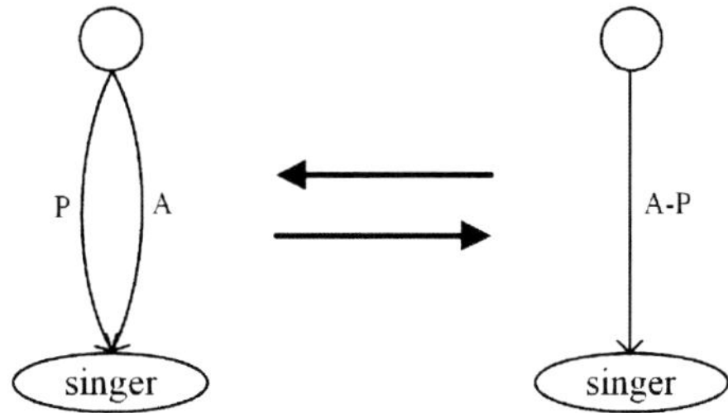

Figure 2: An example of newest version of UCCA.

cross-entropy loss for labels.

$$\ell' = \ell^{label} + \ell^{edge}$$

Lexical Taggers. This SDP task is more difficult than the ealier 2014 and 2015 SDP tasks (Oepen et al., 2014, 2015), since the gold tokenization result, lemmas, and POS tags are not available in the parser input data and the predictions are parts of the MRP evaluation metrics. We use automatic tokenization result and lemmas provided by the datasets; while for POS and frames, we train the taggers with the edge predicter simultaneously under the multi-task learning framework. Figure 1 shows the framework of our SDP parser. The final training loss is :

$$\ell^{sdp} = \ell' + \ell^{frame} + \ell^{pos}$$

where ℓ^{frame} and ℓ^{pos} are both softmax cross-entropy losses.

2.2 UCCA

We directly follow Jiang et al. (2019)'s graph-based UCCA parser. The key idea is to convert a UCCA semantic graph into a constituent tree, and mark remote edges and discontinuous nodes with extra labels for later recovery.

Graph-to-tree Conversion. In the new version of UCCA, one non-terminal node is allowed to point to another by more than one primary edges, e.g., the word "singer" represents a "process" and a "participant" in a semantic scene at the same time (Figure 2 shows the example). Therefore, we keep only one of the edges and concatenate all their tags in the alphabetical order. During the recovery step, the edge with a mixed label is splitted according to the label's length.

Then for the edges that point to the same node, we delete all remote edges and concatenate an extra "remote" to the label of the only primary edge.

To handle discontinuous node, we trace bottom-up from a discontinuous leaf node until we find the specific node whose parent is the lowest common ancestor (LCA) of the discontinuous node and leaf node. Finally we move the edge to make the specific node become the child of the discontinuous, with "-ancestor" added behind the edge label. Please refer to Jiang et al. (2019) for more conversion details.

Constituent Parsing. We directly adopt the minimal span-based parser of Stern et al. (2017). Given an input sentence $X = \{x_0, x_1, \cdots, x_n\}$, each word x_i is mapped into a dense vector $\mathbf{x}_i$ and fed into bidirectional LSTM layers. The top-layer output of each position are used to represent the span as

$$\mathbf{r}_{i,j} = (\mathbf{f}_j - \mathbf{f}_i) \oplus (\mathbf{b}_i - \mathbf{b}_j)$$

where $\mathbf{f}_i$ and $\mathbf{b}_i$ are the output vectors of the top-layer forward and backward LSTMs. The span representations are then fed into MLPs to compute the scores of span splitting and labeling. Finally, a parse tree is derived by a greedy top-down searching. In particular, We start from the span of the whole sentence, assigning it the label with maximum score and choosing the best split point where the sum of two sub-spans' splitting scores are maximum. Then we repeat this process for the left and right sub-spans until the span can no longer be split.

Remote Edge Recovery. To recover remote edges, two seperate MLPs and biaffine operations are applied on remote nodes and other candidate parent nodes representations. They share the same inputs and LSTM encoder with the constituent parser under the MTL framework. The parsing loss and the cross-entropy losses of all remote and non-terminal node pairs are added in the MTL framework.

2.3 EDS

This subsection describes our models on EDS task, which are simple but effective. Since many external resources cannot be used to generate nodes in EDS graph in this shared task, we convert the main task into two sequence labeling subtasks: node prediction and edge prediction.

Node prediction. For each input sentence $X = \{x_0, x_1, \cdots, x_n\}$, our model needs to predict nodes in EDS graph $N = \{n_0, n_1, \cdots, n_m\}$. For each node, it contains such information: id, anchors, labels, properties and values. Taking one node as example, anchors mean the span indicators of characters in the input sentence, like "$< a, b >$". It means this node strides across the sub string from character index a to b in the input sentence string. We can convert anchors from character index provided by the data to word index[4].

From the definition of EDS graph, there is a many-to-many relationship between words and nodes. Lots of nodes stride across more than one word of the underlying sentence according to their anchors. To simplify the alignment between words and nodes, we divide nodes in graphs into two types due to their characteristic.

The first type is those nodes whose labels begin with "_" or properties are not null, e.g., "_fund_n_1". We call them the *original node*, labels of which usually consist of three parts: lemma, coarse part-of-speech(POS) tag and sense according to the role the word plays in the sentence. The second type is the *append node*, e.g., "udf_q". Those nodes do not contain explicit sentence text and many of them stride across several words, which makes us difficult to obtain their anchors.

We align the nodes to input words, so that we predict labels and anchors based on the input word sequence:

For ***original nodes***, we use the lemma of each word provided by organizers and we take POS tag and sense as a joint label and predict them with sequence labeling, like the POS tagger. To generate training data, based on our statistics and analysis, we tag words in the following ways: 1) in most cases, original nodes are aligned to

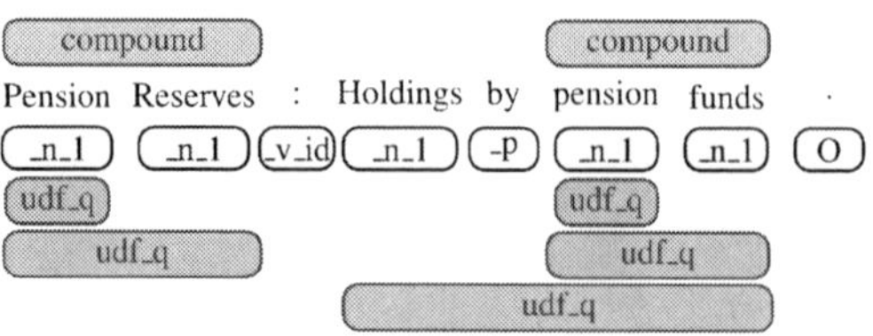

Figure 3: An example for node prediction in the EDS graph. We use nodes with different color shadows to represent different kinds of EDS nodes. Nodes with yellow shadows under the input sentence are *original nodes*. The number of *original nodes* is equal to the length of sentence. Nodes with pink shadows above the sentence are non-terminal *append nodes* and purple nodes below the sentence are leaf nodes. In the example sentence, there are two non-terminal nodes and five leaf nodes. Nodes over across several words means their anchors.

words one by one and these words are tagged with their "POS_sense"[5]; 2) for those compound nodes striding across several words (e.g., "_such+as_p" means it combines "such" and "as" two words), we tag the first word with the true label and other words tagged with "A"; and 3) we tag the input words disappearing in EDS graph with "O". Note that, when one word participates in different *original nodes*, we will concatenate all labels of one word together with separator ":".

For ***append node***, we divide it into two types, leaf nodes and non-terminal nodes[6]. The difference between leaf nodes and non-terminal nodes is that whether they are pointed by other nodes. Both leaf nodes and non-terminal nodes may overlap several words and one input word may participate in different *append nodes* as Figure3 shows. Therefore, we take a similar way like the prediction of SRL predicate and argument[7]. We firstly predict the begin index of each *append node*, like predicate identification in the SRL task, and then, we predict their end index and their labels, like argument prediction. Given the beginning, we tag the end words of nodes with their labels and concatenate labels with separator ":" if more than one node have same anchors. This allows us to solve

---

[4] Index conversion makes us align nodes to words in the input sentence, so that we can simplify our task. And due to the evaluation standard of this shared task, we do not consider punctuation and we can take punctuation as common words if the task needs.

[5] Sometimes, the label only contains POS information.

[6] We take this division originally for edge prediction and task simplification. In EDS graph, leaf nodes should participate in only one edge, but our edge prediction model achieves great performance on all nodes, so we do not distinguish them in the edge prediction.

[7] We did not apply the same sequence labeling method for the *original node*, since it is difficult to recover when continuous words participate in more than nodes.

Detailed errors	Modification
company abbreviation, like Corp., Co., Inc	corporation, company and inc
address forms, like Mr., Mrs., Dr.	corresponding full name
numbers in English	Arabic numerals
country name abbreviation	delete "." in string
some symbol like "%", "#", "$", "&" and ":"	English String

Table 1: Effective post-processing for labels and values in EDS node.

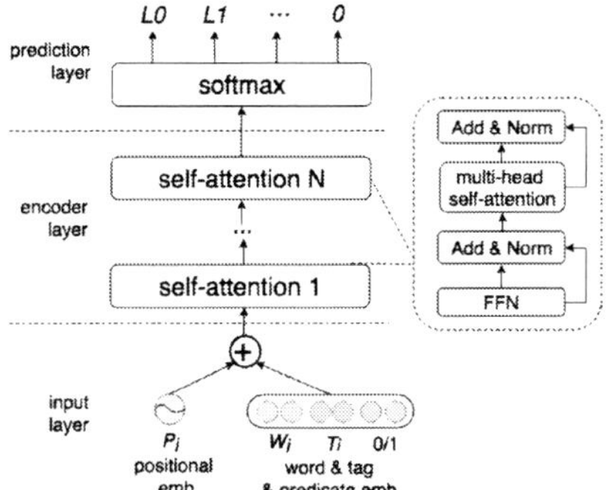

Figure 4: Architecture of our multi-layers self-attention-based model. The dotted box on the right is the detailed composition of the self-attention block.

the problem of the overlap and multi-participation of the *append nodes* elegantly.

We apply a multi-head self-attention model (Tan et al., 2018) for our node prediction, which has been proved effective in SRL task. Details about the attention model please refer to Tan et al. (2018) and Vaswani et al. (2017). For *original nodes* and beginning of append nodes prediction, the input consists of embeddings of words and POS-tags provided by organizers; while for end of *append nodes* prediction, the input contains embedding of the beginning indicator in addition. Then we use simple softmax function to get the index or labels whose scores are the highest.

Edge prediction. Compared with the node prediction, the edge prediction model is more straightforward, which builds links between nodes and generates the final EDS graph.

Labels in edges are used to tag the relation between two nodes, like "ARG1", "BV". If there is no edges between two nodes, we use the relation "O". Note that, we add one pseudo node like the "ROOT" node in the dependency parsing, so that we can get the top node of the graph (which is pointed by the "ROOT" node).

For the edge prediction model, a multi-layered BiLSTM is firstly used to encode the original input sentence, so that we get the representation of each word. Then we represent each node according to its anchors (begin index and end index) as formula in 2.2 shows, so that each node contains information of all words in the anchors. Lastly, we compute the score of each candidate edge relation between two nodes by the biaffine mechanism, and get label whose score is the highest.

Post-processing. We convert our predicted results into nodes according to the predicted begin index and the predicted label (including the end index and corresponding label). We sort them by the anchors of nodes to get the id of each node in the EDS graph. We index these nodes in the *ascending* order by the begin index of anchors and then in the *descending* order by the end of the anchors.

We analysis the results of our splitted development data, and correct some common lemma errors by a post-processing script (Table 1).

For senses, we fix some errors according to the ERG knowledge provided by the organizers. ERG, a external knowledge provided by the shared task, contains all legal sense for each lemma and POS tag. Given a joint string of lemma and POS tag, we judge whether our predicted sense is legal, and for the illegal sense, we use the first one in ERG to replace it.

For compound words containing "-", we find that most of them should split into several parts, but limited by our model, we cannot get their lemma, POS tag and sense. Therefore, we use one split word and the predicted POS tag and sense to replace the originally predicted one after we verify sense legality[8].

---

[8]In dev data, we find that, such split does not work well, but we think, without the replacement, the node is unlikely to be correct.

2.4 AMR

Abstract meaning representation (AMR) (Banarescu et al., 2013) is a semantic formalism to encode the meaning of natural language sentences, which is a broad-coverage sentence-level semantic representation. AMR can be regarded as a rooted labeled directed acyclic graph. We directly follow Lyu and Titov (2018)'s joint modeling of alignments, concepts and relations. In the following, we describe the details of our AMR parser and the modifications we make due to the constrains of the white list of MRP. In general, the training process employs a probability model composed of concept identification, relation identification and alignment, while the testing process only consists of the former two.

Notations. Given a sentence $\mathbf{s} = w_1, w_2, ..., w_n$, where n is the sentence length. Its concepts are defined as $\mathbf{c} = (c_1, c_2, ..., c_m)$, where m is the number of concepts. A relation between c_i and c_j is denoted as $r_i j \in \mathcal{R}$, where $\mathcal{R}$ is the set of all relations. If there is no relation between c_i and c_j, we give them a *NULL* label. We employ $\mathbf{a} = a_1, a_2, ..., a_m$ to denote the concepts, where $a_i \in 1, 2, ..., n$ is the index of a word aligned to c_i. We use $\mathbf{h}_k (k \in 1, 2, ..., l)$ to denote the hidden states of BiLSTM encoders of our model components, where l is the number of the BiLSTM layers.

Concept Identification Model. The concept identification model chooses a concept c conditioned on the aligned word k based on the BiLSTM state $\mathbf{h}_k$, which is defined as $P_\theta(c|\mathbf{h}_k, w_k)$. For more details about the re-categorization and candidate concept, please refer to Lyu and Titov (2018).

Relation Identification Model. The relation identification model is arc-factored as:

$$P_\phi(\mathcal{R}|\mathbf{a}, \mathbf{c}, \mathbf{w}) = \prod_{i,j=1}^{m} P(r_{ij}|\mathbf{h}_{a_i}, \mathbf{c}_i, \mathbf{h}_{a_j}, \mathbf{c}_j)$$

(1)

The model employs a log-linear module with bilinear scorer to compute the probabilities of c_i and c_j.

Alignment Model. The alignment model is only used in training, and thus it only depends on the BiLSTM hidden states $\mathbf{h}_1, \mathbf{h}_2, ..., \mathbf{h}_n$ and the concept list $c_1, c_2, ..., c_m$. Given the concepts list $\mathbf{c}$, the alignment model encodes $\mathbf{c}$ with a BiLSTM encoder, which defines the state of c_i as $\mathbf{g}_i$, $i \in 1, 2, ..., n$. A globally-normalized alignment model is used, which is defined as $Q_\psi(\mathbf{a}|\mathbf{c}, \mathcal{R}, \mathbf{w})$, and the score of the alignment a_i is also computed via a bilinear scorer.

Pre-processing and Post-processing. Since the text format of MRP AMR is different from the original AMR, we need to convert the MRP AMR text to original AMR text, which is same as the input file of the parser (Lyu and Titov, 2018). We utilize Illinois Named Entity Tagger[9] (NER) to generate the NER labels for the AMR data; and we use the Part-of-Speech (PoS) tags and lemmas provided by MRP. After the parser generating the test data output, we convert the AMR form to the MRP form. For details about the pre-processing and post-processing, please refer to the original paper Lyu and Titov (2018) as well.

3 Experiments

This section describes model parameters used in our models, and the overall results of all the five tasks.

3.1 Model Parameters

In both **SDP** and **UCCA** tasks, we use 100-dimensional GloVe (Pennington et al., 2014) as pretrained embedding and random initialized 50-dimensional char embedding. The char lstm output is 100-dimensional. We also utilize the BERT embeddings extracted from the last four transformer layers. The final BERT representation is their normalized weighted sum, which is concatenated with the word embeddings. The other parameters are the same with the previous works (Dozat and Manning, 2018; Jiang et al., 2019).

In **EDS** task, external resources we use are: 1) word embeddings pre-trained with GloVe (Pennington et al., 2014) on the Gigaword corpus for Chinese; and 2) BERT [10] (Devlin et al., 2018), recently proposed effective deep contextualized word representation. We split the provided training data into train/dev/test data, and both dev and test data contain 2500 examples respectively. We evaluate our model on the split data, and before submitting the final result, we train our model on all the data and predict the provided test data as our submission.

In **AMR** task, we randomly choose the samples of the training data according to the proportion of

---

[9] https://cogcomp.org/page/software_view/NETagger

[10] We generate our pre-trained BERT embedding with the released model in https://github.com/google-research/bert.

	DM			PSD			UCCA			EDS			AMR		
	P	R	F1	P	R	F1	P	R	F1	P	R	F1	P	R	F1
Node prediction															
labels	89	90	89.26	83	85	83.80	#	#	#	91	91	91.20	82	81	81.53
properties	90	91	90.65	83	85	84.43	#	#	#	89	91	89.72	77	73	74.96
anchors	#	#	#	#	#	#	96	94	95.02	95	95	94.86	#	#	#
Edge prediction															
top	91	91	91.01	96	79	86.49	100	100	99.56	90	90	89.94	63	63	62.86
edges	88	90	88.69	74	75	74.41	70	65	67.74	90	90	89.66	64	60	61.78
attributes	#	#	#	#	#	#	54	33	40.80	#	#	#	#	#	#
Overall															
all	90	92	91.26	84	86	84.81	81	76	78.43	92	92	91.85	73	70	71.72

Table 2: Experiment results on the provided test data from the shared task. We divide different evaluation criteria into two types: node-related and edge related, which agrees with our task division.

each domain, and compose them as the development data, which contain 2993 samples. We have also attempted to integrate BERT representations into the basic model input, but it did not bring significant improvements. For the model parameters, we directly use the default settings of Lyu and Titov (2018).

3.2 Experiment Results

Our experiment results on the provided test data are shown in Table 2.

SDP. We randomly selected 20% sentences as our development set and the rest as our training set. After tuning on the development set, we train the parser on the whole dataset from scratch and early stop at the best epoch on the development data. The MRP F1 scores of our DM and PSD deveplopment data are 93.37 and 87.89, respectively. After utilizing BERT embeddings, the results rise to 94.06 and 88.79 respectively. As the improvements are not very significant, we will explore better ways of integrating BERT in the future. We achieve 91.26 and 84.81 F1 scores on PSD and SDP test data regarding to the MRP evaluation metrics, which rank the eighth and the ninth respectively.

UCCA. The training strategy is the same as SDP. The MRP F1 scores on our deveplopment data are 79.80 and 73.41, w/o BERT respectively. Unlike SDP, the result is significantly improved after using BERT embeddings. This is consistent with Jiang et al. (2019). We achieve 78.43 F1 score on the test set which ranks the second.

EDS. For nodes prediction, our models cannot assign the labels well compared to the anchors as shown in Table 2, and properties are even worse. This trend is consistent with our model design and the evaluation strategy, since they predict anchors first and the labels second. Another important reason is that provided lemmas of the words are not always correct for EDS task.

For edge prediction, on our split test/dev data, edge model can achieve much better performance based on the gold nodes than predicted nodes, up to ca. 98%. Based on such high performance, we have not considered constraints like leaf node cannot be pointed by other nodes. Edge prediction performance in Table 2 is not optimal mainlly due to the error propagation from node prediction.

External knowledge including BERT and pretrained word embedding are effective; and postprocessing listed in can achieve about 1% improvement on our split dev/test data. Another interesting observation during our experiments is that the complete match score is much higher than the normal dependency parsing (ca. 75% vs. 30%), although the corresponding LAS can be as high as ca. 92%.

Finally, we obtain 91.85 F1 score on the test data, ranks the first.

AMR. We choose the best model that tuned on the development data to generate AMR graphs for the test data, which achieves 69.9 F1 smatch score on development data. Table 2 shows the results of the AMR test data regarding to the MRP evaluation metrics. We achieve 71.72 F1 score on the test data and it ranks the fifth.

Our overall result on all five tasks ranks third, and our results ranks first on EDS and second on UCCA.

4 Conclusions and Future Work

We participate in the shared task on Cross-Framework Meaning Representation Parsing (MRP) at CoNLL-2019. The shared task combines five frameworks for graph-based meaning representation, including DM, PSD, EDS, UCCA, and AMR. Considering the common characteristics of the five semantic formalisms, we treat them as two-stage processing using graph-based methods: node prediction (no need for DM and PSD) and edge prediction. For different graphs, we generate nodes and edges in a joint way or in a pipeline way. BERT is also employed to boost the performance (except AMR). Our system ranked the third on the overall evaluation metrics, the first on EDS and the second on UCCA. For the future work, we plan to jointly handle multiple semantic frameworks (e.g., DM, PSD, and UCCA) at the same time via MTL, in order to facilitate mutual benefits and interactions, and make better use of the non-overlapping training data. Moreover, model ensemble may also further enhance the performance.

References

Omri Abend and Ari Rappoport. 2013. Universal Conceptual Cognitive Annotation (UCCA). In *Proc. of ACL*, pages 228–238.

Laura Banarescu, Claire Bonial, Shu Cai, Madalina Georgescu, Kira Griffitt, Ulf Hermjakob, Kevin Knight, Philipp Koehn, Martha Palmer, and Nathan Schneider. 2013. Abstract meaning representation for sembanking. In *Proceedings of the 7th Linguistic Annotation Workshop and Interoperability with Discourse*, pages 178–186.

Jan Buys and Phil Blunsom. 2017. Robust incremental neural semantic graph parsing. In *Proceedings of the 55th Annual Meeting of the Association for Computational Linguistics (Volume 1: Long Papers)*, pages 1215–1226, Vancouver, Canada. Association for Computational Linguistics.

Yufei Chen, Weiwei Sun, and Xiaojun Wan. 2018. Accurate SHRG-based semantic parsing. In *Proceedings of the 56th Annual Meeting of the Association for Computational Linguistics (Volume 1: Long Papers)*, pages 408–418, Melbourne, Australia. Association for Computational Linguistics.

Jacob Devlin, Ming-Wei Chang, Kenton Lee, and Kristina Toutanova. 2018. BERT: pre-training of deep bidirectional transformers for language understanding. *CoRR*, abs/1810.04805.

Timothy Dozat and Christopher D. Manning. 2017. Deep biaffine attention for neural dependency parsing. In *Proceedings of ICLR*.

Timothy Dozat and Christopher D. Manning. 2018. Simpler but more accurate semantic dependency parsing. In *Proceedings of the 56th Annual Meeting of the Association for Computational Linguistics (Volume 2: Short Papers)*.

Jan Hajič, Eva Hajičová, Jarmila Panevová, Petr Sgall, Ondřej Bojar, Silvie Cinková, Eva Fučíková, Marie Mikulová, Petr Pajas, Jan Popelka, Jiří Semecký, Jana Šindlerová, Jan Štěpánek, Josef Toman, Zdeňka Urešová, and Zdeněk Žabokrtský. 2012. Announcing prague czech-english dependency treebank 2.0. In *Proceedings of the Eight International Conference on Language Resources and Evaluation (LREC'12)*.

Angelina Ivanova, Stephan Oepen, Lilja Øvrelid, and Dan Flickinger. 2012. Who did what to whom? a contrastive study of syntacto-semantic dependencies. In *Proceedings of the Sixth Linguistic Annotation Workshop*.

Wei Jiang, Zhenghua Li, Yu Zhang, and Min Zhang. 2019. Hlt@suda at semeval-2019 task 1: Ucca graph parsing as constituent tree parsing. In *Proceedings of the 13th International Workshop on Semantic Evaluation*, pages 11–15.

Guillaume Lample, Miguel Ballesteros, Sandeep Subramanian, Kazuya Kawakami, and Chris Dyer. 2016. Neural architectures for named entity recognition. In *Proceedings of the 2016 Conference of the North American Chapter of the Association for Computational Linguistics: Human Language Technologies*.

Chunchuan Lyu and Ivan Titov. 2018. Amr parsing as graph prediction with latent alignment. In *Proceedings of the 56th Annual Meeting of the Association for Computational Linguistics (Volume 1: Long Papers)*, pages 397–407.

Yusuke Miyao, Stephan Oepen, and Daniel Zeman. 2014. In-house: An ensemble of pre-existing off-the-shelf parsers. In *Proceedings of the 8th International Workshop on Semantic Evaluation (SemEval 2014)*.

Stephan Oepen, Omri Abend, Jan Hajič, Daniel Hershcovich, Marco Kuhlmann, Tim O'Gorman, Nianwen Xue, Jayeol Chun, Milan Straka, and Zdeňka Urešová. 2019. MRP 2019: Cross-framework Meaning Representation Parsing. In *Proceedings of the Shared Task on Cross-Framework Meaning Representation Parsing at the 2019 Conference on Natural Language Learning*, pages 1–27, Hong Kong, China.

Stephan Oepen, Marco Kuhlmann, Yusuke Miyao, Daniel Zeman, Silvie Cinkova, Dan Flickinger, Jan Hajic, Angelina Ivanova, and Zdenka Uresova. 2016. Towards comparability of linguistic graph banks for semantic parsing. In *Proceedings of the Tenth International Conference on Language Resources and Evaluation (LREC 2016)*.

Stephan Oepen, Marco Kuhlmann, Yusuke Miyao, Daniel Zeman, Silvie Cinková, Dan Flickinger, Jan Hajič, and Zdeňka Urešová. 2015. SemEval 2015 task 18: Broad-coverage semantic dependency parsing. In *Proceedings of the 9th International Workshop on Semantic Evaluation (SemEval 2015)*.

Stephan Oepen, Marco Kuhlmann, Yusuke Miyao, Daniel Zeman, Dan Flickinger, Jan Hajič, Angelina Ivanova, and Yi Zhang. 2014. SemEval 2014 task 8: Broad-coverage semantic dependency parsing. In *Proceedings of the 8th International Workshop on Semantic Evaluation (SemEval 2014)*.

Stephan Oepen and Jan Tore Lønning. 2006. Discriminant-based MRS banking. In *Proceedings of the Fifth International Conference on Language Resources and Evaluation (LREC'06)*, Genoa, Italy. European Language Resources Association (ELRA).

Jeffrey Pennington, Richard Socher, and Christopher D. Manning. 2014. Glove: Global vectors for word representation. In *EMNLP*, pages 1532–1543.

Mitchell Stern, Jacob Andreas, and Dan Klein. 2017. A minimal span-based neural constituency parser. In *Proc. of ACL*, pages 818–827.

Zhixing Tan, Mingxuan Wang, Jun Xie, Yidong Chen, and Xiaodong Shi. 2018. Deep semantic role labeling with self-attention. In *Thirty-Second AAAI Conference on Artificial Intelligence*.

Ashish Vaswani, Noam Shazeer, Niki Parmar, Jakob Uszkoreit, Llion Jones, Aidan N Gomez, Łukasz Kaiser, and Illia Polosukhin. 2017. Attention is all you need. In *Advances in neural information processing systems*, pages 5998–6008.

ÚFAL–Oslo at MRP 2019: Garage Sale Semantic Parsing

Kira Droganova[1], Andrey Kutuzov[2], Nikita Mediankin[1], and Daniel Zeman[1]

[1]Charles University, Faculty of Mathematics and Physics, ÚFAL
[2]University of Oslo, Faculty of Mathematics and Natural Sciences, IFI
{droganova|mediankin|zeman}@ufal.mff.cuni.cz
andreku@ifi.uio.no

Abstract

This paper describes the ÚFAL–Oslo system submission to the shared task on Cross-Framework Meaning Representation Parsing (MRP, Oepen et al. 2019). The submission is based on several third-party parsers. Within the official shared task results, the submission ranked 11th out of 13 participating systems.

1 Introduction

The CoNLL 2019 shared task is on Meaning Representation Parsing, i.e., finding graphs of semantic dependencies for plain-text English sentences. There are numerous frameworks that define various kinds of semantic graphs; five of them have been selected as target representations in this shared task. The five frameworks are: Prague Semantic Dependencies (**PSD**); Delph-In bilexical dependencies (**DM**); Elementary Dependency Structures (**EDS**); Universal Conceptual Cognitive Annotation (**UCCA**); and Abstract Meaning Representation (**AMR**). See the shared task overview paper (Oepen et al., 2019) for a description of the individual frameworks.

Previous parsing experiments have been described for all these frameworks, and some of the parsers are freely available and re-trainable. Being novices in the area of non-tree parsing, we did not aim at implementing our own parser from scratch; instead, we decided to experiment with third-party software and see how far we can get. Our participation can thus be viewed, to some extent, as an exercise in reproducibility. The challenge was in the number and in the diversity of the target frameworks. No single parser can produce all five target representation types (or at least that was the case when the present shared task started).

Within the shared task, data of all five frameworks are represented in a common JSON-based interchange format (the **MRP** format). This format allows to represent an arbitrary graph structure whose nodes may or may not be anchored to spans of the input text. Using a pre-existing parser thus means that data have to be converted between the MRP interchange format and the format used by the parser; such conversion is not always trivial.

The shared task organizers have provided additional *companion data* where both the training and the test data were preprocessed by UDPipe (Straka and Straková, 2017), providing automatic tokenization, lemmatization, part-of-speech tags and syntactic trees in the Universal Dependencies annotation scheme (Nivre et al., 2016). We work solely with the companion data in our experiments; we do not process raw text directly.

2 Related Work

For the purposes of this work we considered previous work matching the following criteria:

- reporting reasonably good results;

- accompanied by open-source code available to use;

- with instructions sufficient to run the code;

- using only the resources from the shared task whitelist.

Peng et al. (2017) presented a neural parser that was designed to work with three semantic dependency graph frameworks, namely, DM, PAS and PSD. The authors proposed a single-task and two multitask learning approaches and extended their work with a new approach (Peng et al., 2018) to learning semantic parsers from multiple datasets.

The first specialized parser for UCCA was presented by Hershcovich et al. (2017). It utilized

Proceedings of the Shared Task on Cross-Framework Meaning Representation Parsing at the 2019 CoNLL, pages 158–165
Hong Kong, November 3, 2019. ©2019 Association for Computational Linguistics
https://doi.org/10.18653/v1/K19-2015

novel transition set and features based on bidirectional LSTMs and was developed to deal with specific features of UCCA graphs, such as DAG structure of the graph, discontinuous structures, and non-terminal nodes corresponding to complex semantic units. The work saw further development in (Hershcovich et al., 2018), where authors presented a generalized solution for transition-based parsing of DAGs and explored multitask learning across several representations, showing that using other formalisms in joint learning significantly improved UCCA parsing.

Buys and Blunsom (2017) proposed a neural encoder-decoder transition-based parser for full MRS-based semantic graphs. The decoder is extended with stack-based embedding features which allows the graphs to be predicted jointly with unlexicalized predicates and their token alignments. The parser was evaluated on DMRS, EDS and AMR graphs. Lexicon extraction partially relies on Propbank (Palmer et al., 2005), which is not in the shared task whitelist. Unfortunately, we were not able to replace it with an analogous white-listed resource, therefore we did not use it.

Flanigan et al. (2014) presented the first approach to AMR parsing, which is based around the idea of identifying concepts and relations in source sentences utilizing a novel training algorithm and additional linguistic knowledge. The parser was further improved for the SemEval 2016 Shared Task 8 (Flanigan et al., 2016). JAMR parser utilizes a rule-based aligner to match word spans in a sentence to concepts they evoke, which is applied in a pipeline before training the parser.

Damonte et al. (2017) proposed a transition-based parser for AMR not dissimilar to the ARC-EAGER transition system for dependency tree parsing, which parses sentences left-to-right in real time.

Lyu and Titov (2018) presented an AMR parser that jointly learns to align and parse treating alignments as latent variables in a joint probabilistic model. The authors argue that simultaneous learning of alignment and parses benefits the parsing in the sense that alignment is directly informed by the parsing objective thus producing overall better alignments.

Zhang et al. (2019a) and (Zhang et al., 2019b) recently reported results that outperform all previously reported SMATCH scores, on both AMR

2.0 and AMR 1.0. The proposed attention-based model is aligner-free and deals with AMR parsing as sequence-to-graph task. Additionally, the authors proposed an alternative view on reentrancy converting an AMR graph into a tree by duplicating nodes that have reentrant relations and then adding an extra layer of annotation by assigning an index to each node so that the duplicates of the same node would have the same id and could be merged to recover the original AMR graph. This series of papers looks very promising, but unfortunately we were not able to test the parser due to them being published after the end of the shared task.

3 System Description

3.1 DM and PSD

To deal with the DM and PSD frameworks we chose a parser that was described in (Peng et al., 2017). This work explores a single-task and two multitask learning approaches using the data from the 2015 SemEval shared task on Broad-Coverage Semantic Dependency Parsing (SDP, Oepen et al. 2015) and reports significant improvements on the state-of-the-art results for semantic dependency parsing. The parser architecture utilizes arc-factored inference and a bidirectional-LSTM composed with a multi-layer perceptron. Our first intention was to adapt the models that utilize the multitask learning approach. Unfortunately, the project seems to be stalled and multitask parsing part is not available. We proceeded with the single-task model (NeurboParser), in which models for each formalism are trained completely separately. To reproduce the experiment from the paper we needed to perform the following steps:

- Convert the training data from the MRP format to the input format required by the parser.[1] The input format is the same as the one used in the 2015 SemEval Shared Task[2] (see Figure 1 for an example).

- Download pre-trained word embeddings (GloVe, Pennington et al. 2014). We use the same version that is described in the

---

[1] All conversion scripts that we created for this shared task are available on GitHub at `https://github.com/ufal/mrptask/tree/master/conll-2019-system`.

[2] See detailed format description at `http://alt.qcri.org/semeval2015/task18/index.php?id=data-and-tools`

paper – 100-dimensional vectors trained on Wikipedia and Gigaword.

- Create training and development splits. We use scripts and id lists provided by the authors. The development set comprises 5% of sentences of the training data.

- Create an additional file with the following information: part-of-speech tag, token ID of the head of the current word, dependency relation. The parser considers syntactic dependencies before it predicts the semantic ones; note that we can obtain this information from the companion data and give it to the parser.

- Run the training script to train the model. The most challenging part was to install and compile the parser. The authors provided the training script with default hyperparameters; however, using some of the documented options resulted in errors on our system. Models are trained up to 20 epochs with Adadelta (Zeiler, 2012).

The single-task model does not predict the frame labels. This is a simple classification problem, similar to lemmatization, so as a quick workaround, we used UDPipe (Straka and Straková, 2017), namely its predictor of morphological features, to simulate such a classifier. First, we converted the training data to the CoNLL-U format[3] replacing morphological features in the sixth column with the frame labels. Next, we trained the model using the instructions from Reproducible Training section of the UDPipe manual.[4]

To produce the final output for the testing data, we first parsed it with the trained models. The input files were produced using companion data. To be more specific, for the UDPipe model input we used tokenization and word forms from companion data. NeurboParser takes the following information as input: token ID, word form, lemma, and part-of-speech tag. Then we merged the frame information predicted by UDPipe with the NeurboParser output and converted it back to the MRP interchange format.

---

[3]https://universaldependencies.org/format.html

[4]http://ufal.mff.cuni.cz/udpipe/models#universal_dependencies_24_reprodusible_training

3.2 EDS

We do not have any parser specifically for EDS. However, EDS is closely related to DM (DM is a lossy conversion of EDS, where nodes that do not represent surface words have been removed (Ivanova et al., 2012)). We thus work with the hypothesis that a DM graph is a subset of the corresponding EDS graph, and we submit our DM graph to be also evaluated as EDS.

This is obviously just an approximation, as EDS parsing is a task inherently more complex than DM parsing. The hope is that the DM parser will be able to identify some EDS edges while others will be missing, and the overall results will still be better than if we did not predict anything at all. To illustrate this, consider Figures 2 and 3. Four DM edges are also present in the EDS graph (in one case, the corresponding nodes have different labels but they are still anchored in the same surface string).

3.3 AMR

For AMR, we chose the JAMR parser (Flanigan et al., 2014, 2016). The parser is based on a two-part algorithm that identifies concepts using a semi-Markov model and then identifies the relations by searching for the maximum spanning connected subgraph (MSCG) from an edge-labeled, directed graph representing all possible relations between the identified concepts. Lagrangian relaxation (Geoffrion, 1974) is used to ensure semantic well-formedness. For our experiments we used the version that was presented at the 2016 SemEval shared task on Meaning Representation Parsing (May, 2016), in which the authors implemented a novel training loss function for structured prediction, added new lists of concepts and improved features, and improved the rule-based aligner.

The instructions and training scripts were provided by the authors. To run the training, we needed to split the data into training and development sets, to create a label-set file, which is a list of unique edge labels collected from the training data, and then convert the training data to the parser input format. Our development split consists of 5% of sentences taken from each text of the training data.

The JAMR parser works with the traditional AMR format, PENMAN, which represents an AMR graph in bracketed form (Banarescu et al.,

1	There	there	EX	-	-	_	_	_	_	_	_
2	is	be	VBZ	+	+	v_there:e-i	_	_	_	_	loc
3	no	no	DT	-	+	q:i-h-h	_	_	_	_	_
4	asbestos	asbestos	NN	-	-	n:x	ARG1	BV	ARG1	_	_
5	in	in	IN	-	+	p:e-u-i	_	_	_	_	_
6	our	we	PRP$	-	+	q:i-h-h	_	_	_	_	_
7	products	product	NNS	-	-	n:x	_	_	ARG2	poss	_
8	now	now	RB	-	+	time_n:x	_	_	_	_	_
9	.	.	.	-	-	_	_	_	_	_	_
10	"	”	' '	-	-	_	_	_	_	_	_

Figure 1: An example of a sentence in the format required by NeurboParser. See Figure 3 for visualization of this DM graph.

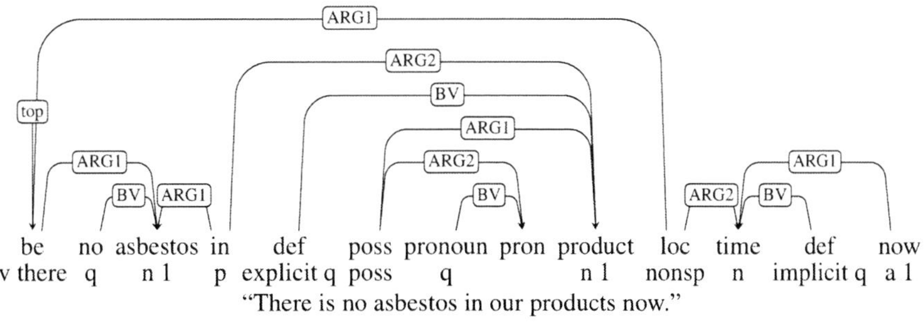

Figure 2: EDS representation of the example sentence.

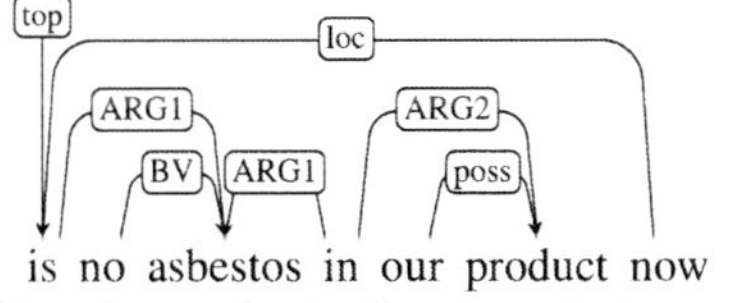

Figure 3: DM representation of the example sentence.

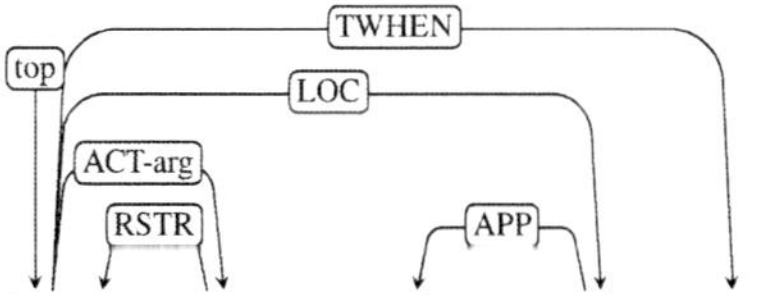

Figure 4: PSD representation of the example sentence.

2013), therefore necessitating a two-way conversion between the MRP and PENMAN formats. The example sentence "There is no asbestos in our products now."" would look the following way in PENMAN format (see also Figure 5 for a visualization of the graph):

```
(a / asbestos :polarity -
   :time (n / now)
   :location (t / thing
       :ARG1-of (p / produce-01
           :ARG0 (w / we))))
```

To facilitate the conversion, we created a Python3 script for each conversion direction.

The main features of conversion from the MRP format to the PENMAN format are as follows:

- For each sentence, a representation of the graph in the form of source-to-target mapping is obtained from the JSON representation of the list of edges.

- The graph is traversed starting from the top using depth-first search algorithm outputting one node on a line in order the nodes are traversed, leading to dropping reentrancies.

- Nodes that were already visited are marked and are not traversed again in order to break

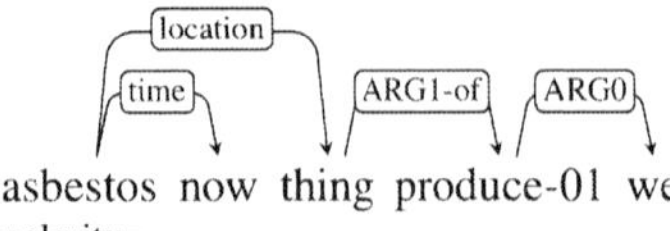

"There is no asbestos in our products now."

Figure 5: AMR representation of the example sentence.

possible infinite loops resulting from the cycles in the graph.

- Numeric node ids are substituted with alphanumeric values standard for PENMAN format: the first letter of the MRP node label is followed by an ordinal number if it is necessary to distinguish multiple nodes starting with the same letter.

- Properties of the node are output on the same line as the node.

- Property values that contain characters that are special for AMR representation, namely a colon (:), are enclosed in straight double quotes, as recommended by the parser documentation, e.g., 20:00 becomes "20:00".

The back conversion has the following features:

- For each sentence, its AMR representation is recursively split into a nested list structure reflecting the nestedness of bracket notation.

- The path starting from the top node is recursively retrieved from the nested list structure.

- The lists of nodes and edges are collected along the path and converted to the MRP format.

- Finally, the alphanumeric node ids are converted to numeric format: the root is assigned 0, then the incremental ids are assigned to the rest of the nodes in order they are visited by depth-first traverse, with the child nodes of the same parent node sorted by rough priority of their connecting edge label:

  - frame arguments are sorted in order of their numbers, e.g., :ARG0 precedes :ARG1;
  - frame arguments precede semantic relations, e.g., :ARG0 precedes :date;

- inverse relations are placed after straight ones of the same name, e.g., :ARG0 precedes :ARG0-of.

3.4 UCCA

We decided to adapt JAMR parser that we had already set up to parse AMR data in order to train on UCCA data as well. We had theorized that a parser suitable for AMR could be trained to predict nonsurface nodes in UCCA graphs. For this, we needed to convert UCCA graphs from the uniform graph interchange format to AMR-like bracketed representation and vice versa, so the parser would be able to work with sentences in familiar format. The example sentence "There is no asbestos in our products now."" would look the following way in the AMR-like representation (see also Figure 6 for a visualization of the graph):

```
(_1 / _root
    :H (_2 / _h
        :S (t / There)
        :F (i / is)
        :D (n / no)
        :A (a / asbestos)
        :A (_3 / _a
            :R (i1 / in)
            :E (_4 / _e
                :S (o / our))
            :C (p / products))
        :T (n1 / now)
        :U (. / .)
        :U (_ / _quot)))
```

As demonstrated by this example, we introduced the following modifications to the PENMAN format in order to adapt it for UCCA:

- Since in UCCA nodes that do not directly correspond to surface tokens lack any labels at all, we assign them placeholder labels during conversion, which start with the underscore to differentiate them from labels of surface nodes. Top node is given the _root label, while the rest are given labels that are the same as the label on the edge connecting it with its parent node.

- In UCCA punctuation gets its own nodes. In most cases we use the punctuation symbol as the node label, with one exception: we replace the double-quote character (") with _quot because the parser treats the double quote as a special character.

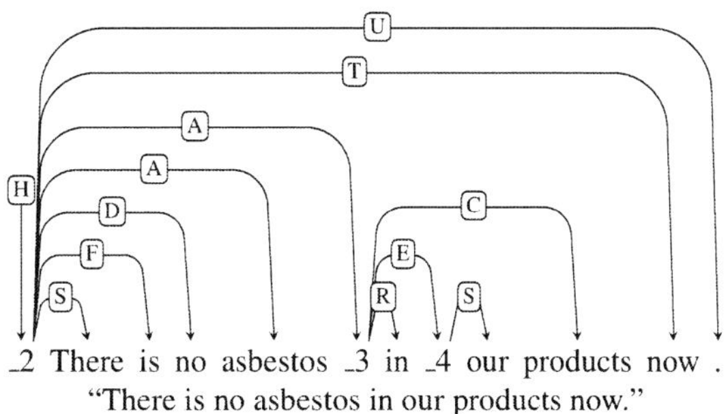

Figure 6: UCCA representation of the example sentence.

The conversion process is mostly the same as for AMR, with the following notable modifications:

- Conversion from MRP to the AMR-like format:
    - labels for the nodes that correspond to surface tokens are obtained by taking parts of the sentence text denoted by corresponding anchors;
    - the list of possible special characters that necessitate the label to be enclosed in double quotes is extended to slash (/) and parentheses;
    - nodes with empty labels are assigned labels as described above;
    - the double-quote label is replaced with _quot as described above.

- Conversion from the AMR-like format to MRP:
    - anchors are recalculated from node labels and sentence text where needed, assuming the order of nodes' occurrences corresponds to the order in which their labels occur in the sentence;
    - alphanumeric ids are reassigned to numeric not based on the order the nodes emerge when depth-first traversing the tree, but first assigned to the surface nodes in order of their occurrence in the sentence, then to the rest of the nodes, which seems to be the preferred way for UCCA graphs.

4 Results

The results are shown in Table 1. Unfortunately, our results for AMR and UCCA testing sentences were corrupted, thus the official results comprise only scores for DM, PSD and EDS frameworks. However, we do provide the scores for the post-evaluation run for AMR and UCCA frameworks. The results for the complete evaluation set and for the LPPS subset, a 100-sentence sample from The Little Prince annotated in all frameworks, are reported for both the official and unofficial runs.

For reference we provide previously reported original results measured by formalism-specific metrics for both the parsers that we use. Our results for DM and PSD are quite close to the original results reported in (Peng et al., 2017). Original SMATCH scores are reported in (May, 2016). The score reported on the LPPS subset is close to the original score, whereas the score measured on the whole test set is much lower. This difference may largely be due to a misinterpreted bug in the back conversion script, which lead to dropping 36% of sentences from the evaluation set. This, however, didn't affect the LPP subset, which comprises relatively simple sentences.

5 Conclusion

We have described the ÚFAL–Oslo submission to the CoNLL 2019 shared task on cross-framework meaning representation parsing. This submission stands on three parsers that were previously proposed, implemented and made available by other researchers: NeurboParser, JAMR, and UDPipe. We added several conversion scripts to make the parsers work with the shared task data. We were not able to implement other improvements within the time span of the shared task; we also do not list other publicly available parsers that we thought of testing but failed to make them work.

The main purpose of the present paper is to provide some context to our numbers in the shared

	MRP	MRP:DM	MRP:PSD	MRP:EDS	MRP:UCCA	MRP:AMR	SDP:DM	SDP:PSD	SMATCH:AMR
Official run	0.344	0.8051	0.6092	0.3064	0.0000	0.0000	0.8803	0.7689	0.0000
	0.334	0.7782	0.5663	0.3260	0.0000	0.0000	0.8879	0.7950	0.0000
Post-evaluation	0.439	0.8051	0.6092	0.3064	0.1118	0.3645	0.8803	0.7689	0.3515
	0.473	0.7782	0.5663	0.3260	0.1748	0.5194	0.8879	0.7950	0.5081
Previously reported							0.894	0.776	0.56

Table 1: Official run: official results; Post-evaluation: results that were achieved after the submission deadline; Previously reported: original results for utilized parsers. For every metric we show F1 score, except for SDP:DM and SDP:PSD, where we show labeled F1 score; for both runs we provide results for the complete evaluation set (upper line) and the LPPS subset (lower line).

task results; the results themselves are far from optimal. Using the official MRP shared task metric (and looking at the unofficial post-evaluation run, which includes AMR and UCCA results), we were relatively successful only in parsing DM. Parsing PSD is obviously harder (these figures are comparable, as we applied the same processing to PSD and DM), and, perhaps unsurprisingly, AMR is the most difficult target of the three. We achieved non-zero score on EDS by simply pretending that the DM graph is EDS. Finally, training an AMR parser on the UCCA representation did not turn out to be a good idea, and our UCCA score is the worst among all the target representations.

Acknowledgements

We thank the authors of the parsers that we used as parts of our system. Their well-documented work allowed us to reproduce their results and conduct our own experiments.

This work is partially supported by the GA UK grant 794417, the SVV project number 260 453, and the grant no. LM2015071 of the Ministry of Education, Youth and Sports of the Czech Republic.

References

Laura Banarescu, Claire Bonial, Shu Cai, Madalina Georgescu, Kira Griffitt, Ulf Hermjakob, Kevin Knight, Philipp Koehn, Martha Palmer, and Nathan Schneider. 2013. Abstract meaning representation for sembanking. In *Proceedings of the 7th Linguistic Annotation Workshop and Interoperability with Discourse*, pages 178–186, Sofia, Bulgaria. Association for Computational Linguistics.

Jan Buys and Phil Blunsom. 2017. Robust incremental neural semantic graph parsing. In *Proceedings of the 55th Annual Meeting of the Association for Computational Linguistics (Volume 1: Long Papers)*, pages 1215–1226, Vancouver, Canada. Association for Computational Linguistics.

Marco Damonte, Shay B. Cohen, and Giorgio Satta. 2017. An incremental parser for abstract meaning representation. In *Proceedings of the 15th Conference of the European Chapter of the Association for Computational Linguistics: Volume 1, Long Papers*, pages 536–546, Valencia, Spain. Association for Computational Linguistics.

Jeffrey Flanigan, Chris Dyer, Noah A. Smith, and Jaime Carbonell. 2016. CMU at SemEval-2016 task 8: Graph-based AMR parsing with infinite ramp loss. In *Proceedings of the 10th International Workshop on Semantic Evaluation (SemEval-2016)*, pages 1202–1206, San Diego, California. Association for Computational Linguistics.

Jeffrey Flanigan, Sam Thomson, Jaime Carbonell, Chris Dyer, and Noah A. Smith. 2014. A discriminative graph-based parser for the abstract meaning representation. In *Proceedings of the 52nd Annual Meeting of the Association for Computational Linguistics (Volume 1: Long Papers)*, pages 1426–1436, Baltimore, Maryland. Association for Computational Linguistics.

Arthur M Geoffrion. 1974. Lagrangean relaxation for integer programming. In *Approaches to integer programming*, pages 82–114. Springer.

Daniel Hershcovich, Omri Abend, and Ari Rappoport. 2017. A transition-based directed acyclic graph parser for UCCA. In *Proceedings of the 55th Annual Meeting of the Association for Computational Linguistics (Volume 1: Long Papers)*, pages 1127–1138, Vancouver, Canada. Association for Computational Linguistics.

Daniel Hershcovich, Omri Abend, and Ari Rappoport. 2018. Multitask parsing across semantic representations. In *Proceedings of the 56th Annual Meeting of the Association for Computational Linguistics (Volume 1: Long Papers)*, pages 373–385, Melbourne, Australia. Association for Computational Linguistics.

Angelina Ivanova, Stephan Oepen, Lilja Øvrelid, and Dan Flickinger. 2012. Who did what to whom? a contrastive study of syntacto-semantic dependencies. In *Proceedings of the Sixth Linguistic Annotation Workshop*, pages 2–11, Jeju, Republic of Korea. Association for Computational Linguistics.

Chunchuan Lyu and Ivan Titov. 2018. AMR parsing as graph prediction with latent alignment. In *Proceedings of the 56th Annual Meeting of the Association for Computational Linguistics (Volume 1: Long Papers)*, pages 397–407, Melbourne, Australia. Association for Computational Linguistics.

Jonathan May. 2016. SemEval-2016 task 8: Meaning representation parsing. In *Proceedings of the 10th International Workshop on Semantic Evaluation (SemEval-2016)*, pages 1063–1073, San Diego, California. Association for Computational Linguistics.

Joakim Nivre, Marie-Catherine de Marneffe, Filip Ginter, Yoav Goldberg, Jan Hajič, Christopher D. Manning, Ryan McDonald, Slav Petrov, Sampo Pyysalo, Natalia Silveira, Reut Tsarfaty, and Daniel Zeman. 2016. Universal dependencies v1: A multilingual treebank collection. In *Proceedings of the Tenth International Conference on Language Resources and Evaluation (LREC 2016)*, pages 1659–1666, Portorož, Slovenia. European Language Resources Association (ELRA).

Stephan Oepen, Omri Abend, Jan Hajič, Daniel Hershcovich, Marco Kuhlmann, Tim O'Gorman, Nianwen Xue, Jayeol Chun, Milan Straka, and Zdeňka Urešová. 2019. MRP 2019: Cross-framework Meaning Representation Parsing. In *Proceedings of the Shared Task on Cross-Framework Meaning Representation Parsing at the 2019 Conference on Natural Language Learning*, pages 1 – 27, Hong Kong, China.

Stephan Oepen, Marco Kuhlmann, Yusuke Miyao, Daniel Zeman, Silvie Cinková, Dan Flickinger, Jan Hajič, and Zdeňka Urešová. 2015. SemEval 2015 task 18: Broad-coverage semantic dependency parsing. In *Proceedings of the 9th International Workshop on Semantic Evaluation (SemEval 2015)*, pages 915–926, Denver, Colorado. Association for Computational Linguistics.

Martha Palmer, Daniel Gildea, and Paul Kingsbury. 2005. The proposition bank: An annotated corpus of semantic roles. *Computational Linguistics*, 31(1):71–106.

Hao Peng, Sam Thomson, and Noah A. Smith. 2017. Deep multitask learning for semantic dependency parsing. In *Proceedings of the 55th Annual Meeting of the Association for Computational Linguistics (Volume 1: Long Papers)*, pages 2037–2048, Vancouver, Canada. Association for Computational Linguistics.

Hao Peng, Sam Thomson, Swabha Swayamdipta, and Noah A. Smith. 2018. Learning joint semantic parsers from disjoint data. In *Proceedings of the 2018 Conference of the North American Chapter of the Association for Computational Linguistics: Human Language Technologies, Volume 1 (Long Papers)*, pages 1492–1502, New Orleans, Louisiana. Association for Computational Linguistics.

Jeffrey Pennington, Richard Socher, and Christopher Manning. 2014. Glove: Global vectors for word representation. In *Proceedings of the 2014 Conference on Empirical Methods in Natural Language Processing (EMNLP)*, pages 1532–1543, Doha, Qatar. Association for Computational Linguistics.

Milan Straka and Jana Straková. 2017. Tokenizing, pos tagging, lemmatizing and parsing ud 2.0 with udpipe. In *Proceedings of the CoNLL 2017 Shared Task: Multilingual Parsing from Raw Text to Universal Dependencies*, pages 88–99, Vancouver, Canada. Association for Computational Linguistics.

Matthew D. Zeiler. 2012. Adadelta: An adaptive learning rate method. *ArXiv*, abs/1212.5701.

Sheng Zhang, Xutai Ma, Kevin Duh, and Benjamin Van Durme. 2019a. AMR parsing as sequence-to-graph transduction. In *Proceedings of the 57th Annual Meeting of the Association for Computational Linguistics*, pages 80–94, Florence, Italy. Association for Computational Linguistics.

Sheng Zhang, Xutai Ma, Kevin Duh, and Benjamin Van Durme. 2019b. Broad-coverage semantic parsing as transduction. *arXiv preprint arXiv:1909.02607*.

Peking at MRP 2019: Factorization- and Composition-Based Parsing for Elementary Dependency Structures

Yufei Chen♠, Yajie Ye♠, Weiwei Sun♠♡
♠ Wangxuan Institute of Computer Technology, Peking University
♠ The MOE Key Laboratory of Computational Linguistics, Peking University
♡ Center for Chinese Linguistics, Peking University
{yufei.chen,yeyajie,ws}@pku.edu.cn

Abstract

We design, implement and evaluate two semantic parsers, which represent factorization- and composition-based approaches respectively, for Elementary Dependency Structures (EDS) at the *CoNLL 2019 Shared Task on Cross-Framework Meaning Representation Parsing*. The detailed evaluation of the two parsers gives us a new perception about parsing into linguistically enriched meaning representations: current neural EDS parsers are able to reach an accuracy at the inter-annotator agreement level in the same-epoch-and-domain setup.

1 Introduction

For the *CoNLL 2019 Shared Task on Cross-Framework Meaning Representation Parsing* (MRP; Oepen et al., 2019), we concentrate on Elementary Dependency Structures (EDS; Oepen and Lønning, 2006), the graph-based meaning representations derived from English Resource Semantics[1] (ERS; Flickinger et al., 2014b) that is the richly detailed semantic annotation associated to English Resource Grammar (ERG; Flickinger, 2000), a domain-independent, linguistically deep and broad-coverage HPSG grammar. The full ERS and EDS annotations include not only basic predicate–argument structures, but also information about quantifiers and scopal operators, e.g. negation, as well as analyses of linguistically complex phenomena such as time and date expressions, conditionals, and comparatives.

Following Koller et al. (2019)'s practice, we divide existing work on string-to-semantic-graph parsing into four types, namely factorization-, composition-, transition- and translation-based approaches. Our previous studies (Chen et al., 2018b; Cao et al., 2019) as well as other investigations on other graph banks indicate that the

factorization- and composition-based approaches obtain currently superior accuracies. In this paper, we fine-tune our factorization- and composition-based parsers and present a detailed evaluation on the MRP data.

Our factorization-based system obtains an overall accuracy of 94.47 in terms of the official MRP evaluation metrics, and out-performs other submission systems by a large margin with respect to the prediction for labels, properties, anchors and edges. We highlight a new perception: Current neural parsers are able to reach an accuracy at the inter-annotator agreement level (Bender et al., 2015) for the linguistically enriched EDS representations in the same-epoch-and-domain setup. Given the information depth of ERS, we think many NLP applications may benefit from a *revisit* of classic discrete semantic representations. The composition-based system reaches a score of 91.84. We do not think the performance gap suggests a weakness of the latter approach, but take it a reflection of the fact that a composition-based parser involves more individual modules that have not been fully optimized yet.

2 Parsing to Semantic Graphs

In this section, we present a summary of factorization-, composition-, transition- and translation-based parsing approaches.

Factorization-Based Approach. This type of approach is inspired by the successful design of graph-based dependency tree parsing (McDonald, 2006). A factorization-based parser explicitly models the target semantic structures by defining a score function that is able to evaluate the *goodness* of any candidate graph. Usually, the set of possible graphs that can be assigned to an input sentence is extremely large. Therefore, a parser also needs to know how to find the highest-scoring graphs from

---

[1] http://moin.delph-in.net/ErgSemantics

Proceedings of the Shared Task on Cross-Framework Meaning Representation Parsing at the 2019 CoNLL, pages 166–176
Hong Kong, November 3, 2019. ©2019 Association for Computational Linguistics
https://doi.org/10.18653/v1/K19-2016

a large set.

To the best of our knowledge, McDonald and Pereira (2006) present the first graph-based syntactic dependency parsing algorithm that removes the tree-shape constraint. In the scenario of semantic dependency parsing, Kuhlmann and Jonsson (2015) generalize the graph-based framework (aka Maximum Spanning Tree parsing) and propose Maximum Subgraph parsing. Given a directed graph $G = (V, E)$ that corresponds to an input sentence $x = w_0, \ldots w_{n-1}$ and a score function SCOREG. The string-to-graph parsing is formulated as a problem of searching for a subset $E' \subseteq E$ with the maximum score. Formally, we have the following optimization problem:

$$(V, E') = \underset{G^*=(V,E^*\subseteq E)}{\arg\max} \text{SCOREG}(G^*) \quad (1)$$

For semantic dependency parsing, V is the set of surface tokens, and G is, usually, the corresponding complete graph.

It is relatively straightforward to extend Kuhlmann and Jonsson's framework to cover more types of semantic graphs as follows,

$$G' = \underset{G^*\in\text{GEN}(x)}{\arg\max} \text{SCOREG}(G^*) \quad (2)$$

where $\text{GEN}(x)$ denotes all plausible semantic graphs that can be assigned to x.

To make the above combinatorial optimization problems solvable, people usually employ a **factorization** strategy, i.e. defining a decomposable score function that enumerates all sub-parts of a candidate graph. This view matches a classic solution to structured prediction which captures elemental and structural information through partwise factorization. For example, the following formula defines a first-order factorization model for semantic dependency parsing,

$$G' = \underset{G^*=(V,E^*\subseteq E)}{\arg\max} \sum_{e \in E^*} \text{SCOREEDGE}(e) \quad (3)$$

The essential computational module in this architecture is the score function, which is usually induced based on moderate-sized annotated sentences. Various deep learning models together with vector-based encodings induced from large-scale raw texts have been making advances in shaping a score function significantly (Dozat and Manning, 2018). We will detail our factorization-based parser in §3.

Composition-Based Approach. Compositionality is a cornerstone for many formal semantic theories. Following a principle of compositionality, a semantic graph can be viewed as the result of a derivation process, in which a set of lexical and syntactico-semantic rules are iteratively applied and evaluated. On the linguistic side, such rules extensively encode explicit knowledge about natural languages. On the computational side, such rules must be governed by a well-defined grammar formalism. In particular, to manipulate graph construction in a principled way, Hyperedge Replacement Grammar (HRG; Drewes et al., 1997) and AM Algebra (Groschwitz et al., 2017) have been applied to build semantic parsers for various graph banks (Chen et al., 2018b; Groschwitz et al., 2018; Lindemann et al., 2019).

A composition-based parser explicitly models derivations that yield semantic graphs by defining a score function SCORED. Assume a derivation $D = r_1, r_2, \ldots, r_m$ is a sequence of rules. Formally, we have the following optimization problem:

$$G' = \underset{G^*\in\text{GEN}(x)}{\arg\max} \sum_{D\in\text{DERIV}(G^*)} \text{SCORED}(D) \quad (4)$$

To make the above problem solvable, people usually employ a **decomposition** strategy, i.e. summing over local scores that correspond to individual derivation steps:

$$\text{SCORED}(D) = \sum_{i=1}^{m} \text{SCORERULE}(r_i) \quad (5)$$

Again, this matches many structured prediction models. Deep learning has been shown very powerful to associate scores to individual rule applications, and thus to provide great models for evaluating a derivation. The general form of (4) is a very complex combinatorial optimization problem. The approximating strategy to search for the best derivation instead has been shown practical yet effective for ERS parsing (Chen et al., 2018b). Formally, we solve the below problem,

$$D' = \underset{\substack{D^*\in\text{GEN}_{\text{DERIV}}(x) \\ D^*=r_1 r_2 \cdots r_m}}{\arg\max} \sum_{i=1}^{m} \text{SCORERULE}(r_i) \quad (6)$$

where $\text{GEN}_{\text{DERIV}}(x)$ denotes all sound derivations that yield x. Then we get a target graph by evaluating D'. We will detail our composition-based parser in §4.

Transition-Based Approach. This type of approach is inspired by the successful design of transition-based dependency tree parsing (Yamada and Matsumoto, 2003; Nivre, 2008). To the best of our knowledge, Sagae and Tsujii (2008) firstly apply this type of approach to predict predicate–argument structures grounded in HPSG (Miyao et al., 2005). A number of new transition systems and disambiguation models have been discussed for parsing into different graphs (Wang et al., 2015; Zhang et al., 2016; Buys and Blunsom, 2017; Gildea et al., 2018; Sun et al., 2019)

Translation-Based Approach. This type of approach is inspired by the success of sequence-to-sequence (seq2seq for short) models that are the heart of modern Neural Machine Translation. A translation-based parser takes a family of semantic graphs as a foreign language, in that a semantic graph is encoded and then viewed as a string from *another* language (Peng et al., 2017b; Konstas et al., 2017; Buys and Blunsom, 2017). A parser knows how to linearize a graph. Data augmentation has been shown very helpful (Konstas et al., 2017), partially reflecting the *data-hungry nature* of seq2seq models.

Simple application of seq2seq models is not successful. However, some basic models can be integrated with other types of approaches. Peng et al. (2018) propose to combine the translation- and transition-based approaches. Zhang et al. (2018) combined the translation- and factorization-based approaches.

3 The Factorization-Based Parser

3.1 Elements in EDS Graphs

The key idea underlying the factorization-based approach is to explicitly model what are expected as elements in target structures. Therefore before introducing the technical details of our parser, we roughly sketch key elements in EDS graphs. Refer to Flickinger et al. (2014a) for more information about the design of ERS.

We distinguish three kinds of elements: (1) labeled nodes, (2) node properties and (3) labeled edges. Nodes are sometimes called concepts[2], where their labels reflect conceptual meaning. The

node labels can be divided into two classes: (1) *surface concepts* that are exclusively introduced by lexical entries, whose orthography is the source form of a core part of a concept symbol, and (2) *abstract concepts* that are used to represent the semantic contribution of grammatical constructions or more specialized lexical entries. Take the output structure in Figure 1 for example: `_go_v_1` and `_want_v_1` indicate surface concepts, while `proper_q` and `named` indicate abstract concepts.

To avoid proliferation of concepts, some concepts are parameterized. The parameters can be viewed as properties of nodes. For example, `named("Tom")` is a `named` concept with a CARG property of "*Tom*". For every EDS graph, there exists a `top` concept, which relates to the `top` handle in its original ERS annotation. In Figure 1, for example, `_want_v_1` is the `top`. In this paper, we practically treat whether a node is *top* as a property whose value can be either *true* or *false*.

Edges are called relations. An edge links exactly two nodes and mainly reflects predicate–argument relations. Edges are assigned with a small, fixed inventory of role labels (e.g. `ARG1`, `ARG2`, ...).

3.2 The Architecture

We employ a four-stage pipeline to incrementally construct an EDS graph. Figure 1 illustrates the four steps with a simple sentence. The core idea is to identify concepts from surface strings, and then detect the relations between them.

3.3 Tokenization

Automatic tokenization for English has been widely viewed as a solved problem for quite a long time. Taking the risk of oversimplifying the situation, tokenization does not have a significant impact on downstream NLP tasks, e.g. POS tagging and syntactic parsing. When we consider semantic parsing, however, it is still a controversial issue which unit is the most basic one that triggers conceptual meaning and semantic construction. Therefore, we need to rethink the tokenization problem in which *tokens* may not be fully consistent with their traditional definitions. Moreover, when we consider other languages like German or Chinese, tokenization brings other issues.

In this paper, we take the most basic **word-level units**[3] as strings that are separated by whitespaces

---

[2] Considering the original design and especially the logic foundation of ERS, the seemly more standard name is *predicate*. In this paper, we call them *concepts*, mainly because we want to follow the new tradition of graph-based meaning representations (Kuhlmann and Oepen, 2016).

[3] We purposely avoid using *words* here. But when we in-

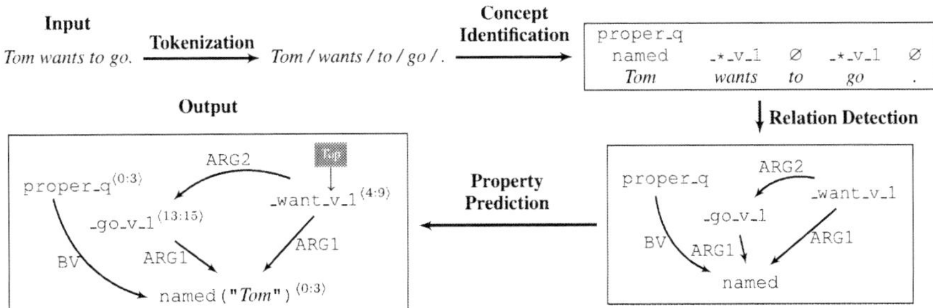

Figure 1: The workflow of our factorization-based parser. Tokenization: To separate an input sentence into semantic parsing-oriented tokens. Concept Identification: To generate concepts with a sequence labeling model. Relation Detection: To link concepts with a semantic dependency parsing model. Property Prediction: To predict node properties by classification.

Input string	*Assets of these short-term funds surged more than $5.5 billion in September.*
RegEx match	*Assets of these short - term funds surged more than $ 5 . 5 billion in September .*
Classification	B B B B BB B B B I B B I I B B B B
Our tokens	*Assets of these short - term funds surged more‿than $ 5‿.‿5 billion in September .*
PTB tokens	*Assets of these short‿-‿term funds surged more than $ 5‿.‿5 billion in September .*

Table 1: A tokenization example. Row "**Our tokens**" shows the result of our tokenizer, while Row "**PTB tokens**" shows the tokenization results defined by the Penn TreeBank (PTB; Marcus et al., 1993).

Concept	**Type**	**String**
_more+than_p	multi-unit	*more‿than*
_asset_n_1	single unit	*Assets*
_short_a_of	sub-unit	*short-term*
_term_n_of	sub-unit	*short-term*
_mis-_a_error	sub-unit	*misinterpreted*
_interpret_v_1	sub-unit	*misinterpreted*

Table 2: Examples to illustrate the relationships between surface concepts and word-level units. '‿' is an escape character for whitespace.

and punctuation markers. In an EDS graph, a surface concept may be aligned with a sub-unit, a single unit or multiple units. Table 2 shows some examples. During concept identification (§3.4), there should exist a surjection from surface concepts to the input tokens. Therefore, tokenization is important for obtaining a reasonable alignment between concepts and input tokens.

We adopt the character-based word segmentation approach for Chinese (Sun, 2010) to find suitable tokens. We first split an input sentence into a sequence of basic elements with simply defined regular expressions. The core part of our tokenizer is a sequence labeling model over this sequence. In particular, each element is assigned with a positional label that indicates token boundaries. The labels can be either **B**, which means the unit is at the begining of a target token, or **I**, which means the unit is inside a token. For sequential classification, we utilize a multi-layer BiLSTM network. Tokens can be retrieved from the predicted labels. See Figure 1 for an example. Note that, Dridan and Oepen (2012) showed that regular expressions are quite powerful to deal with the tokenizaiton problem for different styles.

3.4 Concept Identification

Surface concepts (e.g. quantifier _some_q) and some of the abstract concepts (e.g. named entity named) have a more transparent connection to surface forms and are relatively easier to identify. We call such concepts *lexicalized concepts*, which include all but are not limited to surface concepts. We cast identification of lexicalized concepts as a token-based tagging problem. The lexicalized concepts usually include lemma information in its

---

troduce our neural parsing models, we still use *word* to relate the units to *word embeddings*.

label. For example, _boy_n_1 consists of a lemma (boy) and a *type*, denoted as _*_n_1. As lemmas are much more easily to analyze, our concept identifier targets the type part only.

Some of the rest of abstract concepts are triggered by phrasal constructions. For example, compound is associated to the combination of multiple words. In this case, a concept is originally aligned to a sequence of continuous words. Considering that this type of concepts is a small portion, we propose to handle them in a word-level tagger. To this end, we re-align them to specific tokens with a small set of heuristic rules. For example, compound is re-aligned to the first word of a compound. Re-aligning these concepts means discarding their original anchors. To fully fit the MRP goals, we treat anchors as properties of concepts, and recover them by predicting the start/end boundaries with a classification model, as to be described in §3.6.

We employ a neural sequence labeling model to predict concepts. A multi-layer BiLSTM is utilized to encode tokens and another two softmax layers to predict concept-related labels: One for lexicalized concepts and the other for the rest. We also use recently widely-used contextualized word representation models, including ELMo (Peters et al., 2018) and BERT (Devlin et al., 2018). Figure 2 shows the neural network for concept identication.

3.5 Relation Detection

After finding a set of concepts, the next step is to link them together. Each semantic dependency is treated independently. We use integers as indices to mention concepts nodes. For any two nodes i and j, we give a score $\text{SCOREEDGE}(i, j)$ to the possible arc $i \rightarrow j$. An arc is included to the final graph if and only if its score is greater than 0. We use a first-order model as described in Eq. (3). Figure 2 briefly summarizes the neural network for relation detection.

Following Dozat and Manning (2016, 2018), we use a deep biaffine attention to evaluate a candidate edge:

$$\text{SCOREEDGE}(i, j) = \text{BIAFFINE}(c_i, c_j)$$
$$= c_i^T U c_j + W(c_i + c_j) + b$$

where c_i/c_j is the vector associated to i/j. We consider two information sources to calculate c: a textual part $r_{\text{c2w}(i)}$ and a conceptual part n_i, as

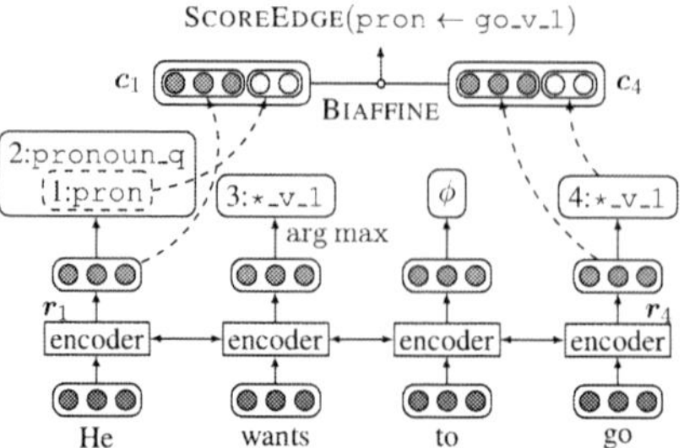

Figure 2: The network architecture for our concept identification and relation detection models which share the same architecture in word embedding and contextual encoder layers but with the same sets of parameters. A softmax layer is used for concept identification. To determine whether the dependency pron ← _go_v_1 exists, i.e. unlabeled dependency parsing, the corresponding embeddings c_1 and c_4, which are the concatenation of textual embeddings (in the red color) and the conceptual embeddings (in the yellow color), are biaffinely transformed into a score.

following,

$$c_i = r_{\text{c2w}(i)} \oplus n_i$$

Due to our concept identification method, we have a function "c2w" that takes as input the index of a node and returns as output the index of its anchored word. $r_{\text{c2w}(i)}$ is the contextual vector of the word aligned to i, which is calculated by the word embedding layer and the encoder layers. n_i is the randomly-initialized embedding of i's concept type, e.g. _*_v_1. We also use the deep biaffine attention function to calculate each edge's scores for all labels, according to which we select the *best* label that achieves the maximum.

For training, we use a margin-based approach to compute loss from the gold graph G^* and the best predicted $\hat{G}$ according to current model parameters. We define the *loss* term as:

$$loss = \max(0, \Delta(G^*, \hat{G}) \\ - \text{SCOREG}(G^*) + \text{SCOREG}(\hat{G})) \tag{7}$$

The margin objective Δ measures the similarity between G^* and $\hat{G}$. Following Peng et al. (2017a), we define Δ as weighted Hamming to trade off between precision and recall.

3.6 Property Prediction

The final stage is to predict properties for each concept that is generated in the previous stages. For the EDS representation at CoNLL2019, we

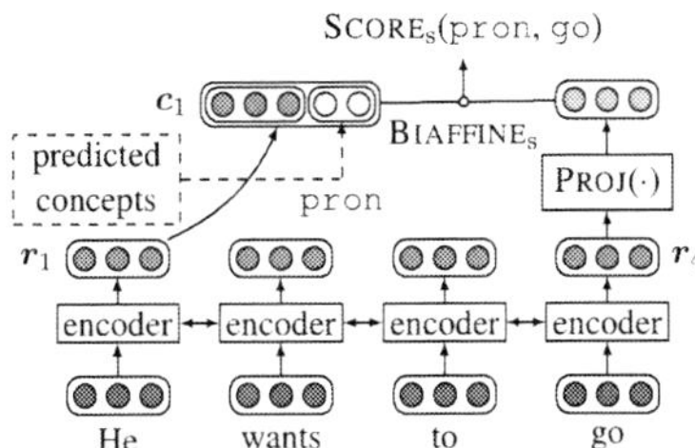

Figure 3: The network architecture for property prediction. The vector representations of concepts are obtained similarly to relation detection. The only difference is that the labels of concepts are provided by previous stages instead of being predicted by a softmax layer.

consider three types of properties and apply different strategies.

Anchors (spans). String anchors are treated as properties of concepts. For a given concept, a classification model is utilized to select two tokens over all input tokens as the start/end boundary of the concept respectively. We use exactly the same neural architecture in §3.5 to encode input tokens. See Figure 3 for a visualized illustration. The score of token j_w being the start/end boundary of node i can be computed by following equation:

$$\text{SCORE}_{\text{s/e}}(i, j_w) = \text{BIAFFINE}_{\text{s/e}}(c_i, \text{PROJ}(r_{j_w}))$$

Here $\text{PROJ}(\cdot)$ represents a feed-forward network with LEAKYRELU activation.

The anchors provided by training dataset are all character-based, so transformation is required before training this model. In the same manner, after retrieving the start/end word of a concept, we need to convert word-based anchors back to character-based anchors. Margin-based loss is used again when training this model and the total loss is the sum of losses for both boundaries.

The CARG property. Since the main function of the CARG attribute is to reduce the size of predicate names by parameterizing them with regularized surface strings, a rule-based system could be effective to predict the CARG information.

Firstly, we decide whether a concept has the CARG property according to its label. For example, `named`, `card` and `ord` need CARGs, but not `_the_q`.

Secondly, we use a dictionary which is extracted automatically from the training dataset. Entries of the dictionary are of the form $\langle\text{label}, \text{string}, \text{CARG}\rangle$. For example, a concept `named` whose *anchoring string* is *D.C.* will be mapped to *WashingtonDC*. Based on a close observation of the data, we introduce several heuristic rules if there is no applicable entry for a concept in the dictionary. For example, one widely applicable rule is to use `1` as the CARG value for concepts labeled `card` and aligned to a float number which is less than 1.

Finally, if no rule is available, we remove punctuation markers at left or right boundaries of anchoring strings and use the remaining part.

Top concept. We cast the precition for `top` as a binary classification problem over all nodes in a final graph. This strategy matches a recent research interest in graph neural networks (Li et al., 2015; Veličković et al., 2017; Defferrard et al., 2016; Chen et al., 2018a; Song et al., 2018), one goal of which is to associate vectors to graph nodes. Such vectors can be more easily to be integrated to neural networks for various purposes. We employ a Graph-based LSTM (Song et al., 2018) to encode an `EDS`graph and a multi-layer feed-forward network to determine whether a node is `top`. Similar as §3.5, margin-based approach is used to compute the *loss* term.

4 The Composition-Based Parser

Our composition-based parser is based on our previous work (Chen et al., 2018b). The core engine is a graph rewriting system that explicitly explores the syntactico-semantic recursive derivations that are governed by a synchronous `HRG` (`SHRG`). See Figure 4 for an example. Our parser constructs `EDS` graphs by explicitly modeling such derivations. In particular, it utilizes a constituent parser to build a syntactic derivation, and then selects semantic `HRG` rules associated to syntactic `CFG` rules to generate a graph. When multiple rules are applicable for a single phrase, a neural network is used to rank them.

One main difference between our submission parer and the parser introduced in Chen et al. (2018b) is that the syntactic parsing model is a re-implementation of Kitaev and Klein (2018). It utilizes transformer layers to capture words' contextual information, denoted as r_i. After encoding an input sentence, a multiple-layer peceptron (MLP) is employed to get span scores. The score of span (i, j) with label L is calculated from its embedding $s_{i,j}$, which is from the contextual vector of

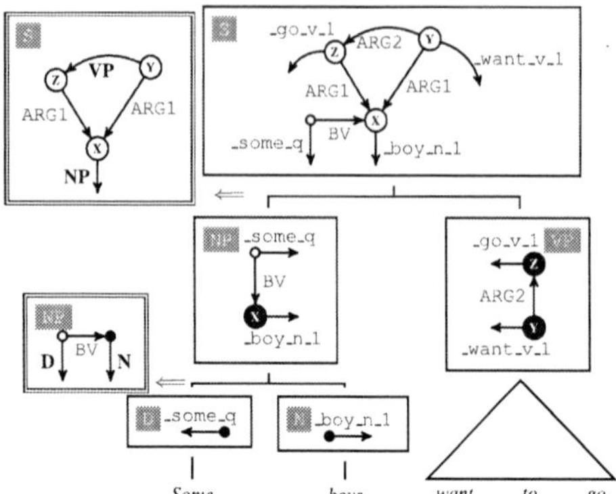

Figure 4: An SHRG-based syntactico-semantic derivation. The derivation can be viewed as a syntactic tree enriched with semantic interpretation rules that are defined by an HRG. Each phrase in the syntactic tree is also assigned with a graph which corresonds to a sub-part in the final semantic graph. Moreover, some particular nodes (filled nodes) in a sub-graph is marked as *communication channels* to other meaning parts in the same sentence. In HRG, these nodes are summarized as a hyperedge. Gluing two sub-graphs according to a construction rule follows the graph substitution principle of HRG. The application of the top rule that introduces a reentrancy structure is such an example. The "X" node in the graph of the left branching phrase is unified with the "X" node in the rule, and so do to the "Y" and "Z" nodes.

the two endpoints, r_i and r_{j-1}:

$$\text{SBCORE}(i, j, L) = \text{MLP}(s_{i,j})[L]$$
$$s_{i,j} = r_i \oplus r_{i-1}$$
$$\text{MLP}(x) = W_2\sigma(W_1 x + b_1) + b_2$$

The operator $[]$ denotes index selection. We perform CKY decoding to retrieve the highest-scored constituent tree that agrees with the syntactic CFG grammar.

When a phrase structure tree is available, semantic interpretation can be regarded as translating this tree to the derivation of graph construction. As multiple subgraph correspondents in each node are available, the beam search strategy is used to balance the search complexity and quality.

To score subgraphs, we use two types of features. The first type is node feature. For a concept n aligned with span (i, j), we use the span embedding $s_{i,j}$ as features, and score with non-linear transformation:

$$\text{SCOREPART}_{\text{concept}}(i, j, p) = \text{MLP}_{\text{concept}}(s_{i,j})[p]$$

The second type is edge feature. Note that a semantic dependency with label L from conceptual node n_a to n_b are aligned to constituents (i_1, j_1) and (i_2, j_2) respectively. We calculate this part of score with non-linear transformation from the span embeddings s_{i_1, j_1}, s_{i_2, j_2} and random initialized concept embeddings n_a, n_b:

$$\text{SCOREPART}_{\text{arc}}(i_1, j_1, i_2, j_2, p_a, p_b, L)$$
$$= \text{MLP}_{\text{arc}}(s_{i_1, j_1} \oplus s_{i_2, j_2} \oplus p_a \oplus p_b)[L]$$

For training, again, we use the margin-based loss.

5 Experiments

The MRP2019 training data consists of 35656 sentences in total. For convenience, the composition- and factorization-based parsers share the same tokenization model. Gold token position labels are extracted from DeepBank (Flickinger et al., 2012). For the composition-based parser, we leverage the syntactic information provided by DeepBank to extract synchronous grammars. Therefore, all sentences in the MRP2019 data that do not appear in DeepBank 1.1 are removed. Following the same preprocessing of semantic graphs in Chen et al. (2018b) and using the recommended setup in DeepBank, there are 33722 samples for training and 1689 samples for validation. The synchronous grammars are extracted from the training data using coarse-grained labels (Chen et al., 2018b). For factorization-based parser, we use heuristic rules to re-align the non-lexicalized concepts to input tokens. We remove all sentences that do not recieve results in this step from our training set. After re-alignment, 33580 sentences are left for training and 1689 for validation.

Table 3 shows the results of both parsers on the validation data using the official evalution tool—*mtool*[4]. Table 4 shows the intermediate results during parsing for both parsers.

For factorization-based parsing, we combine 4 models for concept identification and 5 models for relation detection. We ensemble models by averaging the score functions across all stand-alone models. These models use different initial random seeds, different pretraining methods (ELMo or BERT) or different encoder architectures (Transformer or BiLSTM). All these models achieve a similar performance respectively, but the ensemble one achieves a much better performance, as we can conclude from Table 3.

---

[4]https://github.com/cfmrp/mtool

#	Top	Label	Property	Anchor	Edge	DEVEL.			TEST
						P	R	F_1	F_1
Factorization-based Parsing									
Gold tokenization	88.75	96.92	96.39	96.98	94.88	96.38	96.00	96.19	—
+ensemble stage2	89.23	97.37	97.46	97.16	95.18	96.80	96.26	96.53	—
+ensemble stage2 & 3	89.64	97.37	97.46	97.17	95.53	96.95	96.34	96.64	—
Full pipeline	88.87	96.76	96.03	96.72	94.69	96.20	95.78	95.99	—
+ensemble stage2	89.29	97.12	97.08	96.91	94.98	96.59	96.00	96.30	—
+ensemble stage2 & 3	89.52	97.12	97.10	96.93	95.34	96.74	96.10	96.42	94.47
Composition-based Parsing									
gold tokenization	88.63	95.73	97.37	96.85	93.00	95.38	95.04	95.21	—
Full pipeline	88.27	95.44	97.17	93.62	92.67	94.08	93.86	93.97	91.84

Table 3: Results on the development data set. The evaluation algorithm is Maximum Common Edge Subgraph Isomorphism (MRP). *Gold tokenization* means that the parser uses gold standard tokenization provided by Deep-Bank. *Full pipeline* means that all stages in the pipeline are based on automatic predictions. Columns in the middle block include F_1 scores with respect to basic evaluation items respectively. The right block shows overall precision, recall and F_1. All numbers are obtained by using *mtool*.

Factorization-based Parser	Concept Identification (F_1)			Relation Detection		
	Lexicalized	Non-lexicalized	Overall	Nodes	Edges	Overall
Gold tokenization	97.04	95.72	96.50	96.94	93.43	95.20
+ensemble stage2	97.40	96.20	96.94	97.30	93.85	95.60
+ensemble stage2 & 3		the same as above row		97.28	94.03	95.67

Composition-based Parser	Syntactic Parsing				Semantic Interpretation		
	P	R	F_1	POS	Nodes	Edges	Overall
Gold tokenization	92.16	92.16	92.16	95.01	95.63	91.43	93.56

Table 4: Results of each stage for both parsers on the development data. *Gold tokenization* has the same meaning in Table 3. Columns in the right block are the SMATCH scores ignoring all the node and edge properties for generated graphs. For factorization-based parser, columns in the middle block include the F_1 scores of concept identification with respect to *lexicalized*, *non-lexicalized* and all concepts respectively. For composition-based parser, columns in the middle block are the syntactic parsing results using standard metric and *POS* concerns the prediction of preterminals.

Our factorization-based parser achieves relatively satisfactory performance in all basic evaluation items except top. In the in-domain evaluation, its performace nearly reaches the inter-annotator agreement reported in Bender et al. (2015). To find *top* concepts, our model encodes the semantic graphs and ignores the input sentences. We take the unsatisfactory result as a confirmation of the challenge to encode complex discrete structures into vectors.

The evalution results of our composition-based parser are not as good as the factorization-based one. We believe that the disagreement between our SHRG grammar and the original ERG leads to a major part of the performance gap.

6 Conclusion

Current neural ERS parsers work rapidly and reliably, with an MRP accuracy of over 94% in the same-epoch-and-domain setup. It is comparable to the inter-annotator agreement (in Elementary Dependency Match) reported in Bender et al. (2015). As ERS parsers become more and more accurate, efficient and robust, they have extensive application prospects in downstream deep language understanding-related tasks.

Acknowledgement

We are grateful for the great work of Sheng Huang, Sheng Xu and Xihao Wang on UCCA and AMR parsing tasks. This paper and research behind it would not have been possible without their help.

References

Emily M. Bender, Dan Flickinger, Stephan Oepen, Woodley Packard, and Ann A. Copestake. 2015. Layers of interpretation: On grammar and compositionality. In *Proceedings of the 11th International Conference on Computational Semantics, IWCS 2015, 15-17 April, 2015, Queen Mary University of London, London, UK*, pages 239–249.

Jan Buys and Phil Blunsom. 2017. Robust incremental neural semantic graph parsing. In *Proceedings of the 55th Annual Meeting of the Association for Computational Linguistics (Volume 1: Long Papers)*, pages 1215–1226, Vancouver, Canada. Association for Computational Linguistics.

Junjie Cao, Zi Lin, Weiwei Sun, and Xiaojun Wan. 2019. A comparative analysis of knowledge-intensive and data-intensive semantic parsers. *CoRR*, abs/1907.02298.

Jie Chen, Tengfei Ma, and Cao Xiao. 2018a. Fastgcn: fast learning with graph convolutional networks via importance sampling. *arXiv preprint arXiv:1801.10247*.

Yufei Chen, Weiwei Sun, and Xiaojun Wan. 2018b. Accurate shrg-based semantic parsing. In *Proceedings of the 56th Annual Meeting of the Association for Computational Linguistics (Volume 1: Long Papers)*, pages 408–418. Association for Computational Linguistics.

Michaël Defferrard, Xavier Bresson, and Pierre Vandergheynst. 2016. Convolutional neural networks on graphs with fast localized spectral filtering. In *Advances in neural information processing systems*, pages 3844–3852.

Jacob Devlin, Ming-Wei Chang, Kenton Lee, and Kristina Toutanova. 2018. Bert: Pre-training of deep bidirectional transformers for language understanding. *arXiv preprint arXiv:1810.04805*.

Timothy Dozat and Christopher D. Manning. 2016. Deep biaffine attention for neural dependency parsing. *CoRR*, abs/1611.01734.

Timothy Dozat and Christopher D. Manning. 2018. Simpler but more accurate semantic dependency parsing. In *Proceedings of the 56th Annual Meeting of the Association for Computational Linguistics (Volume 2: Short Papers)*, pages 484–490, Melbourne, Australia. Association for Computational Linguistics.

F. Drewes, H.-J. Kreowski, and A. Habel. 1997. Hyperedge Replacement Graph Grammars. In Grzegorz Rozenberg, editor, *Handbook of Graph Grammars and Computing by Graph Transformation*, pages 95–162. World Scientific Publishing Co., Inc., River Edge, NJ, USA.

Rebecca Dridan and Stephan Oepen. 2012. Tokenization: Returning to a long solved problem — a survey, contrastive experiment, recommendations, and toolkit —. In *Proceedings of the 50th Annual Meeting of the Association for Computational Linguistics (Volume 2: Short Papers)*, pages 378–382, Jeju Island, Korea. Association for Computational Linguistics.

Dan Flickinger. 2000. On building a more efficient grammar by exploiting types. *Natural Language Engineering*, 6(1):15–28.

Dan Flickinger, Emily M. Bender, and Stephan Oepen. 2014a. ERG semantic documentation. Accessed on 2019-09-04.

Dan Flickinger, Emily M. Bender, and Stephan Oepen. 2014b. Towards an encyclopedia of compositional semantics: Documenting the interface of the English Resource Grammar. In *Proceedings of the Ninth International Conference on Language Resources and Evaluation (LREC-2014)*, pages 875–881. European Language Resources Association (ELRA).

Daniel Flickinger, Yi Zhang, and Valia Kordoni. 2012. Deepbank: A dynamically annotated treebank of the wall street journal. In *Proceedings of the Eleventh International Workshop on Treebanks and Linguistic Theories*, pages 85–96.

Daniel Gildea, Giorgio Satta, and Xiaochang Peng. 2018. Cache transition systems for graph parsing. 44(1).

Jonas Groschwitz, Meaghan Fowlie, Mark Johnson, and Alexander Koller. 2017. A constrained graph algebra for semantic parsing with AMRs. In *IWCS 2017 - 12th International Conference on Computational Semantics - Long papers*.

Jonas Groschwitz, Matthias Lindemann, Meaghan Fowlie, Mark Johnson, and Alexander Koller. 2018. AMR dependency parsing with a typed semantic algebra. In *Proceedings of the 56th Annual Meeting of the Association for Computational Linguistics (Volume 1: Long Papers)*, pages 1831–1841. Association for Computational Linguistics.

Nikita Kitaev and Dan Klein. 2018. Constituency parsing with a self-attentive encoder. In *Proceedings of the 56th Annual Meeting of the Association for Computational Linguistics (Volume 1: Long Papers)*, pages 2676–2686. Association for Computational Linguistics.

Alexander Koller, Stephan Oepen, and Weiwei Sun. 2019. Graph-based meaning representations: Design and processing. In *Proceedings of the 57th Annual Meeting of the Association for Computational Linguistics: Tutorial Abstracts*, pages 6–11, Florence, Italy. Association for Computational Linguistics.

Ioannis Konstas, Srinivasan Iyer, Mark Yatskar, Yejin Choi, and Luke Zettlemoyer. 2017. Neural AMR. Sequence-to-sequence models for parsing and generation.

Marco Kuhlmann and Peter Jonsson. 2015. Parsing to noncrossing dependency graphs. *Transactions of the Association for Computational Linguistics*, 3:559–570.

Marco Kuhlmann and Stephan Oepen. 2016. Towards a catalogue of linguistic graph banks. *Computational Linguistics*, 42(4):819–827.

Yujia Li, Daniel Tarlow, Marc Brockschmidt, and Richard Zemel. 2015. Gated graph sequence neural networks. *arXiv preprint arXiv:1511.05493*.

Matthias Lindemann, Jonas Groschwitz, and Alexander Koller. 2019. Compositional semantic parsing across graphbanks.

Mitchell P. Marcus, Mary Ann Marcinkiewicz, and Beatrice Santorini. 1993. Building a large annotated corpus of English: the penn treebank. *Computational Linguistics*, 19(2):313–330.

Ryan McDonald. 2006. *Discriminative learning and spanning tree algorithms for dependency parsing*. Ph.D. thesis, University of Pennsylvania, Philadelphia, PA, USA.

Ryan McDonald and Fernando Pereira. 2006. Online learning of approximate dependency parsing algorithms. In *Proceedings of 11th Conference of the European Chapter of the Association for Computational Linguistics (EACL-2006))*, volume 6, pages 81–88.

Yusuke Miyao, Takashi Ninomiya, and Jun'ichi Tsujii. 2005. Corpus-oriented grammar development for acquiring a head-driven phrase structure grammar from the penn treebank. In *Proceedings of the Second International Joint Conference on Natural Language Processing*, pages 684–693.

Joakim Nivre. 2008. Algorithms for deterministic incremental dependency parsing. *Computational Linguistics*, 34:513–553.

Stephan Oepen, Omri Abend, Jan Hajič, Daniel Hershcovich, Marco Kuhlmann, Tim O'Gorman, Nianwen Xue, and Milan Straka. 2019. MRP 2019: Cross-framework Meaning Representation Parsing. pages 1–26.

Stephan Oepen and Jan Tore Lønning. 2006. Discriminant-based mrs banking. In *Proceedings of the Fifth International Conference on Language Resources and Evaluation (LREC-2006)*, Genoa, Italy. European Language Resources Association (ELRA). ACL Anthology Identifier: L06-1214.

Hao Peng, Sam Thomson, and Noah A. Smith. 2017a. Deep multitask learning for semantic dependency parsing. In *Proceedings of the 55th Annual Meeting of the Association for Computational Linguistics (Volume 1: Long Papers)*, pages 2037–2048, Vancouver, Canada. Association for Computational Linguistics.

Xiaochang Peng, Linfeng Song, Daniel Gildea, and Giorgio Satta. 2018. Sequence-to-sequence models for cache transition systems. pages 1842–1852.

Xiaochang Peng, Chuan Wang, Daniel Gildea, and Nianwen Xue. 2017b. Addressing the data sparsity issue in neural AMR parsing.

Matthew Peters, Mark Neumann, Mohit Iyyer, Matt Gardner, Christopher Clark, Kenton Lee, and Luke Zettlemoyer. 2018. Deep contextualized word representations. In *Proceedings of the 2018 Conference of the North American Chapter of the Association for Computational Linguistics: Human Language Technologies, Volume 1 (Long Papers)*, volume 1, pages 2227–2237.

Kenji Sagae and Jun'ichi Tsujii. 2008. Shift-reduce dependency DAG parsing. In *Proceedings of the 22nd International Conference on Computational Linguistics*, pages 753–760, Manchester, UK.

Linfeng Song, Yue Zhang, Zhiguo Wang, and Daniel Gildea. 2018. A graph-to-sequence model for amr-to-text generation. *arXiv preprint arXiv:1805.02473*.

Weiwei Sun. 2010. Word-based and character-based word segmentation models: Comparison and combination. In *Proceedings of the 23rd International Conference on Computational Linguistics (Coling 2010)*, pages 1211–1219, Beijing, China. Coling 2010 Organizing Committee.

Weiwei Sun, Yufei Chen, Xiaojun Wan, and Meichun Liu. 2019. Parsing Chinese sentences with grammatical relations. 45(1).

Petar Veličković, Guillem Cucurull, Arantxa Casanova, Adriana Romero, Pietro Lio, and Yoshua Bengio. 2017. Graph attention networks. *arXiv preprint arXiv:1710.10903*.

Chuan Wang, Nianwen Xue, and Sameer Pradhan. 2015. A transition-based algorithm for AMR parsing.

Hiroyasu Yamada and Yuji Matsumoto. 2003. Statistical dependency analysis with support vector machines. In *The 8th International Workshop of Parsing Technologies (IWPT2003)*, pages 195–206.

Sheng Zhang, Xutai Ma, Rachel Rudinger, Kevin Duh, and Benjamin Van Durme. 2018. Cross-lingual decompositional semantic parsing. pages 1664–1675.

Xun Zhang, Yantao Du, Weiwei Sun, and Xiaojun
Wan. 2016. Transition-based parsing for deep dependency structures. *Computational Linguistics*,
42(3):353–389.

Author Index

Association for Computational Linguistics
209 N. Eighth Street
Stroudsburg, Pennsylvania 18360

ISBN 978-1-7138-0090-3